Plantation Slavery in Barbados

Plantation Slavery in Barbados
An Archaeological and
Historical Investigation

Jerome S. Handler and Frederick W. Lange
With the assistance of Robert V. Riordan

Harvard University Press
Cambridge, Massachusetts
London, England
1978

Library of Congress Cataloging in Publication Data

Handler, Jerome S
Plantation slavery in Barbados.
Includes index.
1. Slavery in Barbados—History. 2. Barbados—
Antiquities. 3. Plantation life—Barbados—History.
I. Lange, Frederick W., 1944–   joint author.
II. Riordan, Robert V., joint author. III. Title.
HT1105.B3H34   301.44′93′0972981   77–22312
ISBN 0–674–67275–5

For
Holley, Heather, Kathy, Josh, and Lisa
and to the memory of
Robert A. Clarke

Acknowledgments

THE archaeological fieldwork discussed in this book was made possible through a grant from the National Science Foundation and a grant-in-aid from the Wenner-Gren Foundation for Anthropological Research. Most of the data from historical sources were gathered during the several years that Handler held various research grants from the National Science Foundation, National Institute of Mental Health, American Philosophical Society (Johnson Fund), and a Younger Scholar Fellowship from the National Endowment for the Humanities. Handler is particularly indebted to the National Endowment for the Humanities for a Fellowship for Independent Study and Research, awarded for 1975–76, and to Southern Illinois University for a sabbatical leave during which his share in writing this book was accomplished.

During our first archaeological field season, in the winter and spring of 1971–72, the research crew was composed of Richard M. Accola, Michele Hayward, Anthony La Morticella, Dan Schecter, Kristy Scheidenhelm, Darla White, Arthur Zipris, Adam Garson, Hilary Sio, and Holley Lange. We are grateful for their efforts and their contributions to the preliminary analyses of many of the materials excavated during the season. Robert Riordan, the field assistant during the first season, and Crawford Blakeman directed excavations during the second season in the spring of 1973; they were assisted by Sandy Riordan, Sue Blakeman, Neville Daniel, and Cleveland Ashby.

While conducting research in Barbados we received courtesy and cooperation from plantation owners, attorneys, managers, and workers. We would particularly like to thank Lance Bannister, Gerald Briggs, J. W. Chandler, Joseph Clarke, Charles Gill, John Hutson, John St. Hill, Gerald Ward, and Graham Wilkes; we owe a special debt of gratitude to Dorrien Gill, Lionel Ward, and Roy Ward, who generously and hospitably yielded to our impositions. Others in Barbados who assisted our research were Joan and Michael

Chandler, Bently Gibbs, Woodville Marshall, Ronald Taylor, George Warner, and the late Neville Connell.

While analyzing and writing up our materials, we solicited advice and technical assistance from people in a variety of fields and specialties. Colleagues at Southern Illinois University who helped us resolve a variety of problems include Joseph Beatty, Alan Cohn, Philip J. C. Dark, Charles Frank, Jen-Ho Fang, George Gumerman, Stanley Harris, Don Hertz, Brent Kington, Bob Mark, Rose Padgett, and Lon Shelby; Clayton Press compiled some of the ethnographic information on burial customs that we used in chapter 6.

Specialists at other institutions were generous and helpful in attempting to provide us with the technical information we solicited. We are especially obliged to Kenneth J. Boss, Philip D. Curtin, John J. McCusker, Eugenia Herbert, F. Jerome Melbye, William L. Minnerly, Ivor Noël Hume, Irving Rouse, Frank Willett, and Stephen Williams.

Margot Beal and Leonard H. Gant, both associated with Alfred Dunhill, Ltd., of London, graciously helped us with various issues relating to the identification of clay pipes. Clifford Neill, D.D.S., aided in the analysis of dental materials, and Lambros Comitas, Charles Fairbanks, Joan Gibbs, Mildred Hart Higgins, Samuel J. Hough, Kenneth Ingram, Barry Higman, Debbie Teglia, and Rowan Watson provided research materials that we were otherwise unable to obtain.

The Office of Research and Development and the College of Liberal Arts at Southern Illinois University provided most of the funds for preparation of the manuscript for publication. Some of the maps were drawn by Dan Irwin; the illustrations were prepared by Fredda Burton and John Richardson; and Jary Sheppard typed the final manuscript.

J.S.H.
F.W.L.

Contents

Figures

Tables

Plantation Slavery in Barbados

1 / Introduction

THE sociocultural history of black populations in the New World is a subject of considerable study and debate among historians and historically oriented cultural anthropologists. Although not its exclusive interest, Afro-American research in anthropology has traditionally devoted substantial effort to the influence of Africa on specific forms of contemporary cultural behavior and to the study of continuities or changes in African cultural traditions in the New World setting. Conventionally using both an ethnographic and historical approach, this research has examined how Africans and their descendants perpetuated, modified, or lost aspects of their African cultures.

Much of Afro-American research in anthropology has been conducted in the Caribbean where scholars have found a fertile field for exploring questions related to the sociocultural patterns of contemporary Afro-Americans and the historical processes by which these patterns were created. A great deal of this research has examined cultural aspects purported to reflect African influences. Until recently, however, there has been little intensive research on the slave cultures that formed the cultural intermediary between Africa and the present. Consequently, Afro-Americanists in anthropology have often been hindered in their inquiries into the processes of culture change, a major object of their research, and have speculated, often using inadequate information, about the roots of Caribbean cultures. Although slavery is often considered in discussion of these roots, and is particularly significant for understanding Caribbean cultures, a great deal more is known about the institutional aspects of the slave society than about the slaves themselves.[1]

"We need to know in close detail what enslavement did to Africans and then to their Afro-American descendants," Herbert Gutman has recently written in a brilliant and witty critique of the widely discussed *Time on the Cross* (Fogel and Engerman 1974). "But we shall never comprehend slave belief and behavior by just

1

asking that question. We need also to ask what Africans and their Afro-American descendants did as slaves" (1975:170). Although Gutman was specifically concerned with the United States, his remarks are even more applicable to the Caribbean where much less research has been devoted to the sociocultural life of slaves. This book is addressed to the question of what Africans and their descendants "did as slaves" on the southeastern Caribbean island of Barbados from the mid-seventeenth century to 1834, the year in which slavery ended throughout the British Empire.

We report on the procedures, factual results, ethnohistorical interpretations, and theoretical implications of six months of archaeological fieldwork conducted over two seasons in 1971–72 and 1973. Our archaeological investigations were stimulated by Handler's earlier ethnographic and historical research, and in this book we have incorporated a great deal of information derived from this research.[2] By combining archaeological, historical, and, to some extent, ethnographic data, we attempt to portray certain dimensions of plantation slavery and the cultural system that African slaves and their descendants created in the New World; ultimately we focus on the slave mortuary complex, its manifestation of African patterns, and how it developed and changed.

It is to be emphasized that we conceive of this book as a work in cultural anthropology that utilizes more than one data base. We believe that this work illustrates in more detail than has previously been accomplished in the Caribbean (and generally in North America) a particular approach to the study of plantation slavery. We also present a great deal of unique archaeological data and information on Barbados that is otherwise not available in the scholarly literature on Caribbean slavery and slave life. We do not, however, attempt to provide an holistic account of slave behavior and belief over the two centuries of plantation slavery in Barbados. The contours and organization of this book have been greatly influenced by the archaeological research, and we focus on those aspects of slave culture and the plantation system which most directly relate to this research, either having informed our procedural strategies or in permitting interpretations of its results.

In general we follow David Baerreis's conception of the ethnohistorical approach in archaeology. Such an approach, Baerreis wrote, "clearly centers upon the use of documentary sources in conjunction with the study of data derived from archaeological excavation. Its range is broad and not confined solely to the determination of who lived at a particular site and when they occupied that location ... Ethnohistory in conjunction with ethnology

2

provides the means for coordinating diverse kinds of data in the solution of anthropological problems ... For archaeology, an ethnohistoric approach serves as a means whereby a fundamental link in the broad narrative of man's culture history is achieved" (1961: 70).

In this definition the ethnohistorical approach in archaeology in North America has been directed less toward varying groups of European origin and more toward Amerindian and other non-European groups. In such cases, archaeology has provided a broader view and understanding of peoples whose lives have been often hidden or distorted by the historical reporting of white Europeans. Ethnohistory, Richard Dorson has written, "directs its attention to the ethnic groups ordinarily relegated to the shadows in the White man's view of history ... the function of ethnohistory ... is to provide a documentary history of the concealed and officially inarticulate groups in American history" (1961:16–17). Recently, Robert Ascher (1974) suggested a methodology for approaching, among other problems, the "archaeology of the inarticulate." Although Ascher is interested in a variety of traditionally powerless groups in modern, complex society, he stressed that the "largest group of inarticulate Americans were slaves" (p. 11). In this sense, "inarticulate" has a dual meaning: it refers to groups that produced little direct documentation for historical reconstruction (and that scholars interested in these groups must rely on the writings of outsiders); it also implies the minor and incidental position to which such groups have been relegated in conventional historical scholarship—in Ascher's phrase, "those who did not write or who were not written about" (p. 11).[3]

In both senses, African slaves and their descendants in the British Caribbean were as historically inarticulate as their North American brethren, but Caribbean slave culture has attracted the attention of fewer scholars than North American slave culture. In Barbados, in particular, we focused on the sociocultural history of a group who left virtually no written records of their own and about whose lives very little had been written.

In formulating our research project, however, we believed that such persons had left material remains that could be recovered archaeologically. We initially believed that archaeological investigations were more likely to produce new data on specific aspects of Barbadian slave culture and plantation slavery than research into written records. Until the onset of our research, data on Barbadian slaves were collected exclusively from printed and manuscript sources located in libraries and archival repositories in Europe, the

United States, and the West Indies (see Handler 1971a). Despite the difficulties in locating relevant sources, this research yielded a considerable amount of information on the slaves and the society in which they lived. However, the information on social and cultural topics was often fragmentary and highly variable in quality and completeness, particularly for the household and community life of plantation slaves who were an "inarticulate" population *par excellence*. And it is precisely these culture features that require more detailed information to achieve a deeper understanding of slave life and the processes of culture change.

The qualitative or literary historical sources also raised a problem of interpretation. Virtually none of the written sources were produced by the slaves themselves; travelers' descriptions of island life, private letters and journals, and official letters and reports that form the bulk of the historical materials were produced by Europeans, usually Englishmen or creoles of European ancestry.[4] Their accounts of the slave population were generally ethnocentric and often highly prejudicial. Thus, we are faced with the problem of "cultural translation"—viewing one population (the slaves) indirectly through the eyes of another. Overcoming class, racial, and ethnocentric biases in such sources is one of the greater difficulties in interpreting historical materials.

In general, what whites chose to write about the social and cultural life of slaves is relatively limited, selective, and represents a small percentage of the writings available for Barbados during the period of slavery. Descriptions of the recurring and fundamental features of community and household life—dimensions of behavior that concern sociocultural anthropologists when they deal with any human population—are particularly limited.

Our archaeological research project was designed to yield specific information on the life of plantation slaves that was either not available or barely touched on in written sources; we also hoped that this research would raise new questions as well as stimulate fresh perspectives on slave life. Through their material culture and even skeletal remains, we assumed that Africans and their descendants would directly communicate some features of their social and cultural life and that archaeological materials would give an unbiased assessment of human activities under the conditions of the repressive social system of the slave society. As Ascher and Fairbanks noted in a report on their archaeological work in a slave cabin in Georgia, we also believed "that no one expected us to see or touch the things we unearthed" (1971:3).

Ascher and Fairbanks appear to have been the first researchers to

4

recognize explicitly and attempt to exploit the unique and significant means by which archaeological investigations of slavery can supplement the written record. Although other archaeological researchers have shown an interest in the culture of free blacks in North America (see, for example, Bullen and Bullen 1945; Combes 1974; Schuyler 1974; Snow 1969; Weslager 1954), "there is ... a general dearth of reports on the excavation of slave areas in the available literature" (Fairbanks 1974:62). Plantation slave sites have been particularly neglected. Fairbanks has initiated a long-term research project on the Kingsley plantation in Florida, but his published data are presently limited (1974). One of Fairbanks's students, John Otto, has recently completed a dissertation on Cannon's Point plantation in Georgia (1975); his work is an excellent example of the potential of an ethnohistorical approach in archaeology in viewing plantation slavery—in this case, the ways in which status differences between planters, overseers, and slaves were expressed in such areas as housing, material possessions, and food sources. Suzanne McFarlane, also working in the Cannon's Point area, was concerned with the material life of nineteenth-century plantation slaves (1975).

Few researchers have used archaeology to study Caribbean slave cultures and slaves. R. Duncan Mathewson has reported on excavations at Old King's House in Spanish Town, Jamaica's former administrative capital (1972a, 1972b, 1973). Old King's House was originally built as an official residence for the island's governors. Mathewson was initially concerned with delineating construction sequences and architectural features that might have assisted in reconstructing the building. His work, however, subsequently led to a study of the Afro-Jamaican "yabba" pottery found at the site, which in turn led to a consideration of the potential importance this pottery had for the study of sociocultural patterns on the island during the slave period. Though Ebanks (1974) has challenged some of Mathewson's underlying analytical assumptions, Mathewson has made a significant contribution in recognizing the importance of locally produced ceramics (see chapter 5).

Barry Higman and a group from the University of the West Indies have also been working in Jamaica during short field periods. Their work is directed at recovering settlement pattern and household data from two plantations with different economic and ecological backgrounds. Although Higman has regularly reported on the fieldwork, to date results are available in only summary fashion. The plantation that has received the most intensive excavation activity dates from the last quarter of the eighteenth century, but the excavated houses were apparently constructed around 1819 and were occupied for a long period after, perhaps as late as the very end of the nineteenth century. A major problem lies in "distinguishing a slave occupation level from later occupation of the site by free men"; in general, then, the results thus far have been inconclusive with respect to "the nature of slave settlements and slave society" (1976a; see also Higman 1974, 1975).

Archaeological investigations of slaves have also been summarily reported for two other areas in the Caribbean. In 1969–70, the Division of Colonial Archaeology of the Cuban Academy of Sciences excavated in the vicinity of the Ingenio Taoro in the province of Havana. A two-page report describes the limited excavations in structures and in a slave cemetery; dated materials ranged from 1784 to 1853 (Academia de Ciencias de Cuba 1970). Robert Dailey has summarized the "remains of some fifteen or more human skeletons recovered from an eroding beach" at Cinnamon Bay in Saint John, the Virgin Islands. The skeletons "appear to have been predominantly Negroid" and dated "to the 19th century—perhaps earlier" (1974); at one time they were apparently interred in a slave cemetery of "an old Danish sugar plantation" whose property line extended to the shoreline (Lenihan 1974).

Because the archaeological data from other research on slave cultures in the Caribbean are limited, we have only employed these data for comparative purposes in very specific and limited instances. These comparative limitations, we believe, are not a function of the archaeological data potentially recoverable from slave cultures, but rather reflect the present lack of intensive applications of an archaeological-ethnohistorical approach to investigating plantation slavery. Our explicit methodological orientation in the application of this approach was particularly significant for defining our research project in Barbados.

When our archaeological research was initially planned we were specifically interested in excavating plantation slave village sites and recovering information on such topics as settlement patterns, house construction, size and spatial relationships, household furniture and utensils, and culinary practices. We also planned to excavate in cemetery areas to acquire data on mortuary customs and burial practices that would give us insights into the slaves' religious belief system, conceptions of the afterlife, and changes in these ideological patterns. We aimed at recovering artifactual materials in a context that would shed light on domestic and religious life as well as permit some assessment of the survival or modification of African cultural traits.

Although one major archaeological problem lies in establishing

6

reliable time frames for the artifacts we recovered (see chapter 5 and Appendix B), our research design assumed that slaves developed a cultural system and that this system, and elements within it, changed over time. We assumed that Africans who came to Barbados as elsewhere "did not arrive on the shores of the New World with blank minds onto which were impressed ... English culture patterns" (Handler 1969b:337). Although these Africans "could not transfer their cultures to the New World intact," as Sidney Mintz has summarized, they and their descendants "did create viable patterns of life, for which their [African] pasts were pools of available symbolic and material resources" (1970:7–8). We further assumed that over time and within the organizational setting of the plantation, and the society of which it was a part, various dimensions of the African cultural legacy would be lost or modified (for various reasons, including explicitly and consistently enforced prohibitions by whites and loss of adaptive advantage to the sociocultural and physical environments of Barbados). Moreover, historical research led us to expect that the maintenance or modification of African cultural traditions would be archaeologically most evident in domestic and mortuary patterns and their related artifacts—even though we recognized a variety of problems in identifying cultural materials that were distinctively African.

Several research aims could not be realized (see chapter 3) and the field situation caused us to shift our primary orientations. In many cases more archaeological remains were destroyed and fewer preemancipation cultural remains were found than we had anticipated. Mainly because we lack suitable comparative data, we cannot presently tell whether such limited finds from Barbados reflect the selectivity of our sample or a general characteristic of archaeological materials from slave populations, particularly on small islands such as Barbados. In either event, much of our data are at the moment unique and a number of our conclusions are either speculative or incomplete.

Our work ultimately concentrated on Newton plantation, in the parish of Christ Church, and particularly in an apparent slave cemetery on this plantation. We discuss Newton and its slave population, placing both in the context of Barbadian plantation slavery in general (chapter 4). Next we describe in detail the archaeological research and the skeletal and cultural evidence from the cemetery; this evidence is coordinated with available historical and ethnographic data (chapter 5). All sources of data are then employed in a wider discussion of slave mortuary patterns and in a general consideration of the implications of our evidence for an understanding of the culture history of slaves in Barbados (chapter 6). Some of our data also permit testing various assumptions made by archaeologists in interpreting social systems, particularly the "archaeological nature of slavery." Our research also provides materials for a discussion of the relationship between conventionally defined historical archaeology and ethnohistory as methodological approaches to slave culture (chapter 7).

2 / Barbados: Geography, Economy, Demography, and History

ONLY 21 miles long and 14 miles wide, Barbados is the most eastern of the Caribbean islands and lies about 100 miles outside the arc of volcanic islands that constitute the Lesser Antilles. Resting upon the same submarine shelf—a continuation of the Paria peninsula of northeastern Venezuela—as its neighbor Trinidad, some 200 miles to the southwest, Barbados's 166-square-mile surface is largely composed of a coral limestone cap that covers the faulted and folded sedementary rocks underneath. Barbados's relatively low altitudes are arranged for the most part in "a series of gentle undulating plains" (Lowenthal 1957:469) or plateaus that rise gently from the Caribbean coast to the Upland plateau, approximately 1,000 feet above sea level (figure 1). Northeast of Bridgetown, the island's major urban center and political and commercial capital, the road gradually climbs until the eastern edge of the Upland plateau. From there the road drops sharply into the relatively rugged landscape of the Scotland District.

The Scotland District is set off from the rest of Barbados by a natural barrier of a semicircular limestone escarpment that extends for about 14 to 15 miles. The district comprises approximately one-seventh of Barbados's land area; and although its hills are not very high, they give an overall impression of mountainous country in miniature. The Scotland District is a geologically distinct area of Barbados. It lacks the limestone cap covering most of the island and it contains "fertile pockets [of land] alternat[ing] with steep slopes of sand and clay highly susceptible to erosion" (Lowenthal 1957:470–471).

At least nine physiographic regions, including the Scotland District, can be identified for the island (see, for example, Vernon and Carroll 1966:6–11). There are also differences in rainfall and soils. Although "the soils of the Scotland District are quite unlike those of the coral regions" (p. 27), even the coral regions contain approximately ten major soil types which fall into two major categories of red and black soils (Starkey 1961:2, 5; Lowenthal 1957:469). Soils are

9

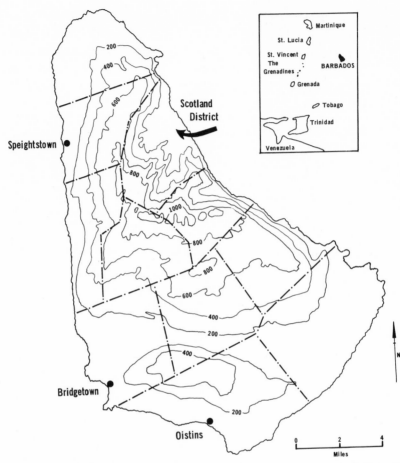

Figure 1. Physical map of Barbados. (Adapted from Vernon and Carroll 1966 and Watts 1968.)

generally rich and well drained, but the depth of soil cover varies; in very general terms, the central and eastern parishes contain the thickest soils, while soil layers are thinnest in the northernmost and southeastern portions of the island.

Rainfall varies with altitude and the location of a region with respect to the northeast and southeast trade winds. In the higher altitudes, annual rainfall averages between 60 and 75 inches; in the lower regions the average is between 40 and 60 inches. Parts of the Scotland District, however, receive an average of 75 to 80 inches (Government of Barbados 1961:108). The overall island average, measured over a 111-year period, is about 60 inches, but rainfall can be highly variable and irregular from year to year and there is also

10

"considerable variation within the year. In general, there is a dry season from January to May and a wet season from June to December, but the inception of the seasons is not the same every year and there are 'transitional' months between them. About three-quarters of the year's rain falls in the wet season and showers are unusually heavy and local" (Vernon and Carroll 1966:4); some regions, particularly the lower ones, experience a longer dry season than others.

Although not as dramatic as the variations in rainfall, some variations in temperature exist. The temperature in Bridgetown can sometimes be uncomfortably high, but the average overall island shade temperature is 79° F (Vernon and Carroll 1966:4). Beyond Bridgetown, "a few hundred feet of elevation modifies the temperatures and in the central uplands the thermometer rarely rises into the middle 80s and may drop into the 60s at night" (Starkey 1961:3). The trade winds blow almost constantly and are generally unimpeded because of the island's relatively low relief; the result is a cooling effect. The winds blowing from the southeast are felt the strongest in the Scotland District, which experiences, on the average, lower temperatures than the rest of the island.

Barbados is marginally located in relation to the Caribbean's hurricane zone, although throughout its history the island has been periodically hit with severe hurricanes—for example, in 1675, 1731, 1780, 1831, and 1898; the most recent major hurricane occurred in 1955. The threat of hurricanes and heavy storms have been more common.

None of the few wild animals are dangerous to man. Two species of snakes are harmless and rarely seen. The mongoose, imported in the late nineteenth century to help destroy rats that were damaging the sugar cane, now often destroys young farm animals and fowls. Monkeys are considered a nuisance because they prey on fruit trees, but they chiefly live in the limited wooded areas, particularly in the Scotland District.

The relatively dense forests that once covered Barbados have virtually disappeared. Most of the forests were destroyed in the 1650s and 1660s while the economy was being rapidly transformed into one based on sugar production under the plantation system; by 1665 "all but the smallest traces of forest had been removed through felling or burning" (Watts 1966:62). Today the only significant reminder of the island's forested past is the fifty-odd acres of Turner's Hall Wood in the Scotland District parish of Saint Andrew. Yet, even the primeval qualities of Turner's Hall Wood have been somewhat diluted. A number of its trees, such as mahogany, were introduced after the island's colonization by Euro-

11

peans in 1627. In fact, a great number of the plants found in Barbados today were introduced after 1627 (Watts 1966:88–92); among these is sugar cane, the omnipresent grass, which has been of fundamental economic importance since the middle of the seventeenth century.

The Barbadian economy is still highly dependent on cultivating and processing sugar cane into raw sugar, molasses, and rum. From 1963 to 1972, for example, the sugar industry accounted for more than 70 percent of the island's total domestic exports and was a major earner of foreign exchange (*West Indies Chronicle* 1973:31). Barbados's growing tourist industry and increased light manufacturing have made significant changes in its economy in the past few years, but to a considerable degree Barbados is still a sugar island.

During the late 1950s and early 1960s, it was estimated that between 67,000 and 69,000 acres of Barbados's 106,000 acres were cultivated, and close to 88 percent of these were planted in sugar cane (Inniss 1961:1–2; Starkey 1961:14); food crops, however, are frequently interspersed among the cane lands. Although the amount of acreage devoted to sugar cane has recently declined as different crops are emphasized or lands are turned to nonagricultural uses, cane fields still give the impression of dominating the countryside.

The vast majority of Barbados's thousands of sugar cane farmers grow the crop on small land units of an acre or less, but the greatest percentage of cane acreage is controlled, as it has been since the middle of the seventeenth century, by plantations; plantations also produce most of the island's sugar (Handler 1966; Barbados Sugar Producers' Association 1970:15–17).[1] The number of plantations has declined during this century (from 329 in 1911 to only 205 by 1969), but many of those operating today have histories that extend well into the period of slavery. As in the past, most Barbadian plantations are relatively small by worldwide sugar plantation standards; anything over 400 acres is considered large, but over 80 percent are under this acreage (p. 17–21). Also continuing a pattern established in an early period of sugar production, relatively few owners hold a considerable percentage of the plantations and arable acreage; in 1970, for example, 54 percent of the arable plantation acreage (exclusive of 2,375 acres—comprising nine plantations—held by a government corporation) was owned by 17.6 percent of the owners; the ten largest owners (7 percent) owned 32 percent of the total arable land.

Most plantations are owned by citizens of Barbados either as individual proprietors or as participants in companies or corporations with other landholdings or economic interests; some plantations,

12

however, are still owned by absentee proprietors, an ownership pattern that extends deep into the island's history.

The number of factories that process sugar cane has steadily declined over the years. In the sugar industry's earlier history, medium and large plantations ground their own cane and processed it into raw sugar; at slave emancipation in 1834, there were close to 400 sugar works. Later, however, smaller unproductive factories were eliminated and the remaining ones were often enlarged; in 1940 about sixty-three factories serviced the island's sugar cane growers, by the early 1960s there were about twenty, and only ten factories were operating in 1973.

Despite the role that sugar plays in the Barbadian economy, a minority of the working population is directly engaged in full-time agricultural pursuits. In the early 1960s approximately 24 percent of those employed were primarily engaged in agricultural work (Barbados Census 1960), but today, with the growth of tourism and related services and construction, light manufacturing, and governmental employment, about 15 percent of employees work in agriculture (Massiah 1976). Recently, in fact, several Barbadian plantations (and many small farmers) have found it increasingly difficult to acquire enough laborers to harvest the sugar crop. As a result, cane cutters are temporarily recruited from neighboring islands, and plantations are beginning to use mechanized harvest equipment. Tillage, however, has been mechanized for a longer period.

Barbados suffers many of the socioeconomic problems—albeit some not as acutely—found in most other Caribbean countries: inflation, vulnerability to international market conditions, extreme dependence on imported goods, widespread poverty, severe unemployment and underemployment, and overpopulation.

Barbados is one of the world's three or four most densely populated countries (United Nations 1974:68), but serious crowding marks much of its history. At the time of slave emancipation in 1834, the island supported approximately 104,000 persons, a density of about 627 people per square mile (Handler 1974:19); over the next century or so, population densities were, on the average, close to 1,000 (Barbados Census 1950:xvii). Preliminary 1970 census figures show a population of 235,229, a density of 1,417 per square mile (Barbados Census 1972).

The large number of Barbadians is not due to their especial fertility as a people. In fact, for many years the rate of natural increase has been the lowest in the Caribbean. In the mid-1950s, the annual natural increase was 2 percent (Lowenthal 1957:448), and over the past decade or so the annual rate of natural increase has been less than 1 percent and is the lowest in the New World (United Nations 1974:68). According to geographer David Lowenthal, "Barbados' superabundant population cannot . . . fairly be attributed to her present demographic character; it is rather historical inertia that is responsible. The island is crowded today partly because it always has been crowded. As one scholar [W. A. Lewis] has written, 'Barbados [was] fully peopled in the seventeenth century and [has] been complaining of over-population for nearly three centuries'" (1957:448–449).

Barbados's population is unevenly distributed. The heaviest concentrations are found along the western and southwestern coast, including Bridgetown and its environs. In the rural areas, as one might expect, population density decreases, but even in the lowest density parish of Saint Andrew (which comprises about 57 percent of the land area in the Scotland District) the population density in 1970 was over 530 persons per square mile (Barbados Census 1972). Most rural peoples live in small villages that are either tenantries (lands owned and rented by plantations) or "free villages" (formed after emancipation by ex-slaves who individually purchased or otherwise acquired plantation lands), or some combination of these two types. Villages are never very far from one another and they are almost exclusively inhabited by persons who are entirely or partially of African descent.

Over 90 percent of Barbadians are black, and an even greater percentage (which includes persons of mixed racial descent)— around 95 percent—can claim some African ancestry; this population composition is a direct consequence of the island's slave past. Barbados's white population has steadily declined over the years. In 1834, whites formed approximately 14 percent of the population (Handler 1974:19); by the early twentieth century, they comprised between 7 and 8 percent (Barbados Census 1950:xvii) and 4.3 percent in 1960 (Barbados Census 1960). The 1970 census reported 9,354 whites, or 3.9 percent of the total population (Barbados Census 1972). This small percentage of whites is higher than in any other territory of the Commonwealth or British Caribbean.[2]

Although a number of Barbadian whites are, and have been, quite poor by island standards (see, for example, Shepherd 1974; Lowenthal 1972:82), until a recent period, whites as a group have controlled, as they have elsewhere in the Commonwealth Caribbean, the national institutions and particularly the island's economic and political life. The general picture has changed dramatically in the last decade or two, especially since Barbados's political independence from Great Britain in 1966. Today persons of African and mixed

14

racial ancestry control governmental and other institutions, and have an increasingly visible role in the economy; nonetheless whites are still disproportionately prominent in commercial and economic life as they have been since the seventeenth century.

HISTORICAL BACKGROUND

Considerable archaeological evidence indicates that various Amer- indian populations visited and inhabited Barbados during pre- Columbian times (Barton 1953; Bullen 1966; Bullen and Bullen 1968; Fewkes 1922:78–88; Hughes 1750:7–8; Roach 1936–39). Early Spanish sources also attest to the presence of Indians on the island during the first few decades of the sixteenth century. By 1541, however, the island appears to have been depopulated largely, it seems, because of Spanish raids in the Lesser Antilles for Indians to work the mines of Hispaniola (Sauer 1966:192–195).[3] Indians from neighboring islands may have visited Barbados during the late six- teenth and early seventeenth centuries, but the island was apparently uninhabited when its first non-Amerindian settlement was established (Handler 1969a:39–40).

In February 1627 a small group of Englishmen arrived directly from England, bringing with them a handful of Africans captured during the sea voyage, to form England's second colony in the Caribbean islands (the first, on St. Christopher—or St. Kitt's— was established in 1624). In its early years, Barbados's cash economy rested on the production of tobacco, cotton, ginger, and indigo, which were primarily grown on relatively small farms of from ten to twenty or thirty acres. The farms were cultivated by free and indentured Europeans assisted by African slaves and occasionally by Amerindians who were imported or captured from neighboring territories in the Caribbean (Handler 1969a).[4]

The island's population rapidly expanded from "but 3 score of Christyanes and fortye slaves of Negeres and indyenes" in late 1627 (Winthrop 1929) to about 1,850 "English, Indians, and others [blacks] ... men, women and children" in 1629 (*True State of the Case* 1644; cf. Smith 1630:56). Around mid-1636, Barbados was "inhabited with about 6,000 English" (Warner 1636), and the al- ready established slave trade continued to bring Africans to Bar- badian shores. By 1643–45, an estimated 5,680 to 6,400 slaves and 18,300 to 18,600 European males or "effective men" lived on the island (Public Record Office 1667; Scott 1668).

Because of marketing and other difficulties with tobacco and cotton, the main cash crops, the commercial growth of sugar cane was encouraged. Although the cane plant (along with other subsistence and commercial crops) had been brought to Barbados from Guiana during the first years of the colony's life, it was not grown as a cash crop until in the late 1630s when Dutchmen from Brazil reintroduced the plant and the technical knowledge to grind the cane and produce sugar. With the aid of Dutch and Sephardic Jewish capital and credit, Barbados became the first British possession in the Caribbean to cultivate sugar on a large scale, and during the 1640s its economy began to be based on plantation production and slave labor.

The emphasis on sugar increased dramatically within a few years: "Provisions for the belly . . . at present is very scarce," wrote a colonist with fifty acres in 1647, because "men are so intent upon planting sugar that they had rather buy foode at very deare rates than produce it by labour, soe infinite is the profitt of sugar workes after once accomplished"; with the assistance of slave labor he was still growing cotton and tobacco, but in "the next yeare I intend for sugar" (Vines 1947). By the 1650s the plantation slave system was firmly entrenched and the island's flourishing sugar-based economy made it (until surpassed by Jamaica in the third decade of the eighteenth century) the richest of England's Caribbean possessions. Around 1651, when sugar production was still in an early phase, an anonymous writer enthusiastically assessed Bardabos as of "so much value that it may [be] reckoned a jewell, & ye most proud state of ye world may wear it as in a ring. Amongst ye Caribbee islands this disserves to be the Empresse" (Ayer Mss.).

As the plantation system expanded, the number of small holdings was severely reduced and the number of landowners declined from between approximately 8,300 to 11,200 in the mid-1640s to 2,639 in 1679 (Public Record Office 1667; Scott 1668; Dunn 1969:8–9). Newton plantation was formed during this period (see chapter 4) the way in which other plantations were established—by buying contiguous land units from small landholders. One well-known mid-seventeenth-century case involved a plantation of "above 800 acres" (an exceptionally large size) whose owner reported that at one time the plantation's acreage had been divided among forty different proprietors (Scott 1688). "I believe," wrote Richard Ligon at a time when the plantation system was beginning to expand, "when the small plantations in poor mens hands, of ten, twenty, or thirty acres, which are too small to lay to that work [sugar production], be bought up by great men, and put together into plantations of five, six, or seven hundred acres, that two thirds of the island will be fit for plantations of sugar, which will make it one of the richest spots of earth under the sun (1657:86).

16

Impelled by the extension of the plantation system, thousands of Europeans left Barbados in search of land and other opportunities elsewhere in the Caribbean and in the mainland colonies. Many of these emigrants were, one contemporary observer wrote, "proprietors and tradesmen—wormed out of their small settlements by their more subtle and greedy neighbors" (Public Record Office 1667), though considerable numbers were indentured servants whose contracts had expired. Although indentured servants continued to be employed,[5] the heightened need for agricultural labor on the sugar plantations intensified the slave trade to Barbados.

Fulfilling Richard Ligon's expectations, a visitor in 1655 exuberantly proclaimed Barbados as "one of the Riches spotes of ground in the wordell" where "the genterey ... doth live far better than ours doue in England" (Whistler 1655). Richard Dunn has written that by 1650 "the big sugar planters had taken charge ... [and] before the close of the century [they] ... monopolized all the best sugar acreage, reaped most of the profits, managed island politics, and dominated their society in every way ... the rise of the Barbados planter class was intoxicating. Virginia might be the Old Dominion and Massachusetts the Bible Commonwealth, but Barbados [in 1679–80] was something more tangible ... the richest and most populous colony in English America" (1972:46–47, 83, 84).

In 1679–1680, 175 Barbados planters (7 percent of all property holders) owned at least 53 percent of the land and 54 percent of the slaves; they were "unquestionably the ... wealthiest men in English America" (pp. 96, 85).[6] The combined efforts of both large and small planters appear "to have produced more sugar and employed more shipping than the other English islands combined" (Dunn 1969:4). Barbados, "that fair jewell of your Majesty's Crown"— wrote the island's governor in 1666 (Willoughby 1666)—reached the zenith of its prosperity in the 1660s and 1670s, but throughout the remainder of the seventeenth century, the value of Barbados's exports to England was greater than that of any other British Caribbean territory, and "more valuable than the total from North America" (Dunn 1969:4–5, n5; cf. Williams 1961:54).

Barbados lost its preeminence in the British Empire during the eighteenth century, but by the end of the seventeenth the basic structural features of Barbadian slave society and the plantation system had been firmly established. These features endured substantially unaltered for the remainder of the slave period. During the 1700s and until 1834, the plantation continued to be a major institution that helped shape the island's polity and society; it remained the major unit of sugar production, but proportionately less of its acreage was devoted to sugar than after emancipation. Despite considerable food importations, Barbadian plantations also grew subsistence crops in their fields, and slaves frequently cultivated food and in the later slave period cash crops in small gardens adjacent to their houses or in various plantation fields. Moreover, sugar and its by-products of rum and molasses continued to be the mainstay of the island's economic life; they accounted for over 95 percent of the value of Barbados's exports during the eighteenth century (Sheridan 1974:144).

Britain not only received most of what Barbados produced, but it also supplied a great deal of the manufactured goods and non-organic materials that the island consumed. These goods ranged from utilitarian items employed in agricultural production and sugar manufacture to clothing materials for slaves and luxury items intended for relatively few of the island's population.[7] In the seventeenth century Britain also supplied provisions, but during the eighteenth century the North American colonies assumed a domiant position in this trade.

Trade with the thirteen continental colonies started early in Barbados's history. At first trade was largely with New England, but later it extended to Pennsylvania, New York, Maryland, Virginia, and the Carolinas. The continental colonies supplied the island with considerable quantities of foodstuffs (such as corn, flour, salt, dried and salt fish, salt beef and pork), and most of its livestock, timber, and timber products (including casks and cask heads, barrel staves and hoops, and wood shingles). Other products, ranging from wax candles to furniture, deerskin gloves, and iron nails, were also involved in this trade, but Britain continued to supply most of the manufactured goods and materials, especially those which might have become archaeologically detectable or identifiable, such as ceramic ware, metal goods, and nonorganic construction materials.[8]

Before the American Revolution, ships from North American ports went straight to the West Indies with their cargoes. Ships from Britain also went directly to the West Indies and probably only a very few first stopped at North American ports, deposited their cargoes or picked up additional goods, and then continued their voyages to Caribbean ports. Although Barbados's trade with North America was severely disrupted during the American Revolution, it was later resumed and continued, albeit with other disruptions and fluctuations, throughout the period of slavery.

In the seventeenth century Barbados also received goods and materials from other European countries and their colonies. During

1652, for example, "several ships arrived from Germany with merchandise to be traded, according to custom" (Gunkel and Handler 1970:94), and a considerable proportion of the foreign trade before the 1660s was with the Dutch whose routes to Barbados were directly from Holland, as well as indirectly from areas such as Brazil.

As a result of the navigation acts of 1650, 1651, and 1660, trade with the Dutch (and "foreigners" in general) was severely curtailed —much to the chagrin of Barbadian planters and merchants; protesting the act of 1650, they stressed their indebtedness to the Dutch and emphasized "how difficult it would have been (without their assistance) ever to have settled this place and even to this day we are sensible what necessary comforts they bring us and how much cheaper they sell their commodities to us than our own nation" (Declaration set forth by the Lord 1651). The navigation acts were changed in later years but the restrictive provisions of the earliest seventeenth century laws "continued to dominate colonial trade" until the last act was repealed in 1849 (Burns 1954:268).

Although the navigation acts all but stopped direct trade with non-British and non-British colonial sources, "foreign" goods, usually relatively small quantities of luxury goods, continued to arrive at Barbados, but generally could only be legally imported if they came in British or British colonial ships. For example, during the 1660s, a Swiss doctor sailed on English ships that sometimes loaded cargoes in Amsterdam and then sailed directly to Barbados (Gunkel and Handler 1969:3, 11), wines from Madeira were imported during the seventeenth and eighteenth centuries, and during the eighteenth century British ships occasionally deposited "German or Dutch linens" (Commissioners for Trade and Plantations 1734:8). From the late seventeenth century to the end of the slave period, however, foreign imports appear to have been inconsequential compared to all Barbados's imports, especially those of nonorganic materials.

In the eighteenth century Barbados conducted "very little" trade with the non-British colonies, although the island sometimes obtained "mill timber" from the Dutch colonies in Berbice and Demerara (Pinfold 1762:459). Small quantities of other goods also might have been funneled into the island from these Dutch sources in Guiana. Moreover, during the seventeenth and eighteenth centuries occasional items of non-British origin were probably brought to Barbados by travelers, traders, colonial officials, and military and naval personnel from continental Europe or from the French Caribbean. Also sporadic contacts with Brazil in the late eighteenth and early nineteenth centuries may have occasionally resulted in the deposition of goods of Portuguese or Brazilian manufacture; referring to this period, a Barbadian writer noted how "Portuguese vessels in distress from the Brazils I have often seen here [in Barbados]; never a Spaniard" (Lucas 1946:161).

In earlier periods, however, some material goods may have derived from Spanish sources.[9] In the early 1660s, the British Crown granted a license to "Spanish subjects in America to purchase from the Caribbee islands and Jamaica supplies of Negro slaves," and from the 1660s through the early eighteenth century, Spanish ships occasionally arrived at Barbados, some coming directly from Spain, and sometimes English ships from Barbados went directly to the Spanish Caribbean colonies (Modyford 1662; Willoughby 1664; Atkins 1677; Crowe 1708a; British Museum 1714–16). The Spanish license to trade directly with the British colonies did not violate the navigation acts for "England still retained the sole right of supplying the colonies with everything they needed." Spanish traders were forbidden from bringing into the British colonies any "goods of the growth of Europe, Asia, or Africa" (Harlow 1926:142). Despite these restrictions it is hard to believe that items of Spanish (or, indirectly, other European) manufacture did not occasionally come to Barbados as a result of the slave trade and other contacts with the Spanish.

Some material goods were brought to Barbados by African slaves during the middle passage; some of these goods, such as glass beads, were of European manufacture, though various types of metal jewelry may have been made in Africa (see chapter 5).

In general, then, throughout the period of slavery, Britain was the overwhelming source of the manufactured goods and materials that arrived in Barbados. One must thus look to the "mother country" for the ultimate origin of most of the materials which would have been most apt to endure in archaeological contexts.

THE SLAVE TRADE, AFRICAN ORIGINS, AND THE SLAVE POPULATION

Importing material goods was one dimension of Barbados's trade, importing human commodities another. It is difficult to achieve a reasonable estimate of the number of slaves destined for the island who died during the middle passage (but cf. Anstey 1975; Curtin 1969:275–284); estimating the numbers who arrived during the entire period of slavery is also difficult, especially for the earliest periods.

In his comprehensive analysis of the Atlantic slave trade, Philip Curtin estimated that 18,700 slaves were imported into Barbados from the time of its colonization to 1650 (1969:119); more recently Richard Sheridan has calculated a rough figure of 29,100 net imports and 33,500 gross imports for the same period (1974:247).

For the 179-year period from 1651 to 1834, we have estimated 353,069 slave imports (table 1). These figures are only approximations of total imports: reported figures are often imprecise or unavailable and reexported slaves were often included in reported figures of total imports.[10]

From 1651 to 1807, the last year of the British slave trade, we estimate that 352,884 slaves arrived at the island; on the other hand, Curtin estimates 368,200 for the same period (1969:55, 119, 140; cf. Sheridan 1974:247). Although we used essentially the same procedures as Curtin for interpolating figures for unreported years, we had access to some late eighteenth- and nineteenth-century figures from primary sources that Curtin did not employ.[11]

Far more slaves were imported from the late seventeenth to the mid-eighteenth century than in the late eighteenth and early nineteenth centuries. The role played by various African coastal areas in supplying these slaves at various periods can be estimated with a certain degree of confidence, but ascertaining the slaves' ethnic origins is another matter.

Ligon wrote that Barbadian slaves in the 1647–50 period "are fetch'd from several parts of Africa... some of them are fetch'd from Guinny and Binny, some from Cutchew, some from Angola, and some from the River of Gambia" (1657:46). From the "River of Gambia" in the north to "Angola" in the south is an enormous area, and throughout the seventeenth and eighteenth centuries the great majority of slaves brought to the island came directly from trading posts along this vast stretch of coastline in western Africa.[12] British traders, who accounted for most of these slaves, largely acquired them along a section of the coast that ranged from the Windward Coast (including the Grain and Ivory Coasts), through the Gold Coast, and to the Bights of Benin (the Slave Coast) and Biafra (see, for example, table 2). The intensity of British slavers' trade from particular coastal areas, however, was greater at certain periods than at others. In the 1680s, for example, an estimated 52.2 percent of the slaves shipped by British slavers came from the Windward and Gold Coasts and 19.9 percent from the Bights of Benin and Biafra; by 1781–90, 21.7 percent derived from the former areas and 52.6 percent from the latter (Curtin 1975:114, 116, 118, 123, 126; Anstey 1975:13). In more general terms, for British traders the Bight of Biafra (from eastern Nigeria, through the Cameroons to northern Gabon) "only began to be significant in the 1730's. Meanwhile, the

TABLE 1. Estimated number of slaves imported into Barbados, 1651–1830.

Period	Years	Slaves	Annual averages of slave imports
1651–1672	22	44,968	2,044
1673–1689	17	36,700	2,159
1690–1697	18	23,300	2,912
1698–1707	10	35,409	3,541
1708–1717	10	31,929	3,193
1718–1725	8	22,079	2,760
1726–1735	10	29,404	2,940
1736–1739	4	11,210	2,802
1740–1748	8	21,320	2,665
1749–1758	10	34,969	3,497
1759–1768	10	32,375	3,237
1769–1773	5	18,776	3,755
1774–1778	5	1,616	323
1779–1780	2	721	360
1781–1787	7	2,785	398
1788–1800	13	3,470	267
1801	1	305	305
1802–1804	3	1,032	344
1805–1807	3	516	172
1808–1814	7	0	0
1815–1819	5	119	24
1820–1826	7	33	5
1827–1828	2	14	7
1829–1830	2	19	9
Total	179	353,069	

Sources: 1651–1672, based on "rough estimates" by Curtin (1969:119) for the twenty-five-year period 1651–1675; Curtin estimates 51,100 slaves imported into Barbados during this period, an annual average of 2,044; we have multiplied this annual average by twenty-two. 1673–1689, Curtin's calculations (1969:54–55, 122) based on materials given by Davies (1957). The Royal African Company's records show 26,245 slaves delivered to Barbados during this period; the remaining number of slaves was estimated from what privateers or interlopers may have delivered. 1690–1697, the total figure is Curtin's estimate (1969:54). 1698–1707, *Account of the Number of Negroes* (1709). During this period, approximately 74 percent of imported slaves were brought by privateers and not by the Royal African Company (Crowe 1708b). 1708–1725, Barbados Department of Archives (1726). 1726–1733, *Calendar of State Papers* (1734).

Gold Coast and the Bight of Benin, which had supplied more than half the British exports of 1701–30, had become minor sources for the trade of the 1790's" (Curtin 1969:154).[13]

Many of the Africans brought to Barbados from the late seventeenth century to the middle of the eighteenth came in ships chartered to the Royal African Company. Although the Company's forts and trading posts were dispersed along Africa's western coast, its major activities were concentrated along the Gold Coast (Commissioners for Trade and Plantations 1750:20–27; Royal African Company ca. 1700; Philopatris 1748; Postlethwayt 1745:36). The general trade patterns during this period were described in 1748: prior to 1697 the Royal African Company "furnished our [Caribbean] plantations with the best Coromantine and other Gold Coast and Whydah Negroes . . . and . . . for the next following 30 years . . . the private traders . . . sent out great numbers of ships to purchase

---

1734–1735, Pitman (1917:72). 1736–1739, no figures are available for this period. We have interpolated the annual average (by taking the mean of the annual averages for the preceding ten-year period and the following eight-year period) and multiplied it by four to arrive at total imports. 1740–1748, Hall (1924:10) had examined the import records of the Barbados Custom House between 1740 and 1748; however, he gives the slave imports only as "a medium of eight years, viz from 1740 to 1748," not the total number imported. We have estimated this number by multiplying the annual average by eight. 1749–1763, Pitman (1917:72). 1764–1778, Barbados Assembly (1790). 1779–1780, no figures are available for this period. We have interpolated the annual average (by taking the mean of the estimated annual averages for the five preceding years and the seven following years) and multiplied it by two to arrive at an estimate of total imports. 1781–1787, Public Record Office (1788; cf. Barbados Assembly 1790). 1788–1800, 1802–1804, Public Record Office (1805). The figures for these years are the slaves who stayed on the island; far more were reexported. 1801, no figures are available. Total imports have been interpolated by taking the mean of the annual averages of the thirteen preceding years and the three following years. 1805–1807, no figures are available. Annual average has been interpolated (by taking the mean of the three preceding years and the seven following) and multiplied by three for an estimate of total imports. 1808–1820, Parliamentary Papers (1823). 1821–1826, Parliamentary Papers (1826, 1831–1832b). All the slaves imported from 1815 to 1826 came from other British West Indian territories. 1827–1828, no figures available. Annual average has been interpolated to calculate the total number of imports. 1829–1830, Parliamentary Papers (1831–1832b). All these slaves were domestics accompanying their masters who came from other British West Indian territories.

TABLE 2. The British slave trade: sources of African slaves and proportions imported into Barbados and other areas.

Period	Estimated percentage of slaves exported from coastal regions[a]								Estimated percentage of imported slaves		
	Senegambia	Sierra Leone	Windward Coast	Gold Coast	Bight of Benin	Bight of Biafra	Central Africa–Angola	Madagascar-Mozambique	Barbados	Jamaica	Other British Caribbean and North American areas
1680s	12.0		32.6	19.6	14.0	5.9	11.6	4.1	38.4	33.6	28.0
1701–1720	14.6	4.1	10.4	31.2	39.5	—	—	—	37.6	29.7	32.7
1721–1740	7.7	10.0	8.7	37.2	19.4	16.7	—	—	22.1	36.1	41.8
1741–1760	8.1	5.9	13.1	23.3	9.4	39.9	—	—	15.5	32.6	51.9
1761–1780	3.5	9.8	21.8	8.4	9.2	41.0	6.0	—	11.7	35.5	52.8
1781–1800	0.8	4.9	6.9	14.5	8.8	37.7	26.1	—	4.2	46.8	49.0
1801–1810	0.6	4.7	7.5	13.8	1.7	40.7	30.8	—			

Sources: Exports from coastal regions: 1680s, the mean of the percentages given by Curtin (1969:129) for 1680–1685 and 1688. 1701–1760, percentages derived from figures in Curtin (1975:114, 116, 118, 123, 126), which have incorporated new data from Anstey (1975). The figures for 1701–1720 are for the period 1711–1720, with the exception of the Bight of Biafra for which no figures are given. During the 1721–1730 period, however, the Bight of Biafra accounted for only about 3.7 percent of the British trade. No figures are given for Central Africa–Angola during 1701–1760, but elsewhere Curtin (1969:129) estimates 14.9 percent and 12.7 percent for 1724 and 1752, respectively, from this region. 1761–1810, percentages for all regions, except Central Africa–Angola, were derived from Curtin (1975:114, 116, 118, 123, 126); for Central Africa–Angola, the percentages have been calculated from figures given by Anstey (1975:13). Import areas: 1680s, percentage given by Curtin (1969:122) for the period 1673–1689. 1701–1810, percentages calculated from Curtin's estimated figures (1969:140).

[a] In defining these regions we follow Curtin (1969:128, 130): Senegambia coincides with the present-day Senegal and Gambia; Sierra Leone roughly with a small portion of Senegal, the coastlines of Guinea-Bissau, Guinea, Sierra Leone, and a small part of Liberia; the Windward Coast stretches through most of coastal Liberia and the Ivory Coast; the Gold Coast is approximately the same as modern Ghana; the Bight of Benin includes a small portion of eastern Ghana, the coasts of Togo and Dahomey (the former slave coast), and western Nigeria to the Benin River; the Bight of Biafra goes from the Benin River, along the coast of eastern Nigeria and through the coastal Cameroons to Cape Lopez in northern Gabon; Central Africa–Angola runs from Cape Lopez in the north, through Angola, and to the Orange River in Southwest Africa (Namibia); Madagascar-Mozambique includes the island and the southeastern Africa coast.

Negroes at Whydah, Anamaboe and other places on the Gold Coast" (Philopatris 1748).

The Dutch also shipped considerable numbers of slaves during the seventeenth century. Although the Dutch were ultimately responsible for only about 10 percent of the Africans taken to the New World over the duration of the Atlantic slave trade (Postma 1975: 33), until the early 1660s they brought most of the slaves who were employed in Barbados (Curtin 1969:55, 117; Harlow 1926:310; Bridenbaugh and Bridenbaugh 1972:248–249, 252); during the early phases of the sugar industry Barbadian planters were particularly dependent on Dutch-supplied slaves (Scott 1688; *Declaration Set forth by the Lord* 1651). Some of these slaves came directly from Africa, primarily from the western parts of the Bight of Benin and bordering on the Gold Coast. Largely using data from Postma (1970), Price reports that, from the 1640s to 1700, 64 percent of the Dutch-shipped slaves derived from the coastal areas of present-day Togo and Dahomey, 2 percent from the Gold Coast, and 34 percent from the Central African-Angola region (1976:13–14; cf. Postma 1975:35, 49), but others were brought from the Guianas and more so from Brazil where they had "been bred up amongst the Portugals" (Ligon 1657:52; see also Handler 1967:67); some slaves who came from Brazil were probably born there while many others were undoubtedly African-born.

Approximately 65.5 percent of the slaves imported to Barbados from 1651 to 1807 were imported between 1651 and 1739 (table 1). During most of the latter period Barbados appears to have accounted for over one-third of the total number of slaves shipped by British slavers (table 2; cf. Sheridan 1972:29) and probably for a considerable percentage of the Dutch-supplied slaves prior to the 1660s. In general, evidence from the slave trade itself indicates that during the period of the most intensive trade to Barbados, the Gold Coast and the Bight of Benin (including the modern areas of Ghana, Togo, Dahomey, and western Nigeria) supplied most of the slaves shipped by British and Dutch slavers. Evidence from Barbados also stresses that slaves from these areas were preferred by planters.

By the late 1600s and during the 1700s, Barbadian planters "universally preferred" creole slaves to Africans (Dickson 1789:88),[14] but they maintained preferences for certain African groups. "I have observed," wrote a wealthy Barbadian planter in the 1670s or early 1680s, "the Caramantines, and Gold-Coast slaves, have always stood and proved best on my plantations"; he therefore stressed that "those [rather] than [Africans] of any other sorts" should be purchased for his property (Drax 1755:67). Captain Thomas Phillips went to

West Africa on a Royal African Company charter in 1693–94 to acquire slaves for Barbados. He ultimately purchased 700 slaves at Whydah, in Dahomey, but, he emphasized, "the negroes most in demand at Barbadoes, are the Gold Coast, or, as they call them, Cormantines"; next in preference were "the Whidaw, or, as they call them, Papa negroes; but these are preferred before the Angola, as they are before the Alampo, which are accounted the worst of all" (1746:230). A group of planters argued around 1749 that "The only proper negroes for the preservation of our sugar colonies are to be purchased no-where but on . . . the Gold-Coast and Whydah . . . the worst kind of Negroes that can be purchased cheap [are] from Calabar, Congo, Angola, and other parts of Africa" (Commissioners for Trade and Plantations 1750:51). These planters were arguing for a Royal African Company monopoly on the slave trade and the areas they extolled were the ones in which the Company had its major trading posts; nonetheless, in Barbados around this period slaves from the Gold Coast were "in general . . . looked upon to be the best for labour" (Hughes 1750:14).

Slaves from the Gold Coast and parts of the Bight of Benin also constituted a significant element of the African-born population during the period Barbados was importing its greatest number of slaves. In 1675, the island's governor reported that "Cormantin negroes . . . are much the greater number from any one country" (Atkins 1675), and by the 1730s and 1740s, although Barbadian slaves "differ[ed] according to the several customs of so many nations intermixed," Africans were imported "chiefly from the kingdoms of Coromantee," "Anamabw" [sic], "Whiddaw," "Ebo," and "Angola" (Hughes 1750:14, 15–16). The first two of these "kingdoms" were located along the Gold Coast, and the third in Dahomey. The importance of these three coastal areas as sources of slaves is corroborated by statistical evidence. And, as Curtin has pointed out, "a [British] colony that imported heavily in the early part of the eighteenth century would receive a correspondingly high proportion of Akan peoples from the southern Gold Coast, and of Fon and Gun from southern Dahomey" (1969:154–155); Barbados clearly "imported heavily" during this period.

The terms used in the historical sources to refer to African cultural groups provide some clues as to the nature of these groups, but they cannot be taken as precise cultural indicators. Although European slave traders and owners recognized "cultural variants" (Curtin 1969:184) among the enslaved African populations, they employed a simplified cultural nomenclature or typology derived from the two general tendencies: "One was the European habit of identifying nationalities customarily shipped from a particular African port by the name of the port... The second was to pick one ethnic or linguistic term to identify a much larger group... These tendencies make for confusion and overlapping terminology... overlapping variants make it difficult to equate ethnic identifications with particular coastal regions of the slave trade... The most common European error was to use a narrow ethnic or linguistic name, or a coastal shipping point, to stand for a larger and more diverse assortment of peoples" (Curtin 1969:184, 190).

"Coromantine" or its variant spellings for example, could refer to several sociocultural groups that spoke Akan languages (including the Ashanti and Fanti), or to peoples who may not have spoken these languages, such as the Ewe-speakers (including the Ga and Adangme and related peoples), but who were shipped from the Gold Coast in general or from the particular town or fort of that name on the Gold Coast. Similarly, Whydah (or Ouidah) could refer to such peoples as the speakers of various Ewe languages (including Fon speakers, such as the Dahomeans, Gun and Popo, and the Ewe proper), who were shipped from that major slaving port in Dahomey, to a wider region which stretched from the Gold Coast to the Benin river in western Nigeria (see, for example, *Abstract of Evidence before a Select Committee* 1791); or Whydah "may have meant people from that part of the coast, not merely those shipped through Ouidah" (Curtin 1969:187).

The specific cultural groupings represented in Barbados were more numerous than the contemporary sources generally indicate by their simplified terminology of African peoples. All evidence, however, supports the view that the island's African-born slave population during the period of greatest importations, roughly prior to 1750, was heavily comprised of persons who came from cultural-linguistic groups that originated in present-day Ghana, Togo, Dahomey, western Nigeria, and neighboring areas and countries. The ethnographically better known groups in these areas in modern times include such peoples as the Adangme, Ashanti, Dahomeans and Ewe, Edo, Fanti, Ga, Ibibio, Ibo, and Yoruba.

It may be surmised that in the earlier periods of the slave trade to Barbados, most of the slaves came from such cultural-linguistic groups that lived near the coastal areas of these countries; later, they also came from areas farther inland. Orlando Patterson is probably generally correct in concluding that "few of the slaves came from an area more than two or three hundred miles inland" (1967:126; cf. Curtin 1969:201–202; Morton-Williams 1964). Most West African slaves brought to Barbados seem to have largely derived from cultural groups that were located in the eastern sector of the "Guinea Coast" culture area, which, according to Melville Herskovits, "follows the line of the West African littoral from the Bight of Biafra to the southern portion of the Republic of Guinea. It is long and narrow, and essentially comprehends the forested belt" (1962:94, 57). This belt is "some two hundred miles deep behind the Guinea coast" (Forde 1960:118).

Although the degree of ethnic and linguistic diversity in this culture area is debatable, many broad sociocultural features were shared by its populations as well as by peoples in culture areas that bordered on the "Guinea Coast" (Herskovits 1962:83–112; Forde 1960; Murdock 1959:237–264, 271–284). We believe these shared cultural characteristics were especially important for the development of slave cultural patterns in Barbados (see, for example, Handler and Frisbie 1972; chapter 6 of this work).

It is difficult to be precise on ethnic origins and the preponderance of specific African cultural groups at varying periods. The "mystery of the ultimate origin of slaves in the African interior" (Postma 1975:33) is not one that we pretend or systematically attempt to solve for Barbados; the problem is simply too complex and cannot be comprehensively treated with our present resources and data. However, these general observations provide a broad idea of the major types of African peoples that composed the island's African-born slave population during the emergence of Afro-Barbadian or slave culture. They also have a direct bearing on the African ethnographic literature we have used to interpret various of our historical and archaeological data.

Through importations and natural increase, particularly in the nineteenth century, Barbados's slave population rose as the white population fell in both proportion and number. During the early phases of the "sugar revolution" whites had greatly outnumbered blacks, but by the 1660s and 1670s, blacks outnumbered whites two to one (Willoughby 1668; Blake 1669; Atkins 1680a; Public Record Office 1679–80), and in the 1680s whites were outnumbered by almost 2.5 to 1 (British Museum 1684). For the remainder of the slave period, blacks constituted the overwhelming majority: in 1715–16, 52,856 slaves were reported (76 percent of the total population); in 1757, about 71,288 (81 percent); and around 1802–03, there were approximately 67,812 slaves (82 percent).[15] Although these and other figures clearly show the preponderance of blacks, until 1817 figures on the number of slaves are based on returns submitted to the island treasurer's office for the annual head tax that slaveowners paid. Earlier figures are invariably underestimates because owners frequently did not declare all their slaves. In 1817 a slave registration system was established; its first census counted 5,000 more slaves "than were hitherto supposed to have been upon the island" (Combermere 1818). The registry was conducted triennially, and for the years 1817, 1820, 1823, 1826, 1829, and 1832, the slave population ranged between 77,493 and 81,902, averaging 79,767, or approximately 80 percent of the island's total population during these years.[16] At emancipation, on August 1, 1834, there were between 82,807 and 83,146 slaves, about 14,592 whites, and 6,584 freedmen.[17]

By emancipation, the vast majority of Barbadian slaves were creoles. This demographic characteristic had been established early, and it increased as a trend as the years progressed. In the 1660s, Barbados contained "many thousands of slaves that speak English, either born there or brought young into the country" (Public Record Office 1667). By the late seventeenth or early eighteenth century, despite large slave importations, most slaves may have been Barbadian-born (see, for example, Oldmixon 1741;2:12), but certainly by the mid to late 1700s, the great majority of them were creoles. For example, in the late 1780s the island's governor submitted to the British parliament detailed information on twenty-two representative plantations of various sizes and number of slaves that were located "in almost every different part of the island." Of the total 3,112 slaves on these plantations, 86 percent were Barbadian-born; the remainder had been born in Africa (Parry 1789c; see also Dickson 1789:88). By the first detailed slave census in 1817, about 93 percent of the island's 77,493 slaves were creoles, a very small number of whom had been born in neighboring West Indian islands; only 7 percent had been born in Africa (Public Record Office 1817). In Jamaica and Trinidad, in contrast, 37 and 44 percent respectively of the slaves in 1817 were of African birth (Higman 1973b:4; personal communication).

PLANTATION SLAVE SETTLEMENTS

In the late 1780s, the governor of Barbados provided a unique estimate when he "imagined" that about 88 percent of the island's slaves were plantation slaves (Parry 1789b). Although we found no other estimates on the number of plantation slaves, official returns on the slave population at emancipation reported that 67 percent were involved in one form or another of agricultural work, 13 percent were defined as domestics, and 20 percent (including small children, the sick, and the aged) were considered without employment (*The Barbadian*, August 13, 1834); many of the unemployed and domestic slaves undoubtedly resided on farm units or plantations.

The life of plantation slaves and their most fundamental social groupings centered in the compact villages that were part of every Barbadian plantation. These villages were located close to the mill yard, not far from the plantation owner's or manager's house, and were small communities in the sociological sense (see M. G. Smith 1956:295). This settlement pattern existed in all sugar plantation areas of the West Indies. Although these communities were not isolated in an island as small as Barbados and slaves from different plantation communities were often in contact, slaves in fact passed more of their working and leisure time with members of their own settlement than with outsiders.

If the word "community" stresses the sociocultural dimensions of the slave settlements, the word "village" can be taken to emphasize their physical features. Aside from the houses, which usually contained small numbers of people who were often related,[18] the major features of Barbadian slave villages were the house plots on which slaves raised subsistence and, occasionally, cash crops, small livestock and poultry; the ponds from which they drew their water; and the communal burial grounds in which they interred their dead (sometimes close kinsmen or friends were also buried under house floors). Although the ponds and burial grounds were not literally in the villages themselves, they were generally located close enough to be considered as intrinsic village features. In the later years of the pre-emancipation period, plantations built "sick houses" and, occasionally, chapels near the villages.

The plantation slave settlement was the center of the slaves' social and cultural life. It was the context for forming household groups, sustaining various family connections, and such activities as music and dance, magicoreligious practices, and curing, as well as other leisure and domestic pursuits.

Slaves did not confine such activities and practices to their own villages. Despite laws that curtailed their movements, slaves left or traveled off their plantations and met slaves from other plantations or towns—for example, when attending weekend dances or seeking to establish or maintain family, marital, and sexual relationships. Moreover, the island's internal marketing system was a powerful inducement to movement off the plantations. The slaves used it to dispose of goods they had produced in the villages, stolen from their masters' properties, or had legally acquired from plantation managements.

The internal marketing system, which existed throughout the slave period (and which is important, we believe, in considering the way in which some archaeologically recovered goods were obtained and distributed), also involved freedmen and whites. Goods "were sold by plying the countryside, and the 'Huckster Negroes' . . . often met incoming ships and sold fresh foods to their passengers and crews. In towns, they sold from door to door . . . established themselves at set locations in the streets or alleys, or set up stalls . . . In Bridgetown, especially on weekends and holidays, many hucksters sat at 'the great market' with their trays or baskets, while others wandered about hawking their wares." In general, despite laws designed to inhibit or eliminate various types of the slaves' and freedmen's trading activities, slaves were active participants in the internal marketing system, a system which was essential to the distribution of foodstuffs and upon which townsmen, including many whites, were particularly dependent (Handler 1974:125–130). It also has important implications for interpreting how some of the archaeologically recovered goods were obtained and distributed.

Most of the nonstolen goods that slaves traded consisted of vegetables (either produced by themselves or part of their food allocations from plantations), small livestock and poultry, and sometimes such materials as animal fodder and firewood that they had gathered. Slaves in Barbados, like those in Jamaica (see Mintz and Hall 1960; Mathewson 1973), probably also disposed of material products they sometimes manufactured, such as baskets, hammocks, wooden stools, ropes, and pottery although direct evidence is sparse (see, for example, *Authentic History of the West Indies* 1810:41; Labat 1722; 4:414–415; Ligon 1657:48; Handler 1963a:139–141).

Stolen goods that slaves traded included plantation food crops, minor cash crops (such as cotton and aloes), and, as one planter complained, "canes, sugar, lead, copper, iron, new and old nails, in fact everything produced or used on a plantation or elsewhere" (Hendy 1833:34; see also chapter 4). The "slave consolidation act," a major law passed in 1826, contained several clauses dealing with slave theft. Clause 23, in particular, suggested the types of materials most apt to have been stolen: "it shall and may be lawful for any person or persons to seize and apprehend any slave or slaves in whose possession may be found any sugar canes, sugar, rum, cotton, ginger, aloes, or other staple and export production of the soil, plate wrought or melted down, iron, lead, copper, pewter, brass, tin, or any other article or thing likely to have been stolen" (*Parliamentary Papers* 1826–27a). Stolen goods were often traded to white (and freedman) middlemen, or hucksters, who, in return, gave the slaves "a mere trifle in money, 'flesh,' fish, or rum" (Hendy 1833:34; see also Handler 1974:125–126).

In general, slaves either exchanged or bartered their products and produce for other foodstuffs, rum, clothing, tobacco, "and other necessaries" or sold them for cash, usually copper coins (G. W. Jordan 1816:15; Pridmore 1965:10) with which they then purchased such items and "whatever additional comforts they prefer" (Pinckard 1806; 1:369). Many of the goods, especially the durable ones, acquired through marketing activities presumably were taken back to the plantation communities.

In their communities, slaves assumed a variety of roles or specialties that were defined independently of the agricultural and associated jobs they were compelled to perform for the plantations. Such roles were associated with kinship and affinity, music (particularly drumming), crafts life basketmaking and pottery (which supplied plantation needs as well as the domestic needs of other slaves), haircutting, storytelling, and midwifery. In the later years of the slave period, literate plantation slaves taught others to read and converts to Christianity proselytized among their peers. Some people who, through their personalities or special talents, were able to influence others; for example, the slaves who assumed leadership positions in plotting revolts and the slave who, after his conversion, used his "superior station" and influence on a plantation to "encourage the Negroes to come to [the Moravian] church and hear something of [the] . . . saviour" (United Brethren 1831; 12:223–224).

The "Negro doctors of the estates," according to an English doctor in the late eighteenth century, "justly vie with [some of the European doctors] . . . in medical knowledge" (Pinckard 1806; 1:389). A "Negro doctor" was particularly adept in using plants or magical procedures, and he could as well have been what was more generally termed an "Obeah Negro." Obeah negroes, who were among the most important members of the slave community, were "physicians and conjurers who can . . . not only fascinate [the slaves] . . . but cure them when they are bewitched by others" (Hughes 1750:15–16). "There is hardly an estate in which there is not some old man or woman who affects to possess some supernatural power. These are called Obeah Negroes, and by the superstitious Negroes [are] much feared" (Barbados Council 1789). Obeah negroes used their talents in sorcery, various forms of divination, and curing. They were held "much in awe" (Hughes 1750:15) and "are the leaders to whom the others are in slavery for fear of being bewitched, from whom they often receive charms to make them successful in any vilanies, and to get deadly doses to dispatch out of the world such masters or other persons as they have conceived a dislike of" (Holt 1729a). As an island resident wrote in 1712, "No Negro that was born in Barbados can do anything of this, only those that are brought from the coast of Africa" (Walduck 1710–12), but by the late eighteenth century "the professors [of Obeah] are as often natives as Africans" and acted "principally as fortune-tellers" and curers (Barbados Council 1789; J. Brathwaite 1789). Obeah was much more than the practice of evil or negative magic; it also used magical practices for such desirable social ends as curing.[19]

Although slaves were surrounded by a variety of repressive laws and social customs that regulated their status and behavior, "the daily life of living," as Sidney Mintz has observed for the New World in general, "did not end with enslavement" (1970:7–8). Barbadian slaves, like those elsewhere, created a cultural system that, although fundamentally based on their African heritages, was significantly shaped by the New World setting. This cultural system was no more wholly African than that of the white creoles was wholly European, but several important features of slave culture undeniably reflected African traditions (see, for example, chapter 6), even though most slaves were born on Barbados by the later years of the slave period. Although slaves can be conceived of in terms of the work roles they performed on the plantations, they also had a variety of roles and specialties that were a function of and defined by their communities and cultural system. The labor they performed for plantations, however, molded the general contours of their lives and structured many of their activities during the year.

In Barbados, as elsewhere on New World sugar plantations, not all of a plantation's slave contingent was employable or employed, but most slaves were put to one form or another of work; children from the ages of five or six and sometimes younger had their share of labor which increased in scope and arduousness as the children became older.

The working slaves on a Barbadian plantation were divided into three broad categories. The field laborers were divided into gangs; the first and second gangs were defined as the effective labor force, while the third (and sometimes a fourth) gang, comprised of small children, was assigned light jobs. Gangs were supervised by black drivers; the driver of the first gang was the head driver. The second category of slaves contained the skilled tradesmen (such as carpenters, coopers, and masons) and others with specialized and valued roles in the sugar manufacture process. The plantation's "officers," adult males with skilled jobs or leadership positions, usually received special privileges. Such officers and sometimes senior domestic servants were also highly valued in monetary terms by plantation managements. The third category included the domestics who performed various chores in the manager's or owner's house, which was frequently called the "dwelling house," "plantation house," or, simply, "the house."

Work roles and labor organization, as well as privileges, rewards, incentives, and ranking among plantation slaves are discussed in greater detail in chapter 4; however, some essential features of plantation labor organization, including the tripartite gang division, task allocations to gangs, and even the terms "gang" and "driver" have persisted into modern times (Handler 1965). Plantations today also employ domestic servants who usually inhabit villages close to the plantation. In the days of slavery, domestic slaves sometimes lived in houses located behind the dwelling house, and personal servants occasionally slept in the house; most domestic slaves, however, probably resided in the slave village itself.

"Most of the plantations in the country," wrote a French priest who visited Barbados in 1654, "are like as many villages whose size varies according to the number of slaves each plantation has" (Handler 1967:65). These villages were generally small. An idea of village size can be gained by viewing available statistics on the slave contingents of individual plantations at various periods. Twenty plantations during the 1650–1693 period had a total of 1,288 slaves (in addition to 128 white indentured servants), an average slave population of 64; the median was 33.5, with a range of from 150 at the highest, to 7 at the lowest (see table 3 for sources for these figures). "Some plantations," according to the priest, contained from 200 to 300 slaves (Handler 1967:65, 69).

Data on slave populations of individual plantations during the eighteenth and nineteenth centuries were also collected from a wide variety of sources; we cannot claim, however, that these data constitute a statistically random sample of all plantations in Barbados. The eighteenth- and nineteenth-century population data are for 177 cases from 1727 to 1834; 165 of the cases (93.2 percent) fall in the 1780–1834 period. The 177 cases include 138 different plantations; in some cases the same plantation was counted twice, but at different times when the size of its slave contingent (and its acreage) varied. The 177 cases included 25,069 slaves, an average of 141.6 slaves for each plantation and a median of 133.5; the range was from 350 slaves per plantation at the highest, to 20 at the lowest (figures derived from sources listed in table 3). During the early 1820s, another group of twenty different plantations (nineteen of which were absentee-owned) had 4,589 slaves, an average of 229 per plantation (Barbados Council 1824:105).

The size of slave settlements, as well as their frequency distribution, is also suggested by individual plantation statistics. Table 3 com-

Table 3. Frequency distribution of slave populations on Barbadian plantations, 1650–1834.

Slaves	Plantations	
	Number	Percentage
50 and under	27	13.7
51–100	39	19.8
101–150	54	27.4
151–200	43	21.8
201–250	23	11.8
251–300	8	4.1
301–350	3	1.5
Total	197[a]	

Sources: Alleyne (1802b, 1802c, 1803); Barbados Assembly (1818:41, 42); Barbados Council (1654–58); Barbados Department of Archives (1780–1834, 1803–04); *Barbados Museum and Historical Society* (1934: 94, 1935:127, 1936:28, 1940b:70–71, 74, 1942:90); Bennett (1958:2, 100–101); Bishop (1759); J. Brathwaite (1789); Cooper and Hawtaine (1652); Cracknell (1934:20, 22–23, 31–32); Dickson (1814:157); Dunn (1972:68); Guinea Plantation (1820); Harewood Archives (1834); Hawtayne (1893:28–35); J. W. Jordan (1824); Lowther Plantation (1756, 1825–35); Lucas (1956:74–75, 125); Newton Papers (523/276, 287, 984, 969–2); Oliver (1910–20; 1:67; 3:65, 366, 372; 5:187, 249, 253–54; 6:133); Parry (1789c); Pasfeild (1727); Rolph (1836:53); Senhouse (1788, 1935:129–30); Shilstone (1933:92); Simmons (1833:25); Society for the Improvement (1811–16); Steele (1789:35); White (1972); *West India Committee Circular* (1911); and notices in the *Barbados Gazette* (November 11, 1761) and *Barbados Mercury* (November 24, 1787; January 19, 1819; February 16 and 27, 1819).

[a] Includes 162 different plantations.

piles information on 197 plantation cases (162 different plantations) from 1650 to 1834. Of the 197 cases, 33.5 percent contained 100 and under slaves, 49.2 percent from 101 to 200, 15.7 percent from 201 to 300, and only 1.5 percent contained over 300 slaves.

Using these figures, we estimate that during the eighteenth century and preemancipation decades of the nineteenth, most slave villages on medium and large plantations held between 100 to 200 people, and that a significant number of villages had populations in the 200s; slave villages that exceeded 300 people were relatively rare. Many small landholdings, often classified as plantations, had commensurately small slave contingents, and thus the size of their settlements was considerably less than our estimated averages. By the index of the size of slave contingent, Newton, the plantation on which our archaeological work concentrated, was among the island's larger plantations. In 1740 and 1750 it had 171 slaves, while from the 1770s to 1834, its slave contingent averaged 265 (table 6).

In the middle of the seventeenth century, Richard Ligon suggested that a plantation's labor force should be equally divided between men and women (1657:115), an opinion probably shared by contemporary planters. This sexual pattern seems to have generally prevailed for most of the slave period. During the eighteenth and nineteenth centuries plantation slave communities were about evenly divided between males and females, but most appear to have contained slightly more women.

Figures on the sexual distribution of slaves on individual plantations were more difficult to acquire than figures on the total size of slave contingents. Sexual data were gathered for eighty-nine cases (including seventy-five different plantations excluding Newton) spread over the 1727–1834 period; these eighty-nine cases included 12,301 slaves. The average percentage of males per plantation case was 48.1 (median percentage, 48.0) and of females 51.8 (median percentage, 52.0). In twenty-five cases (28.0 percent of the total) males exceeded females, but the numerical differences between the two sexes were very slight.[20] "In most plantations there are found among the slaves a greater number of females than males" (Parry 1789a:18), and statistical evidence for individual plantations generally coincides with percentages derived from statistics on the island's total slave population (which included nonplantation slaves). In 1673 and 1675–76, an average of 49 percent of the slaves were males and 51 percent were females (Colleton 1673; Atkins 1676a); although no islandwide sex figures are available for slaves during the eighteenth century, the islandwide population averaged 46 percent males and 54 percent females during the 1801–1834 period (Handler 1974:24–25; *The Barbadian*, August 13, 1834).

NUMBER OF PLANTATION VILLAGES AND PLANTATION SIZE

No statistics or estimates are available on the number of plantation slave villages on Barbados, but a rough idea can be obtained by ascertaining the number of plantations. Even so, difficulties are involved for the number of plantations fluctuated, figures are unavailable for most years, and the definition in the historical sources of what constituted a plantation can be ambiguous.

One way of estimating the number of plantations is by establishing the landholdings that possessed sugar mills or "sugar works"—the complex of buildings and facilities for manufacturing sugar, including the boiling house, and curing house—because many units identified as plantations lacked these facilities. William Mayo's detailed map, based on a systematic survey conducted between 1717 and 1721, provides a clear indication of this pattern (1722). By our count, the map identifies 998 sugar plantations which Mayo classifies into two major types: those lacking and those possessing sugar mills. We identified 332 plantations with one mill (33.2 percent), 70 with two mills (7 percent), and 3 with three mills (0.3 percent). Mayo called the 405 plantations (40.6 percent of the total) with sugar mills "of greatest note"—the other 593 were defined as "of less note." (Newton plantation is identified on Mayo's map as among the 70 plantations with two windmills; by this index, Newton was among the larger plantations on the island.)

We used plantations with at least one sugar mill or "sugar works" to estimate the number of slave villages on medium and large plantations. The historical sources provide figures or estimates on the number of such plantations for only five years or short periods from 1683 to 1834 (table 4). However, there is information for eight additional years on the number of sugar mills; although some plantations had more than one mill, the number of mills can also be used to approximate the number of medium and large plantations. According to Mayo's map, 481 mills were associated with 405 plantations, a ratio of 1.18 mills per plantation. In the 1770s and early 1780s, William Dickson, an Englishman who had lived in Barbados for about thirteen years, estimated that the island contained "upwards of four hundred sugar plantations" (1789:8), while in 1771–73 there were approximately 446 mills (Sheridan 1974:146); we thus estimate a ratio of about 1.11 mills per plantation during the early 1770s. Applying the average of these two ratios, 1.14, to the number of mills in years for which we lack figures on the number of plantations, we can arrive at a rough estimate of the number of medium and large plantations during these years. These estimates are also given in table 4 in brackets.

In the five years or periods for which the sources reported on the number of plantations, there was a range of from 302 to 405 plantations, an average of 373 (median, 399), and in the eight years for which we have estimated the number of plantations the range was from 294 to 516, with an average of 378 (median, 386). Using these two sets of figures, we thus estimate that during most of the plantation slave period there were, on the average, close to 400 medium and large plantations; by extension of these figures we assume there were a comparable number of slave villages.

TABLE 4. Sugar mills and plantations in Barbados, 1683-84 to 1834.

Year	Mills	Plantations with sugar works[a]
1683-1684	—	358
1710	485	[425]
1716	479	[420]
1717-1721	481	405
1731	588	[516]
1755	458	[402]
1767	423	[371]
1771-1773	446	400
1811	341	[299]
1812	337	[296]
1813	335	[294]
1822	—	302
1834	—	399

Sources: 1683-84, British Museum (1684), plantations. 1710, Public Record Office (1710), mills or sugar works only. 1716, H. Hall (1714-17), mills only. 1717-1721, Mayo (1722), mills only. 1731, John Bennett (1738:19), Ashley (1732:27), mills only. 1755, Hall (1924:5), mills only. 1767, Sheridan (1974:146), mills only. 1771-1773, Dickson (1789:8), plantations; Sheridan (1974:146), mills. 1811-1813, Society for the Improvement (1811-16:87, 167, 245), mills only. 1822, Barbados Council (1824:127), sugar works. 1834, Barbados Council and Assembly (1834:83), sugar works.

[a] Bracketed numbers are estimates based on the average number of mills per plantation; these estimates are derived from ratios for 1717-1721 and 1771-1773.

Barbados, however, contained many small plantations or farms, most of which had small groups of slaves living on them. If such units are also considered, the number of slave settlements was much larger than our estimates. For example, smaller units comprised a high percentage of the 844 plantations identified on an elaborate map of the 1670s (R. Forde 1675), but this map did not identify additional small units (Dunn 1972:93). It can be safely assumed that a consequential number of the approximately 1,400 plantations reported in a 1712 census (Public Record Office 1712) were, in fact, relatively small farms, many of which contained slave contingents.

According to the returns of a detailed 1679 census, there were 2,639 property holders (excluding those in Bridgetown), 2,227 of which (84 percent) held less than 30 acres of land; of these 2,227 landowners, 28 percent owned no slaves, but the remaining 72 percent owned between one and nineteen (the average size of a Barbadian farm at this period was 29 acres, the median size, 10 acres; Dunn 1972:88–89, 91–92, 96). In the 1770s and 1780s, William Dickson reported that in addition to "upwards of four hundred sugar plantations" there were "a great number of . . . places and other small possessions" (1789:8); "the properietors of 'places,'" Dickson later wrote, "containing eight or ten acres, or more, with slaves in proportion, form a middle class between the sugar planters and the poor whites" (Dickson 1814:528). By 1834, when there were 399 plantations with "sugar works," most of the reported 2,294 landowners had "no sugar works, [but] nevertheless cultivate canes as the only crop that gives a profitable return" (Barbados Council and Assembly 1834). Small producers milled their cane at neighboring plantations and also cultivated subsistence and minor cash crops (Handler 1971b), but whatever the actual number of plantations at any given period during slavery, it is clear that a significant amount of the island's sugar production took place on medium and large acreage plantations. Acreage statistics were derived from a variety of sources for 180 plantation cases (comprising 153 different plantations) from 1650 to 1834. The average size of a plantation was 265.4 acres; the median was 237.5 with a range of from 861 acres at the highest to 15 at the lowest (based on figures derived from sources listed in table 3). Slightly over 52 percent of the 180 cases fell between 101 and 300 acres, and only 6.1 percent were in excess of 500 acres (table 5).

Although "few Barbados planters worked units larger than 200 acres" in the 1670s (Dunn 1972:95), several planters at this time owned far larger plantations. For example, seventy-two men were named in a 1673 "list of the most eminent planters in Barbados": fifty-one owned between 200 and 499 acres; sixteen from 500 to 699; and five owned from 700 to 1,000 acres (Public Record Office 1673). Such planters tended, as in later periods, to subdivide the very large holdings and work them as separate but contiguous units with their own slave labor forces. They also sometimes had more than one plantation located in different parishes, or their plantations were separated from each other in the same parish. Although we can make no claims for the statistical representativeness of our sample of 180 plantation cases, the sample nonetheless indicates more plantations over 200 acres (65.5 percent) than might be expected, but this distribution might also reflect a trend over time.[21] Newton plantation, with an average of 451 acres during the eighteenth and early nineteenth centuries, was among Barbados's larger plantations and fell in the upper 8.8 percent of our sample.

TABLE 5. Frequency distribution of acreage on Barbadian plantations, 1650–1834.

	Plantations	
Acres	Number	Percentage
50 and under	8	4.4
51–100	11	6.1
101–150	23	12.8
151–200	20	11.1
201–250	34	18.9
251–300	18	10.0
301–350	20	11.1
351–400	16	8.9
401–450	14	7.8
451–500	5	2.8
501–550	4	2.2
551–600	4	2.2
601–650	1	0.5
651–700	1	0.5
701–750	0	0.0
751–800	0	0.0
801–850	0	0.0
851–900	1	0.5
Total	180[a]	

Sources: Same as table 3.
[a] Includes 153 different plantations.

PLANTERS, SLAVEOWNERS, AND INSTITUTIONAL ATTRIBUTES

The vast majority of Barbadian landowners depended on slave labor in agricultural production, but not all slaveowners were landowners. This pattern was already apparent in the seventeenth century (Dunn 1972:96), and by the early 1800s if not earlier the total number of slaveowners exceeded the number of landowners. In 1822 there were 5,206 slaveowners, 3,671 (70 percent) of whom were landless (Barbados Council 1824:77–78); by 1834, 3,055 (57 percent) of the island's 5,349 slaveowners possessed no land (MacGregor 1836; Barbados Council and Assembly 1834). Many landless slaveowners depended for their livelihood on hiring out their slaves for agricultural work or for various types of skilled and unskilled work.

Whites owned the greatest number and proportion of slaves, and most slaveowners were white. Freedmen were also slaveowners, but few of their slaves were plantation slaves for the simple reason that plantation owners were overwhelmingly white; only relatively late in the slave period were a handful of freedmen able to acquire sugar plantations (Handler 1974:121).

Most of Barbados's sugar planters lived on the island. The dual role of plantation owner-manager was not uncommon, but resident owners possessing more than one plantation hired white managers for the plantations on which the owners did not reside; sometimes managers also resided on plantations where owners were resident. Absentee owners hired resident managers over whom there was an "attorney." The attorney, who was usually a large plantation owner himself, was an absentee's "principal agent, who acts for him, by power of attorney; and hence ... the name" (Dickson 1814:526); Newton is a good example of this pattern. An attorney could also assume this function for a number of plantations or absentee owners; in the mid-1820s, for example, John H. Gittens, the Anglican rector of Saint John's parish, owned one plantation and was the attorney for ten others, and Forster Clarke, the owner of one plantation, was the attorney for twenty-one (*Declaration of Inhabitants of Barbados* 1826:3–4).

Throughout most of its history Barbados had a larger percentage of whites than other British West Indian territories. By the late eighteenth century many of these whites were creoles "who have found it possible to forget that England is home ... they possess a real nationality, with characteristics, neither English, Irish, nor Scotch" (Sturge and Harvey 1838:152, 154–55). Most whites were neither plantation owners nor wealthy, and many were quite poor, but as in other slave societies the white group as a whole encouraged a rigid stratification system based on racial origins. Its plantocracy in particular ardently defended the institution of slavery on which the Barbadian social order rested.

Many of the fundamental social, political, and economic institutions that were established during the seventeenth century characterized Barbadian history until fairly recently. For example, the major components of its tripartite political system were a House of Assembly whose twenty-two members, usually large plantation owners and merchants, were elected annually on a narrow franchise based on property, sexual, religious, and (by the early eighteenth century) explicitly defined racial criteria; a twelve-man Council whose members, also leading planters and merchants, were appointed by the Crown on the nomination of the governor; and the governor who was appointed by the Crown and was assigned to represent and protect its interests. All bills passed by the Assembly and Council required the governor's approval to become law. These three bodies composed the island's legislature which structurally and organiza-

41

tionally resembled the system found in Britain's other Caribbean and American mainland colonies. The British legal system in Barbados was supplemented by colonial laws and slave codes reflecting local conditions. These laws were sanctioned by the Crown or its representative when they did not contradict British law or violate metropolitan political and economic interests.

Like other British West Indian territories, Barbados's system of local government was framed around its parishes. The affairs of each parish were controlled by a vestry whose members, all property owners in the parish, were elected under the same franchise that applied to membership in the House of Assembly.

Institutions such as the parish system, a representative assembly, and the common law were of English derivation; they were modified to varying degrees in the Barbadian setting as were other institutions, such as the religious establishment (the Anglican church) and the educational system, which closely paralleled those in the mother country. After emancipation,[22] these institutions continued to exist along with other socioeconomic, demographic, and ideological patterns that had been established earlier: the dependence on sugar and the plantation system (with the descendants of emancipated slaves forming the labor force on plantations); the persistence of various fundamental features of plantation labor organization; an ideology of white racism, nurtured and encouraged during the period of slavery and used to justify and perpetuate the social and legal subordination of nonwhites; the denigration of cultural traits and racial attributes associated with African ancestry; widespread poverty and limited opportunities for social mobility; a rigid stratification system in which class position was intimately linked with racial origins and phenotypic characteristics; and a minority white population that continued to control the society's major internal political and economic institutions until fairly recent times.

3 / The Archaeological Project: Methodology and Survey Summary

OUR archaeological fieldwork in Barbados spanned two seasons. During the first (from late December 1971 to the end of April 1972), a field party of from eleven to thirteen persons conducted a preliminary survey of the island, tested sites in several different areas and conducted extensive excavations at Newton plantation. In the second season (April and May 1973), four to six people concentrated on excavations at Newton cemetery.

We examined fourteen plantations at different locations and physiographic regions for which historical documentation was already in hand or, we believed, readily available. In addition to the work at Newton, limited test excavations were conducted at four plantations (see figure 2).

We initiated research on the fourteen plantations with surveys that tried to establish locations for possible excavation. Surface surveys were made in fields that we suspected were the former sites of slave villages and in other fields from which we wanted to obtain comparative samples. Test excavations were conducted only at locations thought to have contained slave villages. For several reasons outlined at the end of this chapter, the tests were not successful in yielding undisturbed contexts with features resulting from slave activity. On analysis, data from surface surveys and test excavations did not assist in interpreting the archaeological findings at Newton cemetery (where we found the most undisturbed contexts dating from the slave period), and thus detailed results of this work are not presented in this book.[1]

Clues to survey areas on individual plantations were provided by the contemporary names of plantation fields and, to a lesser extent, plantation maps dating from the period of slavery; in one case, we used a plantation drawing made sometime in the immediate post-emancipation period.

From the earliest years of the sugar plantation system in Barbados,

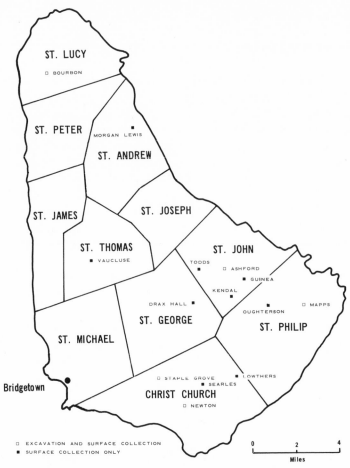

Figure 2. Barbados: parish and plantation locations of archaeological research, 1972 and 1973.

plantations divided their total acreage into fields of varying sizes. In 1796, for example, Newton's fields ranged in size from 1 to 18 acres, but averaged close to 10 acres; at this time the plantation comprised 458 acres, out of which the manager defined 221 acres as "our real cane land" (Newton Papers 523/289). (In 1973, there were many more fields, but the average field size, according to information provided by the plantation manager, was close to 7 acres, with a range from 1 to 14.) Individual fields were named after a former landholder or person who resided in the area or after a physical or cultural feature on the plantation (Cruickshank 1935; J. Chandler 1968): for example, Goddard, Clarke field, Burke field, and North

44

Grand Rock, North Mill field, Garden Wall, Upper Boiling House. A study of plantation field names can provide information about the history of individual plantations (Cruickshank 1935; Barbados Museum and Historical Society 1940a; J. Chandler 1968) because many fields still retain their slave period names. Lowthers, a plantation where surface collections were made, is a good illustration of the endurance of such names. According to an 1825 map, its cultivated lands were divided into twenty-four named fields. By comparing this map with the names of the plantation's contemporary fields and their locations, we found that seventeen of the 1825 fields retained the same names in 1972. Although Lowthers contained forty-eight named fields in 1972, most were simply subdivisions of the earlier ones. For example, the Burnt field of 1825 became Upper Burnt field and Lower Burnt field; Bakers became Upper Bakers and Lower Bakers; Above Mill became Upper Mill field and Lower Mill field. Some names dropped out of use entirely; for example, Negro garden[2] in 1825 became Sour Grass and Hart field.

The persistence of field names is also illustrated at Newton plantation. Ten of the forty-five named fields at Newton today can be found in a 1799 list of thirteen Newton fields (Newton Papers 523/129), but eight of these ten have been subdivided into smaller named units. For example, the Marl Pit field of 1799 became the Lower North Marl Pit, Upper North Marl Pit, and Lower South Marl Pit; similarly, Johnson field in 1799 was Lower Johnson and Upper Johnson at the time of our fieldwork. The Negro yard of the late eighteenth century became four fields: Upper South Negro yard, Lower South Negro yard, Lower North Negro yard, and Upper North Negro yard.

Sir John Chandler, a prominent Barbadian, suggested that contemporary names that included "pasture" and "pond" (for example, Cattle pond and Duck pond) are the most common names found on Barbadian plantations, but included among the "next most frequent names" was Negro yard (1968:135). The Negro yard field is of particular significance, for this term was used for the area of plantations that contained the slave villages or settlements (see, for example, Pinckard 1806; 2:287–288; J. W. Jordan 1824:4; Barbados Assembly 1818:32).

When the villages were moved after emancipation, the former village sites, or parts of them, were converted to sugar cane, other uses, or left barren, but frequently continued to be called Negro yards. Many plantation fields in Barbados today have this name or, as one commonly hears from black and white Barbadians alike, the name "nigger yard." Even if a plantation lacks a Negro yard it is not difficult to find an elderly plantation worker or manager who can remember which field was formerly called Negro yard.

Besides identifying Negro yards, we also located a few sites by using plan ation maps dating from the slave period that showed the location of the slave villages. However, library and archival research over the years had only yielded a handful of these maps. Figure 3 contrasts an eighteenth-century plantation map that shows the slave village and a more modern map that locates the Negro yard field (see also figures 4 and 5).

A manuscript drawing of Ashford plantation, in Saint John parish, shows the plantation house, various outbuildings including the wind-mill, a pond, and the houses of at least some of the laborers who, at the time the drawing was made, were either apprentices or recent freemen (figure 6).[3] During our fieldwork, the plantation house at Ashford was in the same location as shown in the drawing, and the pond, although empty of water and used as a fruit orchard, was clearly observable; the small houses, shown to the left of the planta-tion house, no longer existed, but the drawing gave us a fairly precise idea of where to excavate.

The drawing of Ashford and the maps in figures 3 and 5 show that the slave village, or Negro yard field, was located near the plantation yard, mill yard, or, simply, the yard. "Yard," both during slavery and today refers to the plantation area that includes the owner's or manager's house, the sugar mill or mills, boiling house, and other buildings used in manufacturing sugar; the yard also in-cluded the cattle pens, horse stables, and miscellaneous other build-ings and sheds that served a variety of plantation needs. The figures and other documentary sources, including maps, clearly indicate that the slave village was located relatively close to the plantation yard and, probably with few exceptions, within ready visibility of the owner's or manager's house.[4] The plantations we investigated fell into this general pattern and their Negro yard fields in most cases were adjacent to the yards or, in a few cases, separated from the yards by one or two other named fields.

In general, as far as we can establish, the locations of plantation yards have not shifted since the days of slavery, and the plantation houses, although frequently repaired or reconstructed have remained in essentially their original locations.

All the plantations that we investigated (see figure 2) existed dur-ing the slave period, although not necessarily with the same names they have today, and some have histories that extend into the earliest years of the sugar plantation system. (Because only our fieldwork at Newton is described here we do not provide an overview of these

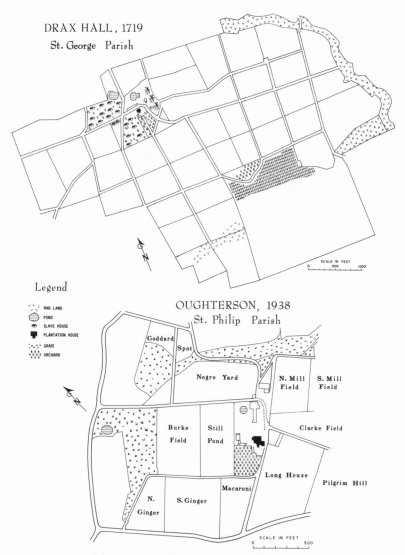

Figure 3. Slave village and plantation yard (Drax Hall) shown in relation to all plantation fields, and modern plantation (Oughterson), showing "Negro yard" field, plantation yard, and adjacent fields. (Maps traced from the originals in the Barbados Department of Archives.)

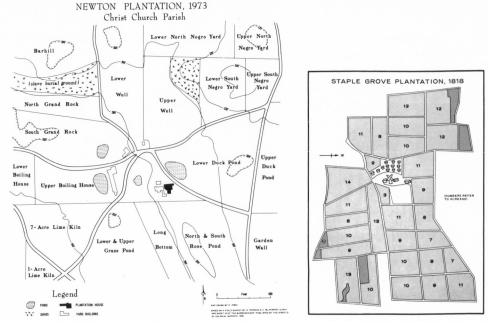

Figure 4. Newton plantation yard and neighboring fields, including "Negro yard" fields and slave cemetery.

Figure 5. Staple Grove slave village and plantation yard in relation to all plantation fields. (Adapted from a drawing by Innes 1967, based on the original located in the Barbados Museum Library.)

Figure 6. "Ashford. The Estate of Henry Hart Esq.," drawn between 1837 and 1845. (Courtesy of Mrs. Mildred Hart Higgins.)

plantations' histories.) These fourteen plantations obviously are only a small sample of Barbadian plantations during the period of slavery. However, they seem typical in, for example, the ways in which they were managed or operated, the location of their slave villages, and the demographic composition, social organization, and cultural patterns of their slave populations.

Weather and agricultural conditions played a significant role in scheduling and executing our research. Fieldwork was initially planned to coincide with the island's dry season, which usually falls between January and May; during these months the cane fields are harvested and are thus most amenable to excavation. However, 1971 was extremely dry and in many parts of the island sugar cane growth was stunted. When unusually heavy and frequent rains began to fall in early 1972, planters delayed the start of the harvest to increase the growth of their cane. The rains impeded some of our surveying and excavations. More important, however, the delay of the harvest meant that some fields in which we wished to work remained under a heavy cover of sugar cane during the early part of our research, and other fields had not been cleared of cane by the end of our first field season.

The amount of work devoted to various plantations differed considerably and was primarily determined by factors such as the density of sugar cane cover in particular fields, artifact yield from surface collections and test excavations, the amount of undisturbed terrain, and the nature and degree of historical documentation on the plantation. In general, we attempted to provide greater proportional emphasis to those plantations for which we had a greater amount of historical information.

The sampling procedures for surface collecting plantation fields varied somewhat and were largely determined by agricultural conditions. All fields we collected were in one stage or another of the cane-producing cycle. Fields covered by large amounts of cane trash (the dried leaves of the sugar cane which are stripped off during the harvest and are used to mulch the fields) were extremely difficult to collect because much of the ground surface was obscured. Fields where trash had been removed by burning prior to harvesting (a procedure increasingly employed to facilitate cutting cane) were also difficult to collect because of concentrations of carbonized debris on the ground surface. Fields with relatively clear ground surfaces were collected with some ease even when cane plants were growing on them; however, when these plants were from 1.5 to 2 meters high, the density of the growth impeded passage through the fields. The easiest fields to collect were those which had been recently plowed, but because of the late harvest in 1972 as well as the widespread practice of "ratooning" (permitting the cut cane stumps to regenerate themselves for several seasons before they are removed and the fields plowed and replanted), we had few opportunities to collect in such fields.

Within the Negro yards and adjacent fields on different plantations, we sought to locate individual house sites to determine, among other things, absolute and relative sizes as well as construction details. The proximity of these fields to plantation yards, however, made them accessible locations for dumping of household debris. Analysis of concentrations of cultural materials in such fields (Accola 1972) indicated a greater contrast in densities between fields (as a group) close to a plantation yard and fields distant from the yard, than the contrast among fields close to the yard. Some materials collected in Negro yard fields were certainly a result of slave occupation, but deep plowing destroyed stratigraphic contexts and we were unable to determine which collected materials were the result of slave occupation and which resulted from dumping. The major components in such collections were earthenware and china, almost all of which dated to post-1762.

The general areas around plantation yards, which in many cases included at least part of the slave villages, have undergone continual functional evolution and alteration since emancipation. Although the sites of plantation yards did not change, over the years new structures such as garages, storage sheds, and workshops were erected and older structures were frequently modified to meet contemporary needs; in addition, vegetable gardens, fruit orchards, or stands of shade trees were often added to the plantation yards or adjacent areas. These changes sometimes affected at least part of the areas in which the former slave villages were located. The village sites have also been altered, for example, by conversion to agricultural production (in recent times involving mechanical deep plowing) and removal of coral limestone for building purposes on plantations or elsewhere.

The tenant village at Kendal plantation was occupied until 1954, when the area was plowed under and planted in sugar cane, but surface collections yielded very little cultural material from any period. This was partially caused by the grading of the tenantry area; large volumes of soil had been scraped from the crest of a hill and pushed down to deepen the soil on the slopes. Similar manmade earth movements occurred at other plantations, and landslides in the Scotland District parish of Saint Andrew also caused substantial movement and soil slippage on the Negro yard at Morgan Lewis plantation.

Most areas we tested had been highly disturbed by debris dump-ing, structural modifications in plantation yard areas, deep plowing, and manmade and natural landscape alterations. We therefore at-tempted to locate either undisturbed sections or substrata that might have preserved materials reflecting slave occupation or activity. We particularly sought plantations where the yards had apparently not been extensively modified in postemancipation times and where the fields appeared to contain enough protective soil to preserve some remains of slave activity. When available, we used old planta-tion maps (not necessarily of the preemancipation period) which showed the location of yards and the names of fields, and we visually compared the features on these maps with the present distribution of roads and structures; in addition, we interviewed plantation per-sonnel about soil depths and cultivation practices to isolate poten-tially productive excavation areas. With the exception of Newton cemetery, however, we were unable to locate any archaeologically productive undisturbed sections. In archaeology, there is always a great dependence on undisturbed, or minimally disturbed, contexts. We anticipated extensive disturbance on Barbados to some extent, but not to the pervasive scale we found. Such disturbance could not have been predicted without an exhaustive preliminary survey and testing operation far in excess of our research design. Because archaeologically productive undisturbed sections were so rare, we turned our efforts toward gathering quantitatively large artifact samples through excavations and surface collections that we hoped would yield diagnostic materials indicative of cultural function or temporal placement.

We found relatively large undisturbed areas only on three planta-tions—Ashford, Bourbon, and Newton—and these areas were uni-formly shallow (30 centimeters deep or less) before bedrock was reached. Excavations at these places mainly consisted of surface stripping various areas in an attempt to reveal evidence of stone house foundations, postholes, hearths, or other similar indicators of cultural activities; following the lead provided by an authoritative late eighteenth-century source, we also looked for burial sites at these (as well as other) plantations. Although plantations normally had special cemetery areas set aside for slave use (see chapter 6), in the late 1780s the island's governor reported: "Negroes are super-stitiously attached to the burial places of their ancestors and friends. These are generally as near as can be to the houses in which they live. It is frequent to inter a near relation under the bed-place on which they sleep . . ." (Parry 1789a:17).

Historical research has established that two or three types of struc-

51

tures were used to house slaves. The most common type was constructed of wattle-and-daub with a packed dirt floor; the low roof was covered with thatch and generally appears to have been somewhat pitched. Wooden poles or stakes were placed in the ground and were interlaced with twigs or the slender branches of trees. When wood was lacking, the wattle was constructed of other materials; for example, Newton's manager reported that "some" of the plantation's slave houses in 1796 were built "of the strong reed or cane of the Guinea corn" (Newton Papers 523/290). Walls were then plastered on the interior (and, perhaps, the exterior as well) with a mud or clay mortar. Roof thatching was made from several materials, including plantain leaves, various types of palm leaves and branches, and the leaves or trash of the sugar cane; historical sources indicate that cane trash was the most common type of thatching.

Although the Barbadian climate does not pose excessive demands for essential shelter requirements, the wattle-and-daub construction was relatively fragile. Historical sources suggest that the houses required frequent repair and were particularly vulnerable to leakage in heavy rains and to destruction by hurricanes, storms, and fires; moreover, the proximity of dwellings within the slave villages and the sea breezes that fanned the island facilitated the spread of fire from one house to another.

Because wattle-and-daub houses were made out of easily perishable materials, their remains probably decayed rapidly from contact with natural elements and traces of them were undetected archaeologically—either because deep plowing had obliterated any surviving wall trenches or postholes or because the houses were built on such shallow soil that no protective deposition could take place. Although large area stripping may have revealed features beneath the plow zone, it was not attempted because fields were planted in crops and because of the low yields of artifactual material from the plow zone. (Barbadian fields today are often plowed in depths of up to two feet in crisscross patterns.) Thus agricultural practices created a dilemma for the archaeological detection of wattle-and-daub structures: if the soil in a field was deep enough to afford some protective deposition, the field was under cultivation; if the soil cover was too shallow to be agriculturally viable, it was also too shallow to preserve wattle-and-daub vestiges, which seem to be quite transient in tropical climates even under nonagricultural conditions (see, for example, Meggers and Evans 1956; Lange and Rydberg 1972). Moreover, several structures may have been entirely removed during the later days of the slave period when different house types were constructed, or when villages were moved after emancipation. In any event, we found no trace of wattle-and-daub structures. Though we do not claim that such traces are impossible to find in Barbados, the evidence suggests they might be preserved only under special conditions, such as immediate postoccupational protective deposition.

Thatched, wattle-and-daub houses persisted as the major house type throughout the period of slavery, but by the late eighteenth and early nineteenth centuries slaves were also increasingly housed in stone-walled dwellings with thatched or occasionally wood shingle roofs.[5] (A few historical sources also suggest that in the late slave period some houses were constructed of rough boards or planks nailed to wooden posts.) Although stone is obviously more permanent than wattle-and-daub, its very permanency caused problems of structural preservation. We conjecture that usable stone blocks would have been reutilized and not simply left standing in place when houses were moved. Moreover, when former village sites were converted to agricultural uses and when, more recently, mechanized cultivation technology was introduced to the sugar industry, there was an organized and systematic removal of stone, invariably broken lumps of coral limestone, from fields; some of this stone may have been, at one time, part of house walls.

Stone has been removed from fields, however, for many years. For example, in a 1796 "Report on the Lands" at Newton, the manager notified the absentee owners in England that on some fields with shallow soil covers he intended, "by blowing up rocks and other means ... to improve our lands considerably, [and] to make those good cane fields which are now not considered as fit for the production of that plant" (Newton Papers 523/289). Today, stone fragments can often be seen collected in piles in plantation yards, and the stone itself is frequently utilized for miscellaneous construction activities such as road fill or building repairs. In Jamaica, during a recent archaeological exploration at the site of a former plantation slave village, the investigators found traces of stone houses, but the area containing these traces had not been under cultivation, and the preservation situation was quite different from what we encountered in Barbados (Higman 1974).[6]

In general, we found no evidence for domestic structures or slave dwellings (or burials under houses) in either undisturbed or disturbed areas. In addition, the quantity of artifactual materials found on the three plantations with undisturbed areas was proportionately far less than the amount recovered from deeper and disturbed fields that had apparently contained slave villages. The shallow soil over the coral bedrock in the undisturbed areas appears to have been largely responsible for why these fields were not cultivated and also seems to have made these areas less favorable for habitation.

In a number of areas of the world where actual house structures cannot be identified archaeologically, hearths and milling stones are often satisfactory indicators of domestic activity. In nineteenth-century Barbados, toward the end of the slave period, plantations sometimes provided the main daily meal for slaves from a central kitchen. Generally, however, each slave household prepared its own meal in or in front of its house. If not overburdened with fatigue from a day's work, and provided they had the necessary utensils and fuel slaves preferred these meals cooked. Foods were either roasted or boiled over open fires, but fireplaces or hearths do not seem to have been permanent fixtures of house construction—although the historical sources are ambiguous and we found no trace of either. Slaves may have used stones to support cooking utensils, such as the iron pots that were sometimes distributed by plantation managements, but we have no documentary evidence that indicates whether these stones were constructed into permanent hearths.

Corn, a food staple of plantation slaves, was ground in their houses "by rubbing it between two stones, by the strength of their arms" (Davies 1791:186). In the middle of the eighteenth century, a windmill was invented that was proclaimed as having a "vast advantage and a great ease... in the beating out and grinding of corn" (Hall 1764:400). By the late eighteenth century many plantations had apparently introduced centrally located windmills or manually driven mills to grind the slaves' corn. Nonetheless, the two "corn stones" of earlier periods persisted as major household utensils. Historical sources do not describe these corn stones in Barbados,[7] and our archaeological work failed to yield a trace of them.

The practice of removing rocks from Negro yard fields under cultivation may have contributed to the lack of evidence of stones that might have been used in milling, fireplaces, or house construction. We also examined, albeit cursorily, a number of rock piles in plantation yards, but we found no evidence of these stones.

Slave houses are also known to have contained other utensils and material objects, some of which were constructed of organic materials and hence were particularly susceptible to the destructive influences of a tropical environment. For example, from at least the middle of the seventeenth century and throughout most, if not all, of the slave period, the most common form of bedding for slaves was a rough board or plank that usually rested directly on the earthen floor of the house. By the latter half of the eighteenth century, and perhaps earlier, these boards were often slightly elevated and gave the appearance, the historical sources suggest, of raised platforms. Slaves occasionally used a matting or crude mattress made from "plantain leaves or some other species of bedding, to defend them from the rough plank" (Pinckard 1806;2:113–114). European-style beds were rare in slave houses. They seem to have been used only in the later years of the preemancipation period, and primarily, if not entirely, by the more favored or "wealthier" slaves such as head drivers and tradesmen.

Aside from bedding materials, the houses of plantation slaves contained little furniture and few tools or utensils although by the early nineteenth century furnishings may have become more elaborate, especially among tradesmen and head drivers. In general, however, furnishings were limited to an occasional wooden stool or bench, or sometimes a table and chair, and the documentary evidence suggests that such items were manufactured by the slaves themselves.

Slaves also manufactured some pottery utensils from local clays (and occasionally used ceramic wares of foreign derivation) and gourd or calabash dishes and containers for storing, cooking, and eating. Slaves were involved in pottery production from an early period in Barbados's history and made the conical pots used in the manufacture of sugar; later, slave potters also made utilitarian household wares, including various types of water jars, some of which are still being made in Barbados today (Handler 1963a, 1963b; see also chapter 5).

A few historical sources that mention the use of gourd and calabash containers give the impression that these materials were more widely used by the slaves than pottery containers. A characteristically African trait was noted by one nineteenth-century writer: the "calabash . . . serves as a bottle to contain rum, etc. Or, by sawing it in half [the slaves] . . . are provided with two vessels, which answer the purposes of basins or dishes. These calabashes are sometimes dyed by the slaves, who carve figures on them with a regularity and order that display much cleverness and ingenuity" (Bayley 1832:90). Plantation managements sometimes provided iron pots in which meals were cooked and occasionally distributed knives and spoons; the last two items appear to have been less common, but a medical doctor reported in 1812 that "some" plantation slaves lacked "utensils for cooking" (Society for the Improvement 1811-16:107).

Houses also probably contained, albeit with less frequency, other items which slaves are known to have used or manufactured: such items could have included various types of baskets, fish nets, ropes, wooden trays and mortars, and musical devices like drums, rattles, and stringed-instruments. Aside from the musical devices (see Handler and Frisbie 1972) and the calabash containers, the historical sources provide no details on the construction or design of utilitarian items made from organic materials.[8]

In general, then, we found no evidence of household furnishings or utensils that were constructed of organic materials and, aside from pottery and other objects associated with burials (see chapter 5), we did not find evidence of nonorganic utilitarian items such as iron pots or eating utensils.

Three major reasons account for the paucity of evidence relating to domestic life that was recovered from our archaeological investigations. First, the island's tropical environment must have played a significant role in obliterating evidence of material culture of an organic nature. In general, it is extremely difficult to preserve such organic materials as baskets, calabashes and gourds, wood stools, and fish nets and such items are rarely recovered archaeologically from contexts other than dry caves.

Second, a great deal of Barbados's arable land has been cultivated for many years and the mechanical deep plowing of fields in recent times, as well as architectural and other alterations in plantation yards and adjacent fields, have undoubtedly assisted in disturbing and even erasing many cultural features associated with slave life. For instance, the drawing of the Ashford plantation yard (figure 6) was a fairly precise guide to locate excavation areas, but our excavations yielded no evidence of occupation. The test excavations we conducted at Staple Grove plantation were also in an area that was clearly marked as the slave village on an 1818 plantation map (figure 5); yet these excavations uncovered no evidence that could be explicitly linked with slave occupation. We believe that such experiences are ample testimony to the effects of time, climate, and agriculture on the archaeological record.

Third, plantation slaves may have been far poorer than we assumed at the beginning of our research. Indeed, from a materialistic perspective slaves were poor in every sense of the word, and they had relatively limited resources for acquiring material goods. Within this context, then, it might be assumed that such goods were considered too valuable and difficult to replace, and thus they were not readily discarded or simply left lying around; when broken and beyond use, evidence of these artifacts can have easily been obliterated by cultural practices and natural forces. The implications of our Barbados experience for the study of slave culture are considered at greater length in chapter 7, where we discuss some of the wider issues involved in an archaeological approach to the study and interpretation of slave culture and the usefulness and limitations of such an approach.

4 / Newton Plantation: History and the Slave Population

URING our fieldwork in Barbados, the multiple
criteria for selecting plantation sites (adequate historical documentation, undisturbed contexts, promise
of remains of mortuary or domestic behavior, and lack of conflict
with the agricultural cycle and sugar production) ultimately co-
alesced on one plantation—Newton plantation in the parish of Christ
Church. From January to April 1972 we spent almost two months
at Newton and an additional six weeks in April and May 1973.

We found evidence of a cemetery at Newton during our first visit
to the plantation,[1] but our initial interest was based on an awareness
of a large collection of manuscripts relating to the plantation's
preemancipation history. With the exception of the two Codrington
plantations, which have been owned since 1710 by the Church of
England's Society for the Propagation of the Gospel in Foreign
Parts (today known as the United Society for the Propagation of
the Gospel), the documentation on Newton exceeds that of any
other plantation in Barbados during the slave period.

Most Newton manuscripts are housed in the University of London
Library where they are collectively referred to as the Newton
Papers (Ms. 523; cited in this book as Newton Papers 523). Well
over 1,000 of these papers deal with Newton and Seawell plantations
(Seawell is now the site of Barbados's airport, but at one time it
was owned by the same persons who owned Newton).[2] The materials on Newton plantation itself span the period from 1683 to the
1920s. The most extensive documentation, however, is from 1794 to
1823 and includes business ledgers and journals as well as a daily
log of work activities for 1796–97 and 1797–98, reports on slaves,
and related documents. In addition, correspondence between the
absentee owners in England and their Barbados managers and attorneys is relatively voluminous; there are also letters to and from
the major Bristol and London firms with which the plantation did
business.

58

The Newton Papers provide considerable materials on the economics of plantation management and the production of sugar and its by-products, agricultural practices and problems, the role of the plantation manager and attorney, and the social customs of the plantocracy for the 1794–1823 period. The papers also contain valuable materials on such topics as the organization of slave labor, the occupational specialization of slaves, plantation discipline, and the physical treatment of slaves.

Despite this extensive documentation, however, data on the social and cultural life of the slaves are relatively sparse. The Newton Papers generally reflect an interest in slaves only as items of property on whose "labours depend," as the plantation's manager wrote in 1804, "the success of the planter" (Newton Papers 523/593). Thus, information on slaves is largely limited to their labor roles and the expenditures on them that were factors in the plantation's profit system. Outside of information that impinges on the slaves' work activities and their "material welfare" (as related to, for example, demographic patterns, disciplinary measures, and plantation expenditures and involvement in food, clothing, shelter, and medical care), the Newton Papers, like the documentary materials from Barbados, often fail to provide data on cultural topics of direct interest to our archaeological research and the wider ethnohistorical project.

Some Newton materials are also located in Barbados. The Barbados Department of Archives has five volumes of account books or ledgers of the plantation and its factory for the 1893–1949 period, and the library of the Barbados Museum contains two "journal" volumes from 1805 to 1867 (the first volume covers the 1805–41 period and is cited in this book as Newton Plantation 1805–1841), a "ledger" for 1805–41, and five volumes of "stock books" for 1828, 1857, 1862, 1866, and 1868. The preemancipation materials in the Barbados Museum include detailed monthly expenditures for the plantation and various demographic materials on the slaves compiled for the slave registry. These materials include names, sex, age, phenotype, employment, births, deaths, and cause of death; information in each category, however, was not consistently reported for each registry year.

The Newton manuscript collections lack a map of the plantation that dates from the period of slavery, although in 1796 the manager referred to such a map in a "Report on the Lands" at Newton that he sent to England (Newton Papers 523/289). At the minimum, this map designated the location of the plantation's fields with letters of the alphabet.[3] Extensive searching over a number of years, however, and numerous queries addressed to archivists and others, have failed to produce this map. To locate various features on the plantation that might have existed during the slave period, we attempted to correlate available written materials with information provided by informants and contemporary features observed during our field-work.

THE PLANTATION YARD AREA

Newton plantation is easily reached from Bridgetown by proceeding east along a major paved inland road or by following the southeastern coastal highway to the village of Oistins and then turning north for a mile or so. The main highways pass through Newton's cane fields, but a short stretch of dirt road leads to the plantation yard.

Dominating the landscape of the yard are the decaying sugar factory buildings whose functions have yielded to the islandwide process of factory centralization. Near the manager's house in the yard are various sheds and stables used for storing equipment and other goods; a short distance away from the manager's house is a more recently constructed dwelling inhabited by the bookkeeper, or manager's assistant. A number of visible depressions in and around the yard once served as ponds for the plantation's slaves and livestock, but they are now empty (see figure 4).[4] The two windmills that once ground the plantation's cane were torn down many years ago (although traces of them still exist close to the bookkeeper's house) and the slave village, of course, is gone. Deep plowing of agricultural fields started in 1947, various stands of trees have been planted in modern times, and the factory ruins postdate the slave period, but in general the ubiquitous cane fields and other features create the impression that the physical layout of Newton has changed little since the days of slavery.

In earlier years, however, less cane was planted, and the yard and its adjacent areas have been altered. In 1796, Sampson Wood, Newton's manager, sent a detailed report to the new absentee owners in England:

> [The] dwelling or manager's house [is] situated on the south side of what forms the square of the buildings on the estate, on a little eminence overlooking the whole aspect to the northward...Detached from the house, through a little yard, are the kitchen, buttery and other offices. Adjoining is the poultry yard, stock house, pigeon house, etc....About forty yards to the westward is the stable...Adjoining to the stable to the westward are two small rooms, the one serving for a store or provision room...the other a cooper's shop...Adjoining to

these rooms and stable, all under one roof, is a small black-smith's shop . . . This building . . . has a covering of shingles . . . [which] are a very light and convenient covering for these climates, and were formerly cheap[er], but have now got to a great price (but nothing in comparison of tile). They come from America, mostly from New England, and are made of Cedar or American Cypress wood. The next building, about fifty yards below the stable, is the curing house, a very strong stone edifice (indeed all the buildings are of stone on the plantation) . . . There is also a shed . . . running out from the southern side of this building . . . This is our [wood shingled] barn or grannery for corn . . . To the westward of this building is the hospital or sick house where Negroes are put . . . This building begins to form the westward side of the square of buildings. On a parallel line, not far from it, is the rum dis-tillery . . . a very substantial stone building covered with tile. We now come to the boiling house, a very strong fine building covered with tile also . . . The mills . . . are two very fine ma-chines . . . (Newton Papers 523/290).

A number of the buildings that Sampson Wood described no longer exist, but his description, compared with contemporary features and information supplied by informants, shows that today's manager's house is still in the same location. Wood also reported that "On the brow of a hill (to the eastward) [of the windmills] are our Negro huts or houses . . . [which] lie scattered about the hill looking very picturesque and pretty amongst a few shrubs they have planted about them." This passage played a key role in our excavation strategy at Newton; the hill still exists and is clearly visible, although today part of it is in grass and the remainder in cane.

By the time of Wood's report, however, considerable changes had taken place in the plantation yard and its adjoining areas. He lamented that "the worst of Newton is that it has no trees," and stated his intention to plant some. The plantation had been seriously affected by a massive hurricane in 1780 that "destroyed every vestige of a house, garden, trees, and every other pleasurable object." Probably, then, much of what Wood described had been recon-structed or repaired after 1780. This construction and other hurri-canes probably also affected the archaeological record on the planta-tion.[5]

One disappointing omission from Wood's description of Newton's buildings, as well as from his detailed reports on the "Negroes" and "lands" of the plantation (Newton Papers 523/288, 289), is his failure to mention a slave cemetery; indeed, none of the documentary sources on Newton mention the cemetery in which we excavated (nor, for that matter, any cemetery). Despite this hiatus in the historical record, the archaeological evidence shows that the cemetery existed during the period of Wood's writing and indicates that people were being buried in the area not long after Newton's establishment as a plantation in the seventeenth century.

ORIGIN AND EARLY OWNERSHIP

Like that of many sugar plantations operating in Barbados today, the history of Newton starts in the second half of the seventeenth century. Its first owner was an Englishman, Samuel Newton, who, from the early 1650s to the early 1660s—a crucial period in the development of the sugar plantation system—accumulated several relatively small parcels of land in Christ Church parish.[6] These parcels were ultimately formed into two plantations, each one bearing the name of its owner.

Although the existence of two Newton plantations in Christ Church in the 1680s is confirmed in early documentary materials (Newton Papers 523/1068, 1110), the earliest clear evidence that Samuel Newton developed two plantations is in Richard Forde's detailed map of Barbados (1675), the first map of the island based on systematic survey. It locates and identifies by name over 800 Barbadian plantations and indicates the number, if any, and type of sugar mills (powered by wind, cattle, or water) associated with each. The two Newton plantations are shown approximately one-and-one-half miles apart on a roughly northeast-southwest axis (figure 7). The southwestern plantation is closest to the village of Oistins (or Oistin's Bay; also known as Charles Town in the seventeenth century), and historical evidence suggests that this plantation was already in existence by at least 1658 (Lucas 1956:117). This southwestern plantation is also shown on Forde's map at about one-and-one-half miles from the coast at Oistins.[7] Allowing for the relative imprecision of a seventeenth-century map, the southwestern plantation is located in an area that very closely corresponds to the area of Newton plantation today.

By the 1670s when Barbados was the "richest colony in English America" (Dunn 1969), Samuel Newton's plantations were operating and their owner was considered one of the island's most prominent planters. The leading planters at this time dominated the island's economy and polity, and in 1672 Newton became a member of the Barbados Council, the upper house of the island's legislature, where he served until his death in 1684. Samuel Newton was considered one "of the most eminent planters in Barbados" in a 1673 list

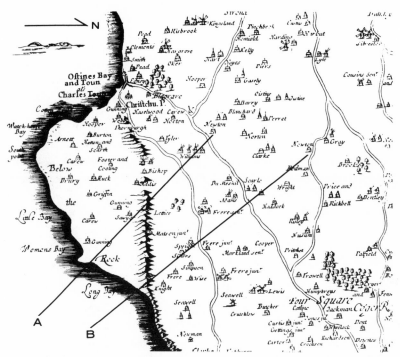

Figure 7. Two Newton plantations, as shown on a section of Richard Forde's *A New Map of the Island of Barbadoes* (ca. 1675). *A:* south-western or "lower plantation"; *B:* northeastern plantation. (Courtesy of the John Carter Brown Library, Brown University.)

containing the names of seventy-two men and the acres owned by each (Public Record Office 1673). Newton was recorded as owning 400 acres of land, but no information was given on the size of each of his two plantations. Although Samuel Newton was not the largest landowner in Barbados at the time (at least twenty-one people owned more land), his property was well within the range of large-scale holdings by Barbadian standards.

Newton, however, continued to increase his landholdings, and by the time of the island's comprehensive 1679 census his property in Christ Church parish included 581 acres of land, to which were attached 15 white indentured servants and 260 slaves (Public Record Office 1679–80), although the census does not indicate how much acreage and slaves each of the two plantations contained. At the time of the census, the twelve men on the Barbados Council "averaged 420 acres and 190 slaves apiece" while "the twenty-two assemblymen averaged 340 acres and 153 slaves apiece" (Dunn 1972:91–92, 96–101).

Upon his death in 1684, Samuel Newton's plantations descended to his wife Barbara and to his son John; Barbara died in 1694 and John in or just before 1706.[8] Around 1706 the financial accounts of Newton suggest that there was only one plantation known by that name. Another indication of only one Newton at this period is in Herman Moll's *A New Map of the Island of Barbadoes*, which was first published in 1708 (see Oldmixon 1708;2:1).[9] Moll did not conduct a survey in Barbados and his map appears to be essentially a copy of Forde's map of the 1670s. Whereas Forde attempted to identify "every . . . plantation" on the island, Moll was only concerned with locating and naming the "principal plantations" and identified fewer plantations than Forde. Moll also may have attempted to update the names of what he considered to be the "principal plantations." Moll's map shows fewer plantations in the general area of Christ Church parish where Newton is located than Forde's map and only identifies the southwestern Newton.

The clearest evidence, however, that only one Newton plantation existed by the early eighteenth century derives from William Mayo's elaborate printed map based on a systematic large-scale survey accomplished between 1717 and 1721 (1722; the sheet showing Newton is reprinted in T. Campbell 1965, plate viii). Of the nearly 1,000 plantations shown on Mayo's map, only one Newton is located in Christ Church; furthermore, this plantation is in approximately the same position as the southwestern Newton shown on Forde's map. Eighteenth- and early nineteenth-century Newton plantation documents that postdate Mayo's map, often refer to the plantation as the "Lower Plantation," the "Lower Estate," or as "Newton's Lower Plantation"; "lower" undoubtedly survived from the period when there were two Newton plantations and the lower was the southwestern one. In Barbadian parlance, then as now, lower refers to the leeward side or the west. In earlier times when the same planter owned two plantations in the parishes east or northeast of Saint Michael the plantation to the west or nearer to Bridgetown was usually referred to as lower. Forde's map shows the lower Newton slightly closer to Bridgetown or somewhat to the west of the northern one (see figure 7). The northern plantation, which no longer exists, was probably sold and then either incorporated into another plantation with a different name or worked as a separate unit and given a new name. Mayo's map shows Barry and Collens plantations in approximately the same general location as the northern Newton shown on Forde's map, but we did not attempt to establish whether either Barry or Collens had ever belonged to Samuel Newton.

After John Newton's death until 1794, Newton plantation remained in the hands of owners, usually absentees, who were direct descendants of the original owner, Samuel Newton. In 1794 the plantation was inherited by two brothers, John and Thomas Lane (a barrister and solicitor, respectively). The period until shortly before the death of both brothers in 1824 yields the richest manuscript materials on the plantation. Thomas, who coordinated the plantation's affairs from London, "kept his accounts and letters received from his managers in Barbados and from his merchants in exemplary order, as well as full copies of almost all his correspondence to them" (Micklem 1969:iv). The Lane brothers were first cousins of Elizabeth Newton, who died in 1794 and who was the last Newton to own the plantation (Armson 1975; Lucas 1949:38). After the brothers died, the plantation descended to one member or another of the Lane family until at least the early part of the twentieth century.

Because we are primarily concerned with establishing a chronological baseline for Newton's origin and indicating the continuity of the plantation's existence through the slave period and up to the time of our fieldwork, it is not necessary to trace in further detail the history of the plantation's ownership. The documentary evidence clearly indicates that Newton has been in existence since the middle of the seventeenth century—in all probability by at least the middle of the 1650s and certainly by the early 1670s. The plantation was thus occupied by slaves for approximately 175 years (until emancipation in 1834) and has been under cultivation continuously for somewhat over 300 years.

ACREAGE AND LAND USE

Newton was one of Barbados's larger plantations in terms of its land acreage, number of sugar mills, and the size of its slave population (see chapter 2). From 1750, the earliest year for which there is information on the Lower plantation's acreage, until recent times, the land area of Newton has remained relatively intact, unlike many other plantations in Barbados (which have been subdivided into smaller units or sold off their marginal agricultural lands). In 1750, the plantation contained 434 acres; by 1784 it had increased to 454; and from 1796 until recently it comprised a little more than 458 (Newton Papers 523/970, 277, 289, 275).

Although the acreage and names of Newton's fields have been modified over the years, the location of the plantation yard has remained stable since the days of slavery, and, as far as we can judge, despite changes in their acreages, the fields surrounding the yard (including those containing the cemetery and site of the former slave village) have been part of the plantation since at least the late seventeenth century.

The slave village started to be abandoned as an occupational site before the termination of the Apprenticeship period on August 1, 1838 when a number of Barbadian plantations began to establish tenantries—plantation villages (usually established on agriculturally marginal lands and on the peripheries of the plantations) that were subdivided into small plots of land and rented to the ex-slaves–apprentices; in the earliest periods, especially, the houses were also owned by the plantations. Newton started its tenantry in July 1838; by the following month, fifty-four allotments had been rented on a weekly basis, although the plantation had surveyed and laid out eighty-one tenant plots.[10] The complete abandonment of the Negro yard as a slave village probably occurred in or shortly after 1838.

Like other Barbadian plantations during preemancipation times, much of Newton's acreage was not planted in sugar cane. In 1693, for example, the plantation attorney reported to the owners in England that "only one hundred acres in canes [are] to be planted yearly"; "to plant more," he added, "would but overwork the strength you have" and prevent effective care of the sugar fields, as well as "your other ground to be kept in provision and . . . for your working cattle, young cattle and breeding cows" (Bate 1693). A century later in 1796, Sampson Wood wrote: "Our real cane land consists of 221 acres and 23 perch, a very small portion out of the total . . . land of the estate"; at the time, however, 184 acres were in sugar, including the acreage being prepared for the planting of new cane plants. Much of the remainder of the plantation's total acreage was in "Guinea" and "Indian" corn or was pasture for the livestock (Newton Papers 523/289). During other years, an average of 172 acres were planted in sugar cane with 60 percent of this acreage to be harvested in each following year (Newton Papers 523/315, 116, 128–1, 586, 593). In 1796, Newton also allotted nearly 25 acres which were divided among nine white militia tenants (Newton Papers 523/289).

Aside from the tenant areas and fields planted in cane, corn, or pasturage, a "provision field" supplied produce for "the use of the [manager's] house, and the Negroes on particular occasions" (Newton Papers 523/289). In 1796, the provision field comprised 15½ acres, half of which were planted in "Indian corn" and the remainder in yams, eddoes, okras, "and other ground provisions." (In 1799 and 1804, the provision fields were 13 and 24 acres, respectively; Newton Papers 523/128–1, 586, 593.) On another 13½-acre field, "pigeon peas,"[11] intercropped among the cane, were grown for the manager's house, but they were also a "very good food occasionally for the Negroes" (Newton Papers 523/289). Newton, unlike some other Barbadian plantations, apparently did not have a Negro garden or Negro ground (see chapter 3, note 2), although the slaves planted "a few shrubs" around their houses where they also probably cultivated small amounts of food crops.

It is difficult to determine the size of the slave village area. We were unable to locate the map that Sampson Wood referred to in his 1796 report; moreover, although Wood systematically described the size and use of each field in his report on the lands, he did not specifically mention the acreage of the Negro yard. In another report, however, Wood did "reckon that the Negro houses, buildings [of the yard], etc. stand on an area of about twenty or twenty odd acres" (Newton Papers 523/290). We can make a crude estimate of the slave village area by using the acreage of Newton's Negro yard fields today. According to the plantation manager at the time of our fieldwork, the four Negro yard fields covered about 15½ acres. Upper North had 2½ acres; Upper South, 2½; Lower North, 5; and Lower South, 5½ (see figure 4). At the time of Wood's writing, the size of the Negro yard was probably much less than 15 acres.

THE SLAVE POPULATION

DEMOGRAPHIC FEATURES

The population of the slave village was relatively large. In the middle of the eighteenth century, Newton's slave contingent numbered 171, but 267 slaves lived on the plantation by 1776. The population fluctuated, largely in the mid-to-upper 200s over the remainder of the preemancipation period (only exceeding 300 in 1825); at emancipation, on August 1, 1834, Newton claimed 261 slaves (table 6).

Although population size from the last half of the eighteenth century to 1834 was in the upper range of Barbadian plantations, the sexual distribution of Newton's slaves generally conformed to that found on other plantations regardless of size. Sex information on Newton's slaves is available for sixteen years during the 1740–1834 period; males averaged 45 percent and females 55 percent. On other plantations during this period, males comprised 48 percent and females 52 percent; islandwide figures indicate a distribution of 46 percent males and 54 percent females during the preemancipation decades of the nineteenth century. Female slaves always outnum-

TABLE 6. Slave population by sex: Newton plantation.

	Male		Female				Male		Female		
Year	Number	Percentage	Number	Percentage	Total	Year	Number	Percentage	Number	Percentage	Total
1740	84	49.1	87	50.8	171	1815	—	—	—	—	258
1750	—	—	—	—	171	1816	—	—	—	—	273
1776	121	45.3	146	54.6	267	1817	121	45.6	144	54.3	265
1782	104	43.3	136	56.6	240	1818	—	—	—	—	275
1783	107	44.2	135	55.7	242	1819	—	—	—	—	275
1784	111	45.8	131	54.1	242	1820	124	44.6	154	55.3	278
1796	109	42.7	146	57.2	255	1821	—	—	—	—	277
1797	109	42.7	146	57.2	255	1822	—	—	—	—	292
1798	—	—	—	—	268	1823	127	45.1	154	54.8	281
1800	111	42.6	149	57.3	260	1824	—	—	—	—	297
1803	114	43.1	150	56.8	264	1825	—	—	—	—	304
1804	—	—	—	—	265	1826	120	44.6	149	55.3	269
1806	—	—	—	—	269	1827	—	—	—	—	278
1807	—	—	—	—	267	1828	—	—	—	—	270
1809	—	—	—	—	263	1829	119	44.2	150	55.7	269
1810	—	—	—	—	255	1830	—	—	—	—	262
1811	—	—	—	—	243	1832	114	44.7	141	55.2	255
1812	—	—	—	—	236	1833	—	—	—	—	259
1813	—	—	—	—	246	1834	117	44.8	144	55.1	261
1814	—	—	—	—	259						

Sources: 1740–1804, Newton Papers (523/970, 270, 271, 272, 277, 288, 116, 131–1, 285, 586). 1806–1819, Newton Plantation (1805–1841). 1820–1834, Newton Papers (523/275); Newton Plantation (1805–1841).

bered males in the years for which there are sexual data on Newton's slaves, reflecting a widespread demographic characteristic on Barbadian plantations.

By the late eighteenth century the vast majority of slaves at Newton, as well as the rest of the island, were creoles. The first birthplace data on slaves are available for 248 of the plantation's 255 slaves in 1796; 242 (98 percent) were born at Newton and another 3 were born elsewhere in Barbados. Only three slaves (a man in his fifties, and two old women) were born in Africa (Newton Papers 523/288). From 1805 to 1834, there were apparently no Africans on the plantation, although one or two creole slaves may have been occasionally acquired from elsewhere on the island (Newton Plantation 1805–1841).

Newton was also fairly typical in terms of the age structure of its slave population. Information on absolute ages for the plantation's slaves, however, is limited to a handful of years; for illustrative and comparative purposes, Newton's age structure in 1796, 1820, and 1834 is compared with that of the islandwide slave population in 1817 and 1834—the last two years are the only ones for which islandwide age figures are available, but in each of these two years the age cohorts vary (see table 7).

In 1817, Barbados's slaves were systematically counted for the first time, and in the sources available to us the age groups were reported by ten-year cohorts, with the exception of infants under age one; to compare the Newton figures for 1796 and 1820 with the

TABLE 7. Slave population by age groups: Newton plantation and Barbados.

Age group	Newton, 1796		Newton, 1820		Barbados, 1817	
	Number	Percent-age	Number	Percent-age	Number	Percent-age
Under 1	3	1.2	14	5.0	2,606	3.3
1–10	64	25.8	75	26.9	20,432	26.3
11–20	55	22.1	51	18.3	16,735	21.5
21–30	23	9.2	60	21.5	14,579	18.8
31–40	43	17.3	19	6.8	10,591	13.6
41–50	31	12.5	23	8.2	6,667	8.6
51–60	20	8.0	21	7.5	3,616	4.6
60+	9	3.6	15	5.3	2,254	2.9
Total	248		278		77,480	

Age group	Newton, 1834		Barbados, 1834	
	Number	Percent-age	Number	Percent-age
Under 6	39	14.9	14,047	16.9
6–12	41	15.7	11,987	14.5
13–21	60	22.9	15,573	18.8
22–50	91	34.9	32,656	39.4
51+	30	11.5	8,544	10.3
Total	261		82,807	

Sources: Newton 1796, Newton Papers (523/288). 1820, 1834, Newton Plantation (1805–1841). Barbados 1817, *Parliamentary Papers* (1831–32 a:520). 1834, *The Barbadian* (August 13, 1834). Seven slaves are excluded in 1796 in Newton for whom no ages are given, and no ages are given for thirteen others in Barbados in 1817.

islandwide statistics for 1817, we have broken down the Newton figures in similar cohorts. Although it cannot be assumed that the ages attributed to slaves were precise or correct in all or most cases, judging from the Newton data (in which ages were reported by the plantation managers), the ages of persons under twenty appear to have been more precisely reported than, for example, the ages of those over forty or fifty. Allowing for imprecision in absolute age attributions, the general age categories are useful for correlating them with demographic characteristics derived from excavated skeletal materials (see Appendix D).

Newton's adult population (those above age twenty) comprised about 50.6 percent of the plantation's slaves in 1796 and 49.3 percent in 1820, percentages which compare favorably with the 48.5 percent of adult slaves in Barbados. Similarly, in what is probably the most precise category in terms of age attributions, those ten and under included 27 percent and 31.9 percent of Newton's slaves in 1796 and 1820, respectively, whereas the Barbados figure in 1817 was 29.6 percent. (Table 8 provides a more detailed breakdown of the absolute ages of Newton's slaves, especially for those under twenty.)

TABLE 8. Slave population by age and sex: Newton plantation, 1796 and 1820.

Age group	1796				1820			
			Total				Total	
	Male	Female	Number	Percentage	Male	Female	Number	Percentage
Under 3	2	10	12	4.8	12	13	25	8.9
3–5	4	13	17	6.8	13	18	31	11.1
6–9	8	16	24	9.7	14	17	31	11.1
10–14	26	14	40	16.1	6	10	16	5.7
15–19	9	11	20	8.0	12	16	28	10.0
20–29	12	9	21	8.5	21	39	60	21.5
30–39	16	25	41	16.5	12	11	23	8.2
40–49	10	22	32	12.5	15	10	25	8.9
50–59	13	16	29	11.7	13	10	23	8.2
60+	4	8	12	4.8	6	10	16	5.7
Total	104	144	248[a]		124	154	278	

Sources: 1796, Newton Papers (523/288). 1820, Newton Plantation (1805–1841).

[a] Excluded are five males and two females for whom no age data are given.

Age cohorts in 1834 were reported differently than in earlier years, but a comparison between Newton and Barbados as a whole reveals a similarity. For example, children under six at Newton comprised 14.9 percent of the population and on the island they formed 16.9 percent; at Newton 11.5 percent of the population was above fifty years compared to 10.3 percent of all Barbadian slaves (table 7).

Other data are available for eleven years on relative age groups of "men," "women," "boys," and "girls" (table 9). The sources suggest that men and women were normally defined as over twenty years; they are classified as adults in table 9. The adult population, then, averaged about 54.7 percent of the total population during the eleven-year period, which is generally consistent with Newton's adult population percentages in 1796, 1820, and 1834 (tables 7 and 8). (In a sample of 43 plantations, dating from 1781 to 1834, for which there are data on the four relative age groups, adults averaged 59.1 percent of the slave contingents; Barbados Department of Archives 1803–04, 1780–1834.) As reported in the sources, boys and girls usually included the smallest infants to people around twenty years old, but in a few cases figures are available on Newton's "infant" population—roughly, children under two years.

The implications of these age data for the archaeological work in Newton cemetery are discussed more fully in Appendix D, which

TABLE 9. Slave population by relative age groups: Newton plantation.

| Year | Adults | | Children | Infants[a] | Total |
	Number	Percentage	Number	Number	
1740	111	64.9	45	15	171
1776	145	54.3	122	—	267
1782	124	51.6	116	—	240
1783	125	51.6	117	—	242
1784	149	61.5	93	—	242
1797	143	56.0	112	—	255
1800	136	52.3	124	—	260
1803	142	53.7	96	26	264
1817	146	55.0	94	25	265
1829	139	51.6	109	21	269
1832	127	49.8	112	16	255

Sources: 1740–1803, Newton Papers (523/970, 270, 271, 272, 277, 288, 131–1, 285). 1817–1832, Newton Plantation (1805–1841).

[a] Dashes indicate that no separate figures could be estimated for infants; infants are included with children.

also considers some of the plantation's other demographic data, including death rates.[12]

WORK ROLES, RANK, AND REWARDS

Age was one of the factors that determined the tasks a slave would be assigned in meeting labor requirements on Barbadian plantations. In general, Newton's work organization and the jobs assigned its slaves reflect the pattern found on other Barbadian plantations of comparable size.[13]

"One of the most important parts of management," advised a prominent Barbadian planter in the late eighteenth century, "is a judicious division of Negroes into gangs" (Gibbes 1797:69–70); the organizing of field laborers, who comprised the largest single category of plantation slaves, into gangs goes deep into the history of the island's sugar plantation system (Ligon 1657:113–114). Field laborers were divided into three, and sometimes four, gangs. The first and second gangs (the first was of crucial importance) together constituted what plantation managements considered their effective labor force; these two gangs comprised, on the average, about 30 to 40 percent of a plantation's total slave contingent.[14]

The first or "great gang" was composed of mature men and women (from the late teens upward); in actual field operations, this gang could also be further subdivided by sex or relative strength. As a group, however, the first gang performed the most physically demanding work on the plantation. Work followed, as it does today, a two-season agricultural cycle. During "crop time" (from January to April or early May), when "more hours of continued hard labour are required than at any other time" (Steele 1789:30), the first gang cut the cane, carried it to and operated the mills, and made sugar; during the out-of-crop season the gang was occupied with such tasks as tilling the fields, digging cane holes, planting canes and food crops, and collecting animal dung, which was carried to the fields and used as fertilizer. The last operation, in particular, slaves considered the "most disagreeable and distressing duty" they were compelled to perform (Parry 1789a:23).

The second gang, sometimes called the "little" or "young people" gang, was composed of adolescents and for particular tasks it was sometimes subdivided by sex. Generally, the second gang weeded the fields and sometimes planted food crops, especially corn; during the harvest season the second gang also gathered cane trash for sugar factory fuel and thatching material for slave houses. In addition, some members of the second gang were usually assigned to tend the plantation's livestock.

Depending on the agricultural season, some first and second gang members performed specialized jobs outside of the field. For example, during the harvest season, male boatswains supervised the positioning of the windmill arms in relation to the wind as well as feeding the canes into the mill rollers; other men were distillers, clayers, clarifiers, and boilers (roles associated with various phases of sugar and rum manufacture). The head boiler was especially highly skilled and among the most valuable of all slaves to a plantation's management. During the out-of-crop season some of these people might have performed such other specialized jobs as watchmen or livestock keepers; plantations also had full-time watchmen or livestock keepers who did not engage in field labor. Slaves who performed various domestic chores for other slaves, such as the older women who cooked meals for the small children or tended infants while their mothers were in the fields, the "sick nurses" in the plantation's infirmary, and carters were other specialized roles.

The first and second gangs at Newton, the plantation's effective labor force, averaged about 43 percent of the slaves. An average of eighty-one slaves on the first gang followed the same agricultural cycle and task performance found on other sugar plantations. On occasions, Newton was underhanded for certain field tasks, particularly cultivating the land preparatory to cane planting; in such cases the plantation followed a common practice on the island and hired "additional labor to perform such jobs as require immediate dispatch" (Newton Papers 523/653). People generally joined the first gang by the time they were in their early twenties and, according to figures for 1796 and 1820, the average age of Newton's first gang members was in the mid-thirties.

From three to five of Newton's slaves, usually middle-aged or older women who might otherwise have been in the first gang, were assigned tasks to assist other slaves. Depending on circumstances, from one to three women were "sick nurses," another two or three prepared meals and took care of the small children (as on other Barbadian plantations, nursing infants were usually taken out to the fields by their mothers), and in the late eighteenth century, if not earlier, from one to three people were assigned to "beat corn" for the other slaves; in 1825, however, Newton purchased "a corn mill for the use of the Negroes" (Newton Plantation 1805–1841).

The second gang at Newton was largely composed of teenagers. They usually entered the gang when they were thirteen and their average age was around sixteen or seventeen. The second gang averaged approximately thirty people, but its size could be enlarged by adding from among those who tended the livestock. Several teenaged males assumed responsibility for Newton's livestock. An adult male was sometimes designated "head cattle keeper," while others were usually charged with each variety of livestock, such as cattle, horses, sheep, and hogs. Between 3 and 9 percent of the total slave contingent (excluding small children who collected fodder) was involved in one form or another of livestock care. In addition, one or two older females were usually assigned to care for the "feathered stock."

On Barbadian plantations the third gang (also variously known as the "childrens' gang," "meat pickers' gang," "hog meat gang," or "grass gatherers") was composed of small children from the ages of five or six to eleven or twelve. The older members of the third gang sometimes weeded fields, but the gang's major function was such light work as collecting grass or other fodder for the plantation's livestock—hence the name "meat pickers" or "hog meat gang" —the word "meat" is still used in Barbados to refer to animal fodder. Some children in this gang also tended the plantation's small livestock and domestic fowl. Although all the children could be included in the third gang, sometimes the smallest children were put into a fourth "pot" gang. As the gang's name indicates, these children received a cooked meal prepared for them by an older female slave who was specifically charged with this task. The fourth gang could also be called the "hog meat gang," indicating its primary task of collecting vines and insects to feed the plantation's small livestock and fowl. If the plantation did not have a fourth gang, small children, sometimes as young as four years old, were included in the third gang and assigned tasks commensurate with their physical abilities.

Newton did not have a fourth gang. Children generally entered the plantation's third gang by the time they were seven years old (on occasion at six), but the average age was between nine and ten in 1796 and 1820; during these years, most children under seven were considered "not fit to be employed."

In the late 1780s, Barbados's governor reported that, in general, if one deducted "the aged and infirm, the sick, the pregnant, the young, and the absent, there are seldom more than two thirds of the slaves on a plantation who contribute to its cultivation" (Parry 1789b). Data on the number of unemployed slaves could be gathered in ten specific cases, which include nine different plantations (exclusive of Newton) over the 1781–1834 period. These cases included 2,287 slaves, of which 519 (22.6 percent) were unemployable or unemployed; in only two cases were more than 25 percent in this category. These figures, however, do not include people who were temporarily ill or permanent or temporary absentees; see Bennett (1958:12); Harewood Archives (1834); Rolph (1836:53); Barbados Department of Archives, Deed Books (vol. 287, pp. 322–328); Guinea Plantation (1820); and Newton Papers (523/276, 285).

Roughly 18 to 25 percent of Newton's slaves were considered unemployable, including the "superannuated," permanently disabled, and "young children not fit to do anything." Occasionally, people in these categories were given light jobs commensurate with their physical abilities, and thus the actual percentage of unemployed slaves was lower than the figures indicate. As Newton's manager wrote in 1796: "All who can be of any service in the plantation are put to some occupation or other. All have something to do, except diseased people and cripples" (Newton Papers 523/288).

On Barbadian plantations slaves who had "something to do" and who were placed in gangs were directed by a "black overseer" or slave "driver." Plantation managements considered the driver of the first gang (who was always a man) among the most important slaves on the plantation. Large first gangs sometimes had two or three drivers, but in such cases only one was called the head driver. The driver of the second gang was usually an adult, either male or female, while the driver of the third (and fourth) gang was invariably a mature woman. The first gang at Newton sometimes had two drivers; one directed the labor of the older women in the gang. The drivers of the first and second gangs were men in their late twenties to mid-thirties, while an older woman drove the third gang.

Drivers did not engage in common field labor, and the head boiler and the senior tradesmen or skilled craftsmen were usually also exempt. (Younger men or boys apprenticing as tradesmen, however, were sometimes put into the field or performed other chores related to agriculture or livestock tending.) Most plantations had at least one mason, carpenter, and cooper in addition to other tradesmen such as saddlers, blacksmiths, and, on occasion, potters who manufactured the conical earthenware pots employed during sugar manufacture.

Adult male slaves who performed skilled jobs or who held leadership positions on Barbadian plantations were considered the officers of a plantation (the concept of "officer" or rank occurs early in the historical literature; see Ligon 1657:48–49). Officers included the senior tradesmen, those skilled in various phases of the sugar manufacture process, the senior drivers, and rangers. The position of ranger had emerged by the late eighteenth century, and it was filled by "a principal slave ... appointed to superintend the field work"

(Clarke 1828); at Newton, the manager defined the ranger as the "head man of the estate who superintends all the Negroes and the land" (Newton Papers 523/288).

On plantations with rangers, the manager's orders were issued directly to the ranger who then conveyed them to the drivers. If a plantation had a ranger, it also had drivers of the first, second, and third gangs; if there was no ranger, however, presumably a white suboverseer issued the manager's orders to the drivers.

The management of Newton considered the ranger and, especially, the driver of the first gang as among the more valuable slaves. In 1784, when Newton's 242 slaves were appraised at an average value of £31 (with a range of from £88 to £5—excluding "superannuated" and permanently disabled persons to whom no monetary value was attached), the head driver was valued at £60, as were a few first gang members, two of the coopers, and some others with specialties in the sugar manufacturing process; only four other slaves were valued in excess of £60 (Newton Papers 523/277).[15] But in 1803, when the plantation's 264 slaves had an average value of £83, the head driver was valued at £300, the highest of all the slaves (523/285, 287).

Newton's tradesmen, like others in Barbados, as a group were among the most highly valued slaves. In 1784, the average value of a Newton slave was £31, but the senior tradesmen averaged £77; in 1803, when the average slave's value was £83, the tradesmen averaged £202 (cf. Bennett 1958:16–17). The most highly valued tradesmen at Newton were the senior carpenters, coopers, joiners, and masons, all of whom were adult males. Newton usually had two or three carpenters, three masons, three to five coopers, one joiner, and two or three blacksmiths; in addition, for some of the years for which there is information, the plantation maintained an older man identified as a basketmaker (although this was not a position to which a great deal of monetary value was attached, and was apparently given to persons who had passed their prime in other capacities; see Bennett 1958:16, 18). Other highly valued specialized positions at Newton included the head carters, boatswains, boilers, clayers, clarifiers, and distillers; during the out-of-crop season, some of these people worked at field jobs or performed tasks such as caring for livestock or guarding the plantation's fields and storehouses.

Newton's domestic slaves catered to the manager and his family. The domestics or house Negroes on Barbadian plantations occupied positions as cooks, chamber maids, personal servants, washerwomen, coachmen, grooms, and gardeners. The number of domestics and the degree of their specializations varied with the size of a plantation and the opulence of its owner or manager. Because Newton did not have a resident owner, the number and variety of its domestics was probably somewhat less than on large plantations where the owner resided. Over the years Newton averaged about nine domestic slaves, including butlers and other personal servants, cooks and kitchen assistants, and a groom, washerwoman, and gardener; sometimes, as elsewhere, the head cook or another senior domestic slave was highly valued in monetary (and personal) terms.

The distinctions or ranks among slaves on Barbadian plantations as related to occupational categories were noted by several observers. Early in Barbados's plantation history, Richard Ligon alluded to distinctions and concomitant "privileges" when he reported on Macow who, one day, came into the plantation house "which none of the Negroes ... do unless an officer, as he was" (1657:48); in later years such distinctions became even more apparent. An observer of the island's slave system, William Dickson (who had lived in Barbados for about thirteen years from 1772 as secretary to the governor), described these distinctions in unusual detail:

> Although slavery, properly speaking, admit[s] of no distinctions of rank, yet some slaves live and are treated so very differently from others, that a superficial observer would take it for granted they belong to classes of men who hold distinct ranks in society, so to speak, by tenures essentially different ... The black drivers, boilers, watchmen, and other black officers on estates; the mechanics; and, above all, the numerous and useless domestics, both in town and country: All of these, *comparatively*, and many of them *really*, live in ease and plenty; nor can they be said to feel any of the hardships of slavery, but such as arise from the caprices of their owners which, however, are sometimes intolerable enough. To these I may add most of the slaves who ... find employment for themselves, and make their owners a weekly return out of their earnings ...
>
> On the other hand ... the great body of the slaves, the field-people on sugar-plantations, are generally treated more like beasts of burden than like human creatures; since they cultivate the land with no assistance from cattle and suffer every hardship which can be supposed to attend oppressive toil, coarse and scanty fare, bad lodging, want of covering in the wet season, and a degree of severity which frequently borders on, and too often amounts to, inhumanity.
>
> In order ... to form anything like a just idea of the condition of the slaves, it is absolutely necessary to attend to the distinctions (1789:6).

In 1812, a group of planters emphasized that "one of the causes of depression among our slaves ... is derived from a source the least likely perhaps to attract the notice of a superficial observer. We mean the inequality among them" (Society for the Improvement 1811–16:133–134). Although by the late eighteenth and early nineteenth centuries efforts were made to improve the material conditions under which slaves lived, distinctions persisted until the end of the slave period and there continued to be slaves who received relatively better treatment and accumulated more material goods than others.

On Newton plantation "distinctions" and "inequality" existed, and Newton followed the Barbadian pattern wherein adult slaves were ranked by plantation managements. This ranking was generally linked to the work roles or job categories that slaves assumed, and the ranking, in turn, was reflected in the monetary values that plantations attached to their slaves and the "privileges" and "rewards" that some, especially the plantation officers, received.

However, rewards were not only distributed to plantation officers but also to others as positive incentives or inducements to conform to plantation disciplinary and labor norms and to protect whatever other self-interests the planters defined. Rewards included (but were not exclusively limited to) legally codified incentives, such as manumitting slaves who informed on revolt plots (Handler 1974:30–31), the granting of such special favors as permission to attend the funeral of a kinsman on another plantation, the payment of small sums of money, and the allocation of material goods that were not normally distributed by plantation managements.

By the late eighteenth century, a systematic distribution of rewards was increasingly recognized as an important element of plantation management and as an essential device in the successful governance of a slave labor force. The utility of positively reinforcing and encouraging the slaves was well expressed in 1812 by a committee of planters. Charged by an agricultural society "to draw up a plan for the regulation of plantations," it recommended

a system of rewards [which] would undoubtedly be attended with the most beneficial effects since it would give ambition & vanity [and] something to work for. Every Negro who distinguishes himself for regularity, sobriety & industry should be distinguished by some reward useful to him. Every mother who is careful of their family should be similarly compensated ... It is a common & highly laudable custom to give each mother a dollar on bringing out her child after the expiration of the month[16] ... [The slaves in general] ... should be ... encour-

78

aged to realize a comfortable peculium of their own, feel themselves to have an interest at stake & a regard for home. Every possible encouragement should be given to good morals and domestic virtues . . . We know nothing that so strongly attaches a slave to the plantation . . . as being in the possession of a comfortable house, which is generally accompanied with a suitable portion of stock, a fondness for home, & general habits of industry . . . to furnish proper houses to a whole set of slaves is certainly a very expensive & tedious work, but it is one to be overcome by constant perserverance, & which will amply repay all the trouble & expense it may have cost . . . we think it right to mention that occasionally gratuities of iron pots, knives, spoons, etc. are encouragements to the slaves which should be given as bounties for good behavior (Society for the Improvement 1811–16:131–146).

Plantation officers clearly benefited the most from the system of rewards and had privileges that normally were not shared by other slaves, particularly the members of the field gangs. "The principal negroes in [the] estates," wrote the chaplain to the Codrington plantations in 1789, "enjoy several privileges & advantages above . . . their inferiors"; "their importance to the estates was marked by many tokens of special status [and] . . . the leading men received many unusual favors" (Bennett 1958:18). For example, on Barbadian plantations in general, slaves considered common field labor as the hallmark of their status,[17] but officers were usually exempt from most kinds of agricultural work.[18] Officers and similarly privileged slaves also had somewhat greater access to material goods, received larger supplies of clothing and food,[19] sometimes had more elaborate houses and household furnishings, and even received monetary payments or rewards distributed in local currency.[20] In addition, tradesmen were sometimes hired out for wages (or were permitted to hire themselves out)—one reason why they were valued so highly—and were able to retain part of what they earned; occasionally they could achieve manumission through a customary (but not legally codified) device locally known as self-purchase (Handler 1974:34–36).

The son of a black woman and a white man, George Saer, the head cooper at Newton, was highly valued in practical and personal terms; Saer's case illustrates dimensions of the plantation's system of rewards for those who conformed—or appeared to conform—to white-defined norms for slave behavior. In his 1796 report on Newton's slaves, Sampson Wood effusively spoke of Saer as "a most valuable member" of the slave contingent who "would be a treasure in any society. He is an excellent workman in his own trade, a good carpenter, almost a good anything; always at work, always willing, and always ready and good humoured—strictly honest and sober." At this time, Saer was ill with "consumption." "He was so ill," Wood wrote, "that I thought it best ... tho a little expensive, not to trust to our common apothecary, but to consult a physician on his case ... We let [Saer] do just as he likes, work or work not ... His loss would be irreparable to us. I cannot say too much of him" (Newton Papers 523/288).

Saer's medical condition fluctuated, but within two years he was clearly dying. "I have done everything that the greatest care, affection, and tenderness could. He has been nourished from our own table ... He dies a Christian by baptism and a true one in spirit. I mean to give him a handsome burial—what they [the slaves] esteem the best reward of services after death—and he's richly deserved anything ... Poor fellow! I shall miss him sincerely and your interest too as much. He was worth anything to it" (523/352–1). After Saer's death, at the age of forty-seven, "or thereabout," Wood reported: "I gave him a handsome funeral ... as an encouragement to others and as a small tribute to faithful services, and I would make one request in his name, that if there be not much expense in it, you would send over [from England] a small plain stone for the head of his grave. He was a Christian and expressing the approbation of his owners for his faithful services t'would, I think, have a good effect [on the other slaves]" (523/381–1).

Expenditures on slave funerals were another reflection of plantation rewards and incentives, but these expenditures were not regular and only made in certain cases. "Extraordinary recognition was accorded" to one of the drivers on the Codrington plantations when, in the late 1780s, he was given money "to assist in burying his sister" (Bennett 1958:18), and the pattern is further illustrated by data in Newton's financial accounts from 1805 to 1811 (Newton Plantation 1805–1841). In 1805, the plantation spent close to £2 for the "funeral fees of Ned Thomas"; in 1807, about £3½ for "hearse hire and church fees for [the] funeral of Old Mary Ann"; and in 1811, a little over £2 for the fees of a clerk, sexton, and clergyman for the "funeral of Old Doll." The plantation thus expended funds for the funerals of only three slaves of the approximately sixty who died during the 1805–1811 period. The three slaves were members of George Saer's family (one was a full sister, another a half sister, and the third a nephew), had been baptized, and were or had been domestics. Other indications that funerals and burials were associated with the plantation reward-incentive system are suggested by the practice of assigning plantation carpenters-coopers to build coffins for some deceased slaves (see chapter 6).

One question that arises in viewing slave culture relates to the criteria slaves used in according rank and prestige within their own plantation communities, and the relationship, if any, of these criteria to occupational positions—particularly those of plantation officers with their concomitant privileges and rewards—in the plantation's labor system. Phrased another way, was there any relationship between how a slave was ranked or personally viewed by plantation owners or managers, on the one hand, and his or her position, prestige, influence, or esteem in the slave community itself, on the other? Slaves perceived distinctions among themselves and some had more influence on their peers than others. Moreover, certain influential people in the slave communities, such as Obeah men or women, were universally disapproved of by plantation managements, and these persons do not appear to have held positions that would have been included among a list of plantation officers. In general, the historical data on Barbadian and Newton slave life are ambiguous about the relationship between rank within the labor hierarchy and influence or prestige within the slave community itself. At least occasional positive correlations between plantation rank and peer influence or prestige is suggested by evidence that plantation officers were prominent among the leaders in plotting revolts. Several of these plots occurred in the seventeenth century, and an investigation of a particularly threatening plot in 1692 yielded the information that the leaders and the "greatest villains" included drivers, carpenters, masons, wheelwrights, sawyers, blacksmiths, grooms, "and such others that have more favor shown them by their masters, which adds abundantly to their crimes" (Public Record Office 1692). Among the leaders of Barbados's only actual revolt in 1816 were slaves "who had gained an ascendency over their fellows by being enabled to read and write" as well as various plantation officers (Barbados Assembly 1818:6). In 1789, the chaplain of the Codrington plantations also observed how, in general, "the principal negroes ... have a surprising influence over their inferiors," and suggested that "they would if occasion required it, readily sacrifice their lives in the defence of [their owners] ... and their property" (quoted in Bennett 1958:18). Some fifty years earlier, however, the Codrington manager stressed that those slaves "who are our chiefest favorites & such that we put most confidence in are generally the first & greatest conspirators"; "the best of them," he wrote, "are at all times ready to joyn in a conspiracy" (pp. 28–29). At this time, and without the

81

manager's permission, a group of these slaves had led "a considerable body" of the Codrington slaves to Bridgetown where they complained to one of the plantation attorneys about their labor conditions, food, and clothing supplies. Although the archaeological record does not illuminate the relationship between work role and rank in the labor hierarchy and prestige in the slave community, it suggests some social distinctions among the slaves (see chapters 5 and 6).

The longest and most intensive labor of plantation slaves occurred during the harvest season. However, during this season plantation slaves were normally released from work on Sundays. Not until 1826 did Barbadian law specify that slaves should be released from work demands from Saturday night to early Monday morning, but release from plantation labor on Sundays was established in custom by at least the middle of the seventeenth century. Although this custom was not universally observed by plantation owners in the early periods, by the middle of the eighteenth century it was widespread and firmly entrenched in island life. In addition, slaves were generally released from labor on Christmas day, Easter Monday, and Good Friday, and occasionally on special days of thanksgiving (set aside to commemorate deliverance from events such as hurricanes or epidemics), Saturday afternoons, or other holidays (Handler and Frisbie 1972:10–11).

During such holidays, plantation slaves were relatively free to follow their own inclinations: their activities ranged from cultivating their small house plots, trading and marketing in the countryside and towns, engaging in crafts, and making and repairing their houses and household furnishings, to visiting, sexual courtship, gossiping, drinking, and gambling. A number of these last activities took place in association with one of the most important social events in the slaves' cultural system—the weekend and holiday dance; and in general, musical activities played a vital role in the life of the slaves, especially on days when they were released from plantation labor (Handler and Frisbie 1972).

William Dickson agreed with the observations of a late eighteenth-century planter and reported that, with Sundays, other holidays, and bad weather, plantation slaves had at least sixty-one days off during the year (Dickson 1814:433). Dickson's estimate is generally confirmed by the daily work logs of Newton and Seawell plantations in 1796–97; on Newton, the slaves had fifty-four days off, while at Seawell they had at least fifty-six (Newton Papers 523/110, 111).

By the time the work logs were compiled, the management of

Newton, along with that of other plantations in Barbados, was showing special interest in the treatment, material welfare, and natural increase of its slaves. In fact, these topics continued as major themes in the managers' and attorneys' letters to the owners in England during the preemancipation decades of the nineteenth century. The Newton letters, in turn, reflect changes that were occurring in the Barbadian plantocracy during this period; these changes involved a greater explicit interest than in earlier periods in the material existence of the slaves and their treatment in law and custom.

PLANTERS' VIEWS ON THE TREATMENT OF SLAVES

The period during which the treatment of slaves and the quality of their material life were of intense plantocratic interest was also a time of relatively significant changes in Barbadian society as a whole; moreover, these changes had bearing on the sociocultural life of the slaves.

The "material comfort" and humane treatment of slaves were not important issues to Barbadian or British West Indian planters until the late eighteenth century. The controversy surrounding the abolition of the slave trade provoked discussion of these issues and generated enormous arguments on both sides of the Atlantic. These arguments reached major proportions after abolition in 1807, and became especially intense over subsequent years as the British government moved, first, toward favoring reform of colonial slave laws and, then, in 1823, formally declared itself in favor of eventual emancipation.

The treatment of slaves was usually discussed by planters in the context of slave mortality rates and the need to provide an environment conducive to their natural increase. Natural increase, of course, became an issue of vital concern after the abolition of the slave trade. Debates centered on, for example, how this increase was affected by wanton brutality, the use of the whip (and other social control devices), as well as by the slaves' food and clothing allowances, housing conditions, and medical treatment.

Despite the fact that some owners and managers were, as a manager of Newton wrote in 1804, "activated by the calls of humanity toward them [the slaves] as fellow creatures" (Newton Plantation 523/593), it must not be forgotten that plantations were profit-seeking enterprises that attempted to guard their slave expenditures stringently; moreover, plantation owners and managers were overwhelmingly committed to maintaining the slave system. Whatever humanitarian values influenced some masters in the treatment of their slaves, a widespread plantocratic conception of the word "humanitarian" derived from the belief that if "slaves be well fed, properly clothed, comfortably lodged, not overworked, and duly taken care of when sick . . . the owner's humanity will in a few years be amply rewarded by a valuable increase in his property" (Senhouse 1788). This "increase is the only test," asserted a planter in the late eighteenth century, "of the care with which [the slaves] are treated" (*Instructions for the Management of a Plantation in Barbadoes* 1786: 2). In general, planters adhered to the notion that emphasized the slave as property on whose "labours depend the success of the planter" (Newton Papers 523/593). The attorney for Newton and Seawell plantations (a prominent creole planter), stressed that "Independent of any other idea tis to the interest of a planter to take the utmost care of his slaves, for land is not worth holding without slaves to cultivate it" (523/765–1).

"The preservation of the Negroes" became a policy of increasing importance in the management of sugar plantations in the late eighteenth and, especially, during the early nineteenth centuries. Manifestations of this policy were evident in a variety of areas ranging from reform in the slave code (after considerable prodding by the British government) to greater support for the Christianization of slaves, as well as to increased interest in their food and clothing allowances, shelter, and medical treatment.

Newton's managers and attorneys frequently apprised the owners in England of the health and welfare of the slaves, their birth rates, and the increase (or decrease) in their population. For example, in 1815, the attorney for Newton and Seawell discussed the state of the plantations in a periodic report; mentioning, with satisfaction, "the increase" in the number of slaves over the two preceding years, he advised Thomas Lane to send the manager of each plantation "a piece of plate of 15 to 20 guinea value" because of "their unwearied and uncommon attention to your slaves" (Newton Papers 523/741). The inscription on the "plate" received by Newton's manager comments on "his particular attention and humanity towards the Negroes on Newton's plantation; evinced by their increase since he was overseer" (523/759). Pleased with the gift, the manager expressed his "hope that my future exertions for the welfare of the people who are . . . in so especial a manner committed to my care, will be attended with the success which they hitherto have been" (523/761).[21] An earlier manager of Newton, Sampson Wood, shared these sentiments; in one of his many letters reporting in glowing terms his concern for the slaves, he wrote: "All things are as usual with your Negroes, well clothed, strong, healthy and well fed . . . The grown-ups are my friends, the young my children. They want nothing. Everything they ask they have. They are indulged 'tis true, but I am disciplinarian enough to correct severely too when there is occasion" (523/345).

Wood's position on slave treatment and slavery and his self-conception as a manager were often revealed in his writings. In his 1796 "Report on the Negroes," for example, Wood requested extra clothing allowances for the "officers, or those who behave well"; he stressed "these unfortunate people should be indulged any little thing that does not run to any injurious expence. One cannot help pitying their condition, at the same time one knows there is an absolute necessity of keeping them to business and employment, and to have a proper control over them, without which all must be anarchy ... They are a race of discontented beings (indeed it is natural; how can slavery be contented) and hard to be pleased." Wood left "little matters of discipline" to the white overseers, but "in things of greater magnitude, which are brought before me, I never order a blow but confine them [to a dungeon located in the plantation house], and never relax a moment 'till the time fixed for confinement is fulfilled. If they in the interim show repentance they are released; if not, the period is prolonged. I tell them that if they are good Negroes and behave well you are determined they shall want for nothing and have every indulgence, but that they must work and do the business of the estate" (Newton Papers 523/288).

In a letter to Lane, Wood wrote: "If I am lavish in anything, 'tis in my kindness to the poor Negroes—but 'tis to the worthy only and such as really deserve it. I treat them as a father, yet preserve the strictest discipline. When I punish, they see 'tis done with reluctance and with pain; yet when it is done, 'tis done with firmness, and they see a determination in me to do it; hurt me as it may" (523/340–1). "Go tell it to St. Wilberforce," he wrote in another letter to Lane, "West Indian oppression [indeed]! Your slaves are my family and my children have not more attention paid them—well or sick. 'Tis nature to hate the hand which obliges it to work, but I think most of these people love me" (523/381–1).

Wood's views on slaves (and blacks in general) and his professed treatment of them typified those of many other "enlightened" planters—a paternalistic self-image as well as racist and ethnocentric perceptions. The slaves, Wood wrote in 1800, "are the most extraordinary animals to deal with in the world, and there is no such thing as knowing their passions, propensities, or humours for two days together. Discipline and indulgence are tried by us in a thousand ways, the one consistent with all the forms and tenderness and humanity and the other kept from excess, but there is no such thing as finding out a medium that will hold for any time" (523/423).

Regardless of the motives and attitudes of individual white planters, their overriding concern was profit—even when they assumed financial obligations in pursuing the "preservation of the Negroes." Such expenses occurred in four major areas relating to the physical "welfare" of their slave populations: food, clothing, shelter, and medical care.

FOOD SUPPLIES

By the later years of the slave period, plantations sometimes provided a cooked noonday meal for their slaves, in addition to an allowance of "undressed provisions" which the slaves cooked themselves.[22] However, throughout the preemancipation period slaves generally prepared most of their own meals and derived much of their foodstuffs from the formal allocations of plantation managements.

From the late seventeenth century to the preemancipation decades of the nineteenth, corn, primarily "Guinea" corn, was the staple food of the plantation slave.[23] Guinea corn, which was also fed to cattle, "will grow on any land without much tillage or cultivation," wrote Sampson Wood in 1796, "and is our great stand by of food and provision for our Negroes"; to a lesser extent, the plantation grew "Indian corn [which] requires more care and trouble and richer land" (Newton Papers 523/289). In the late 1790s, for example, an annual average of 265 of Newton's total 458 acres was planted in corn (91 in Indian and 174 in Guinea); the Indian variety, in particular, was sometimes intercropped among the cane fields (523/289, 290, 315, 128–1).

When the plantation's corn supplies were insufficient, Newton purchased "American corn," but only made these purchases when circumstances, such as a drought, forced it to do so. Such purchases were a general practice on Barbadian plantations; for example, as the agent for Barbados reported to a committee of the British Parliament in the late eighteenth century, "the allowance of corn to a Negro must depend on the circumstances of his master. If the planter fails in his own crop of corn, he must purchase. Should the price demanded be greater than he is able to pay, his Negroes must suffer" (J. Brathwaite 1789).

Barbadian plantations usually distributed the slaves' corn supplies weekly or daily; Newton, judging from its daily work log for 1796–

97, generally gave daily portions. During that year, corn was distributed on 303 days; for 255 of these days, 400 pints were distributed (no information is given on the amount distributed during the other 48 days), an overall average of 1½ pints per day per slave (Newton Papers 523/110). This figure is consistent with estimates on corn allocations for other Barbadian plantations during the eighteenth and nineteenth centuries. These estimates usually place the maximum daily allowance for adult working slaves at from 1 to 1½ pints, or from 6 to 9 pints weekly. Children, slaves "passed labour," and "women not working in the field," however, received less than the average amounts of corn (and other foods) and often drivers, senior tradesmen, and similarly "privileged" slaves received more; presumably Newton adhered to this practice as well.

Salt fish, usually cod or mackerel imported from North America, was "the meat of all the slaves in all the West Indies" (*Substance of the Evidence on the Petition* 1775:14), and in Barbados, including Newton, it was second to corn in terms of frequency of distribution to adult plantation slaves. Often arriving from North America "in a state of ... putridity" (Nicholls 1790:349), fish was ideally distributed once a week although, in actual fact, it was sometimes distributed no more than three or four times a year. At Newton during 1796–97, "working" slaves received approximately a half pound of salt fish about once every two weeks, while at Christmas and at another holiday special allowances doubled this amount.[24] Late eighteenth and early nineteenth century islandwide, and individual plantation, estimates for salt fish allocations to adult, or "working," slaves suggest a usual average of one pound per week, sometimes from one and a half to two pounds.

In addition other foodstuffs were distributed, albeit less frequently. By the late eighteenth century, plantains were occasionally provided, but they appear to have been more common during the seventeenth century. Following the general practice on Barbadian plantations, "on particular occasions" Newton allocated various crops (usually yams, sweet potatoes, and eddoes) from its provision field. But provision crops were distributed irregularly and infrequently, and even proslavery sources generally acknowledge that provision crops assumed a secondary position in the food allocations made by plantation managements. Plantation slaves also received pigeon peas, which were a "very good food occasionally" (Newton Papers 523/289); during 1796–97 the Newton work log showed that peas were distributed only one day, in an unspecified amount (523/110).

In the late eighteenth century, one well-known planter conceived that Barbadian slaves were generally given "too scanty an allowance of salt [their need for which was] only casually relieved by ordinary salt fish, or ... half putrid herrings" (Steele 1789:26), but salt was another item plantation managements were expected to distribute. Various planters in the second and third decades of the nineteenth century maintained that they provided a weekly salt allowance of from a quarter to a half pint per slave, and the Newton log for 1796–97 showed that forty pints of salt were distributed about every two weeks, a weekly average that came closer to a half pint for each five "working" slaves.

Small amounts of rum and molasses were also "periodically distributed" to plantation slaves, usually when they undertook such exceptionally strenuous tasks as holing the ground for cane planting or when the weather was especially damp. In 1796 Sampson Wood reported that Newton stocked "jars of molasses reserved for the Negroes, upwards of 600 gallons being appropriated for this purpose" (Newton Papers 523/290), a rough annual average of about four gallons for each adult slave. In the late 1780s, the island's governor reported that, on the average, plantation slaves annually "consume each" six gallons of molasses (Parry 1789a:14), and in the 1820s a planter noted that his slaves received about 6½ gallons a year (Barbados Council 1824:106). The only quantitative estimate available on rum distribution suggests that, on the average, plantation slaves were allocated about 1½ gallons each on an annual basis (Parry 1789a:14).

Slaves also regularly chewed sugar cane during the harvest season, and acquired "syrup from the boiling-houses when at work." In addition, special vegetable items were occasionally imported. At Newton, for example, the manager expressed his appreciation to the owner for having sent from England, among other goods, "beans"; they will be of "great service to the Negroes," he wrote, because "a change of food to the Negroes is wholesome, and I know very agreeable" (Newton Papers 523/401; see also 523/459).

Sometimes small amounts of meat were provided, but usually the recipients were officers of one kind or another. In the late eighteenth century, William Dickson reported that "when in health, the field-Negroes never do taste, at least they are not allowed, butchers meat, milk, butter, or any kind of fresh animal substance (flying-fish sometimes excepted) which, when cheap, those who are near enough to the towns occasionally buy with the money they receive, at nights for horse-meat and other stolen articles" (1789:14). Salt beef and pork were allocated, but only "as a great indulgence in small quantities" (Nicholls 1790:349). If given at all, salt or fresh meat was usually distributed on special occasions, such as Christmas, Easter, or the "harvest home." The last holiday celebrated the end of the crop season, and started being observed on some Barbadian plantations including Newton by the end of the eighteenth century (Newton Papers 523/381-1; cf. Handler and Frisbie 1972:11).

Perhaps overstating the case, Sampson Wood concluded his 1796 "Report on the Negroes" at Newton by telling the owners: "It would delight you to see their little possessions, their stock, their poultry of all sorts, their goats, their hogs, their milch cows" (Newton Papers 523/288). Like many other plantation slaves, Newton's slaves supplemented their food allowances by consuming the small livestock, poultry, and food crops they raised on their house plots or had stolen, and by exchanging or selling their produce and stolen goods on the internal marketing system.[25] Throughout Barbados, however, the major portion of the slaves' subsistence derived from what the plantations provided, and the types of food available indicate that the diet was consistent, if not monotonous. As George Pinckard, an English medical doctor, observed in 1796: "The food of the Negroes ... is very simple and but little varied ... [meals] being similar to each other, and for the most part the same throughout the year" (Pinckard 1806; 2:115). "The quality of [the slaves'] ... diet, in the gross," William Dickson generalized for Barbados, "is, perhaps, not nearly so objectionable as its quantity; which, in general, is far from being proportioned to the toil [field slaves] ... undergo" (1789:14).

Although food types were consistent, the amounts distributed were not and fluctuated with weather and agricultural conditions,[26] external trading patterns (for example, the disruptions caused by the American Revolution), and the expenditures that plantations were willing to assume. "It is the greatest misfortune in this island," wrote the manager of the Codrington plantations in 1711, "that few planters give [the slaves] ... a bellyfull" of corn; the reason, he added, was that the slave population was "so great and corn so dear" (Smalridge 1711). The manager also noted that in earlier times corn supplies came from "abroad," but because of increased prices he was planting the crop and encouraging his slaves to do the same. In the seventeenth century, it appears that Newton also purchased most of its corn supplies (Bate 1693), but by the late eighteenth century Newton and other Barbadian plantations attempted to grow all or most of the corn they believed necessary for their slave contingents. Nonetheless, slaves often went hungry and attempted to augment their food allowances by various means, including stealing from plantation provision fields. Indeed, one wonders what was going on at Newton when, in 1801, its manager complained how "rats molest us most terribly, and destroy a great deal of provisions"; but, he lamented, despite his efforts "to establish cats . . . the Negroes either steal or destroy them" (Newton Papers 523/459).[27]

Planters frequently complained about theft from their fields and storehouses. For example, in the late seventeenth century Newton's attorney wrote the owners in England that "your Negroes have been so long used to steal rum, they cannot yet forbear. I have made several discoveries and used severe correction, but all will not yet do" (Bate 1693). Based on his experiences in Barbados during the 1670s, an Anglican minister observed that in general theft was one "effect" of the "scant allowance of food" given to the slaves (Godwyn 1680: 83). Later observers also noted that stealing, especially from provision grounds, was fairly common. Sampson Wood attributed the chronic stealing of Seawell's slaves to their insufficient food supply; he related this insufficiency not only to poor managerial practices in the past, but also to a recent drought and the destruction of corn supplies by insects (Newton Papers 523/434).

On Barbadian plantations, because of the frequency of theft, "the most trusty" slaves were appointed watchmen to guard the fields, storehouses, and other plantation property (see, for example, Pinckard 1806; 2:118; Nicholls 1790:331). In the seventeenth and early eighteenth centuries, watchmen carried wood "lances and darts," but by the 1740s "custom hath allowed these the use of swords" (Hughes 1750:155). " 'Tis law here," explained Sampson Wood in 1798, "to kill any Negro you find plundering on your lands and the watchmen are generally armed with swords—frequent are the murders this way" (Newton Papers 523/381–1).

Another kind of theft from plantations (though we cannot say how "typical" or frequent it was) is illustrated by what transpired at Newton before Sampson Wood assumed the management in early-to-mid-1796. Newton's previous manager had taken a black mistress who was a member of a large slave family on the plantation. The woman was brought to live in the plantation house where she took advantage of "the opportunities . . . of pilfering." She was assisted by her nephew who was already a servant in the house when she came to live in it. "This boy was in great confidence with his master and trusted with everything; even lay in his chamber, by which means he had an opportunity of stealing the key, of the box which held the key of the buildings, out of his pocket . . . when asleep, which gave them an entree to the rum, sugar, corn, and everything else which lay at their mercy." One day, however, two plantation watchmen caught the boy in the act of "loading himself with sugar"; he was ultimately "put upon his trial . . . and executed accordingly." Wood reported that most of the family was "concerned in these rogueries. I hear that their houses were perfect shops for dry goods, rum, sugar, and other commodities." In fact, the mother of the boy referred to above, a black woman, "was married to a huckster (a man who retails rum etc. to Negroes) and [she] ... supplied him plentifully with everything, I presume from your rum and your curing-house" (Newton Papers 523/288).

Planters also complained of "the facility with which stolen goods are disposed of by [slaves] ... to the numerous receivers of these contraband articles—called hucksters ... everything produced or used on a plantation or elsewhere, the worshipful company of 'cadgers' receive from the slaves" (Hendy 1833:34). "The Negroes steal without feeling any sense of wrong, and without any apprehension, except that of being detected ... They feel peculiarly prone to robbing their masters; and this they do not even consider a theft, as is too evident by an expression very common among them, viz. '*Me no tief him; me take him from Massa*'" (Pinckard 1806;2:118). A number of years later Thome and Kimball, the American emancipationists, learned: "For a slave to steal from his master was never considered wrong, but rather a meritorious act. He who could rob the most without being detected was the best fellow. The blacks in several of the islands have a proverb, that 'for a thief to steal from a thief makes God laugh'" (1838:56).

However conceived of by either slaves or slaveowners, theft was an important device by which slaves acquired food and various types of material goods, and could have accounted for the presence of at least some of the objects excavated during the archaeological research at Newton cemetery; theft also permitted slaves to acquire goods that could be further traded and exchanged for other items such as clothing or clothing materials.

CLOTHING

Nothing in the slave code of Barbados specified the food allowances slaves should receive, but a 1688 law ordered that slaves "shall have cloaths once every year (that is to say) drawers and caps for men, and petty-coats and caps for women" (Rawlin 1699:158). The law, however, seems to have had little effect, especially during the seventeenth and early to mid-eighteenth centuries; although it probably served as a general guide for plantation practices in later periods, there were considerable deviations from it. When revised in the 1820s, "the law respecting clothing," a British official wrote in 1827, was "too indefinite to produce any practical results" (Huskisson 1827: 40).

"It is notorious," a well-known "liberal" planter observed in 1788, "that many small planters, and slave owners without land, as well as some greater proprietors, seldom, and some never, give their slaves any clothing; while, for the most part, in the greater plantations, they are regularly clothed" (Steele 1789:25). "Regularly clothed," however, implied the allotments suggested by the 1688 law, and, in general, even "the greater" plantations rarely went beyond the minimal allowances and assumed what were defined as unnecessary expenditures for slave clothing. "It is not the practice to load the slaves with superfluity of clothing" (Pinckard 1806;2:113), and Newton, as best as we can tell, was no exception to this rule.

In the early years of the slave period, especially during the seventeenth and early eighteenth centuries, plantation slaves of both sexes usually wore no more than a band of cloth around their waists to cover their pubic areas. Even in later periods, when European-type clothing became more common on a number of plantations, "the Negro slaves in general have [but] a small rag to cover their nakedness," a 1782 visitor reported (Rees 1790:247). A few years earlier, another visitor noticed that slaves "are often so near naked that they are ashamed to be seen" (Colley 1779), and an American who spent six months in Barbados in 1814 observed that "the field gangs went naked, with the exception of a cloth around their loins" (Browne 1926:112). In addition, "newly-imported Negroes ... of whatever age or sex, are seen going about with no other covering than a handkerchief round the waist" (Waller 1820:13). By the late eighteenth and early nineteenth centuries, however, the ideal (as far as the plantocracy was concerned) standard dress for plantation slaves was a "jacket" or "waist coat" for both men and women, as well as one pair of breeches or trousers for the former and a "petticoat" for the latter; in addition, in the late eighteenth century, some plantations (including Newton) provided shirts for adult males, and by the nineteenth, "one suit annually" for children. (Evidence that plantations gave children clothing only derives from the later years of the slave period—children, up to the age of ten or so, usually went naked.)

At the most, clothing was distributed once a year, and was made from inexpensive and rough fabrics imported from Britain. In the earlier periods, the major fabric was Osnaburg, and throughout the slave period it was used for men's breeches and trousers and women's petticoats; by the middle to late eighteenth century, however, penistone, a coarse wool, or flannel was used for jackets. In general, trousers and petticoats wore out fairly rapidly, and "their poor one Pennistone jacket for the year," wrote Newton's manager in 1798, "gets soon wet and quickly rotten" (Newton Papers 523/353).

When a new attorney assumed his duties at Newton in 1804, he requested the owners to send "out immediately the Negroes' clothing ... [they] have suffered very much for the want of their clothing and will continue to do so until it arrives" (523/585). Each adult slave also was annually issued (ideally, at least) an imported woolen or flannel cap, and the evidence suggests that by the late eighteenth century, if not earlier, some plantations distributed "handkerchiefs" in lieu of caps to serve as head ties for women.

Imported fabrics were made into clothing on each plantation. At Codrington during the early decades of the eighteenth century, lower-class white women were hired to do the sewing, but, Bennett conjectured, they "must have had slaves to help them," and slaves later took "over the sewing operations" (1958:36). The pattern on other Barbadian plantations was probably similar, and during the latter part of the eighteenth century at Newton and Seawell "cutting up and making the Negro's clothing" was done by plantation slaves who were assigned the task by the manager; this work was only done "once a year" and lasted "but for a few days" (Newton Papers 523/288, 111). Plantation accounts for Newton in later years do not show expenditures for making clothes and we assume that at Newton, as at Codrington and, presumably, many other plantations, sewing was done by members of the plantation's own labor force. At the Codrington plantations by the nineteenth century, "most slaves, it seems, were ... responsible for fashioning their own garments from the materials supplied to them, or for having clothes made at their own expense" (Bennett 1958:104), and a similar pattern probably existed at Newton and other plantations.

Aside from these items and quantities, plantations did not regularly provide additional articles of clothing or such accessories as belt buckles. Occasionally, however, Newton's management (and presumably the managements of other plantations) requested special items for particular working slaves. In 1798, for example, the owners in England were asked to forward "a dozen ... large cloaks" for the watchmen and cattle keepers "who are exposed to all weathers in bad seasons ... night and day" (Newton Papers 523/353), and a similar request was made in 1807 (523/633); it is not known, however, if the owners complied with these requests. Newton's managers sometimes made other requests for special articles of clothing as elements in the plantation's "system of rewards": in 1796 Sampson Wood wrote "Will you send me for the women some common figured cotton, or linen, the gayer the colours the better ... or some coarse blue or red common pocket handkerchiefs with which they dress their heads. One of these as a reward when they behave well, and said to come as a present from their mistress in England, will stir up a great spirit of pride and emulation. It will not cost much, and will have a wonderful good effect" (523/288).

There is no indication if slaves sometimes made or used sandals, but plantation slaves were overwhelmingly barefooted and thus "often get chigoes and sores in their feet and toes" (J. Hendy 1784: 32) and were "more subject" to tetanus "than the white people usually are" (Hillary 1766:227); on rare occasions, however, certain favored slaves were given a pair of shoes. For example, the accounts of "Negro expenses" for Lowther plantation during the late 1820s record that a man called Edward received a pair of shoes annually; during this period, around 211 slaves lived on the plantation (Lowther Plantation 1825–35; cf. Bennett 1958:18).

By the late seventeenth century, if not earlier, higher ranking slaves sometimes received greater clothing allowances than others, and special items of clothing were distributed to encourage slaves who conformed to plantation disciplinary and behavioral norms. A plantation owner, for example, instructed his manager on the standard clothing allocation for his slaves, but, he added, "for encouragement to particular Negroes, give what you think fit" (Drax 1755: 67). In 1801, another owner sent his plantation's annual supply of penistone from England, but notified the manager that another type of cloth, "of a better quality than the pennistone," was being sent "to give the tradesmen and officers" (Alleyne 1801a). And in 1796, Sampson Wood requested "two or three dozen of ready made check or very coarse white linen shirts for the officers, or those who behave well. Coming as your present they will esteem it the more" (Newton Papers 523/288). In general, however, the sources convey the impression that, for the island as a whole, certain tradesmen, drivers, or similarly "privileged" slaves received the same fabrics as other slaves, but in somewhat greater proportions. Some of the domestic slaves, such as favored personal servants and footmen, were "more elaborately clothed" in material and style, especially when their masters attended or hosted various social functions.

In the 1820s, a prominent member of the Barbadian plantocracy acknowledged that "the quantity of clothing [allotted the slaves] may appear insufficient for a year" (Barbados Council 1824:107), and close to forty years earlier the agent for Barbados, among others, also admitted that "upon the whole [the slaves] ... are [in]sufficiently clothed"; the agent, in particular, did not believe "this is a point of much importance ... in a hot climate" (J. Brathwaite 1789). Slaves felt otherwise and frequently used various means (for example, the exchange of foodstuffs, small livestock, and stolen goods in the internal marketing system, as well as the small amounts of money they sometimes acquired) to augment their clothing allowances and to acquire "personal ornaments."

The evidence strongly indicates that slaves valued clothing and body ornaments, and from an early period they distinguished their everyday wear from that worn on Sundays and other special occasions. In the 1650s, for example, a French priest observed that "the slaves go around almost entirely naked, except on Sundays when they put on some worthless canvas breeches and a shirt" (Handler 1967:66). Over a century later a white creole wrote that plantation slaves "find means of their own to supply themselves" with more elaborate clothing for "occasions of their meeting together, for festive or solemn purposes" (Holder 1788:23). In fact, a planter with over twenty-five years of experience in Barbados reported that "slaves generally have already a strong desire to dress themselves in finery"; he explicitly suggested that this "disposition" should be encouraged by plantation managements as a reward element—by increasing "their wants artificially . . . we shall enlarge the motive to labor, by encreasing the desire to satisfy them" (Hendy 1833:24–26).

SHELTER

For most of the preemancipation period, plantation slaves were expected to construct and provide their own shelter. The slave code of Barbados contained no provisions for slave housing, and Barbadian plantations often followed different policies in providing housing materials and incurring expenses in the construction and repair of houses.

Seventeenth- and early eighteenth-century historical sources provide little evidence that plantation managements paid much formal attention to slave shelter, but later, usually proslavery sources indicate that slave houses were sometimes constructed and maintained at the financial expense of the plantations. The most common pattern in Barbados is illustrated by the practices on the Codrington plantations: throughout the eighteenth century and until around 1820, "shelter was regarded as the slave['s] own problem . . . [and he] was left to build, repair, and furnish his hut with such materials as he could find for himself"; the managers sometimes assisted in emergencies (such as after a storm), and during the late eighteenth century the plantations' account books began to show occasional small expenditures to aid favored slaves, usually drivers and tradesmen, in the construction and repair of their houses. As late as the second decade of the nineteenth century, however, "most of the slaves continued to find housing for themselves, with only occasional help" from the plantations' management (Bennett 1958:32–33, 43, 101, 138).

As a committee of resident planters observed in 1812, "to furnish proper houses to a whole set of slaves is certainly a very expensive & tedious work" (Society for the Improvement 1811–16:143–144), and when slave houses were constructed of stone or wood planking and roofed with wood shingles, plantations incurred some expenses—especially because boards and shingles were imported, usually from North America. Yet, throughout the preemancipation period, as noted in chapter 3, most houses were wattle-and-daub with thatched roofs and were thus fabricated out of locally obtained materials; although planters occasionally gave their slaves "some assistance with materials," it is doubtful that this "assistance" involved much, if any, financial expenditure or sacrifice.

By the late 1700s and early 1800s, plantation tradesmen were sometimes employed in house construction or repair. In 1824, while stressing that slaves on his three plantations were well treated, a planter reported that their houses were "regularly repaired . . . with the labour of the estate" (J. W. Jordan 1824:3). The 1796–97 Newton work log shows that during the out-of-crop season, the plantation's three carpenters-coopers worked for thirty-four days in building and "mending" slave houses, while the two masons worked for seventy-seven days at the same tasks; on Seawell, during the same year, a carpenter and two coopers were employed for twelve days, and the plantation's two masons for thirty-three days, on slave houses. On both plantations, slaves from the first gang were also assigned to "tying trash" for roof thatching; on Newton, two slaves worked for twenty-eight days at this task, while at Seawell one was employed for nine days (Newton Papers 523/110, 111).

Although tradesmen on Barbadian plantations were sometimes assigned to work on the houses of field slaves, we do not know whether this pattern was widespread. Because of traditional plantation policies, most slaves constructed or repaired their own houses. However, when stone and plank houses became more common in the late eighteenth and early nineteenth centuries, skilled workmen were probably employed to a greater extent by plantation managements; the increased use of more substantial housing materials during this period, in turn, reflected the growing interest among planters in their slaves' material existence.

Little specific data are available on the housing of Newton's slaves, but our sources suggest that house types and management policies toward shelter generally reflected islandwide patterns. A 1796 report by Sampson Wood contains the earliest direct evidence about slave houses at the plantation: "some of . . . our Negro huts or houses

... [are] built of stone (and they shall all be built of that material before long as most convenient for them), others of the strong reed or cane of the Guinea corn. They are all thatched with the cane-trash, and lie scattered about the hill" (Newton Papers 523/290). Although Wood intended to have all the houses constructed of stone in the near future, he died in 1803 and we are uncertain if his intentions materialized. If Newton reflected wider Barbadian practices, we can assume an increase in the number of stone houses. This increase is also suggested by the fact that the plantation's two masons worked on slave dwellings for seventy-seven days in 1796–97. In the mid-1820s, Newton's accounts show expenditures on materials such as "deal boards," "planks," and nails "for building Negro houses," which suggests that wooden houses were also increasing and probably replacing wattle-and-daub structures.

Medical Care

In his 1796 report Sampson Wood also discussed "the hospital or sick house where Negroes are put ... [which] is a horrid unhealthy hole, most ill contrived, and men and women are most indecently mixed together, with other detestable circumstances"; "I mean to make a great alteration here," Wood added, "I hope at not much expense" (Newton Papers 523/290). The "alteration" Wood planned was not prompted by any legal norms; the Barbadian slave code ignored the medical care of slaves as well as housing and food. Any such law would probably not have been enforced with any regularity or consistency—any more than the law respecting clothing was enforced by the plantocracy that had written the law in the first place.

From the middle of the seventeenth century, plantations employed a European "apothecary" who "we call doctor" (Ligon 1657:93) to administer medicaments and perform various services for slaves, white servants, and others; by the last quarter of the eighteenth century plantations usually employed both apothecaries and "physicians or surgeons," and this system prevailed until the end of slavery.

"There is not a single estate in Barbadoes," William Dickson categorically asserted, "that does not pay a doctor ... annually for each Negroe, sick or well. The doctors either attend themselves, or send their journeymen, at least once a week, at all times" (1789:11). The "doctor," or apothecary, was retained on an annual salary based on a flat fee per individual slave; he made daily (according to some sources) or weekly (according to others) visits. "Physicians or surgeons," who were paid by the visit, were called "in cases of danger or difficulty" (Parry 1789a:15) or for such special occasions as innoculations against smallpox. Sometimes "physicians" assumed the apothecary role as well and were paid extra for their services. Both apothecaries and physicians or surgeons (slaves called the surgeon the "Great Doctor"; Orderson 1842:113) usually worked for a number of plantations and visited the "sick house" of each when they made their rounds.

We do not know if sick houses, infirmaries, and hospitals existed during the seventeenth century, but by the late eighteenth and early nineteenth centuries, they were common features on Barbadian plantations especially, it can be assumed, of the medium to large ones. Appraisals of the quality and facilities of "sick houses" ranged from Sampson Wood's description of a "horrid unhealthy hole" to a leading planter's claim in 1823 that "there is a good hospital on almost every estate, which is generally a clean well-ventilated building" (Barbados Council 1824:109). Although the evidence suggests that plantations devoted greater attention to their sick houses and medical services in the 1810s and 1820s, it would be fatuous to evaluate these by modern standards. Nineteenth-century sources, in particular, positively evaluate plantation medical facilities, but these sources usually defended, in one way or another, the slave system and the ways in which planters treated their slaves.

Barbadian slaves frequently had accidents of one kind or another, particularly workers in the mills or boiling houses. Slaves also suffered and succumbed to a variety of ailments, illnesses, and contagious diseases including body sores, colds, "consumption," coughs, diarrhea, dysentery, "dropsy," elephantiasis, "fevers," "influenza," leprosy, loss of limbs or joints, measles, mumps, ruptures, smallpox, sore throats, stomach aches, tetanus, toothaches, yaws, and yellow fever; dirt-eating, or geophagy, also occurred.

Whites were also plagued by some of the same afflictions and diseases, but certain problems were more common among the slaves. The frequency of these problems varied over the years or as a result of specific conditions. For example, more deaths occurred after droughts or during epidemics, and malnutrition seems to have been more widespread among the slaves; also, by the late eighteenth century, leprosy and yaws were less common than in earlier periods.

Newton's slaves succumbed to similar illnesses and periodic epidemics (see, for example, Newton Papers 523/423, 593, 899). Although the diagnoses of Newton's managers and medical practitioners cannot be taken as precise indicators of the causes of death, their observations provide a rough illustration of the types and frequency of causes. Causes of death for 146 of the 169 slaves who died in a twenty-year period are given in table 10. Consumption, dropsy, dysentery, leprosy, and measles accounted for 41 percent of the deaths, while

TABLE 10. Slave deaths by cause of death and relative age groups: Newton plantation, 1796–1801 and 1811–1825.

Cause of death	Age group[a]					Total	
	Infant	Boy-Girl		Man-Woman		Number	Percentage
Accident in infancy	2	—	—	—	—	2	1.1
Accident at work	—	—	1	—	—	1	0.5
Childbirth	—	—	—	—	2	2	1.1
Cold	—	3	1	—	1	5	2.9
Consumption	—	2	1	5	6	14	8.2
Convulsed	—	1	—	2	—	3	1.7
Cough	—	—	—	—	2	2	1.1
Croup	—	—	1	—	—	1	0.5
Dirt eating	—	1	—	—	—	1	0.5
Dropsy	—	6	—	3	5	14	8.2
Dysentery	—	—	1	2	9	12	7.1
Fever	—	2	4	—	1	7	4.1
Fits	—	—	2	—	—	2	1.1
Gunshot	—	—	1	—	—	1	0.5
Inflammation	—	—	1	—	—	1	0.5
Invalid	—	—	—	—	2	2	1.1
Joint evil	—	—	—	—	1	1	0.5
Leprosy	—	1	—	4	6	11	6.5
Lockjaw	—	—	—	1	—	1	0.5
Measles	1	2	6	—	—	9	5.3
Merasmus	—	2	2	—	—	4	2.3
Obstruction	—	—	—	—	1	1	0.5
Old age	—	—	—	9	13	22	13.0
Palsy	—	1	—	—	—	1	0.5
Rheumatism	—	1	—	—	—	1	0.5
Scrofula	—	1	2	4	1	8	4.7
Sore throat	—	3	1	—	—	4	2.3
Teething	4	3	1	—	—	8	4.7
Worms	—	4	—	—	—	4	2.3
No cause given	9	4	—	6	5	4	14.2
Total	16	37	25	36	55	169	

Sources: 1796–1801, Newton Papers (523/315, 116, 128, 131–1, 282). 1811–1825, Newton Plantation (1805–1841).

[a] Infants, roughly under age 2; men and women, above 20.

twenty-four other causes (aside from old age) were given for the remainder.

As elsewhere in Barbados (and the New World) Newton's slaves sometimes feigned sickness to evade work. "Many of them," wrote Sampson Wood, "run, without reason, into the sick house" (Newton Papers 523/288), but in his report on Newton's hospital he expressed his dilemma in distinguishing between those who were ill and those who used illness as a pretext. The building contained slaves "who are not very sick, but either in reality or from pretence not fit to work. Of the latter I am afraid we have a great many, but as it [is] impossible to tell when a person is sick or not, except he be really ill, for fear of accidents they are confined here till they profess themselves ready to go to work again" (523/290). Wood later recalled that when he first assumed the managership of Newton, the slaves were "under no discipline" and lax in their work performance. This condition was illustrated for him by the number of slaves who evaded work by claiming illness to be placed in the hospital: "For sometime after I came to the place I found the sick house, constantly, to have from fifteen to twenty invalids in it—now 'tis a rare thing [to have] four there at a time. I suffer no idlers to remain when the doctor declares that they need no physic, that their pulse is regular, and [when] I find their digestion good and their appetite keen, I send them to work" (523/321).[28]

Like other plantations, Newton employed a "doctor" in the seventeenth century, and in later periods the plantation's sick house was visited by an apothecary as well as by a physician or surgeon; in 1808, when a doctor was retained to perform both roles, the owner in England was reassured that, despite the fee increase, he would "pay no more than other people in the neighborhood" (Newton Papers 523/653). Also reflecting the wider pattern, Newton occasionally hired a midwife if one of its slaves could not, for whatever reason, perform this role; in the late eighteenth century, for example, one of the female slaves was a midwife or "Granny," but when she became too old and "totally incapable of it," a "white woman [was] employed" (523/381–1). In addition, as elsewhere on Barbadian plantations, Newton regularly assigned one or two older female slaves as "sick nurses" to feed and otherwise care for patients in the "hospital," and incurred additional medical expenses aside from the fees to medical practitioners. For example, from 1805 to 1808, Newton expended an annual average of about £13.10 on "sundries for sick Negroes" such as "flour biscuit and rice" and "porte wine" (Newton Plantation 1805–1841).

The historical sources for Barbados provide little detailed information on the specific practices that plantation slaves, including those on Newton, used to cope with their many and varied ailments. However, they developed a pharmacopoeia from local flora and concocted various types of medicaments; moreover, curing often took place within a magicoreligious context. "The ... Negro doctors of the estates," observed George Pinckard—himself a doctor—in 1796, "justly vie with [some of the local white doctors] ... in medical knowledge" (1806;1:389). Writing about yaws, William Hillary, another doctor who lived in Barbados for more than six years during the 1740s and 1750s, reported how "the Negroes have by long observation and experience, found out a method of curing this disease," which involved various plant preparations taken internally and applied externally; "they keep [their knowledge] ... as a secret from the white people, but preserve [it] among themselves by tradition with which they sometimes perform notable cures, both in [yaws] ... and some other diseases" (1766:341). In 1790, a white Barbadian creole recommended "a herbal medicine [not identified] for treating skin disorders and venereal disease 'which has done wonders and like many great discoveries originated from the Negroes' " (K. Watson 1975:235). We can assume that medical practices among Newton's slaves resembled those on other plantations, and that Newton also had its share of "Negro doctors."

In this chapter we have suggested that in all major physical, agricultural, social, labor organizational, and demographic characteristics Newton seems to have typified medium- to large-scale Barbadian sugar plantations. Although the written sources do not contain a great deal of detailed information on the sociocultural life of Newton's slaves, we can assume that their cultural practices, social activities, and value system reflected those found in other plantation slave communities. Newton's slaves, for example, absented themselves without managerial permission, negatively viewed field labor, and their conception of theft was shared by other Barbadian slaves. Newton's slaves also wore the same types of clothing, made out of the same fabrics, ate the same types of foods, and were subject to the same ailments, accidents, and diseases. There is no reason to assume that slaves at Newton had significantly different family forms and household types, household furnishings, courtship and sexual activities, marketing and curing practices, recreational and musical activities, and community defined roles; and when Sampson Wood reported that before he became manager "dances, cock-fights [and] gaming-tables were plenty on the estate" (Newton Papers 523/288), he may have been exaggerating, but his comments on the existence of such activities could have been echoed by many other planters in Barbados.

Because Newton so well reflected islandwide plantation characteristics and because its slave community also seems to have typified the Barbadian pattern, we suggest that in mortuary beliefs and practices, Newton's slaves also displayed characteristics that were found elsewhere. We thus believe that the findings of the archaeological investigations at Newton, particularly those relating to the cemetery excavations, can be extended to indicate patterns that also existed in other Barbadian plantations and slave communities.

5 / Newton Plantation: Archaeological Investigations

EWTON'S manager described the slave village in 1796 as "on the brow of a hill" near the plantation yard (Newton Papers 523/290). In 1972 we compared this description with contemporary plantation features and projected the western margin of the former slave village to a grassland west of today's Lower South Negro Yard field (figure 4). As in many other areas of Barbados, this area was not cultivated because of its shallow and rocky soil. The soil of the Negro Yard fields east and north of the knoll is deeper, and it is likely that the major portion of the slave village was in these fields at the time of the 1796 report. These fields, however, had been severely disturbed by agriculture, and were planted in yams or sugar cane at the time of our work. We therefore decided to focus our efforts on the less desirable, but undisturbed, area of the knoll.

Our initial surface collecting yielded a general scatter of china and redware ceramic fragments across the top of the knoll. We laid out a north-south baseline and later an east-west line. Ten 1-meter square units demarcated along these lines were excavated. In all locations we reached bedrock by 30 centimeters below the surface. The extremely low artifact yield was confined to an occasional piece of china, redware, and two pipestems. With these limited returns from surface collecting and testing at what we assumed was the site of at least part of the former slave village, we turned our efforts toward the cemetery.[1]

Given the potential importance of the slave village site, it seems, in retrospect, that we might have expended more effort in this location. In reality, however, the Upper and Lower North and Upper and Lower South Negro Yard fields were under cultivation during both field seasons, and the fields could only be surface collected with difficulty. All four fields had been deep-plowed, and surface collections from Upper and Lower South Negro Yard fields yielded very thin artifact concentrations; moreover, cultural and economic considerations in Barbados mitigated against the removal of crops to permit excavation.[2]

THE SLAVE CEMETERY

Though other slave cemeteries undoubtedly exist in Barbados Newton was the only one we encountered. Before our archaeological research at the plantation, however, the only suggestion that the burial ground contained a slave population derived from information given by Barbadian informants.

Positive identification of a cemetery of slaves, as opposed to another group, was a problem that had to be resolved in the early stages of fieldwork. Human bones were found in the burial ground when holes were dug for planting trees over the past few decades. During interviews the plantation manager at that time provided conflicting information as to what was found, but he consistently emphasized that some human bones and coffin furniture, such as handles, were excavated; there was little doubt about the presence of interments, but their antiquity was not known.

Several suggestions indicated that the burials were slave rather than European or Amerindian. A Newton employee, a black man in his seventies or early eighties, assured us that, as a child, his grandparents had told him that the burial area was where the "old people" were interred and that these "old people" antedated his own childhood. A more important indicator that the burials were of a pre-emancipation, non-European group was that the bodies had been buried on the plantation rather than in an Anglican churchyard or the grounds of a Protestant mission station. Europeans, especially in early Barbadian history, were sometimes buried on plantations, but these interments were usually well marked with tombstones or vaults. Documentary evidence (reviewed in chapter 6) had established that most slaves were buried in either plantation communal burial grounds or under houses in the slave villages. The proximity of the cemetery to Newton's former slave village also supported the suggestion of the cemetery's slave association, and the presence of European artifactual materials, such as manufactured whole pipes and pipestems, indicated that we were not dealing with a precolonial Amerindian population.

We also had to consider the possibility that we were exhuming the victims of a great cholera epidemic of 1854 or of some other postemancipation natural disaster such as a hurricane. No massive hurricanes affected Barbados after emancipation and for the remainder of the nineteenth century; the only large hurricane occurred in 1898 and resulted in eighty-five deaths (Starkey 1939:128). This number was too small to necessitate separate burial grounds, and the historical sources do not suggest that separate burial grounds were established during the slave period for those who died in hurricanes or epidemics. If the Newton cemetery, however, contains victims from the 1854 cholera epidemic then it would, of course, postdate emancipation and thus contain a nonslave population. New burial grounds were established on some plantations during this epidemic (see, for example, Barbados Museum and Historical Society 1940a: 114), which caused the deaths of 20,727 persons, "chiefly colored, black, and Scotland district whites" (Starkey 1939:122). Aside from artifactual materials dating the cemetery to preemancipation times, the interment patterns at Newton indicate repeated burials over many years rather than the simultaneous burials that would suggest mass deaths. Also, although partial or complete cranial indices could have been used to distinguish African from European or Amerindian skulls, the excavated fragmented skulls were not reconstructed. Though study of the skulls would have probably identified the group racially as Negroid and might have provided additional information on the overall physical nature of the slave population, the measurements would not have distinguished between a slave and a nonslave population.

In all, the conjecture that Newton's burial ground was a slave cemetery is based largely on nonarchaeological evidence, and the excavations at Newton *did not in themselves* establish that the interments were those of slaves; this important issue of interpretation is discussed in chapter 7.

The Newton cemetery area is in an uncultivated belt of grassland (figure 4); because of its shallow soil cover, it is apparently one of the few areas on the plantation that has never been plowed. The grassland includes a rise in slope of approximately 8 meters; the slope is at its most gradual within the cemetery area and most distinct to the west, where it joins a short, abrupt cliff and ridgeline.

Our excavations showed that the mortuary activity within the cemetery was concentrated in a relatively flat section just north of North Grand Rock field (figure 4). North of the main burial area, an upward slope begins that extends to a flat area which forms the southern boundary of Barhill field. Test excavations on this upper ridge revealed very shallow soil conditions, and no burial remains were found.

The main burial area contained several low mounds, some of which were barely visible. Even the largest, Mound 1 (figure 8), was still small enough to be mistaken originally for a natural feature of the terrain. The numbers indicate the sequence in which the mounds were mapped or located. Numbered square designations (30N9W and so forth; see figure 9) refer to the southeast corners of the

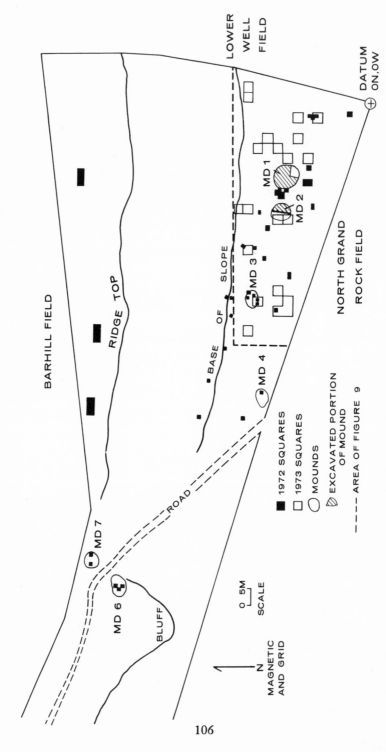

Figure 8. Newton cemetery: excavation locations, 1972 and 1973.

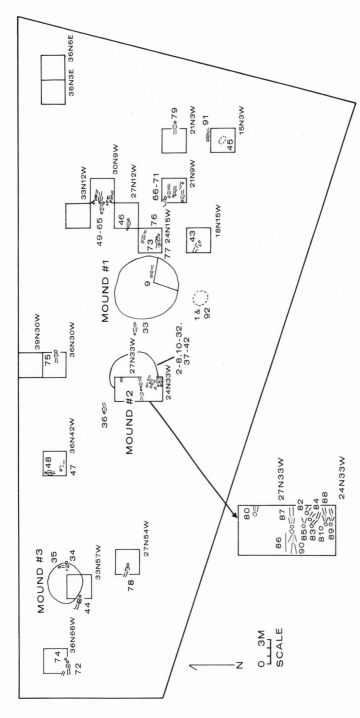

Figure 9. Newton cemetery: locations and orientations of burials (except those in the eastern portion of Mound 2) in southeastern section.

107

squares. Mounds were generally absent from the ridgetop along the southern margin of Barhill field; however, at the western end of the ridgetop (where it joins the bluff outcrop) and for approximately 100 meters to the west, seventeen distinct low mounds bordered the cane field. Limited testing of these mounds identified all but two (Mounds 6 and 7) as piles of rock, presumably cleared from the adjacent fields when they were prepared for planting.

In addition to the slope within the grassland, the main cemetery is bordered by North Grand Rock field on the south and by Lower Well field to the east (figure 4). Dirt roads, locally known as "cart roads," now separate these fields from the grassland. Though it is likely that these roads existed during the slave period, it is also possible that a section of the cemetery was located in the parts of these fields that border the grassland area. We did not test the fields, however, because they were under cultivation in sugar cane; surface collections in North Grand Rock field, made from a 25-meter-wide strip adjacent to the road, included china, redware, and a few pipestems.

ARCHAEOLOGICAL STRATEGIES

Because the initial results from the 1972 excavations in the grassland area showed great promise for acquiring extensive data on slave mortuary practices, we devoted a significant amount of time to the cemetery. However, surface collections, test excavations, and archival research were conducted elsewhere on the island throughout the 1972 season. Thus, although the cemetery excavations constituted the largest portion of archaeological research in 1972, they were never our exclusive focus. For this reason, they can be characterized as exploratory, and our nonrandom excavation strategy was designed to yield an idea of the variability in mortuary practices manifested in the cemetery.

Early in the 1972 season we mapped the grassland containing the cemetery with a plane table and telescopic alidade, utilizing three datum points at widely spaced locations. Secondary lines of measurements were also made with a compass and metric tapes, and the baselines were oriented to magnetic north—although the field deviates slightly from this alignment. Obvious surface features, such as the mounds, were included on the map.

Faced with a large area of unknown archaeological content that was almost certain to contain some human remains, we decided to place selective test excavations in four areas: the northern ridgetop, the ridge extension to the west, the sloping portion of the main field, and the flat section of the grassland including the mounds. The ridgetop tests conducted first immediately demonstrated the extreme shallowness of the soil and yielded virtually no cultural materials; test pits on the slope also yielded no positive results.

Only when excavations were begun in Mounds 1 and 2 (see figure 9) did we find any evidence to confirm the use of the field as a cemetery. The first burials were encountered in a test trench south of Mound 1, and soon after a complex of burials was located in Mound 2. Tests were also conducted in the mounds along the ridge extension to the west, but most of these mounds proved to be piles of rocks removed from fields, although Mounds 6 and 7 contained fragmentary skeletal remains.

We soon found that Mound 2 was a complex area with multiple burials clustered in a limited space. To gain a good record of the patterns of interment and to recover a skeletal series as large as possible, we excavated the entire eastern section of the mound. This work occupied the entire crew for six weeks. With Mound 2 nearly finished late in the 1972 season, more testing was conducted in selectively placed squares in the southern portion of the grassland. These tests yielded additional burials and indicated that interments existed in nonmound areas. We also tested Mound 3 during this period, and it yielded two burials.

Our 1972 experience guided the continuation of the cemetery excavations in 1973, when we excavated the southern portion of the grassland more extensively. All but the extreme western end of the grassland was incorporated into 3-meter-square grids. We selected excavated squares by using a table of random numbers except when randomly selected squares extended into one of the field roads; in such cases, the next randomly selected square was excavated instead.

Of seventeen squares, thirteen contained burials. Although excavating more squares would have increased the reliability of the sample, the brief field season and the small crew prevented more extensive sampling. Burials that extended into adjacent squares were also excavated. The elimination of bias in the sample through random sampling procedures did not, as we expected, result in the excavation of many sterile squares. This can only be attributed to the extensive use of the grassland area as a cemetery. In addition to demonstrating the extensive use of the field as a burial area, we uncovered different temporal and interment patterns.

We spent the last phase of the 1973 season excavating two squares in the western half of Mound 2 that had not been randomly selected. The additional concentration of burials we found confirmed our 1972 observation that Mound 2 had been the site of repeated and extensive mortuary activity.

In general, many skeletons in the cemetery were located close to the surface, which usually resulted in poor bone condition. Also, many interments had been disturbed by subsequent burials and a considerable amount of disarticulated skeletal and unassociated artifactual material was found; in some cases, these materials could be reasonably associated with nearby incomplete skeletons.[3]

The following sections describe various excavated areas and the types of materials recovered. The mortuary contents of the burial mounds were sufficiently different from each other to warrant individual discussion. In the nonmound interments, particular groups, or individuals, have been selected as representative examples which illustrate the full range of physical and cultural variables present in the cemetery.

MOUND EXCAVATIONS

Mound 1. Mound 1 was approximately 7.5 meters wide and 0.8 meters above the present ground surface (figure 10); its size suggests that a substantial effort had been made in bringing soil from some source—perhaps from one of the adjoining fields. Initially, a 2-by-5-meter strip was plotted as a southern approach to the mound, and the first skeletal material was encountered in this strip less than 2 centimeters below the surface. Mound 1 was 80 percent excavated and one burial (Burial 9) was discovered under the mound. We did

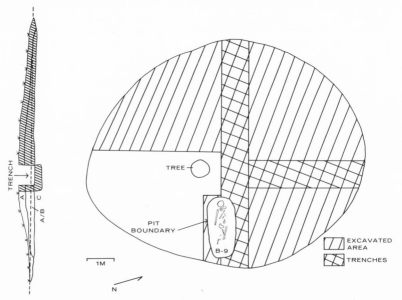

Figure 10. Mound 1, Burial 9, Newton cemetery.

not excavate the remainder of Mound 1 because we did not wish to remove a tree rooted on the southeastern portion. Though it is not absolutely certain that no other burials were present, related evidence from the mound suggests that Burial 9 was its only interment.

Burial 9 was not only the sole burial in Mound 1 but also the only prone burial uncovered in the cemetery. The individual was oriented with its head to the west. There was no evidence of a coffin. The corpse had been placed in a prepared subsurface pit (figure 10), a shallow excavation into the underlying bedrock. This pit sloped inward from the edges; the head was slightly raised and rested against the western end of the pit. The individual was an adult female; its left arm was extremely fragmented and folded under the chest and the skeleton was fully articulated (bones in normal anatomical relationships).

No artifacts were associated with the burial, although two pipe-stem fragments were recovered from the fill around the skeleton. The first stem has a bore diameter of 7/64 inches, giving a bracket date of 1620–1710, while the second has a diameter of 9/64 inches, yielding a potential date of 1620–1650. The problems of using bore diameter measurements for dating, especially from single examples, are fully discussed in Appendix B. However, both stems provide tentative evidence for construction of this mound sometime during the late seventeenth or early eighteenth centuries.

Another reason for inferring the early construction of Mound 1 is the absence of imported earthenware or china from its fill, although a single redware sherd was present. Such materials, mostly post-1762, were found in the fill of Mounds 2 and 3. The 1762 date is based on known dates of manufacture in England, and thus the date of archaeological deposition was somewhat later.

In addition, it is perhaps significant that no other burials were found beneath Mound 1, although burials were located nearby on three sides. This also seems to indicate that the mound is one of the earlier burial sites in the cemetery and dates from an early period in the plantation's history.

If we are correct in believing that Mound 1 was an early burial site, it is relevant to ask why it was not reused, especially because the adjacent Mound 2 was intensively used for a long period. The answer must remain conjectural. A tradition respecting Mound 1 may have been perpetuated among Newton's slaves, possibly because of the way in which the burial in the mound was viewed. The solitary interment of Burial 9 in a mound and its prone position make it a unique case in the cemetery. These features suggest that the individual died under special circumstances or possessed special characteristics. No unusual physical features were observed in the skeleton, and a tentative interpretation, relating to negatively perceived social characteristics of the individual, is offered in chapter 6 which discusses the possible cultural meanings of body position and orientation in general.

Mound 2. Mound 2 was located immediately west of Mound 1. Despite its smaller size it contained forty-seven of the ninety-two burials recovered in the cemetery. The range of burial modes and artifactual materials associated with the interments suggests that Mound 2 was utilized over a long period of time. Although we found a number of skeletons in the mound (figures 9, 11, 12), Mound 2 was not a mass grave, but rather a mortuary area that developed because of repeated use.

The physical, contextual, and chronological data for Mound 2 are summarized in table 11. Particularly noteworthy are the variations

TABLE 11. Mound 2 burials, Newton cemetery: physical, contextual, and chronological data.

Burial	Articu- lated	Orien- tation	Coffin	Age	Sex	Pipe date	Ceramic date
2	n	—	P	OA	M	n	n
3	+	W	P	YA	M	n	n
4	n	—	P	—	F	+	+
5	+	W	+	OA	M	n	n
6	A/D	W	+	YA	F	n	+
7	n	—	+	—	M	n	+
8	+	W	+	YA	F	+	+
10	+	W	+	YA	F	+	n
11	n	—	—	C	—	n	n
12	n	—	—	—	—	n	n
13	n	N	+	YA	M	n	+
14	n	—	P	C	—	n	n
15	A/D	W	+	OA	—	n	+
16	n	—	+	C	F?	n	+
17	n	—	+	I/C	—	n	n
18	n	—	+	OA	—	n	n
19	n	—	+	I	—	n	+
20	+	W	+	OA	M	+	n
21	n	—	+	I	—	n	n
22	A/D	W	+	YA	F	n	+
23	n	—	P	OA	—	n	n
24	A/D	W	P	YA	M	n	+
25	n	—	P	YA	—	n	n
26	n	W	P	YA	—	n	n

Burial	Articu-lated	Orien-tation	Coffin	Age	Sex	Pipe date	Ceramic date
27	n	W	P	OA	M	n	n
28	+	W	+	YA	—	+	n
29	n	—	P	YA	—	n	n
30	n	—	n	OA	M	n	n
31	+	W	+	YA	F	n	+
32	n	—	P	—	—	n	n
37	n	—	P	OA	—	n	n
38	n	—	+	OA	—	+	n
39	n	—	P	YA	—	n	n
40	n	—	n	YA	—	n	n
41	n	—	n	—	—	n	n
42	n	—	n	YA	—	n	n
80	n	W	+	AD	—	n	+
81	n	—	—	YA	M	++	n
82	n	W	n	C	—	n	n
83	+	W	+	A	F	++	n
84	+	W	+	C	—	n	n
85	+	W	+	OA	M?	+	n
87	A/D	W	P	A	—	n	n
88	+	W	P	OA	—	n	n
89	+	W	P	AD	—	+	n

Key: A/D, skeleton largely articulated, but had been disturbed. N, north. W, west. P, possible coffin use. OA, old adult. A, adult. YA, young adult. AD, adolescent. C, child. I, infant. M, male. F, female. —, insufficient data. ?, provisional identification. +, yes. ++, yes, associated with either Burial 81 or 83. n, no.

in body orientation; twenty-one of the skeletons for whom there are data were buried with their heads to the west and only one appears to have been buried with its head to the east. The last was buried under the mound, rather than in the mound, and thus the interpretation of its relationship to the mound and other interments at that location is somewhat ambiguous. One skeleton also had its head to the north. Twenty-one individuals were definitely buried in coffins in Mound 2 and four were definitely coffinless; in addition, coffin burial was evaluated as a possibility for sixteen others, reflecting the high level of postinterment disturbance in the mound. We found few grave goods or even items indicating clothing.

Small quantities of locally made and imported ceramic sherds were recovered from the mound fill; in a few cases these were in direct association with interments, but they are all fragmentary and are not

113

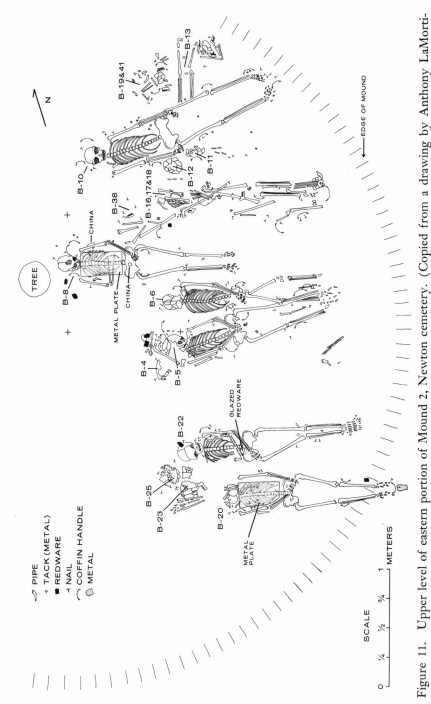

Figure 11. Upper level of eastern portion of Mound 2, Newton cemetery. (Copied from a drawing by Anthony LaMorticella and Hilary J. Sio.)

114

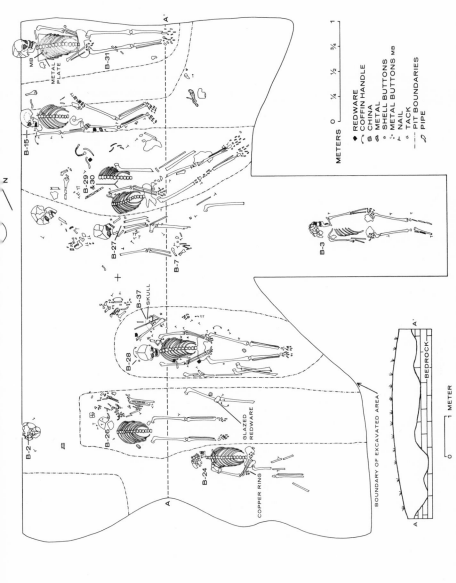

Figure 12. Lower level of eastern portion of Mound 2, Newton cemetery. (Copied from a drawing by Anthony LaMorti-cella and Hilary J. Sio.)

interpreted as grave goods. The bulk of the ceramics suggests a post-1762 date for most Mound 2 interments, although the lowest minimum date could be as early as 1670. These dates are derived from ceramic data compiled by Noël Hume (1970:102–45).

We can also date the use of Mound 2 by analyzing the pipes associated with it. A mean date of the pipe bowls from Mound 2 is 1749 (table 24), but other dates support an inference for burials in this mound over a long period. Individual whole pipe bowl median dates range from a probable 1680, with a range from 1670 to 1690, to a probable 1815, with a range from 1780 to 1850 (table 20). Although bore diameter dates from the whole pipes would shift the median date to 1737, this shift would not alter the relative chronology of the mound.

Pipestem fragments in the Mound 2 fill probably reflect redeposition from fill sources and extend the median date back to approximately 1707, with a range from 1608 to 1806 (table 23). These dates are disregarded for specific temporal interpretation because the pipestems were not in a primary context. The dates, however, generally support an eighteenth-century development for most of Mound 2. The dates derived from all sources of pipe data span most of Newton's preemancipation history. This large span places some limits on the specific reliability of the pipe dating, but the general temporal patterns are independently supported by ceramic and stratigraphic data.

Mound 3. Mound 3 (figure 9) was approximately 0.6 meters high and 4.5 meters wide. After it was cleared of grass cover, a series of 1-meter squares were plotted over its eastern half. Surface collecting yielded redware sherds, and we began a trench from the eastern edge of the mound toward its center. We found human skeletal material in this trench, and excavated Burials 34 and 35. We also placed test pits in the center of the mound to determine if there was a concentration of interments like that in Mound 2. These tests only yielded redware sherds and no further excavation was conducted in Mound 3 until 1973, when part of one excavation square overlapped the southern part of the mound; no additional burials were found.

Burial 34 was a young adult female, with an east head orientation and possible evidence of a coffin. A whole pipe associated with the skeleton yielded a median bowl date of 1690 (range 1670 to 1710); the range of the bore diameter date is 1620 to 1680.

Burial 35 was one of three burials of ninety-two in the cemetery that was oriented with its head to the north. The two others were Burial 13 in Mound 2 (figure 11) and Burial 48 from a nonmound context (figure 9). Burial 35 was an adult male buried without a coffin. A creamware sherd, found in the fill around the body, suggests a minimum date of 1762; we found no associated cultural materials except for a metal belt buckle, one of the few artifacts in the cemetery suggesting clothing. Burials 35 and 48 were the only two in the cemetery with filed incisors. This strongly indicates African birth, unless we assume that tooth filing was practiced by some creole slaves in Barbados; the practice is not, however, reported in written sources.

Burials 34 and 35 were placed in Mound 3 at different times, and their interrelationship is clearly shown by the fact that Burial 34 was placed over and partially cut through the earlier Burial 35. The difference between the 1690 pipe date and the 1762 (or later) ceramic date is difficult to reconcile, but additional soil may have been added to the mound after Burial 34 was interred.

Mounds 6 and 7. These mounds, or mound remnants, were located on top of the low bluff at the western end of the cemetery (figure 8). Test excavations in these areas attempted to verify information from local informants that burial mounds had once been present but had been leveled within the past thirty years.

Three 1-meter-square test excavations were conducted in Mound 6, and bedrock was reached at approximately 50 centimeters below the surface. All three test excavations yielded human bone fragments and redware sherds; however, no complete or semiarticulated skeletal remains were encountered. A copper tack recovered may have been from a coffin. In general, it appears that Mound 6 was once a burial site, but not on the scale represented by Mound 2.

Two 1-meter squares excavated in Mound 7 were even less productive. We recovered only one human incisor, two bricks, one iron nail, and several small, unidentifiable, bone fragments. Mound 7 apparently had been a burial area at one time.

NONMOUND BURIAL CONCENTRATIONS

Unit 30N9W Burial Complex. The 3-meter-square excavation unit 30N9W (figures 13–15) is the main example of nonmound mortuary practices; with the exception of north-headed individuals, this complex incorporates all the significant variables found outside the man-made burial mounds. In addition, the seventeen burials in this complex clearly indicate the stratigraphic relationships between a variety of burial styles, with east-headed coffinless burials underlying or displaced by west-headed coffin burials. Information on specific interments in this complex is given in Appendix A and physical and contextual data are summarized in table 12.

The superficial level of interments in this complex consists of

TABLE 12. Excavation unit 30N9W, Newton cemetery: relative depths of burials and related physical and contextual data.

Burial	Depth	Articulated	Orientation	Coffin	Sex
49	surface	n	—	—	—
50	surface	n	—	—	—
51	surface	n	—	—	—
52	surface	n	—	—	—
53	surface	n	W	+	M
57	40 cm	n	—	—	—
59	40 cm	n	—	—	—
62	53 cm	n	—	—	—
65[a]	12–26 cm	n	—	—	—
55	55–62 cm	+	E	n	M
61	56–62 cm	+	E	n	F?
63	62–65 cm	+	E	n	—
54	29–32 cm	+	W	+	F
56[b]	42–56 cm	+	W	+	M
58[b]	62 cm	+	W	+	M
60	48 cm	+	W	n	F
64[b]	55 cm	+	W	+	M

Note: See table 11 for key to symbols.

[a] A cluster of three skulls, exclusive of postcranial material, found in association with Burial 65 may represent some of the disarticulated skeletons in Burials 49–53.

[b] Metal flakes.

highly disturbed and disarticulated human bone resulting from repeated use of the area. This skeletal material can be considered as backfill with no contextual validity. Figure 13 shows the shallowest west-headed coffin burial, Burial 54; it was almost directly above Burial 58 (figure 14) and lacked jewelry or grave goods. We found a pipestem by the right patella, but its placement may have resulted from the disturbance of underlying interments. It should be noted that Burials 54 and 58 were articulated. Burial 54 was either placed in the ground at the same time as Burial 58, or else the position of Burial 58 was not disturbed in the process of interring Burial 54.

Figures 14 and 15 indicate the relationship between Burials 56, 58, and 64; all were males in deep-placed west-headed coffin burials, with the rusted remnants of thin, rectangular iron plates over the chest areas of the skeletons. The function of the metal plates is unknown, but they appear to have been part of the coffins. In comparison with three individuals with metal plates in Mound 2

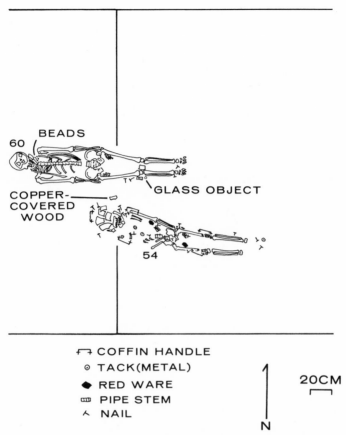

Figure 13. Excavation unit 30N9W, Burials 54 and 60, Newton ceme-tery, showing examples of different burial orientations, contexts, and patterns of artifact associations.

(Burials 8, 20, and 31), the presence of a metal plate is clearly not sex-related; Burials 8 and 31 were females but Burial 20 was the only male with a plate.

Burials 56, 58, and 64 were probably interred at the same time. During excavation we observed that the area including 56 and 64 was one continuous pit; data for the area around 58, however, were inconclusive. There was an apparent overlap along the boundary between 56 and 64, but because neither skeleton was disarticulated along this boundary and both were at almost exactly the same depth, the overlapping is best interpreted as postdepositional shifting in the soil as the coffins decayed.

Although difficult to illustrate with precision, figures 13–15 and table 12 show that several earlier burials, at least one of which was

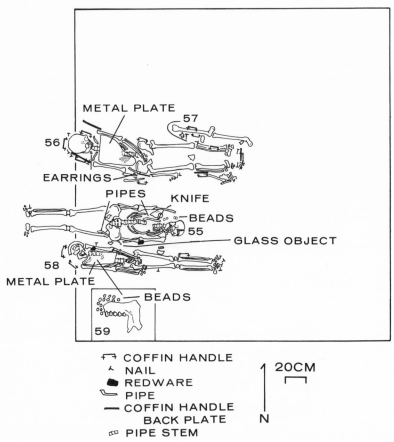

Figure 14. Excavation unit 30N9W, Burials 55–59, Newton cemetery, showing examples of different burial orientations, contexts, and patterns of artifact associations.

identified as east-headed, were displaced by the coffin burials; moreover, just as the deeper-lying Burial 58 was apparently not disturbed by the subsequent Burial 54, so east-headed and deep-lying skeletons such as Burials 55, 61, and 63 were not disturbed.

Burial 60, found 48 centimeters below the surface, was a coffinless, west-headed female partially overlapping earlier Burial 56. The nails around the lower leg and foot region of Burial 60 were probably part of the general debris in the square, rather than having been associated with the burial. A pipestem was found by the right knee, with a small glass object in close association.[4]

The small glass object with Burial 60 is one of two such objects found in the cemetery. Both are similar in number of facets, size,

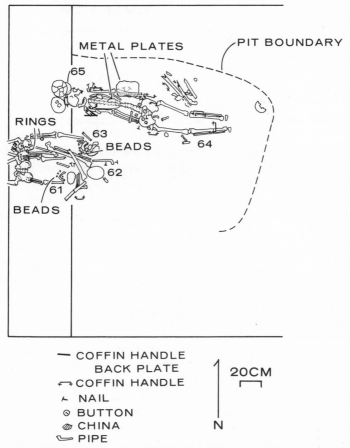

Figure 15. Excavation unit 30N9W, Burials 61–65, Newton cemetery, showing examples of different burial orientations, contexts, and patterns of artifact associations.

shape, and weight, and both were found in association with pipes that were excavated from coffinless burials in 30N9W. One object was with a long-stemmed pipe by the pelvis of Burial 55 (pipe 1; see table 20); the other, as indicated above, lay next to a section of pipestem found by the right knee of Burial 60 (see figures 13 and 14). The objects are of translucent glass, roughly conical, and have circular flat bases (figure 16). The facets are irregularly and crudely shaped; under magnification they show no evidence of having been ground or chipped, and almost certainly the objects were pressed or mold-made.[5]

The original function of these glass objects is uncertain. Neither the published literature nor persons familiar with colonial pipes

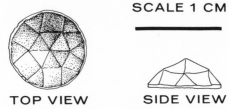

Figure 16.   Glass object with Burial 60, Newton cemetery.

indicate that the objects had any traditional functional relationship in Europe or Colonial America to pipes or pipe smoking. Ivor Noël Hume has suggested that the objects may have been "from an item of paste jewelry and would have originally been backed with metallic foil or perhaps by colored paper"; the objects may have been originally associated with finger rings or, possibly, shoe buckles that "generally date from the second half of the eighteenth century" (personal communication; see also Abbitt 1973:28). Because neither Burial 55 nor 60 had rings or shoe buckles associated with them, it is quite likely that the slaves' use of the glass objects was secondary. However the objects (or the rings or buckles to which they might have originally belonged) were acquired, we do not know what burial function they might have performed. The two contexts in which the glass objects were found (especially in Burial 55), and their total absence in other contexts, suggests a relationship between the objects and the pipes. This relationship may have been functional, but it is more likely that the objects were placed with the burials simply because they had been of personal value to the decedents. Whatever meaning these objects had to the slaves, we can assume that their function was unaffected by temporal and cultural changes, given the stratigraphic, orientation, and sex differences between Burials 55 and 60. Both burials were from deep positions within 30N9W and were coffinless—and therefore probably early in date—but Burial 55 was an east-headed male while Burial 60 was a west-headed female.

In general, the artifacts associated with burials in the 30N9W complex represent a cross-section of grave goods, jewelry, and apparel found in the cemetery. Such artifacts included small fragments of china, redware, glass, and pipestems, all found in the fill around the bodies; intentional inclusions with interments were complete pipes, glass beads from necklaces and bracelets, metal knives and finger rings, and buttons. Although these items are a diverse inventory, it must be emphasized that a very limited quantity of material occurred with any single individual and no individual had all types of items associated with it. Correlations of various grave goods with age, sex, and orientation patterns was attempted but with inconclusive results.

Two complete clay pipes with median bowl dates of 1705 were recovered from Burial 55; a single complete pipe found with Burial 62 had a median bowl date of 1700 (table 20 and figures 34C, D, and 33B). Using the bore-stem diameter dating method, the two pipes with Burial 55 yielded a date of 1710–1750; the pipe from Burial 62 yielded a late seventeenth- and early eighteenth-century date (see table 20 and figure 35). Along with the east-headed orientation and absence of coffins, these pipe dates suggest that this area of the cemetery was used in an early period.

Unit 21N9W Burial Complex. In some ways this complex mirrors features observed in 30N9W, but 21N9W also manifests additional nonmound burial traits. Six individuals were interred in this complex: two heads were to the east and four to the west. Data from this complex are summarized in Appendix A.

Burials 67 and 71 (see figure 17) are the only examples in the cemetery where a later east-headed, noncoffin burial (Burial 67) was superimposed over an earlier west-headed burial with a coffin (Burial 71). In the general cemetery pattern burials with a western head orientation occurred later than those with an eastern orientation.

None of the west-headed bodies (Burials 66 and 69–70—a multiple interment[6] counted as one burial) shown in figure 17 intrudes on another's space. Such spacing suggests that either the location of these burials was marked by some visible sign or they were interred simultaneously. Although not clearly shown in figure 17, Burial 68 was oriented with its head to the east and was the only partially flexed interment of the ninety-two excavated burials. Because it was located very close to the surface (less than 5 centimeters below ground level), its bones were in an advanced state of decay; we could not estimate age or sex. No grave goods were found in Burial 68; nor was there any evidence of clothing or jewelry. It is difficult to explain the unique partial flexing of this burial as well as the fact that more flexed burials were not found in the cemetery. Although flexed burials were not characteristically European they were common in West Africa; and West African mortuary practices in general clearly influenced those found in Barbadian slave culture (see chapter 6).

Burials 69 and 70 were the interment of an adult and child, apparently in a coffin. They represent one of the two examples of multiple interments in the cemetery; the other was Burials 20 and 21 in Mound 2. In both cases, the adults were classified as "old

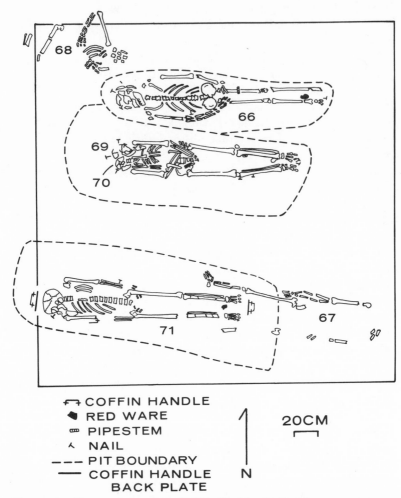

COFFIN HANDLE
RED WARE
PIPESTEM
NAIL
PIT BOUNDARY
COFFIN HANDLE
BACK PLATE

20CM

N

Figure 17. Excavation unit 21N9W, Burials 66–71, Newton cemetery, showing burial orientations, contexts, and adult-child interment (Burials 69–70).

males," whereas Burial 70 was classified as a "child" (less than five years old at death) and Burial 21 as an "infant" (but not newborn). Although it may be initially surprising that both adult individuals were probably males, because the child and infant were not newborns, it is possible that specific but unknown cultural or social factors operated in these interments. These burials are also interesting because of the apparent lack of attention given to nonadult burials in Barbadian slave and African mortuary practices (chapter 7) and the general lack of nonadult burials in the cemetery as a whole. Artifactual and other supporting data provide no additional assistance in interpreting these multiple interments.

Burial 72 Unit. In terms of associated cultural material, Burial 72 was the richest in the cemetery and dramatically contrasts with the total absence or very limited quantity of grave goods with other interments. This individual was an "old" adult male whose head was oriented to the east; we found no evidence of a coffin.

Burial 72 displaced and disturbed an earlier interment (Burial 74) of the same sex and approximate age. Both burials provide the only clear case of two interments outside of the major burial concentration areas (for example, Mound 2, 30N9W), where two bodies are superimposed in the same space and share the major characteristics of sex, approximate age, eastern head orientation, and absence of coffins. The correlation of physical, contextual, and locational data makes this a unique case in the cemetery (although there is one other possible example). However, there is a distinct contrast in accompanying artifactual material: only a European clay pipe was associated with Burial 74 (see figure 33C) while Burial 72 had relatively numerous artifacts. We are not sure if the interment of these two individuals in the same area had any cultural significance or if it was merely a result of fortuitous circumstances.

Two copper or copper alloy bracelets were on the lower left arm of Burial 72 (figures 18E, D and 20 A, C) while another bracelet was on the lower right arm (figures 18C and 20B; see also figure 19). One copper and two identical white metal rings were on the middle finger of the left hand (figure 18F). The bracelets and rings were in excellent condition, but a metal knife at the end of the left hand (figure 18G) was badly corroded.

Textile fragments were found on the exterior surface of one of the copper bracelets (figure 20B). Microscopic analysis showed these fragments to be the same open or "coarse" plain weave fabric, suggesting the type of manufactured textile that we would expect to find in slave clothing. The poor state of preservation, however, precluded identification of the fibers.

A unique and elaborate necklace with obvious, but generalized, African characteristics, was also found with Burial 72 (figure 18A). The necklace is composed of seven cowrie shells, twenty-one drilled dog canines, fourteen glass beads of various types, five drilled isospondylous vertebrae from a comparatively large teleost or true bony fish (not shark), and one large reddish-orange agate bead (figure 21; see also figure 26ff, left); part of the necklace's stringing pattern was reconstructed during the process of its excavation (figure 22).

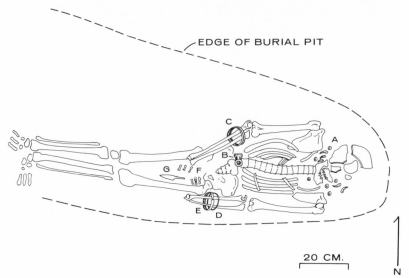

Figure 18. Burial 72, Newton cemetery, with associated artifacts. *A:* necklace (see figure 21); *B:* pipe (see figure 23); *C:* bracelet (see figure 20*B*); *D:* bracelet (see figure 20*A*); *E:* bracelet (see figure 20*C*); *F:* rings (see figure 20*D,E*); *G:* iron knife blade (not illustrated in detail because of advanced state of corrosion).

Figure 19. Burial 72, Newton cemetery, upper portion of skeleton and associated artifacts in situ.

126

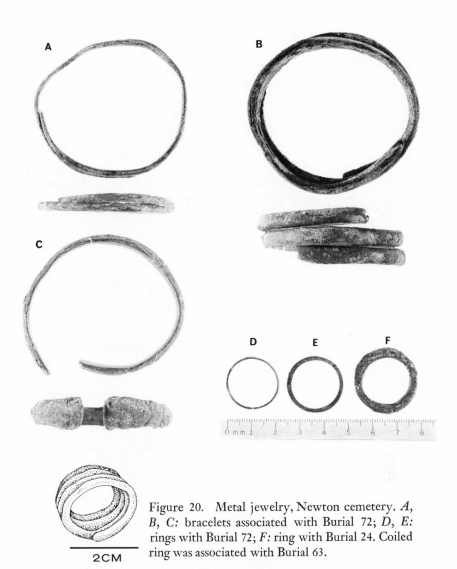

Figure 20. Metal jewelry, Newton cemetery. *A*, *B*, *C*: bracelets associated with Burial 72; *D*, *E*: rings with Burial 72; *F*: ring with Burial 24. Coiled ring was associated with Burial 63.

The beads are discussed in a subsequent section of this chapter, but the cowries are *Cyprea moneta*, one of the world's best-known cowries; it is a highly variable species with an extremely broad Indo-Pacific zoogeographic range from Durban, South Africa, to Hawaii and including the area of Mozambique and Madagascar. This species does not inhabit the Atlantic ocean in Caribbean, European, or West African areas. Although we have been unable to establish the ultimate provenance of our shell specimens (and it is highly unlikely that a specific locality can be identified), the shells clearly

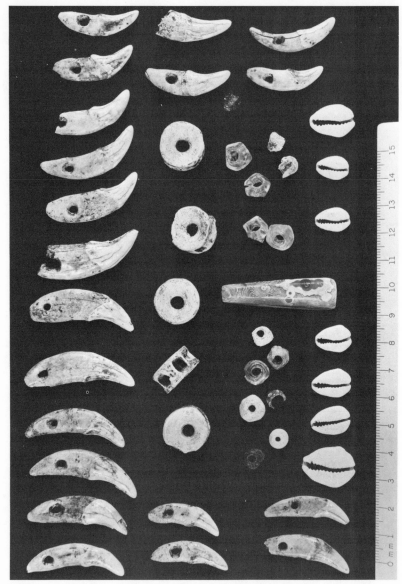

Figure 21. Components of necklace with Burial 72, Newton cemetery.

were brought to Barbados by some human agent. Europeans could have brought the shells in any number of ways and either slaves or Europeans could have brought them during the middle passage. European slavers, for example, used cowries in their business transactions along the West African coasts. Captain Thomas Phillips's

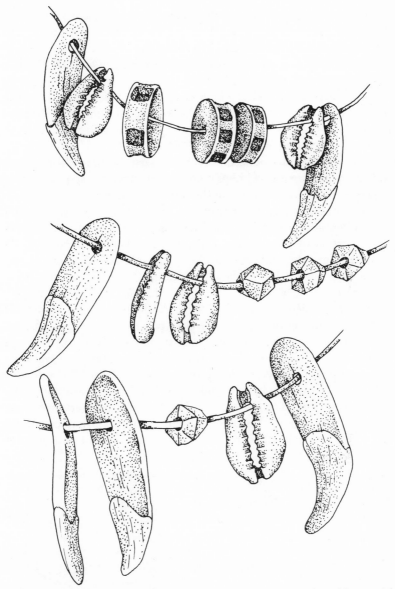

Figure 22. Reconstructed stringing pattern, sections of necklace with Burial 72, Newton cemetery.

account of a slaving voyage to West Africa in 1693–94 to acquire slaves for the Barbadian market describes the use of cowries by both Europeans and Africans. While at Whydah (or Ouidah) in Dahomey, he reported: "The best goods to purchase slaves here are cowries... The only money they have here are these cowries or shells we carry them, being brought from the East-Indies... as soon as the negroes have them, they bore holes in the backs of them, and string them on rushes, forty shells on each, which they call a foggy; and five of such foggys being tied together, is called a galina, being two hundred shells, which is their way of accounting their shell-money. When they go to market to buy anything they bargain for so many cowries, foggys, or so many galinas, and without these shells they can purchase nothing" (1746:243–244).

However, the shells need not have been brought from West Africa. At the time of Phillips's voyage, slaves were acquired from Madagascar, an area included in the term "East Indies."

We have been unable to identify the type of dog from which the canines in the Burial 72 necklace came, but it is of interest that an excavation of a nineteenth-century slave burial ground in Cuba yielded "algunos pendientes hechos con colmillos de perros perforados—de indudable tradicion africana" ("some pendants made of perforated dog canines, undoubtedly of African tradition"; Academia de Ciencias de Cuba 1970). Although the dog canines in Barbados could have come from elsewhere, various types of dogs were on the island during the slave period (Ligon 1657:98, 105; Walduck 1710–1712; Cadbury 1943:123; Schomburgk 1848:683).

A clay pipe discovered on top of the pelvis of Burial 72 (figures 18B and 19) was apparently undisturbed since interment. It is the only pipe we found in Barbados and at Newton cemetery not made of white clay (figure 23). Its apparent mode of manufacture and distinctive form and decorative features suggest that it is not of European origin.[7]

After searching the literature and consulting with people familiar with clay pipes and Caribbean artifacts, we cannot positively identify

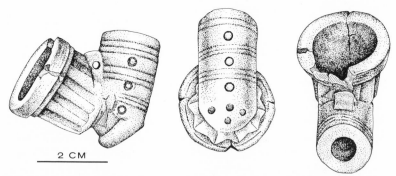

2 CM

Figure 23. Short-stem pipe with Burial 72, Newton cemetery.

where this pipe originated or the style provenance it represents. It is unlikely that the pipe was manufactured in Barbados; the color and qualities of the clay, the absence of archaeological evidence for similar pipes, and the fact that the written sources do not indicate any kind of pipe manufacturing on the island suggest that the pipe was brought from elsewhere.

Leonard H. Gant, a pipe specialist associated with Alfred Dunhill Ltd. of London, though fairly certain that the pipe is neither African nor European and positive that it is not English, suggested a Brazilian origin. The shape and decoration of the pipe, Gant claimed, especially the relief dots and impressed circles along the sides and bottom of the stem, are characteristic of Brazilian Amerindian pipes (personal communication). We have been unable to verify this suggestion although in the seventeenth century, especially prior to the 1650s, slaves were brought to Barbados from northern Brazil and the Guianas.

José Cruxent, the Venezuelan archaeologist, also attested to the rarity of this type of pipe. He believes it is not Amerindian, but resembles pipes of late sixteenth- or seventeenth-century Spanish colonial manufacture; such pipes were manufactured in various Spanish colonies so that the ultimate provenance of the Newton example would be very difficult to ascertain (personal communication). Barbados also had trade contacts with various Spanish colonies in the New World during the seventeenth and early eighteenth centuries.

Paul Ozanne, in dealing with the archaeology of the early historic period in the area of Accra in Ghana (Gold Coast), discusses various types of clay pipes (1962). Most of these pipes were "collected from the surface of old settlements, or from road-cuttings and industrial workings." Some pipes from the "early historic site" of Asafo (west of Accra) bear the closest resemblance we have found to the pipe associated with Burial 72. These pipes were surface collected, but by cross-dating various pipes with materials found in excavated contexts elsewhere, Ozanne concludes the pipes were not only of African manufacture, but also date from the late seventeenth century (1962:51–58).

Although the pipe from Burial 72 does not appear to resemble modern or relatively modern African pipes, we tentatively conclude, following Ozanne's lead, that the pipe is of African origin. Other materials found with the burial, including the necklace and various of the metal jewelry, probably also originated in Africa.

The relative richness and distinctiveness of the artifacts associated with Burial 72, strongly suggest that the individual held a special position in the slave community. He was "old" at the time of death and he may well have been a positively viewed Obeah practitioner or folk doctor. The east-headed orientation, absence of a coffin, and the fact that grave goods in the cemetery were generally associated with earlier burials all suggest an early burial. Moreover, the man was probably of African birth, because of some of his associated artifacts and because Barbados contained more African-born individuals in the earlier periods of slavery than in the later ones.

Burial 33. This burial of an adult male was oriented with its head to the west and was found between Mounds 1 and 2 (figure 9). Burial 33 is unique because we found large hinges beneath the shoulder and lower ends of the femurs. The hinges indicate that the individual was buried either on a door or in a handleless coffin for which a door had been used for the bottom (at one time, the door may have been used as a form of bed).[8] Near its left shoulder was a complete pipe (figure 32*A*) that was dated between 1650 and 1680 using its stem bore diameter and bowl shape. Aside from metal nails, we found no other associated artifacts.

ARTIFACTUAL MATERIAL RECOVERED FROM EXCAVATIONS

The assemblage of collected and excavated artifacts from Newton cemetery and its adjacent fields consists almost entirely of materials that could have been available to or utilized by freedmen and whites of various socioeconomic strata as well as by slaves. The content of some of the island's material culture during the slave period was discussed in earlier chapters, and here it need only be emphasized that imported goods of European origin found their way to the slave population through a variety of means.

Establishing reliable time frames for the skeletons and associated artifacts was a major analytical problem. Most recent archaeological literature on historic New World artifact types or styles is based on data from North American sites where the American Revolution and other factors were important in accounting for the presence or absence and quantity of diagnostic artifacts. The North American colonies and the English colonies in the West Indies used similar, often identical, goods manufactured in Europe. However, because of differences in the economic and social development of North America and the English Caribbean, different sets of historical, demographic, and economic factors affected the quantities, content, and timing of the introduction of European artifacts to Barbados. As a simple illustration, glass beads were extensively used in North America in the Indian fur trade. No comparable exchanges occurred in Barbados and there is no indication that glass beads were an import of any consequence. Similarly, both North America and Barbados imported European white clay pipes, but the larger population of the first area ensured its acquiring a greater number of pipes. Although iron tools for woodworking were used in both areas, the vaster forest expanses of North America, as well as its larger population, required greater quantities of such tools. In all, the lack of a solid time frame based on historical and economic data specific to the southern Caribbean during the period of slavery is a great deficiency at present. As Walker (1972:132) has cautioned, the failure to consider historical factors and processes when dating historic materials may lead to serious chronological difficulties and skewed interpretations of culture processes.

Our chronological base is somewhat more limited and less precise than we would like, but we are satisfied that it is adequate for tracing the development of Newton cemetery and related changes in mortuary patterns during the slave period. The available dates span a period from before the known establishment of Newton as a plantation to a terminal date well beyond emancipation. These extremes are achieved by utilizing the full ranges of dates in terms of potential error; medians of all dates and grouped dates fall well within the period of slavery. The length of the temporal sequence is important here and is an essential factor in subsequent discussions of behavioral practices and changes.

Clay Pipes. With the exception of the pipe associated with Burial 72, whole white clay pipes and pipestem fragments are fully analyzed and discussed in Appendix B. The Appendix also discusses the methodology used in dating these pipes, and the pipes, in turn, provide the most effective means for dating the cemetery. All the white clay pipes appear to be of English manufacture or European origin.

Although clay pipes have been smoked on Barbados until fairly modern times, the preemancipation historical record seldom mentions pipe use by slaves. Several sources indicate that the slaves valued and smoked tobacco, but only a few sources mention the use of pipes and only one in any detail. George Pinckard, who visited Barbados in 1796, recorded an evening scene in the "negro-yard," or slave village. Some people were "at rest, or moving in busy occupation," others "passing from hut to hut, some dancing to their favorite music, some sitting at the door with the pipe in their mouths, and others smoking their loved sagar under the broad leaf of the plantain" (1806;1:369). Pinckard observed, that

> Smoking is an universal custom among [the slaves] ... In order to be at all moments provided for this enjoyment, they carry

133

in their breeches pocket a short pipe, about an inch in length from the bowl; or, instead of this a leaf of tobacco rolled into a sagar. Very often the pipe is so short, or the sagar so closely smoked away, as to be in danger of burning the nose, or even the lips. I have frequently seen them smoking with the pipe so short as to hold it in the mouth by pressing with the lips upon the lower part of the bowl. They often kindle their pipes from one another's mouths, by putting bowl to bowl and nose to nose, and smoking into each others eyes, until the tobacco has taken fire (1806;2:115).

The pipes recovered from the cemetery plainly show the "short" pipe reported by Pinckard was not the only type used by slaves (see, for example, figures 32E, 33B, and 34C, D); indeed Pinckard may not have observed a distinct type at all, but rather pipes whose stems had broken off and which may have been given to the slaves, otherwise acquired by them, or were discarded by their original (European?) owners.[9] Because they were so poor, slaves probably would have used their pipes, even with broken stems, longer than Europeans for whom the pipes were cheap and readily accessible.

Tobacco was a major cash crop in Barbados before the sugar revolution of the middle of the seventeenth century, and it continued to be grown in later periods. By the 1730s and 1740s Griffith Hughes reported that tobacco was "here planted but very sparingly, and that chiefly by the slaves, and the poorer sort of white inhabitants, but none for exportation" (1750:171). Pipes, however, were imported from England from the seventeenth century and throughout the eighteenth (and later), and early evidence in Barbados's sugar plantation history shows that tobacco, whether locally grown or later imported, was considered a treat and a reward for the slaves (Handler 1967:66; Drax 1755:66). Reporting on the late seventeenth and early eighteenth centuries, John Oldmixon noted how "a pipe of tobacco and a dram [of rum] is the most acceptable present that can be made" to the slaves (1741;2:132–133). On the Codrington plantations in the middle of the eighteenth century, "the Negroes were given pipes and tobacco, which served some of them as a marketable commodity when they bargained on a Sunday for food" (Bennett 1958:39). In the late eighteenth century, a prominent Barbadian planter instructed his manager to "keep a constant supply of pipes and tobacco in the plantation, and to distribute them, occasionally, to those who smoke" (Gibbes 1797:85).

In general, then, slaves were not limited to picking up discarded pipes, stealing them, or acquiring them through the internal marketing system or other forms of exchange. Some pipes were received directly from the plantation managements. However they were acquired, pipes were given a secondary use as grave goods or mortuary offerings.[10]

Except for coffin furniture, white clay pipes were the most frequent artifacts associated with burials. We found pipes with both a bowl and at least part of a stem in association with seventeen of the ninety-two skeletons we excavated and pipestem and bowl fragments in the fill surrounding thirty-one (see Appendix B). One whole pipe, with a bowl and stem, was collected from the surface of the cemetery field, and twenty-eight stem fragments were recovered from the fill of excavated squares that did not contain burials.

Whole pipes were interred in a variety of burial conditions and there is no statistical correlation between the presence of whole pipes and other significant burial characteristics such as age, sex, head orientation, presence or absence of coffins, or presence or absence of other grave goods.

Ceramics. We cannot use the chronology provided by the limited occurrence of ceramics with or around some of the interments to arrive at precise dates, but it does provide limits and ranges. Locally manufactured and imported ceramics were also found through surface collecting and test excavations in other parts of the island, but these materials generally lack specific archaeological context and have little interpretive value. Thus, only ceramic materials from Newton cemetery and comparable data from other Newton fields are discussed here.

Based on the imported ceramics alone, we can be sure that no associated burials were made before 1670, at the earliest. However, there is a greater tendency for ceramic dates to cluster around the 1760s; this date is probably much more accurate, and the limited earlier material was probably simply incorporated in the soil used for grave fill. The 1760s date correlates closely with the beginning of the manufacture of Creamware and similar pottery in England. Production of these types greatly increased the availability of well-made ceramics in the West Indies. In Jamaica, for example, it was "only after 1750, with the increase in popularity of blue and white Chinese porcelain, and 1762 with the creation of Creamware, that the range of wares offered was much more exactly economically differentiated" (Ebanks 1974:2).

China was probably not imported into Barbados during the seventeenth century "since it was only being imported into England in the last quarter of the 17th. century" (Connell 1957:121); however, by the 1750s, if not earlier, china from England was found in the homes of well-to-do Barbadians (see, for example, the 1757 inventory of William Barwick's estate in Connell 1959:179; see also Frere 1768:120–21). Manufacturers' marks and identifiable styles of the preemancipation china from Newton cemetery seem to confirm this general period of introduction of china to the island; according to Noël Hume (1970:102–145), the initial production dates of the china we recovered fall within the late eighteenth and early nineteenth centuries. We also collected china and other imported ceramics of postemancipation manufacture in fields adjacent to the cemetery, but none was encountered in the cemetery itself. Appendix A shows the distribution of imported and locally made ceramics from excavation contexts within Newton cemetery.

China was a luxury item in Barbados. Until the late eighteenth century, if not later, it was used mainly by the middle and upper strata of the white population (see, for example, Connell 1959) and probably the upper stratum of freedmen as well. Toward the end of the slave period, however, a few sources suggest that sometimes plantation slaves of higher ranks occasionally may have had access to china which they kept in their houses (Bayley 1832:91; Coleridge 1832:126). However, such possession was uncommon and occurred late in the period of slavery. Some china may have been obtained after it had been broken and discarded, while other pieces may have been stolen or acquired through the internal marketing system; it is also possible that china was occasionally given to some slaves as a reward.

The glazed earthenwares or "redwares" are similar to materials being manufactured in Barbados today (Handler 1963b), but we were unable to establish their chronological value. Glaze colors range from dark green through light green and from yellow to brown, depending on the glaze and the temperature at firing.

A large fragment of a shallow glazed redware bowl was found immediately beneath the pelvis of Burial 22 in Mound 2 (figure 24). This vessel is the only positive instance of an apparent association between a burial and a pottery container. The vessel was wheel-made and has an interior light green lead glaze. Although its form differs from conventionally manufactured vessels in Barbados in modern times, the method of manufacture, type of clay, and glaze is very similar to contemporary pottery made in the village of Chalky Mount (Handler 1963b). This bowl appears to have been locally made. The relative age of Burial 22 suggests an early date of the vessel's manufacture and this date provides supportive evidence that domestic wares in general were made on the island in an early period (see Handler 1963a).

Other nonglazed earthenware sherds recovered in archaeological

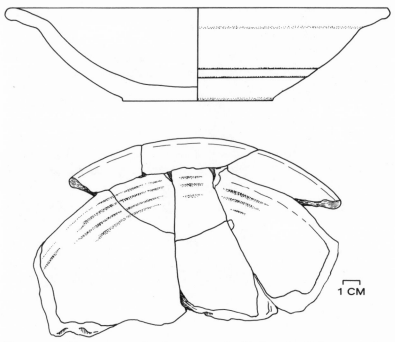

Figure 24. Reconstructed redware vessel with interior light green glaze from beneath the pelvis of Burial 22, Mound 2, Newton cemetery.

contexts also appear to be similar to the type of wheel-made pottery manufactured on the island today, although earthenwares were also imported from England and North America during the period of slavery in Barbados.

Buckley ware, a generally thick ceramic with a dark brown sur-face is distinguished by its marbled paste (figure 25*A*, *B*). Charac-teristic of the Buckley district of North Wales, it was found in the fill of Mound 2, although not directly associated with any particular burial. Buckley ware was also widely collected from field surfaces throughout the island as well as from test excavations at Staple Grove plantation. Its occurrence in Newton cemetery, however, is the only case in which it was found in a firm archaeological context.

In dating Buckley ware in Colonial America, Noël Hume wrote "I have yet to see this ware in contexts dating earlier than 1720 (though I am told it has been found in one of the late seventeenth century), but it becomes increasingly common thereafter, the trade seemingly terminating at the time of the Revolution" (1970:133). In accordance with this dating, South (1972) dates Buckley ware from 1720 (which he assumes to be the beginning of manufacture

Figure 25. Dated ceramic types, Newton cemetery. *A* and *B:* Buckley ware (1720–1803); *C:* blue-edged pearlware (1780–1830); *D:* green-edged pearlware (1780–1830); *E:* lead-glazed slipware, combed yellow (1670–1795); *F:* Burslem stoneware (1705–1740).

in Britain) to 1775 (the revolutionary war). However, the Revolution affected British trade to the Caribbean differently than trade to North America, and Buckley ware probably continued to be exported to Barbados throughout the final quarter of the eighteenth century. Barton gave a dated manufactured range of ca. 1740 to 1803 for Buckley ware recovered from Prescot's Pottery, "one of the earliest kilns recorded" in the Buckley district (1955:63). The presence of Buckley ware in the fill of Mound 2 extends the earliest minimum date for the mound to the 1720s, which is somewhat later than the minimum date we established from the analysis of pipes; however, the major clustering of pipe and ceramic materials seems to represent activity that postdates 1762.

The spatial distribution of datable china from the excavations at Newton indicates that dirt fill was brought to the cemetery from the plantation yard area. As Appendix A shows, most definite associations occurred in Mound 2 and the only exceptions were Burials 1 and 35. Burial 1 follows the general Mound 2 traits of a western head orientation and the presence of a coffin, while Burial

138

35 is a north-headed burial in Mound 3. In general, no ceramics other than common redwares were associated with skeletons whose heads were to the east. In other limited instances where general associations occurred (as, for example, in the 30N9W group and in Burial 22), the associations can be explained by the addition of earth during later interments.

Thus, the presence and absence of china in relation to east- and west-headed burials has chronological significance and supports an interpretation, based on stratigraphic relationships as well as artifactual materials, that the east-headed burials were generally earlier than the west-headed ones.

In tested cemetery areas lacking burials, no china fragments were recovered, although we continued to find redware fragments in these areas. These redware fragments may represent portions of liquid or food containers that were possibly used in burial or postinterment activities (see chapter 6). The fragments, however, may simply reflect the remains of food or drink vessels that were carried by workers in adjacent fields. These redware sherds are only bodysherds and no rims, spouts, or other vessel portions are represented in the collections. This suggests that the excavated and surface collected redware sherds in Newton cemetery were not from vessels placed in or near the graves, and that if food containers were left or buried they were made from organic materials.

Historical sources indicate that earthenware manufacture began in Barbados between 1650 and the 1670s. Slaves were involved in this manufacture by the late seventeenth century or no later than the first decade of the eighteenth century. The male slave potters employed a wheel and kiln technology of European derivation to manufacture conical sugar pots that were used for draining the molasses from the raw sugar (Handler 1963a). Earthenware sugar pots were made by a number of Barbadian plantations for their own use and for sale to other plantations; these sugar pots as well as household earthenwares were also imported from England in very large quantities throughout the 1700s and early 1800s.[11]

We found some indications that slaves were making and using household or domestic earthenwares by the first half of the eighteenth century, if not earlier. In his *Natural History of Barbados*, based on observations made during the mid-1730s and 1740s, Griffith Hughes speculated on the precolonial Amerindian inhabitants of the island: "several earthen vessels of different sizes have been dug up ... within these thirty years last past. These were generally of a globular figure, of a slate colour, but very brittle otherwise, far surpassing the earthen-ware made here by Negroes, in thinness, smoothness and beauty" (1750:8). Hughes also reported the use of "earthen basons" by an Obeah practitioner and noted that "a great many Negroes have a notion that if they kill one [of a particular type of insect] . . . they will be very unlucky in breaking all earthen wares they handle" (pp. 15, 67–68).[12] William Dickson, who lived in Barbados during the 1770s and 1780s, reported that slave musicians used "a common earthen jar" as a substitute for drums made out of wood (1789:74). By the end of the eighteenth century or the first decade of the nineteenth, a visitor to the island observed that the slave's "pots, he manufactures himself; his dishes are composed of gourds" (*Authentic History of the West Indies* 1810:41), and another visitor in the 1820s saw "Negro" hawkers in Bridgetown selling, among other goods, "gurglets for holding water" (Bayley 1830:61; see also Handler 1963a:146–147).

Despite the sparse evidence, slaves probably made domestic wares and applied the wheel and kiln technology of sugar pot manufacture to the manufacture of such wares. Wheel and kiln production is the only pottery technology used in Barbados today; moreover it is the only technology reported in the oral traditions of contemporary Barbadian potters and is the only one suggested in all historical sources. Although historical evidence is lacking and the archaeological evidence is very weak, some slave potters, including women, possibly employed a nonkiln and nonwheel technology with African or Africanlike methods. Such manufactures have been found in recent times in other British West Indian islands with sugar plantation histories, such as Antigua and Nevis.[13]

Before our archaeological research began we anticipated that at least some pottery we recovered would reflect an African tradition or influence. We found some suggestive but noncorroborated documentary evidence for an African influence in Richard Ligon's seventeenth-century account of Barbados. During his stay on the island in 1647–50, European colonists, at least, were not making pottery although they were aware of the island's clays and had attempted, with little success, to make bricks. After his return to England, Ligon met "an ancient Captain . . . one of those that first landed on the island" and who had lived in Barbados for a number of years thereafter: "This Captain . . . inform'd me for certain that [pots found by early Barbadian colonists and attributed by them to former Amerindian inhabitants] . . . were brought by the Negroes, which they fetcht from Angola, and some other parts of Africa; and that he had seen them make of them at Angola with the greatest art that may be. Though I am willing to believe this Captain, who delivered upon his knowledge that the Negroes brought some pots

140

thither, and very finely and artificially made, yet it does not hinder any man from believing that the Indians brought some too, and who knows which were the most exactly made" (1657:23–24, 42).

Recent archaeological work at Old King's House at Spanish Town has yielded evidence of a tradition of African-influenced pottery in Jamaica:

> This ceramic folk tradition has not hitherto been duly recognized in Jamaica as having had a long history of development in West Africa prior to its introduction into this country by Akan peoples from the country now known as Ghana. Initial examination has revealed that many of the locally developed earthenwares exhibit a number of ceramic traits showing a strong African element and influence, which clearly indicates that the vessels were made here in Jamaica by Africans... Although the existence of basal foot rings, flat bottoms, strap handles and lead glazes fully document the English influence in many of the earthenwares, the general overall proportion and firing characteristics of these vessels vividly reflect the cultural bias of the African potter himself (Mathewson 1972b:54–55).

Ebanks, though disagreeing with parts of Mathewson's methodological approach to the ceramic materials, agrees that the cast of much of the local material is basically African: "One of our major wares is the Yabbah collection, which has so far been divided into three major groups. This ware was created in the ancient African way and there is no evidence of corruption of tradition. In addition to this, there are two other groups which, although using non-African techniques and shapes, seem to have been created by African potters under the supervision of Europeans" (1974:2).

At Old King's House, at least "five major Afro-Jamaican wares have been identified, of which two have been finished with a lead glaze." The pottery assemblage at this site consisted of over 2,000 sherds from a wide variety of vessel forms. They clearly reflect the African heritage of the potters (Mathewson 1973:29). In contrast, we identified only three nonwheel-made sherds at Newton cemetery, and none had a specific burial association. These sherds were clearly distinguishable from the more common wheel-made redware. No nonwheel-made sherds (other than Amerindian remains) were found elsewhere in Barbados, either in surface collections or from test excavations. The nonwheel-made sherds from Newton may represent vessels that were made in Barbados, and at least some of the wheel-made wares undoubtedly were produced on the island as well.

Unspecified types of "earthen wares" were manufactured in the Chalky Mount area of the Scotland District parish of Saint Andrew by at least the 1670s (Handler 1963a:131, 148), and a cottage-type pottery industry producing "coarse ware" for domestic use was already established in the Scotland District by at least the first decade of the nineteenth century (Skey 1816:241–242). By the early nineteenth century this pottery industry involved black potters (Handler 1963a:141–146).

Major preemancipation pottery production took place in the Scotland District; the district contains abundant clay supplies and today supports the only group of cottage potters in Barbados (Handler 1963b). In 1830, a doctor reported that "the clay, which is plentifully distributed through the hilly district . . . answers sufficiently well for the manufacture of coarse ware and bricks, and accordingly there are several pot-kilns in the parishes of St. John, St. Joseph, and St. Andrew" (Maycock 1830:10). Though some of these pot kilns may have belonged to cottage potters who were free blacks, others were plantation kilns; in either event, in earlier times these three parishes were important to the island's pottery industry although pottery was also being made in some bordering parishes.

The number of pottery kilns on plantations is a good indication of the distribution of pottery-making. With a few exceptions, such as the Codrington plantations,[14] we do not know which plantations possessed kilns, but table 13 shows that kilns were located in several

TABLE 13. Pottery kilns in Barbados during the eighteenth century.

Parish	1710	1716	1731	1750–1751	1752–1753	1755	1757	1758–1759	1760
Saint Andrew	8	9	—	—	—	6	—	—	—
Saint Joseph	4	7	—	—	—	3	—	—	—
Saint John	2	2	—	—	—	4	—	—	—
Saint Philip	5	9	—	—	—	4	—	—	—
Saint Thomas	4	0	—	—	—	2	—	—	—
Saint Peter	1	0	—	—	—	0	—	—	—
Saint Lucy	0	0	—	—	—	0	—	—	—
Saint James	0	0	—	—	—	0	—	—	—
Saint Michael	0	0	—	—	—	0	—	—	—
Saint George	0	0	—	—	—	0	—	—	—
Christ Church	0	0	—	—	—	0	—	—	—
Total	24	27	26	18	19	19	20	18	15

Sources: 1710, Public Record Office (1710). 1716, H. Hall (1714–17). 1731, John Bennett (1738:19) and Ashley (1732:27). 1750–1753, Pinfold (1762). 1755, Hall (1924:5). 1757–1760, Pinfold (1762). For all years the information is based on tax returns in the island Treasurer's Office; thus there may have been more kilns in any given year.

parishes during the eighteenth century; no kilns, however, were in parishes that were outside of, or did not border on, the Scotland District.

Thus slaves from a number of plantations in a relatively limited and well-defined region of Barbados manufactured pottery. In earlier periods they made sugar pots and probably also made domestic wares. If at times during the slave period nonwheel and non-kiln domestic pottery was made, the manufacture of these wares was probably also localized in the Scotland District. Furthermore, slave potters in Barbados like slave craftsmen in Jamaica probably exchanged or sold at least some of their products on the internal marketing system (Mintz and Hall 1960).

The temporal classification of Barbadian-made redwares requires more concerted and systematic archaeological research than we were able to accomplish. We attempted to deal with this problem by surface collecting at abandoned kiln sites in the vicinity of Chalky Mount. These kilns had belonged to former cottage potters, but because we were entirely dependent on surface materials the data were generally nonproductive. The possible significance of local redwares was not clearly recognized or defined sufficiently early in the research to permit a meaningful focus on these kiln sites, and more extensive research, particularly excavation, is needed.

In all, Mathewson's comment on Jamaica that "the study of eighteenth century . . . ceramic utilization patterns is still very much in its infancy" (1973:27) is even more appropriate archaeologically to Barbados. However, Mathewson's attempt to deal with sociocultural differences in the eighteenth-century population of Jamaica by interpreting locally produced ceramics is a new and useful approach, especially because it utilizes ceramic data as cultural rather than purely temporal indicators. Mathewson has identified a level of residual Africanisms in eighteenth-century Jamaican ceramics not seen in the Barbadian materials.[15] However, Barbadian slave potters who used the wheel technology of sugar pot manufacture in producing domestic earthenwares may have applied some African practices in surface finish or decoration, and there may have been some female potters who made household wares with a nonwheel technology that reflected an African influence.

The differences in African influences on ceramic traditions in Jamaica and Barbados can probably be attributed to a combination of geographical, ecological, and historical factors. For example, the greater number and higher percentage of native-born African slaves in Jamaica during the eighteenth century provided greater opportunities for exposure to African ideas and techniques through the continuing arrival of new immigrants. Clay resources were more widely distributed in Jamaica than in Barbados and indications are that craft traditions in general had a greater development in Jamaica. From early in the slave period, runaway slaves found havens in the mountains of Jamaica where African traditions could be maintained. These havens persisted throughout the period of slavery. Although Barbadian slaves escaped and sought refuge in caves and forested areas, by the second half of the seventeenth century the island was · fully occupied, the forests were mostly removed, and there were no opportunities for the establishment of maroon communities. Barbados's small size, extensive development and settlement, and proportionately larger white population subjected the slaves to more continuing and direct European influences than slaves in Jamaica.

Although the Barbadian sugar industry used wooden sugar pots in early periods, they were ultimately supplanted by clay pots. Both clay and wooden pots were used in Jamaica, but wood was apparently more common in the eighteenth century (see, for example, W. Hughes 1672:34–35; *Account of a Voyage to Jamaica* 1776:73–74; Renny 1807:136) even though the island's clays were used to produce "water-jarrs and other conveniences of the like nature" (Browne 1789:61). The difference in dependence on and manufacture of sugar pots also probably affected the way in which wheel-made pottery was encouraged in Barbados and, to a lesser degree, in Jamaica. We realize that these factors may not be sufficient to explain the apparent lack of development of an African-based ceramic tradition in Barbados, but it seems likely that the differences between Barbados and Jamaica with respect to African influences on local ceramic traditions result, at least partially, from such reasons.

Glass Beads. Newton cemetery yielded glass beads of European manufacture in specific association with a limited number of burials (table 14). The bead sample includes those made by the hollow cane (tube) and by the Mandrel wound (wire wound) methods (Stone 1974:88). We found thirty different types of beads (figure 26), many of them appearing only in single instances, or in very limited quantities.

The largest number of beads was found in association with six interments from burial complex 30N9W; a few additional beads were associated with Burials 22 and 87 in Mound 2 and in limited nonmound contexts.

The archaeological and historical data show that slaves used beads primarily in necklaces, bracelets, and anklets. The archaeological materials, in particular, not only indicate bead use, but also provide a detailed idea of the types of beads that were employed. Although

144

TABLE 14. Bead types, Newton cemetery: distribution and related contexual data.

| | Burial number | | | | | | | | | | |
| | Mound 2 | | 30N9W excavation unit | | | | | | Open field | | |
Bead type[a]	22	87	55	58	59	60	61	63	36	72	77
CI,SA,T1,Vb	—	—	—	—	34	—	1	37	—	—	—
CI,SA,T1,Ve	—	—	—	—	—	—	127	—	—	—	39
CI,SA,T1,Vf	7	—	—	—	—	4	1	—	30	—	—
CI,SA,T1,Vg	—	—	—	—	—	—	1	—	—	—	—
CI,SA,T1,Vk	—	—	—	—	—	—	1	—	—	—	6
CI,SA,T1,Vq	—	—	—	—	—	—	46	—	—	—	—
CI,SA,T1,Vw	—	—	—	—	—	—	2	—	—	—	—
CI,SA,T1,Vy	—	—	—	—	—	—	—	—	—	—	14
*CI,SA,T3,Vg	—	—	—	—	—	4	—	—	—	1	—
CI,SA,T4,Vb	—	—	—	—	11	152	21	9	—	—	—
CI,SA,T9,Vd	—	—	1	1	—	—	2	—	—	—	3
*CI,SA,T9,Ve	—	—	—	—	3	—	1	5	—	—	—
CI,SA,T10,Va	—	—	1	—	—	34	—	—	—	—	—
CI,SA,T11,Vc	—	—	—	—	1	—	—	—	—	—	—
CI,SA,T12,Vd	—	—	—	—	—	—	—	2	—	—	—
CI,SB,T2,Va	—	—	—	1	32	1	5	—	—	—	26
CI,SB,T2,Vc	—	—	—	—	—	—	—	1	—	—	—
*CI,SB,T2,Vd	—	—	—	—	—	86	49	—	—	—	—
CI,SC,T1,Ve	—	—	—	—	—	—	—	2	—	—	—
CI,SC,T3,Vg	—	—	—	—	—	1	—	4	—	—	—
CII,SA,T1,Va	—	—	—	—	—	—	15	—	—	2	—
CII,SA,T1,Vf	—	—	—	—	—	—	4	—	—	—	—
CII,SA,T1,Vh	—	—	—	—	—	—	—	—	—	9	—
CII,SA,T1,Vj	—	4	—	—	—	—	7	1	—	1	—
*CII,SA,T1,Vk	—	—	—	—	—	—	3	—	—	—	—
CII,SA,T2,Va	—	—	—	—	—	—	1	—	—	—	—
CII,SA,T6,Va	1	—	—	—	—	—	—	—	—	—	—
CII,SA,T8,Va	—	—	—	—	—	—	3	—	—	—	—
CII,SA,T10,Ve	—	—	—	—	—	1	—	—	—	—	—
Agate	—	—	—	—	—	—	—	1	—	1	—
Eroded	—	—	6	—	—	4	23	—	1	1	—

[a] Bead types are described in Appendix C.

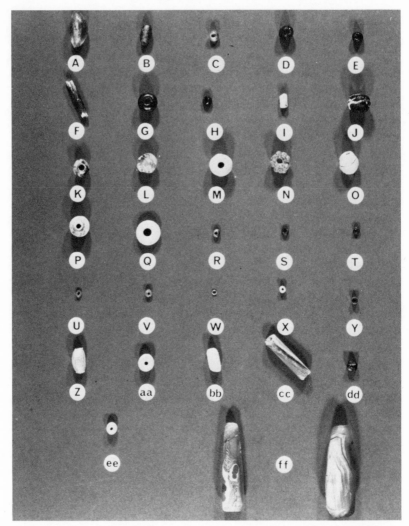

Figure 26. Bead types, Newton cemetery (see table 14 for distribution). Type designations after Stone 1974, with additions preceded by an asterisk by Minnerly (personal communication). *A:* CISAT12Vd; *B:* CISAT1Vb; *C:* CISAT1Vg; *D:* CISAT4Vb; *E:* CISAT4Vb; *F:* CISBT-2Vc; *G:* CISAT10Va; *H:* CISAT11Vc; *I:* CISAT9Vd; *J:* CISCT3Vg; *K:* CIISAT1Va; *L:* CIISAT1Vf; *M:* CIISAT1Vj; *N:* CIISAT2Va; *O:* CIISAT6Va; *P:* CIISAT8Va; *Q:* CIISAT10Ve; *R:* CISAT1Vf; *S:* CISAT-1Vb; *T:* CISAT1Ve; *U:* CISAT1Vk; *V:* CISAT1Vq; *W:* CISAT1Vw; *X:* CISAT1Vy; *Y:* CISBT2Va; *Z:* CISCT1Ve; *aa:* larger specimen of *CISAT3Vg(ee); bb:* *CISAT9Ve; cc:* *CISBT2Vd; dd:* *CIISAT1Vk; *ee:* *CISAT3Vg; ff:* agate beads associated with Burials 72 (left) and 63 (right). Scale: Agate bead (*ff*) on right is 44 mm long. (See Appendix C for bead decriptions.)

only a few historical sources mention beads, they suggest that the use of beads of one kind or another in various types of jewelry was relatively widespread among the slave population.

Griffith Hughes, reporting on the 1730s and 1740s, wrote: "Our slaves, in their mirth and diversions, differ according to the several customs of so many nations intermixed. However, all agree in this one universal custom of adorning their bodies, by wearing strings of beads of various colors, intermixed sometimes by the richer sort of house Negroes with pieces of money. These beads are in great numbers twined around their arms, necks, and legs" (1750:15–16). When Lady Maria Nugent arrived at Carlisle Bay in Bridgetown during the summer of 1801, her ship was "immediately surrounded by boats, with naked men and women covered with beads, and bringing us all sorts of tropical fruits" (Cundall 1934:10–11).

The beads noted by Hughes and Nugent could have been imported glass ones as well as those made from local flora. Hughes, for example, observed that the nut of the "Palm Oil Tree" was "bored and emptied of its kernel, [and] is much worn by several nations of Negroes by way of ornament, about their necks." Slaves also used the multicolored pea-sized seeds of a plant locally known as "Job's Tears"; the seeds were "strung upon silk, and used instead of bracelets by some of the poorer sort [of whites], but especially by the Negroes." Seeds in the pods of the "Moabite" or "Mangrove Beard Tree" were also "strung upon silk and made use of by the Negro women for bracelets" (1750:111–112, 193, 254); local flora was used in a similar fashion by Jamaican slaves (Brathwaite 1971:233).

Europeans used glass beads during the African slave trade (see, for example, Phillips 1746:233), and some beads found among Barbadian slaves were clearly brought from Africa during the middle passage. The Reverend Cooper Willyams observed a slave sale in Barbados in 1794 and noted that "some of them were decorated with beads, given to them by their captors, and bracelets round their wrists and ancles" (1796:12–13). During his visit to Barbados in early 1796, General William Dyott boarded a newly arrived English slaver at anchor in Carlisle Bay: "I observed the females had all a number of different coloured glass beads hung around their necks. The master of the ship told me the chief employment, and indeed amusement, they had was in new-stringing their beads, and that very frequently [they] broke the string on purpose to set them to work" (Jefferey 1907:93–94).

There is no way of demonstrating whether organic or nonorganic bead types were the most common among the slaves, although we expect that they increasingly used local floral materials as the slave trade decreased and as the number of creole slaves rose. Furthermore, there does not appear to have been a ready supply of glass beads on the island. Glass beads may have been occasionally distributed by plantation authorities as a reward, but we have no direct evidence for this or the distribution of jewelry of any kind. Nor is there any direct evidence that such beads might have been distributed through the island's internal marketing system. Beads made of organic materials would not be expected to survive under most geographical and archaeological conditions, and no seeds of vegetal origin were found during our excavations.

In discussing the glass beads found at Newton cemetery, we employ the classification system developed by Stone (1974) for materials from Fort Michilimackinac in Michigan. This system is based on the initial division between tubular and wound beads and then on distinctions in form, design, and color. The system is open-ended so that new varieties can be added as they are encountered. We found five bead types (figure 26*aa*, *bb*, *cc*, *dd*, *ee*) that do not appear in Stone's study, a reflection of the myriad types of beads produced in Europe.

At present, the cultural and chronological significance of the glass beads at Newton is quite limited. As Stone has observed: "Any attempt to date a bead assemblage on comparative and typological grounds should acknowledge the following potential sources of error: (1) certain bead types are virtually useless as temporal indicators (except in very general terms); (2) one or several bead-type associations from two sites does not necessarily define contemporaneous (or even near contemporaneous) site occupations; and (3) sites from widely separated areas may have experienced the introduction of the same bead type at different points in time" (1971:84).

The last observation again emphasizes the need to consider historical factors when interpreting colonial period artifactual material. There are no published comparative references from the Caribbean for the Newton beads, and the only reliable data come from North American sites (see, for example, Stone 1971, 1974; Jelks et al. 1967). Although Higman reports that beads were found at New Montpelier in Jamaica, he does not describe them (1975:8). Stone's extensive bibliography of bead references in his Fort Michilimackinac study utilizes a wide range of sources, but "In several of these reports, only the compound, complex, or composite could be correlated with those from Fort Michilimackinac since simple beads were often so inadequately described that it is often impossible to compare the two" (1974:89). Stone's type descriptions of the principal bead types and descriptions of beads we found that are

148

not considered by Stone are given in Appendix C. Here we briefly indicate the cultural, chronological, and interpretative difficulties presented by the Newton beads.

The most quantitatively significant bead types at Newton were not as popular at Fort Michilimackinac. This is not surprising in light of the different geographical locations and cultural or historical associations of the two areas; but where comparable materials were found, without exception, the ones at Newton are the same as those associated with the fort's French component that dates from 1715 to 1761. Chronologically, Stone's careful comparisons with other sites (1974:108–09) indicates the wide temporal occurrence of most of the Newton bead types. However, Stone's type CII,SA,T1,Va, a seed bead (figure 26K), is present at Newton in small quantities and is dated from 1714 to 1803 at the Southern Compress site and from the "early" eighteenth century at the Fish Hatchery site. These Louisiana sites were studied by Webb and Gregory (cited in Stone 1974:108). At both sites the seed beads are either French or Spanish in origin or manufacture. It is not unusual to find a common form of seed bead so widespread, but CII,SA,T8,Va, a larger necklace bead also found at the Fish Hatchery site, has been assigned dates from 1700 to 1820 by Harris and Harris (cited in Stone 1974:109). Though we found only three examples of this bead with Burial 61 (see figure 26P), it provides a valuable illustration of the wide distribution of various bead types and the difficulty in using beads to ascertain precise chronologies (cf. Noël Hume 1970:54).

Glass beads probably came into Barbados throughout the period of slavery (for example, after the abolition of the slave trade in 1808, the British Navy occasionally deposited Africans, taken from foreign slavers, in Barbados), but the limited quantity of beads at Newton, the repeated examples of single occurrences of individual types, and the concentrations with very few burials suggest that glass beads were uncommon and not regularly obtainable. This suggestion reinforces an interpretation derived from the historical sources. Because slaves apparently valued beads for various forms of jewelry, they may have considered the glass ones particularly valuable. In turn, glass beads might not have been placed in graves on all possible occasions. Thus, although the relative sparsity of beads in the burials can suggest their general sparsity in the slave population, it might be that glass beads were more widespread, although still not abundant, especially in the later years of the slave period.

Both reddish-orange agate beads, found only with Burials 72 and 63 (figure 26ff; see also figure 21), have eight facets and similar shapes and sizes. Each has a hole bored through its length. Although the facets were first chipped or ground, they were polished to a smooth surface. The beads (or agate) came from somewhere other than Barbados.

Burials 63 and 72 had more than the usual amounts of grave goods associated with them. The goods with Burial 72 have been noted previously, while Burial 63 had a glass bead necklace, which included the agate bead, and two metal rings. Other comparisons between these burials are inhibited because age and sex data are lacking for Burial 63. Both burials, however, were east-headed and coffinless, and are thus probably early in date; the relatively early placement of Burial 63 is demonstrated stratigraphically by its depth below the surface in the 30N9W excavation unit (see table 12 and figure 13).

Coffins. Aside from clay pipes, coffin artifacts were the most common type encountered in Newton cemetery. Twenty-nine people definitely were buried in coffins, and twenty-three others were possibly buried in coffins. Coffins were archaeologically detected by the presence of square or round metal handles (both styles are illustrated in figure 27), iron nails, and copper and brass tacks (see, for example, figures 11–15). In some cases nails were found around the peripheries of skeletons, but without evidence of handles. The absence of handles indicated a more rudimentary and probably relatively earlier type of coffin; for example, in Colonial North America until the middle of the eighteenth century, coffin hardware was only occasionally used (Habenstein and Lamers 1962: 206, 255). Some Newton coffins had both square and round handles; the type of handle used appears to reflect the supply of handles on the island, and the types themselves do not appear to have chronological significance.

Chapter 6 provides a fuller discussion of coffin use among slaves, and the presence of coffins with Newton burials is summarized in Appendix A. The correlation of the presence or absence of coffins with other characteristics such as age, sex, and body orientation is discussed below.

Metal Flakes over Chest Areas. Six bodies were found with concentrations of thin, rusted metal flakes, decomposed from rectangular iron sheeting, covering the chest and abdominal areas. All six had a west-headed orientation and all were buried in coffins; there were no other significant correlations.

The thin rectangular form of the metal flakes clearly indicated that they were not the remnants of metal dishes; they were apparently the remains of some sort of metal plate that probably formed part of the coffins. There was no evidence of handles

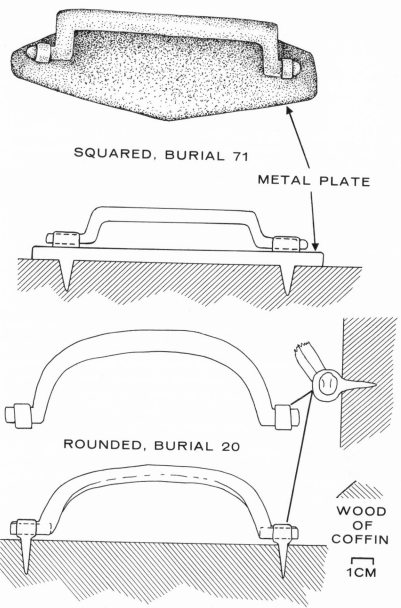

SQUARED, BURIAL 71

METAL PLATE

ROUNDED, BURIAL 20

WOOD
OF
COFFIN

1CM

Figure 27.   Coffin handle styles, Newton cemetery.

attached to these plates, and their nature or function is unknown. The distribution of the plates with burials is given in Appendix A, and their locations are illustrated in figures 11, 12, 14, and 15.

Iron Knives. Iron knives were associated with six burials (Appendix A; see also examples of locations illustrated in figures 14 and 18). All the knives were less than 30 centimeters long and badly corroded; our attempts to analyze the nature and construction of these knives through X-ray examination were nonproductive. Skeletal and artifactual data were correlated against the presence of knives, but these correlations yielded no significant results.

Clothing. European-type clothing was apparently more common among plantation slaves by the mid to late eighteenth century than in earlier periods. (Clothing was discussed in chapter 4 and the questions of how and if slave corpses were clothed or covered are considered in chapter 6.) Archaeological evidence for clothing in association with burials was quite limited. The evidence includes a metal belt buckle with Burial 35 and the textile fragments that had adhered to the coils on one of the bracelets excavated with Burial 72. A few small metal fasteners and buttons were also found (see Appendix A).

Four bone buttons (figure 28) with Burial 64 resemble Stanley South's type 20, which he dated from 1800 to 1865, although he seriated the main popularity of these buttons from 1800 to 1830 in dated contexts from two North American sites (1964:121). The 1800–1830 period is within the terminal phase of Barbadian slavery, and a relatively late date for Burial 64 is supported by its west-headed orientation and the presence of a coffin. Although Noël Hume (1970:90) adjusted South's dates for this button type to from 1837 to 1865, he does not explain the time differential between his range and that of South. Without this explanation and specification of criteria by Noël Hume, we prefer South's original dates; otherwise Noël Hume's entire range lies outside the period of slavery, which is clearly not supported by the Newton cemetery evidence.

Five small shell buttons (figure 28) were associated with Burial 31, but we have been unable to interpret these buttons chronologically. Burial 31 was a young adult female in a west-oriented coffin. A similar button was found with Burial 58, a young adult male, also west-oriented and buried in a coffin.

A metal, possibly brass, button was excavated from square 15N3W (figure 28). Although the square contained two burials, the association of the button with either could not be ascertained. This button appears to most closely resemble Stanley South's type 7 from the 1726–1776 period (as illustrated and discussed in Noël Hume 1970: 90–92). However, as Noël Hume has stressed, this and similar button types "continued into the early nineteenth century" in North America.

The dates given for various buttons cannot be taken as definitive,

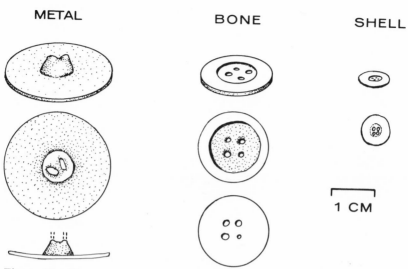

Figure 28. Button types, Newton cemetery.

and the buttons at Newton cannot be used as precise chronological indicators of the burials. The numerous varieties of buttons known from Colonial America, of which the Newton types are common examples, have been an effective deterrent to detailed studies of colonial button types. We must also consider slave clothing types at different periods as well as the probable effect of differential trade patterns between the North American colonies and the Caribbean and England. The buttons found at Newton were almost certainly made in England. Although the four bone buttons with Burial 64 were most probably associated with an item of clothing, the metal and shell buttons may not have been associated with clothing, but may have had a secondary use as part of a piece of decorative jewelry.

Metal Jewelry. Historical sources attest to the slaves' use of bead jewelry; a few also suggest that slaves occasionally wore metal jewelry. Griffith Hughes reported "the wearing of ear-rings amongst the richest of the Negroes," but did not describe these earrings. Although he also mentioned the "use of bracelets," he implied or directly stated they normally were composed of beads (1750:15–16, 193, 254). In 1794, a visitor observed that some of the newly arrived Africans at a slave sale wore beads as well as "bracelets round their wrists and ancles" (Willyams 1796:12–13), but it is unclear if the "bracelets" were metal. A prominent Barbadian planter described a visit he made to a Birmingham, England, factory in 1801. This factory manufactured "finger rings, such [as] you may have seen our Negroes wear"; although the metal rings were not described, the planter noted they were cheap, produced in large quantities, and "sent abroad, particularly to Germany, Spain, and Russia, the common people of those countries having a great passion for ornamenting their fingers with such baubles" (Alleyne 1801b).

Thus, the historical evidence for the slaves' use of metal jewelry is minimal; the archaeological evidence, however, clearly indicates its use and provides examples of various types. Although we cannot determine how frequently metal jewelry was worn by the wider slave population, the archaeological evidence appears to corroborate the implicit historical evidence that such jewelry was not very widespread and secondary in importance (though not necessarily in value) to that composed of beads.

Eleven metal jewelry objects were excavated. Burial 72 had six, while the remaining five were distributed among Burials 24, 56, and 63. We found three different copper or copper alloy bracelets on the forearms of Burial 72. One of these objects is a thin undecorated wire that was bent into a roughly circular shape; the interior is irregularly flat and the exterior slightly rounded (figures 20A, 18D). Evidence for the manufacture of the wire is not clear: it could have been crudely cast in an "open mould" (Cline 1937:82; Hodges 1964:70) and then slightly beaten to produce the tapered ends, or the wire could have been entirely beaten. In either event, the wire was bent into shape after manufacture.

The second bracelet is thicker and coiled (figures 20B, 18C). Holes on the interior and at each tip provide evidence of forging and indicate that a good deal of hammering stretched various areas of the metal; cracks around the side of the coils also show the overlay from rough forging. In his comprehensive survey of mining and metallurgy in sub-Saharan Africa, Walter Cline refers to "metal ribbon produced by hammering and cutting" and manufactured by various peoples of Central Africa into coiled bracelets; the BaNgala of the northern Congo, for example, "make brass ribbon by beating out brass currency rods to the required width" (1937:112). Coiled bracelets are generally widespread in West Africa.

The third bracelet from Burial 72 is relatively thick; it has a rounded exterior, smoothly flattened interior, and a simple design at its flanged ends (figures 20C, 18E). It was apparently roughcast in a straight form and then bent into its circular shape; the design on each end appears to have been hammered into the piece. Although the interior may have been beaten flat after the object was cast, there does not appear to have been a great deal of forging.

None of the rings found in Newton cemetery were decorated,

inscribed, or otherwise marked. Burial 72 had three simple band rings (resembling modern wedding bands) on the middle phalanx of the left hand (figure 18F). Two of the rings (found together at the distal part of the phalanx) are a white metal, possibly a silver alloy, and are identical in size and shape (one ring is illustrated in figure 20D). With smooth flat interiors and smooth slightly convex exteriors, they are extremely regular in construction and were clearly made from a wire pulled through a drawplate. The clean break in each ring was the original solder seam, and the ring was probably formed on some kind of a tapering rod. "Silver was probably never smelted, and very rarely worked in the indigenous Negro cultures" of Africa (Cline 1937:16; but see, for example, Herskovits 1938;2: 356), and silver "was apparently never as prized nor as widely in demand in Black Africa as was copper" (Herbert 1973:193); whatever the case, the rings appear to have been made in Europe.[16]

The third ring excavated with Burial 72 (figure 20E) was found at the proximal part of the phalanx. It is of a copper alloy and was probably made from a wire pulled through a drawplate. The interior diameter of the ring is perfectly circular with a flat surface, suggesting the ring's formation on a tapering rod; the exterior is slightly rounded. The top and bottom of the ring are somewhat irregularly flattened, probably as a result of some sort of natural abrasion.

Two copper or copper alloy rings were associated with Burial 63. One of these (not illustrated) was located over the pelvic area, among the (probably) left fingers. Although fragmented when found, it is a simple round wire band (approximately 2.5 millimeters thick and 2 centimeters in diameter). The other ring with Burial 63 was found intact below the right forearm. It too was made from a round copper wire (approximately 2 millimeters thick), but the wire was bent into four somewhat irregularly shaped coils (figure 20; see also figure 15).

A copper alloy ring from the middle phalanx of the right hand of Burial 24 (figure 12) differs from the Burials 63 and 72 rings in its width, form, and apparent method of manufacture (figure 20F). Its interior surface is irregularly flattened while the exterior is rounded. Casting, perhaps by the lost-wax method, is suggested by the absence of a joining seam and the general irregularity of the ring's form.

We excavated two very small copper or copper alloy rings with Burial 56. We found one ring next to the right side of the mandible and the other by the right side of the pelvis (figure 14). The rings are plain round wire bands (approximately 1–1.5 millimeters thick) and have an inner diameter of 7–8 millimeters. The small size (too small for an adult finger) and the circular shape of these apparently paired items suggest they were earrings. Although a small fragment of one of the rings was broken off and could not be located, the other ring (found near the pelvic area) was intact, but still had a small gap between the ends. This gap, which differs from the clean break found in solder seams, for example, further suggests that the object is an earring. We are unable to explain its location near the individual's pelvis, but this location may indicate a secondary use of the earring, similar to that ascribed to the glass objects with Burials 55 and 60.

The metal jewelry we excavated appears to have no specific chronological value, and the ultimate source of the various copper objects is difficult to establish. Copper and its alloys "were always luxury materials in West Africa" and were highly valued by many of its peoples. Unlike other areas of the Old World, where copper was also used for utilitarian objects, iron was the traditional everyday metal in West Africa and copper was employed almost exclusively as an exchange medium, in material symbols of rank and authority, in ritualistic paraphernalia, and in the manufacture of objects of personal adornment. Although copper in its natural state was rare in sub-Saharan West Africa and was traditionally mined and smelted in only a few areas, it was widely traded and used by smiths in cultural groups that were distant from the copper-producing zones. Copper products were manufactured in pre-European times, but Africans valued copper and its alloys so highly that they willingly traded gold and slaves. From the late fifteenth and early sixteenth centuries, brass as well as "brass and copper bracelets" were used by Portuguese traders in West Africa, and as other Europeans came to the area they also extensively used copper and its alloys as trade goods (see Cline 1937 and Herbert 1973).

For example, in 1694 Captain Thomas Phillips purchased a large contingent of slaves destined for Barbados. In Whydah he found that cowries were "the best goods [with which] to purchase slaves," but "next in demand are brass neptunes or basons, very large, thin, and flat; for after they have bought them they cut them in pieces to make anilias or bracelets, and collars for their arms, legs and necks."[17] Phillips also traded such goods as textiles, brandy, and iron bars, but, he stressed, "without the cowries and brass" the Dahomeans refused other goods or, at best, only took small quantities (1746:243).

The manufacture of bronze and brass, in particular, was very limited in West Africa, and during the period of the slave trade most, if not all, these metals were apparently acquired from Europeans and Arabs (Cline 1937:78–79). The ready-made brass or bronze acquired from such sources was reworked by the smiths of several West African cultural groups. Phillips's observations in Whydah and the celebrated Benin bronzes are good illustrations. Although bronze-casting existed in Benin from the early fourteenth century, the great bronze casting period began after European contacts in the late fifteenth century; Europe became the major supplier of metals for Benin artists (Dark 1973:2–12). Also, although the wire-drawing technique was traditionally found in tropical West Africa, external trade was widespread and the wire used by African crafts-men during the period of the slave trade was not necessarily African-produced. By the seventeenth century, for example, Dutch and Portuguese traded wire in Angola, but Africans sometimes took the coarse trade wire and drew finger gauges from it with their own drawplates (Cline 1937:109; Herbert 1973:180).

It is difficult to determine the ultimate source of the metals used in the objects excavated from Newton cemetery; even detailed mod-ern studies of well-known African art, such as the archaeologically recovered bronzes from Ife, have failed to establish "the sources of the metals from which these bronzes were made" (Willett 1967:56; but cf. Werner and Willett 1975). Some of the Newton objects, such as the rings of a white metal with Burial 72, were probably of European manufacture, but they could have been acquired in Barbados or brought by slaves from elsewhere. Some of the copper objects also could have been European, though others, particularly the three bracelets with Burial 72, could have been made by Africans (in Africa or elsewhere) of African or European copper. Although metal bracelets and rings were widespread forms of jewelry in West Africa, we have been unable to identify the types from Newton cemetery with any particular cultural tradition or congeries of related cultures. Coiled or spiral bracelets, for example, were found among various West African peoples, but so were simple band bracelets and rings. Although there are a wide variety of bracelet types, considerable variations in design can occur within the same cultural group (see, for example, Roth 1903:28, 29, 31). Moreover, the types of metal jewelry illustrated and described in the West Afri-can ethnographic literature are usually ones of more elaborate con-struction, decoration, and intricate workmanship. Also, it is quite possible that the forms of jewelry found in earlier periods were some-what different from those reported in modern times.

It is also possible that some of the slaves brought to Barbados were versed in traditional African techniques of metal work and, of course, slave blacksmiths had access to plantation forges. As noted in earlier chapters, slaves acquired raw metal or metal objects in a variety of ways. Wire and wire jewelry objects were simple enough to produce; items rough cast in open molds did not require an elaborate technology and also could have been made under plantation conditions. The possibility that metal jewelry (although not necessarily the items found in Newton cemetery) was occasionally manufactured by Barbadian slaves should not be discarded, despite the lack of direct historical or archaeological evidence.

In general, the archaeological research did not yield evidence for a number of items that historical sources indicate were commonly used by slaves. Most of these items were organic (see chapters 3 and 4) and environmental conditions easily explain their absence. In the case of nonorganic materials, it may be again suggested that we are dealing with goods that were too scarce to be interred with the dead. Artifacts other than coffin hardware were relatively limited in the kinds or quantity of material with any one individual. Clay pipes and beads were the most common types of artifacts but only the former are chronologically significant. Some chronological data were also gained from china but these data only demonstrated certain minimum dates of possible burial, and most dates centered around the mid-eighteenth century. Beyond minimum dates, the materials could not be used for chronological purposes because of the disturbed nature of the burial contexts.

When buttons and other evidence for clothing are included slightly more than one-third of the burials had some associated artifactual material other than coffin hardware. The occurrence of any single type of artifact, however, was so small that no significant statistical correlations could be made between artifact types and variables such as age, sex, and burial context.

HUMAN SKELETAL MATERIAL

Skeletal remains are quantitatively the largest body of data recovered from Newton cemetery. Because the state of bone preservation was generally quite poor, we encountered several problems in trying to assess sex and age.[18] Much of the information in this section would be enhanced had we been able to specifically determine sex for a larger number of skeletons. Our inability to identify sex precisely for many individuals contrasted with our ability to estimate age for a large number; this disparity affected correlations in which age and sex may have been important variables.

Relative age was determined by using skeletal and dental criteria. Infants and children were classified on the basis of stature and deciduous dentition; adolescents were differentiated from the "young adult" category on the basis of incompletely fused long bones and by the pattern of adult molar eruption. The distinction between young and old adults was a subjective assessment based on the comparative degree of tooth wear. Our terms "young" and "old" have meaning only for the skeletal population under study. Cultural and dietary practices on Newton plantation (such as the type of stone used to grind corn) might have resulted in a degree of tooth wear in an old person who would be considered a young adult in modern society.

Determination of age and sex from skeletal material has a number of well known problems. Weiss has summarized these problems:

> Traditional aging criteria have one apparently chronic problem in that they seem systematically to under-age adults. In many skeletal studies there are no individuals at older ages, and everyone is reported to have died before age 45 or 50 . . . in such cases either the sample is not representative or the aging criteria are incorrect . . . If a population is large enough to contemplate demographic analysis, but is not well enough preserved to be sexed with multivariate populational methods (generally requiring the skull and pelvis from most individuals, at a minimum), at least one alternative method will usually accomplish accurate sexing. In most cases, culturally and biologically related populations have been excavated already in the same area (1973:58, 59).

Though we have no comparative collections from Barbados, population statistics from Newton during the eighteenth and nineteenth centuries (see tables 6–9) give an exact idea of the distribution of age and sex categories we should have expected to find had no selective criteria been involved in interment. Appendix A shows that in many cases general age classifications were possible, and these data are conservative estimates in which we have confidence. Our problem was eased by the fact that we were more interested in differentiating between juveniles and adults in general than with ascertaining more specific age groups and our sample contained relatively few infants and children. Although the skeletal data comprise a wide range of individual ages, we do not have the distribution of sex and age groups that would have been expected in terms of the population data from archival sources (see Appendix D).

Determining sex presented a different problem from that of age. Appendix A shows that we could not determine sex in many cases. The poor state of skeletal preservation prevented using the pelvis as a sexing device in almost all cases. Skulls were usually in better condition, and such nonmetric data as the ramus angle, mastoid size, chin shape, and tooth size were used as sexual criteria as well as the general robustness of the long bones. Weiss noted that these standard sexing criteria tend "to produce a systematic bias in favor of males [by] about 12% ... The adult sex ratio of more primitive populations ... was very close to 50% male. If the sexing procedures applied to a skeletal population result in a sex ratio very different from this, then either the sexing criteria or the data are suspect. In this case ... one should ... examine the cultural evidence for reasons which would account for the observed sex ratio" (1973:58).

The male-female ratio from the Newton burials appears to have significance when compared to expected frequencies derived from archival data regarding the living slave population at Newton. Females exceeded males from at least the middle of the eighteenth century, if not earlier, to emancipation (table 6 and Appendix D).

Some analytical problems arose because of the absence of a comparative population from another source; thus, the study collection from Newton cemetery became its own comparative base. However, we recovered enough skeletons to note general physical characteristics of the population, and we believe that our examination has resulted in reliable sex identifications in the cases where these have been made.[19]

Many of the people buried at Newton were not originally derived or descended from the same gene pools, and inherent genetic differences were incorporated into an initially artificial population. A degree of Caucasoid admixture in the burial population is also suggested by available phenotype information on Newton's slaves (see table 15). Some Amerindian admixture in the burial population is also possible; if it occurs, however, it would be far less significant than the Caucasoid element because the number of Amerindians in Barbados was extremely small (Handler 1969a, 1970).

The skeletal population data are compared with historical statistics

TABLE 15. Slave population of Newton by percentage of phenotypes.

Year	Black	Colored/Mulatto
1796	89.8	10.1
1817	84.5	15.4
1820	84.5	15.4
1829	84.8	15.1

Sources: 1796, Newton Papers (523/288). 1817, 1820, 1829, Newton Plantation (1805–1841).

on Newton's slave population in Appendix D. The appendix also contrasts and discusses expected and observed frequencies of interments according to age and sex.

Distribution of Interments by Age and Sex. The most widely identified characteristic was general age. Age categories were assignable to eighty-two of the ninety-two excavated bodies (Appendix A). Even in cases where burials had been severely disturbed, or had undergone serious decomposition, sufficient dental information was available for aging.

Concentrations of burials occurred in Mound 2 and in the 30N9W excavation unit; the burials in each area, however, represented a range of age categories, and with the exception of small infants, there appears to have been no cultural exclusion of age categories. (In general, no distinction between mound and nonmound burials in terms of age categories appears to have taken place.)

The data, however, indicate that interment was biased in favor of males. As shown in Appendix A sex was definitely assignable to thirty-nine of the ninety-two interments; twenty-four (62 percent) were identified as male, and fifteen (38 percent) as female. If we assume the unsexed portion of the total burial sample follows approximately the same distribution as the sexed portion, then our sample includes considerably more males than would be found in a normal population (see Weiss 1973:58). Such an assumption about the unsexed portion of the sample seems warranted: in seven provisional cases of sex identification, four were identified as males and three as females.

The skeletal data contrast with population estimates and statistics on Barbados and Newton derived from written sources. Females composed over 50 percent of the island's slave population. A similar pattern existed at Newton; data for sixteen years during the eighteenth and nineteenth centuries indicate that females averaged 55 percent (table 6). The excess of males over females in the archaeological sample is significant beyond the 12 percent error that Weiss (1973:56) described as the typical bias favoring male sex identification in most skeleton populations he analyzed (see also Appendix D).

Body Orientation and Position. Orientation data are available for 63 percent of the excavated individuals; after general age, orientations provide the most complete body of data relative to the total number of interments. Nearly all bodies were interred with their heads to the east or to the west; only three were north-headed and none were oriented to the south.

Possible explanations of orientation patterns and their cultural significance are considered in chapter 6. It can be noted here, however, that with the exception of the extended prone Burial 9 in Mound 1 and the partially flexed Burial 68, all individuals were found in extended supine positions. Some tentative explanations of Burial 9 were advanced earlier in this chapter. The problems of interpreting Burial 68, however, are complicated by the facts that it was not associated with a burial grouping, was not in a mound, and did not have associated artifacts.

Preference for east-west orientations prevailed, and west-headed burials predominated (Appendix A). Stratigraphic superposition of west-headed burials over east-headed ones (the reverse was observed only once, in the 21N9W complex) as well as comparison between dates for whole pipes associated with the respective orientations strongly argues for the temporal precedence of the east orientation pattern. However, individual whole pipe median dates clearly indicate this was a trend rather than an absolute shift. West-headed Burials 28, 33, and 81 and/or 83 were essentially contemporaneous with east-headed Burials 43, 55, and 74.

Strong stratigraphic evidence, then, indicates that most east-headed burials preceded most west-headed ones; it must be emphasized, however, that a limited number of west-headed burials were probably contemporary with east-headed ones. The west-headed orientation is correlated with the presence of coffins. Coffin and west-headed orientation data are available in thirty-eight cases: 53 percent of the west-headed individuals were definitely buried in coffins, while an additional 31 percent were probably interred in coffins; only 16 percent were definitely coffinless. Coffins, in turn, reflect a greater European influence on burial practices, and this influence was more apparent in the later phases of the slave period than in the earlier ones; moreover, west-headed orientations were generally more characteristic of European populations than they apparently were of African ones (see chapter 6). In sum, the gradual shift in burial orientation at Newton cemetery may be explained in terms of the increasing influence of European practices in the mortuary complex in general; these issues are discussed at greater length in the following chapter.

Articulation. Because no purposeful secondary or bundle interments were uncovered, we assume that all burials were initially articulated, and that disarticulation was a result of subsequent disturbance. This interpretation is also supported by the fact that no burials in individual contexts (as contrasted to multiple burial contexts; for example, Mound 2) were disarticulated. In most cases, those who buried the dead appear to have been unconcerned by the disturbance of previous interments when reutilizing the same burial area. One cluster of skulls, located in 30N9W, involved the redeposition of three complete skulls, suggesting that at least some instances of more careful treatment may have occurred.

We observed one possible case of intentional disarticulation in Burial 56. The head of the right femur was completely reversed and directed away from, rather than toward, the acetabulum. F. Jerome Melbye, a physical anthropologist, suggested that this could not have resulted from postinterment slippage in the skeleton, especially because the body was perfectly articulated with this one exception (personal communication).

To one degree or another, forty-two of the ninety-two skeletons were disarticulated, reflecting the repeated use of such multiple burial areas as unit 30N9W and Mound 2.

Distribution of Coffin Interments. The twenty-nine definite coffin burials were highly localized in Mound 2 and in two other excavation units of major multiple interments in nonmound areas (30N9W and 21N9W; Appendix A). Determining whether a particular individual had been buried in a coffin was often hampered by the disturbed condition of many of the burials in these areas of repeated use. In many cases we could not determine with which of the disturbed skeletons particular coffin hardware was associated. We can assume that most of the possible coffin interments in Mound 2 (see Appendix A) were, in fact, coffin burials, although the number could not be ascertained.

The distribution of coffins provides another view of the correlation of west-headed burials with coffins and the apparent absence of coffins from east-headed burials. Noncoffin interments clearly tended to be in nonmound areas, and most of them tended to be east-headed. All coffin burials, however, were west-headed and occurred in concentrated areas of multiple interments. We found no clearly defined example of an east-headed burial in a coffin, although three or four questionable cases suggest the possibility of this combination in either mound or nonmound contexts.

Coffins, Mounds, Locations, and Orientations. Twenty-one coffin burials were in mounds, while seven coffin burials occurred in nonmound areas. Probably more coffin burials took place than were explicitly identified, especially in Mound 2. Of the coffin burials in Mound 2, all were west-headed (although one was possibly east-headed). In nonmound areas, all coffin burials were oriented to the west and were concentrated in the 30N9W and 21N9W excavation units (Appendix A).

In addition to five west-headed coffin burials in 30N9W, the unit contained nine cases of postinterment disturbance and four noncoffin articulated skeletons (three east-headed and one west-headed); the one west-headed individual was from an upper level of the burial area, while the three east-headed specimens were from the basal levels. Similarly, the possible east-headed individual from Mound 2 was from the lowest level. Unit 21N9W yielded one disturbed skeleton and one west-headed individual without a coffin, in addition to three west-headed coffin burials.

Twenty-two burials without coffins were found outside the mounds. Four in the 30N9W unit, and three in the 21N9W unit. Most of the remaining fifteen coffinless burials were individual interments whose common distinguishing characteristic was that of having been buried extremely close to the surface.

The concentration of coffin burials in Mound 2 and in units 30N9W and 21N9W may imply cultural or practical significance. Though the presence of coffins for only a portion of the burials certainly had cultural significance (see chapter 6), the concentration of coffin interments in limited areas may have been solely a function of soil depths in the cemetery field. Only limited areas in the field contained sufficient soil depth to accommodate coffins. Because age, sex, orientation, or grave good patterning apparently does not occur among the individuals interred in these areas, we infer that reuse of the areas was primarily determined by practical rather than cultural considerations. Although analysis of the burials and their contexts was often difficult, especially in areas of heavy burial concentration, some general observations can be made.

West-headed individuals were generally interred in coffins, while east-headed individuals were not. This contrast in orientation has apparent cultural and temporal significance, although other data suggest that the generalization should not be extended too far. For example, pairs of clay pipes were associated with Burials 28 and 55. While some caution must be followed in placing too great a reliance on bowl form dates for individual pipes, both sets of pipes have a median date of 1705. Both these burials were from multiple use areas, but Burial 28 was west-headed and buried in a coffin, while Burial 55 was east-headed and coffinless. Although the contrasts in orientation and coffin use support our generalization that east-headed, coffinless burials occurred earlier and west-headed coffin burials were later, in some cases variations in the orientation of the body and utilization of coffins have a significance other than a temporal one.

Position of the Hands. We found several variations in hand positions. In some burials, hands were at the sides, in others they were folded over the chest or pelvis, while in still others each hand was in a different position. In an attempt to detect patterned differences, we analyzed these data in the articulated skeletons. Hand position

164

was observed in fifty-one of the ninety-two skeletons, but in many cases data for only one hand could be recovered. Analysis yielded no significant patterns or correlations with other burial features.

Dental Alteration. Two forms of dental alteration occurred in the skeletons. In Burials 35 and 48 the incisors were filed. Burial 35 was a male while Burial 48 was unsexed, and we therefore cannot determine whether filed teeth were sex-linked. However, this characteristic probably identifies these individuals as having been African-born.

In twenty cases a definite pattern of wear on canines, incisors, and, most frequently, premolars, resulted from habitual clay pipe smoking (see Appendix A). Slight pipe wear is obviously difficult to identify, and our numerical figures are a conservative interpretation of the data. Dental materials were inadequate for analysis in thirty-five cases.

Correlation of Pipe Wear with the Presence or Absence of Pipes. The Newton data suggest no relationship between dental pipe wear and the presence of whole pipes. A positive correlation between individuals with pipe wear and whole pipes might have been expected if the pipes had been placed with the burials for the practical purpose of ensuring the deceased was equipped to continue a favorite habit in the afterworld (see chapter 6).

However, the lack of a correlation between pipe wear and pipe presence suggests the placement of one or more pipes with a particular individual may have had other ritualistic implications. Seventeen burials had one or more whole pipes; of these, five showed indications of pipe wear (table 20). Dental information was inadequate for four of the remaining twelve. Two burials with pipe wear were definitely males, one was possibly male, one was female, and one could not be sexed; two were east-headed, two were west-headed, and one was disarticulated. From another perspective, of the total ninety-two burials we excavated, twenty-one showed some signs of pipe wear. Only five burials showing pipe wear were associated with whole pipes. No children or infants were interred with whole pipes.

Because minor cases of pipe wear are difficult to recognize, it would be unwise to conclude that whole pipes buried with persons not exhibiting pipe wear reflect solely ritualistic behavior. Even in cases where the pipes can be regarded as possibly ritualistic, it is uncertain whether they were the personal property of the deceased, offerings or contributions made by fellow slaves, or tokens of respect or reward from the plantation management.

Age, Sex, and Artifacts. Appendix A summarizes basic age, sex, and artifactual information, as well as data on burial locations, orientations, and coffins. The sample size of ninety-two individuals is large enough to ask questions regarding distributions of age, sex, artifactual, and contextual data. The distribution of interments and their association with varied quantities of grave goods, as shown in table 16, should also permit questions of broader cultural significance to be approached. As Appendix A indicates, however, the substantial data gaps in several different categories limit our comparisons of the skeletal population.

Age categories could be assigned to eighty-two of the ninety-two individuals (Appendix A) because dental data permitted age determinations even when the remains had been disturbed. The orientation category more clearly indicates the high level of postinterment

TABLE 16. Burials with associated nonceramic artifacts, Newton cemetery: artifactual distributions and related physical and contextual data.

Burial	Orien- tation	Mound or field	Coffin	Age	Sex	Whole pipes	Beads	Other artifacts
44	E	33N57W	n	OA	M	—	—	1 button
55	E	30N9W	n	OA	M	2	8	1 iron knife, 1 metal fastener, 1 glass object
61	E	30N9W	n	AD	F?	—	313	—
63	E	30N9W	n	—	—	—	62	2 finger rings
72	E	36N66W	n	OA	M	1	14	1 iron knife, 3 finger rings
77	E	24N15W	n	A	—	1	88	—
86	E	24N33W	P	A	—		—	1 iron knife
22	W	2	+	YA	F		8	—
28	W	2	+	YA	—	2	—	1 iron knife
31	W	2	+	YA	F		—	1 iron knife, 6 metal fasteners, 5 buttons
36	W	31N37W	P	YA	M		31	1 iron knife
54	W	30N9W	+	YA	F		—	1 metal fastener
56	W	30N9W	+	YA	M		—	2 earrings
58	W	30N9W	+	OA	M		2	2 metal fasteners
59	W	30N9W	—	AD	—		81	—
60	W	30N9W	n	OA	F		287	1 glass object
64	W	30N9W	Y	OA	M		—	6 buttons
69	W	21N9W	P	OA	M		—	1 metal fastener
85	W	2	Y	OA	M?	1	—	1 copper pin
87	W	2	P	A			4	—

Note: See table 11 for key to symbols.

disturbance; only fifty-eight orientations could be assessed with certainty. Fifty-seven of the ninety-two were determined to have been definitely buried in coffins or definitely buried without coffins. In several other cases, postinterment disturbances had scattered coffin hardware and nails. Although more were very probably buried in coffins, the additional number of such burials could not be identified.

Sex may have been a factor in determining burial location, orientation, and the presence or absence of a coffin; sex, however, could be determined with certainty in only thirty-nine cases.

Exclusive of coffin hardware, grave goods were associated with thirty-three burials, although in eleven cases these goods comprised no more than one whole pipe, and in four cases only buttons or metal fasteners. Two factors may account for the very limited number of buttons and fasteners: either they may have not been generally used on slave clothing or they were valued so highly that they would not have been deposited with burials except, perhaps, in unusual cases. If, however, buttons and fasteners were simply utilitarian, their identification as grave goods masks the predominant association of grave goods with noncoffin, east-oriented, and earlier burials.

The distribution of artifactual data has no significant correlation with other categories of data, although artifacts do not appear to have been associated with children. In general, artifacts were limited in both diversity and quantity, and this is perhaps another good indication of the material poverty of the slave population; moreover, certain classes of material goods might have been so difficult to acquire and considered of such value that they would not be generally relinquished for placement with a burial. Other factors that might help to account for the general absence of grave goods derive from suggestions in the written sources. Although there is no direct historical evidence from Barbados for grave offerings of any kind, comparative evidence from Jamaica and West Africa suggest that food and drink offerings were made. If such offerings took place in Barbados, they were probably placed in gourd or calabash containers —materials that were widely used by Barbadian slaves. In either case, organic materials were not archaeologically detectable. A related possibility is that food and drink offerings were placed on top of the grave after it was filled in and during postinterment rites. The historical evidence indicates that postinterment rites were as or even more important as interment rites and that food and drink were placed on or strewn over gravesites during postinterment activities (see chapter 6).

Grave goods tended to be associated with east-oriented and coffinless burials more often than with west-oriented burials, with or without coffins (table 16). Following the stratigraphic inference that east-oriented burials were generally earlier, it appears that inclusion of grave goods was more prevalent in the earlier phases of the slave period than in the later ones.

In most cases artifactual materials were associated with individuals for whom there are data from the four main categories of age, sex, orientation, and presence or absence of a coffin (Appendix A). However, the limits of this information are evident. Data in all four categories are available for only twenty-five burials out of the total ninety-two, and in three categories for an additional twenty-seven. This total of fifty-two cases for which there are sufficient sex and contextual data made correlations with other data categories non-productive. The twenty-one burials for which no or only one category of data were available almost equaled those for which all categories were available; for the remaining nineteen, two categories of data were present.

Most of the interments with insufficient burial data were those which had been disturbed; in some cases these disturbances were minor and did not interfere with analytical procedures, while in others significant observations were entirely precluded.

THE GROWTH AND DEVELOPMENT OF NEWTON CEMETERY

Utilizing data from the archaeological excavations as well as some information from historical sources, we can delineate the general sequence of cemetery development. The earliest burials, made soon after the plantation was established in the 1650s and 1660s, were single nonmound interments in the flat area of what is now the grass-land west of Lower Well field (figure 4). Most of these interments were oriented with heads to the east and apparently lacked coffins; however, examples of west-headed and coffin burials also occurred relatively early in the cemetery's history. The earliest burials were more likely to have had associated artifactual materials.

Although single interments without mounds continued to be made, sometime later mounds were constructed over some inter-ments. Mound 1, for example, was apparently constructed during the late seventeenth or early eighteenth century but prior to 1760. Mound 2 was used later; despite its smaller size, it was reutilized a number of times and contained at least forty-five burials. Although Mound 1 was used only once, Mound 2 grew slowly through accre-tion over the years. Though the ceramic evidence indicates a great deal of activity in the mound after 1760, whole pipes associated with disturbed clusters of bones or with individuals laying on the bed-rock (basal level of the mound) predate 1760. Earlier dates from pipes suggest that Mound 2 was used over a long period and that additional soil was added to it from time to time, probably when fresh interments were made.

The increased use of Mound 2 after 1760 is perhaps most easily explained by an increase in Newton's slave population from 171 in the 1740s to 267 in 1776, and more than 235 for all subsequent years until emancipation (see table 6). This increase in the size of the slave population would have resulted in a greater number of annual deaths than in earlier periods and thus a greater use of the cemetery area. Some increased use of Mound 2 and other multiple burial areas possibly also occurred in 1780 as a result of the massive hurricane (see chapter 4).

The 30N9W excavation unit seems to have begun in much the same way as Mound 2 and, perhaps, at around the same period. Like Mound 2, the 30N9W unit was extensively used over a long period, but it never had a constructed or accumulated mound. Major use of the 30N9W unit seems to have been essentially completed by the middle of the eighteenth century, but the area may have continued in use thereafter.

Although age, sex, or artifactual data are not adequate to explain the differential use of the Mound 1, 2, and 30N9W areas, sometime during or after the 1760s coffin burials that were west-headed and rarely accompanied by artifactual materials apparently became a relatively more acceptable style of burial; after these years and with the exception of Mound 1, coffin burials were made in all areas of the cemetery that were physically capable of accepting a coffin.

Use of Newton cemetery continued into the first quarter of the nineteenth century and perhaps up to emancipation. The mortuary patterns in the early years of the plantation's history (pre-1725) generally included eastern head orientations, lack of coffins, and a greater emphasis on placing artifactual materials in the graves. By the middle decades of the eighteenth century, burials showed more European characteristics, particularly in the increased use of coffins and the decreased emphasis on grave goods. A major change in the orientation of the body also occurred, and west-headed interments became more prevalent. The full implications of body orientation changes are not clearly understood and we have not considered this burial characteristic as being particularly diagnostic of either European or African traditions (see chapter 6). In many ways the activities in the cemetery reflect the development and sociocultural changes in the slave population at Newton plantation and presumably on Barbados during the period of slavery.

The general time period of the shift to major use of coffins and the prevalence of west-headed orientations roughly corresponds to the period when the large majority of Barbadian slaves were creoles rather than having come from Africa. By the late 1780s, as was noted in chapter 2, more than 85 percent of the slaves were of Barbadian birth while by 1817, 93 percent were creoles. These population data suggest that creole patterns or European influences were probably reflected in the mortuary complex by this period; this suggestion is supported by the archaeological evidence and information derived from written sources.

6 / The Mortuary Patterns of Plantation Slaves

MATERIALS on the mortuary patterns of Barbadian slaves derive from the archaeological research at Newton cemetery and from manuscript and printed sources; by integrating both sets of data we follow the archaeological approach to ethnohistory outlined by Baerreis (1961). Comparative data on other West Indian slave cultures, particularly Jamaica, and West Africa suggest possible Barbadian patterns when specific information is lacking; these data are also used to help elucidate information in the written sources on Barbados or the archaeological record. Comparative archaeological data from other Caribbean slave cultures are negligible.

In general, the archaeological record from Newton provides some information not available in written sources, but it also defines the inherent limitations of archaeology with respect to reconstruction of ideological and behavioral patterns. Thus, although archaeological data helped us reconstruct this important aspect of slave culture, its limits required greater reliance on written sources.

Despite their importance, however, the written sources do not provide detailed and systematic descriptions of mortuary patterns; also, written information is generally superficial, scattered, and fragmentary; particularly when compared to Jamaica where "the material on the subject is comparatively rich" (Patterson 1967:195).[1] The only relatively detailed source for Barbados describes an urban funeral of a domestic slave in 1796 (Pinckard 1806; 1:270–274).

Although the written sources span the slave period, they do not consistently report on the same topics. We often had to guess dates within broad time periods and also frequently speculate about how common a particular custom or belief was at any given period. Another important limitation of the written sources on mortuary patterns is the Eurocentric bias underlying all observations and descriptions of slave values, ideas, and behavior.

The relatively limited archaeological and written evidence means

171

that a variety of specific questions and issues related to the mortuary patterns of any society, whether viewed diachronically or synchronically, can only be minimally treated. Other significant features cannot be dealt with at all, or else must remain highly conjectural. Nonetheless, we can delineate a number of the more fundamental and general components of the beliefs and practices surrounding death with a reasonable degree of confidence, even if we cannot recapture many details and variations. Moreover, despite the shortcomings in the archaeological and written record, we are confident that this chapter shows how mortuary patterns formed only one dimension of a total ideological and behavioral system that can be identified as slave culture.

SLAVE DEATHS

Tens of thousands of slaves died on Barbados from the inception of the sugar plantation system to emancipation, but we cannot determine the actual number of deaths. Until the second decade of the nineteenth century, when a slave registry was established, the island's central government kept no records of slave deaths or births because, as the governor reported in 1681, "few of them [are] ... Christened" (Dutton 1681). By the late eighteenth century, if not earlier, plantations usually kept complete records of slave deaths, but few of these records have survived and they are insufficient to

TABLE 17. Deaths of Barbadian slaves by sex, 1817–1832.

| | Males | | Females | | | Buried by Anglican church during triennium | |
| | | | | | | | |
Triennium	Num-ber	Percent-age	Num-ber	Percent-age	Total	Num-ber	Percentage of total deaths
1817–1820	3,317	50.2	3,286	49.7	6,603	558	8.4
1820–1823	3,487	51.9	3,228	48.0	6,715	528	7.8
1823–1826	3,409	50.7	3,304	49.2	6,713	739	11.0
1826–1829	3,494	51.2	3,320	48.7	6,814	919	13.4
1829–1832	—	—	—	—	8,587	956	11.1
Total					35,432	3,700	

Sources: 1817–1829, *Parliamentary Papers* (1833a). 1829–1832, *Parliamentary Papers* (1833b). All figures are from the triennial registry returns which ran from July to July. The 1829–1832 figures include the approximately 1,189 slaves who died during the 1831 hurricane. Anglican burials are derived from table 18.

project islandwide statistics effectively for any given year or for the duration of the slave period.

The available islandwide figures, derived from the slave registry, do reflect the number of people who died during some years of the nineteenth century before emancipation. The earliest figures are for the triennium July 1817 to July 1820, and later figures are from subsequent trienniums until 1832. Over this fifteen-year period there were 35,432 deaths, an annual average of 2,362 or about 2.9 to 3.0 percent of the total slave population (table 17). Although this percentage could be projected against available earlier islandwide population statistics to arrive at a crude estimate of the total deaths during the slave period, it is not necessary for present purposes. The point to be stressed is that, taking the island's plantation slave population as a whole, death was not a rare or infrequent phenomenon, and that slaves responded to death, as men and women have done everywhere and at all periods, with a variety of beliefs and socioreligious customs.

GRAVESITES AND CEMETERIES

PLANTATION BURIAL SITES

"The Negroes . . . bury one another in the ground of the plantation where they die," wrote Barbados's governor in 1676, "and not without ceremonies of their own" (Atkins 1676b). A ceremonial context and the slaves' responsibility for burying their own dead on plantations had been established in earlier years (Ligon 1657:50), and these features continued to mark the mortuary complex throughout the slave period.

In 1828, a London-based Anglican missionary society asked the rectors of the island's eleven parishes "in what places are slaves usually interred?"[2] The ministers variously reported that unbaptized slaves (and some baptized ones) were buried "in their usual burying places on the estates," "on the plantations to which they belong," and "in places set apart for that purpose on each plantation" (Society for the Conversion 1829); in no case, however, did a minister suggest where these "usual burying places" were located or indicate if a common pattern was followed on plantations in situating these "places." In fact, the historical sources are generally silent or vague about where plantation burial grounds or gravesites were located.

No known maps show the locations of plantation burial grounds, although a few sources suggest an area in the vicinity of the mill yard or slave village. For example, 1812 records show that among Edgecombe plantation's 210 acres there were two acres of "a bottom containing a pond, trees, & bamboos which has the common burial place." This delineation may imply an area not far from the mill or Negro yard—where ponds were usually placed—but the record does not specify where the "bottom" was located in relation to the three acres "in Negro houses" (that is, the Negro yard) and the four additional acres which included roads and the mill yard (Society for the Improvement 1811–16:43).

Two written sources, however, provide a relatively specific indication of where the burial grounds or graves were located. In 1788 the governor reported

> Negroes are superstitiously attached to the burial places of their ancestors and friends. These are generally as near as can be to the houses in which they live. It is frequent to inter a near relation under the bed-place on which they sleep, an unwholesome and dangerous practice which they would think it the utmost tyranny to alter. These houses are in many estates injudiciously placed in unwholesome situations, where the Negroes are perpetually, in spite of every care, decreasing; and to remove their habitations unto healthier spots, has been found, from that very attachment I have mentioned above, a most dangerous experiment (Parry 1789a:17).[3]

During the same period, the Council of Barbados also noted that slave mortality could be partially explained by "the injudicious situation of their houses, which it would be dangerous to alter, on account of their superstitious attachment to the burying places of their ancestors" (1789).[4]

The written evidence indicates and the location of Newton cemetery clearly shows that graves were located either within the slave villages or in nearby burial grounds. Historical sources as well as the archaeological investigations at Newton and other plantations suggest that common burial grounds were more frequently used than subfloor house graves for interments; moreover, although the direct evidence is slim, the locations of these burial grounds were probably determined by plantation managements who not only considered the agricultural potential of the plantation's lands but also the positive value that slaves attached to having their burial grounds located close to their villages.[5]

ANGLICAN BURIALS: CHURCH CEMETERIES AND PLANTATION SITES

A few slaves were buried in cemeteries attached to Protestant mission stations or, more frequently, Anglican church and, late in the slave period, chapel yards. The Anglican church was the island's official church, its ministers derived salaries from public funds, and from early in the seventeenth century its churches were located in each of the island's parishes. In general, the religious influence of the Anglican church overwhelmingly surpassed that of any other European denomination.

During most of the period of slavery relatively few slaves, especially plantation slaves, were baptized in the church[6]; baptism, of course, was a prerequisite for church burial. There were comparatively few church burials during the seventeenth century and much of the eighteenth. Anglican slave burials did not significantly increase until the early nineteenth century (table 18). Because Anglican clergymen sometimes did not record slave burials and baptisms in the parish registers, in 1826 a law, popularly known as the "Sunday and marriage act," directed all clergymen "to keep a register of the several baptisms, marriages, and burials of slaves ... celebrated and performed in their ... parishes according to the rites and ceremonies of the Church of England."[7] This law resulted in more systematic records of slave burials, but as the rector of Saint Thomas reported in 1821 (in a remark that could as easily have been expressed by other parochial ministers in earlier and later years), "there are many deaths of persons unbaptized which the parish register does not notice" (Maynard 1821). During this period, the island's Anglican church, as a result of external pressures, was beginning to convert the slave population. A few ministers had made sporadic efforts in earlier periods, but it was not until the 1820s that these efforts were more or less systematically pursued. Slave conversion was increasingly emphasized for the rest of the preemancipation period (Handler 1974:172–189).

Although the number and proportion of slaves buried by the Church of England was much greater in the later years of the slave period, a sampling of surviving parish registers for the eighteenth and nineteenth centuries indicates that the church buried relatively few slaves. Most were in Saint Michael (table 18). Probably a majority of the Saint Michael burials were in Bridgetown, where the urban environment provided greater opportunities and incentives for the adoption of European-derived beliefs and practices than existed in the plantation areas of the parish (or the rural areas of the island in general).

The infrequency of Anglican slave burials, especially outside of Saint Michael, is clearest when the number of these burials is compared with the total number of slave deaths. Islandwide statistics on

175

TABLE 18. Anglican burials of Barbadian slaves by parish.

Year	Saint Michael		Other parishes	All parishes
	Number	Percentage[a]		
1678–1679	2	66.6	1	3
1700	0	—	0	0
1720	0	—	0	0
1740	2	100.0	0	2
1760	0	0.0	3	3
1780	14	82.3	3	17
1800	37	82.2	8	45
1810	117	85.4	20	137
1818	138	79.7	35	173
1819	168	81.9	37	205
1820	147	81.6	33	180
1821	162	77.1	48	210
1822	104	71.7	41	145
1823	132	76.3	41	173
1824	160	75.8	51	211
1825	166	69.4	73	239
1826	206	71.2	83	289
1827	152	62.5	91	243
1828	167	65.7	87	254
1829	281	66.5	141	422
1830	178	65.6	93	271
1831	221	61.0	141	362
1832	200	61.9	123	323
1833	229	49.3	235	464

Sources: 1678–1679, Public Record Office (1679/80). 1700, 1720, 1740, 1760, 1780, 1800, 1810, Barbados Department of Archives (1700–1833). Figures for all years are only available for Saint Michael and Christ Church, the most heavily populated parishes; except for Saint Andrew and Saint James, figures for other parishes are available for various years. The totals for parishes, aside from Saint Michael and Christ Church, have been estimated by applying the average of the known parishes to the unknown ones. 1818–1820, *Parliamentary Papers* (1823), all parishes except Christ Church. Figures for Christ Church are from Barbados Department of Archives (1700–1833). 1821, Barbados Department of Archives (1700–1833). Data are lacking for the parishes of Saint John, Saint Andrew, and Saint James; totals have been estimated by applying the average of the other parishes, exclusive of Saint Michael. 1822, Public Record Office (1823). 1823–1833, Barbados Department of Archives (1700–1833). No data are available for Saint Andrew and Saint James for 1823, 1824, and 1825; average for other parishes, exclusive of Saint Michael, has been applied to estimate total.

[a] Percentage of all Anglican slave burials.

slave deaths for fifteen years can be correlated with Anglican burials for the same period. From 1817 to 1832, 35,432 slave deaths were reported to the island's central administration, but only about 3,700 slaves (10.4 percent) received Anglican burials (table 17). Of these 3,700 burials, however, 2,582 (69.7 percent) were in Saint Michael. During this fifteen-year period, the maximum percentage of slave decedents buried by the Anglican church was only 13.4 percent and the percentage was lower in the earlier years.

What, then, was the general practice that determined where Anglican-baptized slaves were interred? In 1817 the rector of Saint Peter reported that baptized slaves in his parish were "interred in the same manner as the whites and free coloured people in the church or chapel yard" (Neblett 1817). The clearest answer to this question, however, derives from information supplied by the eleven parochial rectors in 1828 (Society for the Conversion 1829). They stressed that a crucial determinant of church burial was baptism; baptized slaves were always buried according to Church of England rites, often in the burial grounds of the parish church or chapel where the service was performed by the rector or catechist. However, baptized slaves were also buried in plantation burial grounds. On such occasions, the funeral rites could be performed by the rector, a catechist, or a white member of the plantation staff. Saint Michael was an exception to the general pattern; baptized plantation slaves there were "always interred in places set apart for that purpose on each plantation." Bridgetown's baptized slaves were buried in the yard of Saint Mary's chapel (but not in the cemetery of Saint Michael's Cathedral).[8] The ministers also implied or directly stated that neither they nor their catechists attended the burials of unbaptized slaves and that these slaves were always buried "in their usual burying places on the estates"—never in church cemeteries.

The ministers' information is from quite late in the slave period and probably does not adequately reflect earlier practices. In fact, we suspect that even baptized plantation slaves tended to be buried on the plantations rather than in church grounds during the seventeenth, and much of the eighteenth centuries (see, for example, Godwyn 1680:136). By the 1820s (if not earlier), according to the parochial ministers, baptized slaves were buried in either location—church grounds, with the exception of Saint Michael, being more common. However, baptized slaves were a minority in the slave population and constituted a small percentage of the total slave deaths. Thus, although the number of plantation burials cannot be quantified, the number of baptized slaves buried on the plantations added to the number of unbaptized slaves also interred on plantations clearly indicates that the overwhelming majority of slaves were buried on plantation lands.

MORAVIAN AND METHODIST BURIALS

Other European denominations—the United Brethren (or Moravians), Methodists, Quakers, Catholics, and Jews—may have had some direct effect on where and how plantation slaves were buried. As a whole, however, they played a minor role in comparison with the Church of England. From the early eighteenth century, a catechist was assigned to work among the slaves of the Codrington plantations (although his "religious work was not permitted to interfere in any significant way with the usual pattern of plantation management"; Bennett 1958:140), but United Brethren missionaries were the first who came to work specifically among the slave population. The earliest missionaries arrived in 1765, but some fifty years later, only 480 slaves had been baptized (United Brethren 1814; 6: 436–437). By contrast the Anglicans had baptized over 2,500 slaves from 1812 to 1817 (Handler 1974:164); this number also far exceeded the additional 1,339 Moravian baptisms from 1818 through 1834 (United Brethren 1834; 13:291–292).

From their two mission stations (the second one was established in 1825), the Moravians confined their efforts to the rural areas and almost exclusively to plantation slaves. Although the missionaries regularly reported on their activities and problems, they rarely mentioned the funerals of slave congregants (United Brethren 1790–1836; 1–13). When these slaves died "most of them were interred" in the cemetery attached to the mission station (United Brethren 1831; 12:42–43); however, some Moravian slaves were buried on plantations, a practice which must have been more common in earlier periods.

The number of Moravian burials, whether on mission grounds or plantations, was relatively small. In 1827, 1829, 1831, and 1832, years when slave membership in the Moravian church was rapidly increasing, missionaries reported the deaths of 120 adult and children congregants (United Brethren 1826; 10:357–358; 1829; 11:269; 1831; 12:134–135, 330). Even if we assume that all 120 received Moravian burials, far more were buried under Anglican auspices. During the same four years, 1,350 slaves were buried according to Anglican ritual and practice (table 18). Thus, the Moravians had a much slighter impact than the Anglicans on plantation slave burials.

The Methodists, who started their missionary activities in 1788, had an even weaker, indeed negligible, influence. They generally had difficulty in receiving permission to preach to plantation slaves;

unlike the Moravians, therefore, their activities were largely confined to Bridgetown. Not until 1821 did Methodist missionaries proclaim some success among plantation slaves: on *one* plantation they "selected" for baptism six adults who they regarded "as the first fruits of this mission amongst the thousands of pagan slaves ... living on the island" (Shrewsbury and Nelson 1821a); by 1829–30, only thirty-two slaves belonged to the mission and most, if not all, lived in Bridgetown (*Parliamentary Papers* 1831–32b); at the same time, the Moravians had 620 slave members (United Brethren 1831; 12:42–43).

Methodist missionaries believed that one of their problems in proselytization was the lack of a mission burial ground. Efforts to purchase land started in 1804 (Bradnack 1804), but were not realized for a number of years, a source of considerable frustration. As one missionary despairingly wrote in 1814, as an elder congregant (race not specified) was dying, the Anglican "clergy declare they will not bury her because she was not baptized by them. We have not a foot of land in which we can put her and she must either be buried in some private place or thrown into the sea" (Boothby 1814). When their first chapel was constructed in Bridgetown in 1820, the Methodists gained their cemetery, but it is doubtful if more than a handful if any plantation slaves were buried in it.

QUAKER, CATHOLIC, AND JEWISH BURIALS

In the 1670s and 1680s, Quakers composed the second largest Christian denomination in Barbados. By the late seventeenth century, however, death and migration had greatly reduced the Quaker community. In 1743 less than one hundred, including children, were concentrated in Bridgetown and Speightstown (Peckover 1742–43). By 1810, if not earlier, no Quakers were living on the island (Schomburgk 1848:94–95; Sturge 1908).

During George Fox's visit to Barbados in late 1671 and early 1672, the Quakers became the first group to attempt to Christianize their slaves and to bring them to their meetings. Pressure from the wider white community, including a 1676 law forbidding the practice (Rawlin 1699:120–121), ultimately inhibited proselytization. In general, the influence of Quakers on slaves, beyond a short period during the 1670s, appears to have been slight.

We do not know whether any slaves were permitted to become Quakers, and there is no specific information on the influence that Quakers may have had on slave burials. A 1671 visitor observed that Quakers "in many places ... bury their own in their gardens" (Hull 1671), or, as the governor reported ten years later, "bury their dead in fields and hedges" (Dutton 1681).[9] Although the Quakers developed some community burial grounds, there is no evidence that slaves were buried in them; if, indeed, any plantation slaves were ever buried under Quaker auspices they were probably buried on plantation lands in the same cemeteries as other slaves.

Catholicism was of some importance in Barbados during the seventeenth century, especially among the Irish who were usually indentured servants. But during the eighteenth century and preemancipation decades of the nineteenth, there were virtually no European Catholics on the island. Even those in earlier periods appear to have had a negligible religious impact on the slave population. By the middle of the seventeenth century, however, slaves had been imported (presumably by Dutchmen) from Brazil where they had "been bred up amongst the Portugals" (Ligon 1657:52). Some of these slaves were probably Catholics. In 1654 a handful of Catholic slaves was also brought from the English colony in Surinam by a group of Frenchmen.

Commenting on the religion of Barbadian slaves in general, one of these Frenchmen, a priest, observed that "if any of them have any tinge of the Catholic religion, which they received among the Portuguese, they keep it the best they can, doing their prayers and worshipping God in their hearts." When some of the slaves brought by the French party were sold, the priest reported "they were extremely sorrowed to see themselves sold as slaves in an island of heretics" (Handler 1967:61, 67, 71). We have no evidence beyond the mid-seventeenth century for Catholic slaves. If, during that period, any plantation slaves died as Catholics, they were presumably buried on the lands of their owners because Barbados had no Catholic church or cemetery during the slave period.

During the seventeenth century, the island's small Sephardic Jewish community, whose members had largely come from Brazil, was almost entirely confined to Bridgetown, although some lived in Speightstown. Of about 260 Jews of all ages and sexes in 1681, only three or four men owned very small plantations (Dutton 1681; Samuel 1936). The Jewish community steadily decreased and by the preemancipation decades of the nineteenth century, it comprised about 100 persons, all residents of Bridgetown and all white (*Parliamentary Papers* 1814–15; Shilstone 1966:4). Slaveholding was common among Jews although the number they could own was sometimes legally restricted. The total number of slaves owned by Jews, however, was very small; for example, in 1679–80, when the Jewish community was relatively large, Jews owned only 304 slaves, approximately 0.7 percent of the total slave population (Samuel

1936:51, 63, 90, 91; Public Record Office 1679–80). No evidence exists that Jews ever attempted to convert their slaves and there is no clear evidence that the slaves of Jewish owners were ever buried in the Jewish cemeteries (see, for example, Shilstone 1956, 1966: 7–8).

In all, during the slave period, the vast majority of Barbadian slaves were buried on plantations; of those buried in nonplantation cemeteries, the largest number (but still a fraction of the total burials) was interred in Anglican church or chapel grounds. The Newton data show that many deceased slaves on that plantation were buried in a cemetery, and written sources indicate that on other plantations specific burial grounds were also set aside for slave interments. However, the population data from Newton suggest that some persons, such as infants and small children, were buried apart from these designated areas, but the written sources are silent as to where these interments took place.[10] Baptized plantation slaves were in a minority, and they also often adhered to the beliefs and practices of their nonbaptized peers. The Society for the Propagation of the Gospel, for example, baptized "many slaves" during the eighteenth century, but "very few learned anything of Christian doctrines" (Bennett 1958:140).

BELIEFS SURROUNDING DEATH

Barbadian slaves believed that death was usually the result of supernatural causes, particularly witchcraft or sorcery.[11] Belief in these causes was apparently more common in the earlier years of the slave period (for example, in the 1730s and 1740s, "but few Negroes ... believe that they die a natural death"; Hughes 1750:15–16; see also Holt 1729a), but such beliefs were also widespread in later times. "Even the better sort amongst them," reported Governor Parry in the late 1780s, "almost universally believe in witchcraft, and are so firmly persuaded of its effects ... [that] many of them despond and die when they conceive themselves bewitched" (Parry 1789b; see also J. Brathwaite 1789 and Barbados Council 1789). An 1806 law making Obeah a felony punishable by death stated that "many slaves have lost their lives or have otherwise been materially injured in their health by the wicked acts ... of Obeahmen and women" (Public Record Office 1806). Another law, passed twelve years later, found the earlier one "ineffectual" and attempted to more rigorously circumscribe those who would "injure and affect the life or health of any other person" (Public Record Office 1818).

The belief in witchcraft or sorcery was, of course, found in

Europe, but the conviction that witchcraft and sorcery not only caused death but also were major causes of death was much more common, indeed ubiquitous, as a cultural rationale among West African populations. The fact that Barbadian slaves subscribed to such a widespread rationale in the belief systems of African peoples clearly suggests African influence.

In the earliest years of the slave period, the magicoreligious beliefs of Barbadian slaves were fundamentally African. Even though these beliefs were modified over the years, slaves (whether ultimately influenced by African or European religious thought) also retained a profound adherence to the notion of an afterlife and "the survivance of departed souls" (Steele 1787–88).[12]

The written sources provide few details on how the nature of this afterlife was defined or perceived, but it is apparent that African-born slaves (and perhaps creoles as well) believed in a return to Africa. "They imagine that if they die they will go to another land where riches, honor, and splendor will not be lacking, but where there will be an abundance of everything," observed a visitor in 1661 (Gunkel and Handler 1969:7). And Ligon, who lived in Barbados from 1647 to 1650, noted that non-Christian slaves "believe a resurrection, and that they shall go into their own countrey again, and have their youth renewed" (1657:51). "When these Negroes die a natural death, or especially when they destroy themselves," observed Hughes during the 1730s and 1740s, "they believe that they shall return to their own country . . . and what they mean by their own country is that they shall, after this life, enjoy the company of their friends and relations in another world" (1750:16). Pinckard, commenting on an African-born domestic slave's funeral in Bridgetown in 1796, also stressed how the participants "had full faith in Jenny's transmigration to meet her friends, at her place of nativity; and their persuasion that death was only a removal from their present to their former home—a mere change from a state of slavery to a state of freedom . . . They confidently expected to hear from poor Jenny, or to know her influence . . . before morning." The women who helped inter "poor Jenny" bade her good-bye while asking her to "remember me to all friends t'other side of the sea" (1806; 1:273–274).[13]

By Pinckard's time most slaves in Barbados were creole and at least some of the participants in the funeral he described were probably Barbadian-born. The sources, however, generally do not clearly distinguish between the beliefs held by creole and African-born slaves or provide information that can be interpreted as specifically creole.

In the early eighteenth century, John Oldmixon (who never visited Barbados but had received his information from planters and merchants familiar with the island) wrote: "The foreign slaves believe they return to their own country, which belief they brought from thence with them"; he did not specifically mention the conception of the afterlife held by creole slaves although he implied that most slaves were creoles at the time of his writing (1741;2:12, 135). Similarly, in 1788, when a knowledgeable planter reported "many Negroes ... believe in a supreme being, in the survivance of their spiritual part, and in the expectation of future rewards and punishments," he was referring to non-Christian slaves (by this time creoles were in a majority). He pointed to the "universality" of a conception of life after death as one of "these three points of faith" among the slave population (Steele 1789:28). This belief, whether or not tempered by the influence of European thought, was shared by baptized and nonbaptized slaves (for the latter, in particular, it meant they did not have to relinquish a fundamental belief when they became Christians[14]). Even though their interpretations of slave beliefs and behavior are Eurocentric, the sources agree that an important component of slave religion was a conceptualization of a soul that survived after death and was able to move through space.[15] (Indeed, although not specifically reported in the sources, slaves may have adhered to the notion of multiple souls, a common notion in West African religious thought.) The archaeological evidence, in the form of grave goods with at least some of the burials, seems to support this interpretation.

Jamaican slaves' belief in a return to Africa was "clearly the retention and slight reinterpretation of the common African belief that on death one rejoins one's ancestors. Indeed, the very notion of 'returning home' after death was held by many of the tribes in Africa from which the slaves came" (Patterson 1967:198); Patterson's observations can be extended to Barbados as well. And, in general, beliefs which were fundamental and widespread in West African indigenous religious systems—such as the survival of souls, a journey to the spirit world where the dead reside, and an afterlife (and even reincarnation)—could have been easily adhered to by both African-born slaves in Barbados and creoles.

Regardless of whether possible variations in belief were, for example, a result of different African ethnic backgrounds, cultural exchange among slaves in Barbados, or differential acculturation to European thought, all Barbadian slaves—Christian and non-Christian, creole and African-born—placed great emphasis on the funeral. The funeral had a number of functions in slave life, but its importance was clearly related to a "strongly marked...characteristic," a visitor in 1833 ethnocentrically reported, which is "their superstitious veneration for the dead"; "it is impossible to pay them a higher compliment or please them more than by attending the funeral of any of their deceased relatives or friends" (Rolph 1836:38). And when, in the late 1790s, the manager of Newton wrote about the death of one of his favorite slaves, a Christian, he expressed his intention to provide "a handsome burial—what...[the slaves] esteem the best reward of services after death" (Newton Papers 523/352–1); the slave received his "handsome funeral...as a small tribute to faithful services" and "as an encouragement to others" (523/381–1).

THE FUNERAL

"The funeral is the true climax of life," wrote Melville Herskovits, the pioneer in anthropological studies of Afro-American cultures, "and no belief drives deeper into the traditions of West African thought...The elaborateness of funeral rites in the area is cast in terms of the role of the ancestors in the lives of their descendants, and because it is important to have the assurance of the ancestral good will, the dead are honored with extended and costly rituals...whatever else has been lost of [African]...custom, the attitudes toward the dead as manifested in meticulous rituals cast in the mold of West African patterns have survived" in the New World (1958:63).

For several reasons, including removal from their natal social groupings, the fracturing of their kinship and community ties, the heterogeneity of their ethnic backgrounds, and the plantation regimen and its behavioral restrictions, African slaves could not reconstitute the rituals and funeral patterns of their homelands. The concept of a funeral, however, and the importance attached to the disposition of the dead and the veneration of ancestors continued into the New World setting and provided the foundation for the mortuary patterns that evolved in slave cultures.

Slaves on Barbadian plantations, like those elsewhere, developed a ritualistic complex from an early period in the history of slavery on the island. Judging by the way in which Europeans commented on, or alluded to, this complex it was clearly alien to them in many respects. For example, the island's governor stressed that slaves buried their dead with "ceremonies of their own" (Atkins 1676b). Ligon also suggested the patterned nature of such "ceremonies" when he reported that "when any [plantation slaves]... dye, they dig a grave, and at evening they bury him, clapping and wringing their hands, and making a doleful sound with their voices" (1657:50).[16]

To describe the mortuary complex and to suggest the changes it underwent over time, we outline the sequence of activities from the time of death through the funeral, interment or burial, and postinterment period.

PREPARATION OF THE CORPSE

Various West African cultures prescribed definite lengths of time to elapse between death and burial, and some societies employed diviners to ascertain the most propitious time for interment. We do not know to what extent, if any, such norms were operative among Barbadian slaves. Following either their own beliefs or, more likely, the exigencies of plantation demands, slaves were usually buried on the day of their death or within a day afterward (Ligon 1657:50; Madin 1779; Newton Papers 523/110, 111). Burials took place in the evenings and associated activities lasted late, according to a clause in the major and comprehensive "slave consolidation act" of 1826 which forbade plantation managements from permitting "the funeral of any slave...after the hour of seven o'clock at night" (*Parliamentary Papers* 1826–27a:210).

The historical sources do not mention if slaves were buried in shrouds or clothing, but the archaeological evidence suggests the latter (and also makes it plain that people were occasionally buried with jewelry as well). As noted in chapter 5, excavated artifacts included buttons and a metal belt buckle; also textile fragments had adhered to the coils of one of the bracelets excavated with Burial 72.

Although the direct historical and archaeological evidence is weak, it seems reasonable to assume that slaves were usually, if not always, buried in clothing. There is no record that plantations provided shrouding materials, and the material poverty of the slaves makes the use of shrouds unlikely. The European practice involved clothing or shrouding. Although West African practices varied, most bodies were clothed or wrapped in some manner. In West Africa, both clothing as well as some type of wrapping could occur simultaneously, and occasionally only genital coverings were used. European and African practices and the social conventions of Barbados make it doubtful that slaves were buried naked; although nude burials are occasionally reported for West Africa, they were unusual and apparently occurred only in special cases in cultures where clothing or wrapping was the more customary practice (see, for example, Cardinall 1920:109; cf. Ffoulkes 1909:155, 158). Also, if nude burials had occurred in Barbados, they probably would have been reported because of their alien nature to European practice.

Corpses were probably prepared for burial in their houses or in the homes of close kinsmen or friends. The historical sources do not indicate if corpses were placed on formal display or treated in any ritualistic manner before being transported to the burial ground; however, because such practices are not mentioned may mean very little. In Jamaica in the late eighteenth century, if not earlier, the decedent was laid out and "an assemblage of slaves from the neighborhood appears; the body is ornamented with linen and other apparel, which has been previously purchased, as is often the custom ... and all the trinkets of the defunct are exposed in the coffin" (Beckford 1790; 2:388, quoted in Brathwaite 1971:216).[17]

Only one Barbadian source records that bodies were kept for any length of time after death. In 1806, Major Richard Wyvill, a British Army officer stationed in Barbados, wrote in his diary: "A funeral of black people passed our windows, the attendants all in black. The corpse was excessively offensive in its effluvia, as we are informed that those Negroes who wish to have a handsome funeral for their dead friends keep the body as long as possible, and until they can raise a sufficient sum of money to pay the expense of hiring clothes, etc" (Handler 1975:23). Wyvill's observations referred to townsmen who probably included freedmen (some of whom at one time may have been slaves) as well as slaves. Although the plantation regimen would probably have inhibited delaying the funeral, Wyvill did point to the importance attached to the funeral and also to the emphasis placed on special attire for the occasion.

MOURNERS AND THE FUNERAL PROCESSION

In the late eighteenth century, a Barbadian creole reported that slaves attempted to wear more elaborate attire on "occasion of their meeting together, for festive or solemn purposes" (Holder 1788: 23). This practice was already apparent earlier and persisted in later times. Only by the late eighteenth century, however, do the sources indicate that those who were "decently and respectably clad" (Rolph 1836:38) at funerals wore attire that was marked by a standardization in color. Without mentioning how men were dressed, Pinckard noted that at the funeral he viewed in 1796, the women were "neatly clad ... and mostly in white" (1806;1: 271). Wyvill, also reporting on two funerals he witnessed in Bridgetown some ten years later, observed, without specifying sex, that the "attendants" wore black (Handler 1975:23, 26). In 1833

186

another observer stressed that black was worn by mourners at slave funerals (Rolph 1836:24, 38), while a Moravian missionary in 1830 reported that the women were dressed in white, without mentioning the color worn by men (United Brethren 1829;11:407–408). The sparsity of references and their lack of generalization make it difficult to establish a clear pattern, yet it is apparent that by the later days of the slave period the color of attire had significance within the context of the funeral. Today in Barbados in the funerals of the rural working class, white is the standard color for females while men wear black (or dark) suits.[18]

There are strict standards of dress at contemporary funerals and people only wear their finest clothes. Plantation workers who ordinarily go barefoot and wear tattered, worn clothing would not conceive of attending a funeral without wearing shoes. Men wear their only suits and women white dresses. This dress, usually an altered version of the dress in which she was married, is a married woman's finest piece of clothing. Men, women, and children are as well groomed as possible. Their appearance (and often their demeanor) dramatically contrasts to that of everyday life.

A Barbadian informant described funerals in the days of his youth—at around the time of World War I—before the advent of automobiles in the rural areas. On the day of the burial, the procession left the house of the deceased for the parish church. First came the horse-drawn hearse with the coffin; the immediate family walked behind and was followed by the other mourners. The mourners walked in pairs; the women, dressed in white, preceded the men, dressed in dark, preferably serge, suits. The ambience of the procession was solemn—no noise, no music. Today, however, the automobile plays a key role in the funerals of rural Barbados. Mourners are transported from the house of the deceased where they congregate to the churchyard for interment. Preceded by the hearse carrying the corpse and the car carrying the immediate family, the remaining autos are strung out into a procession that winds over country roads until it reaches the church. Barbadians place great value on riding to church in a car and often gauge the elaborateness of funerals by the number of automobiles in the procession.

Even during the slave period a procession of some kind was an important element in the complex surrounding the disposition of the dead. By the end of the slave period, this procession already had many of the overtones or features that endure in rural Barbados today. In 1833, Thomas Rolph observed "the funeral of a Negro woman," probably in the area of Vaucluse plantation in the parish

187

of Saint Thomas, where he had spent some time during his three-month visit: "The long procession winding along the mountain's brow had a solemn, yet picturesque effect. The mourners were all very decently attired in black" (1836:24). Later Rolph provided a more detailed description of another "spectacle of a Negro funeral":

> On reaching the house, I observed several long forms covered with mourners, all most decently and respectably clad in black. Many females were also assembled in black crape dresses, with black bonnets and veils. Groups of Negroes continued arriving for an hour; at length a large party having congregated, they formed themselves into a procession. They had an abundance of fruit, cake, wine and refreshments. The hearse, a sort of funeral car, drawn by a black horse, containing the coffin, which was covered with small ornaments, and surmounted by a large pall, went first; then the mourners followed, forming a parade, two by two, carrying umbrellas, and extending a long distance. The procession was closed by two mourners on horseback. The whole appearance was decent and respectable, and resembled more the funeral of a wealthy tradesman, than a slave (1836:38).

This was probably not the funeral of an ordinary field worker, and the description clearly implies the funeral of a baptized slave destined for burial in a churchyard. The processions in most slave funerals were undoubtedly more spartan. Funerals were probably also much less elaborate in earlier times than toward the close of the slave period.

The Reverend Griffith Hughes, a careful observer of slave customs from the mid-1730s through the 1740s, reported a procession while alluding to beliefs and practices clearly of African origin: "There are but few Negroes who believe that they die a natural death, but rather that they are fascinated, or bewitched. The bearers, in carrying the corpse of such a one to the grave, when they come opposite to, or in sight of, the house of the person who is supposed to have bewitched the deceased, pretend to stagger, and say that the corpse is unwilling, and will not permit them to carry it to the grave until it is suffered to stop near, or opposite to, that house. After this is complied with for a few minutes, the corpse is, as they think, appeased, and then the bearers, without difficulty, carry it to the grave" (1750:15).

An identical custom was described for Jamaica around the same period and persisted, in one form or another, into the nineteenth century (Patterson 1967:196–197; Lewis 1834:98). Rattray described "carrying the corpse" among the Ashanti as a "ceremony by means of which it was hoped to discover the person who by witchcraft had caused the death of the deceased" (1927:166, 167–170; cf. Danquah 1928:238). The custom was also found among, at least, other peoples of the Gold Coast and in Dahomey (Field 1961:200; Parrinder 1961:152); a similar custom also existed on the Niger delta (Talbot 1932:243). The practice reported for Jamaica and Barbados—and other areas of the Caribbean (Mintz and Price 1976:28)—is so similar to the West African one that its origin in the West Indies can clearly be attributed to a West African source. Because Hughes was the only one to report "carrying the corpse" in Barbados, it is difficult to establish to what extent the custom continued as part of the slaves' mortuary complex. Apparently nothing similar has survived into modern times.

The procession itself became more elaborate in later years and may have been modeled along European lines. Information on processions is largely confined to the preemancipation decades of the nineteenth century and, to some extent, the late eighteenth. In general, descriptions of or allusions to these processions refer to townsmen or those buried in church or chapel grounds. Later, however, as more slaves were buried in church grounds, the procession took on more elaboration and importance probably because church cemeteries were distant from the plantations. Without information, we cannot describe plantation burials (especially those of nonbaptized slaves) or determine if a formal procession accompanied the corpse to the plantation burial ground.

Although slaves, through compulsion or otherwise, sometimes attended the funerals of their owners (Hutchins 1817; Handler 1975:26; Orderson 1842:209–210), the sources convey the impression that whites rarely attended the funerals of nonbaptized slaves. We doubt that whites participated in the processions preceding interment even for baptized slaves. For all intents and purposes, then, the participants in slave funerals were "fellow slaves only" (Madin 1779:22).

The funerals could be limited to a handful of people or could include a good portion of the slaves on a plantation. On the Codrington plantations from 1819, "on the death of any one [slave], the relatives have the intermediate time between the decease and interment, and all on the estate leave their work one hour earlier than usual to attend the funeral," according to *The Christian Remembrancer* (1823:408). We do not know if the Codrington practice was followed on other plantations during the nineteenth century or whether, in earlier periods, plantation managements permitted all their slaves to attend a funeral. A suggestion that close kin of the deceased sometimes had special privileges is found in the work log of Seawell plantation for 1796–97. In one case, five slaves were given the day off from work "because of death in family," and in another "children of a Negro woman" were given "two days off from their work in the 1st and 2nd gang" (Newton Papers 523/111). Although the Newton log for the same year does not specify this practice, it probably occurred at Newton and on other plantations. Throughout slavery, however, the permission of plantation managers or owners was required to attend funerals (permission was apparently not usually denied in the case of close kinsmen), especially if interment were in a churchyard or cemetery.

Sometimes a special group was permitted to attend a funeral. In 1741, for example, a Christian slave died on the Codrington plantations and "all the Christians [slaves] ... attend[ed] his funeral" (A. Alleyne 1741). And, when a slave member of the Moravian church died, the missionary wrote that the plantation manager "gave a holiday to the people who belonged to our church, for attendance at the funeral." She was interred at the churchyard, "the distance being nearly five miles" from the plantation where she died (United Brethren 1829; 11:407–408).

The Moravian missionary also found "the appearance of the funeral procession ... very striking. The women dressed in white, walking in pairs after the corpse, followed by the men." Pinckard, on the other hand, observed that males preceded females: after the hearse came "six boys, twelve men, and forty-eight women [who] walked behind, in pairs, as followers" (1806;1:271). Pinckard accounted for the large number of females in terms of their being the "sud-associates" of the deceased who was a "washerwoman." A few other sources that mention processions suggest that formation in pairs was a feature of at least some processions in the later years of the slave period. Moreover, by the late eighteenth century, in the funerals of freedmen (some of whom at one time may have been slaves), "the kindred of the deceased" followed the corpse "as chief mourners, and after these all that were their friends and acquaintances" (Steele 1789:35); a similar pattern may have been followed by slaves at this period or in later years. The general order of these funerals and specifically the procession of mourners walking in pairs behind the corpse, seems to have been of European derivation (see, for example, Ashton 1883:44; Sidney 1891;1:71; Grant 1961:369; Besant 1925:270).

The degree to which funeral processions were formally organized in the earlier years of the slave period is not known. However, by the late eighteenth century funerals appear to have had a number

of culturally prescribed organizational aspects, such as the precedence of the corpse, the mourners walking in pairs, and the color
and nature of attire. The evidence also suggests that the organization and content of the processional became more formalized and
elaborate as the years progressed.

Hearses and Coffins. The hearse was one manifestation of the
more elaborate funeral content. Evidence for hearses, however, is
meager. Pinckard in 1796 and Rolph in 1833 both witnessed small
horse-drawn hearses in slave funerals. In 1807 Newton plantation
expended over three pounds for "hearse hire & church fees for
[the] funeral of Old Mary Ann," a favored domestic (Newton
Plantation 1805–1841), the only case in the plantation's records on
slave expenditures that a hearse is mentioned.

On Barbadian plantations in general, hearses may have been
occasionally used in the funerals of baptized slaves whose bodies
were transported to a church burial ground and more frequently in
the towns (even for nonbaptized slaves—as suggested by Pinckard),
but the cost of renting them inhibited their use. In any event, the
evidence implicitly suggests that hearses were not common in the
funerals of plantation slaves and were not employed in these funerals
until fairly late in the slave period.[19]

Although each source that mentions a hearse also mentions a
coffin, coffins were more widely used; not all slaves, however, were
buried in coffins. At Newton cemetery, for example, twenty-nine
burials definitely had coffins (additional coffins could not be associated with particular individuals because of postburial disturbance).
In some cases these coffin burials dated from the early eighteenth
century. The earliest explicit historical references to coffins for
slaves, however, are in Pinckard's 1796 description of a Bridgetown
funeral, and the 1796–97 work logs of Newton and Seawell plantations; the latter record that plantation carpenters and coopers constructed coffins for some of the slaves who died (Newton Papers
523/110, 111).

The limited documentary evidence that permits correlating the
deaths of individual slaves with the construction of coffins supports
the archaeological observations that not all slaves were buried in
coffins. On Seawell plantation from April 28, 1796, to April 25,
1797, six slaves died, but coffins were only made for three; at Newton, from May 5, 1796, to April 26, 1797, four slaves died, but
coffins were made for two (table 19). The plantation's carpenters or
coopers made each coffin on the day of death, and apparently were
only called on to construct coffins as they were needed and on an
individual basis.

The sample of deaths shown in table 19 is too small to establish

TABLE 19. Coffin construction and slave deaths: Newton and Seawell plantations, 1796–1797.

Planta-tion	Date of death	Date of coffin con-struc-tion	Sex	Age	Place of birth	Occupation	Cause of death
					Decedent		
Seawell	Sept. 7	none	M	"old"	—	retired	old age
Seawell	Oct. 6	none	F	50+	Africa	field	—
Seawell	Nov. 17	Nov. 17	F	50+	Seawell	sick nurse	old age?
Seawell	Nov. 21	Nov. 21	F	30+	Seawell	unemployed	leprosy
Seawell	Jan. 1	none	M	40	Seawell	field	—
Seawell	Jan. 11	Jan. 11	F	30	Seawell	field	childbirth
Newton	Oct. 18	none	M	60+	Newton	retired	old age
Newton	Nov. 21	Nov. 21	F	50+	Newton	livestock	dysentery
Newton	Nov. 27	none	F	21	Newton	field	dysentery
Newton	March 9	March 9	M	60+	Newton	basketmaker	old age

Sources: Seawell, Newton Papers (523/111, 316). Newton, Newton Papers (523/110, 315). Deaths and coffin-building could only be correlated for Newton from May 5, 1796, to April 26, 1797, and for Seawell from April 28, 1796, to April 25, 1797. All the decedents were phenotypically black; no data show whether any were baptized.

a pattern of what categories of slaves received coffins or what criteria were significant in determining who would be buried in a coffin. Baptism, which may have been an important variable in coffin use, is not recorded for the plantations' slaves. In any event, we suspect that the most important factor was the personal value that the plantation manager placed on a slave; the coffin was, in effect, a plantation reward and one of the items that, for example, the manager of Seawell and Newton had in mind when he emphasized that slaves attached great weight to having a "handsome burial" (Newton Papers 523/352–1). In general, coffins were probably more regularly used on Newton, Seawell, and other Barbadian plantations as the slave period drew to a close.

Only one source mentions that the coffin in a slave funeral was "covered with small ornaments" (Rolph 1836:38), but the failure of other historical sources to mention ornamentation or, indeed, the early use of coffins means very little. The archaeological evidence shows that some coffins had ornaments or furniture—at least in the form of metal handles and plates—and date from the early eighteenth century. There is no reason to suppose that coffin use at Newton deviated from the pattern that existed on other Barbadian plantations.[20]

In general, coffin use among Barbadian slaves appears to have been the result of European influence. Although we do not know the shape or design of the coffins, the historical sources implicitly suggest (by not commenting that there was anything exceptional about them) that they were probably of "a conventional Old World form"—that is, octagonal—a coffin type that was also widespread in Colonial America (Habenstein and Lamers 1962:256).

Both the archaeological and historical evidence also indicate that normally only one corpse was placed in a coffin. However, when great numbers of people died at one time during epidemics or as a result of hurricanes, practical expediency dictated that a coffin contained more than one corpse. An eyewitness account of the massive hurricane of 1831 mentioned that "wherever one turns, there are coffins to be met with, in each of which two poor creatures are in many instances conveyed to the grave" (quoted in Schomburgk 1848:59–60). Although not specifically mentioned, we assume that in some cases the comment applied to slaves because they accounted for about 75 percent of the deaths caused by this hurricane.

Under normal circumstances, multiple interments (with or without coffins) were not a characteristic feature of the slave mortuary complex. The historical sources imply that single interments were the rule, and, aside from the hurricane-related deaths there is no other direct evidence of multiple interments in historical sources. Among the ninety-two burials we identified at Newton cemetery, only two pairs, in both cases a probable man and a small child (but not a newborn infant), could be positively identified as multiple interments. We find it difficult to explain these cases, although the persons involved in each case probably died at the same time.[21] In any event, except for reasons of epidemics or natural disasters, the number of people who died annually on Newton plantation (and, presumably, on other plantations), including women in childbirth, would have generally mitigated against the possibility of multiple interments (see Appendix D).

Whether buried in a coffin or whether a hearse was used, the corpse was "conveyed to the grave" by bearers, but the historical sources do not specify if any norms governed their selection and number. The two sources that mention bearers imply that they were men (Hughes 1750:19; Pinckard 1806; 1:271–272). The coffin bearers themselves were participants in the funeral procession.

Ambience. In 1796, Pinckard described a Bridgetown funeral of an African-born "washerwoman" slave. The participants followed the coffin, "but I cannot say as deeply afflicted mourners ... Grief and lamentations were not among them; nor was even the semblance thereof assumed. No solemn dirge was heard ... no fearful silence held. It seemed a period of mirth and joy. Instead of weeping and bewailing, the followers jumped and sported as they passed along, and talked and laughed with each other, in high festivity. The procession was closed by five robust negro fishermen, who followed behind playing antic gambols, and dancing all the way to the grave." While the coffin was lowered into the grave, "many [of the participants at the funeral] were laughing and sporting the whole time" (1806; 1:271–272).

The white Barbadian author of the novel *Creoleana* alluded to a similar atmosphere. The novel was written in the late 1830s but its setting was Barbados in the last quarter of the eighteenth century. Slave funerals were marked with "hilarity which ... amounted to little less than revelry and debauch, created by the profuse introduction of 'burnt wine' and 'sangaree' " (Orderson 1842:117). The novel, however, described the death of a "mulatto" domestic slave whose "remains ... were attended to the grave by a solemn procession of all the most respectable negroes and mulattoes of Staffords and the neighboring estates," and the novelist expressed, "with Christian satisfaction," that, at the time of his writing, "the solemnity of these occasions" was more widespread.[22]

Other references to slave funerals in the 1830s (United Brethren 1829;11:407; Rolph 1836:24, 38) also convey a picture of more "solemn" processions than those of earlier times. Neither reference alludes to an air of "high festivity" or "hilarity" nor an ambience of "mirth and joy." However these later references, including the slave funeral mentioned in *Creoleana*, refer to the funerals of baptized plantation slaves who were destined for churchyard burials. Similarly, a comment on the funerals held by "Free Negroes" in Bridgetown during the late 1780s, when one of their number had been "wantonly shot by some angry white man," described the atmosphere as "solemn ... quite peaceable, silent, and inoffensive" (Steele 1789:35). Although the atmosphere at these funerals may have been tempered by the protest freedmen were expressing, at this period "the greater part" of "Free Negroes" were baptized (Parry 1789a:18), and many subscribed to the values and shared the cultural practices of the white population (Handler 1974:208–217). Slaves probably also attended the funerals of freedmen (freedmen often had slave kinsmen and mates), and by the nineteenth century, if not earlier, the funeral processions of Christian slaves probably had the character and general atmosphere found, or expected, in the processions of Europeans or white creoles. To what extent this atmosphere existed in the funerals of unbaptized plantation slaves, even during the late period of slavery, is difficult to say. Whatever this ambience, however, the important role of music, including singing, dancing, and instrumentation was one of the major differences between European and slave funerals.

In Barbados in general, musical forms and expression were one of the more prominent complexes in slave culture. From an early period of slavery, music was "an integral part of the slaves' system of religious beliefs and practices," manifesting itself in mortuary patterns and strongly reflecting the West African influence (Handler and Frisbie 1972:6, 14, 33–34).[23] For example, Ligon reported that while burying their dead, slaves were "clapping and wringing their hands, and making a doleful sound with their voices" (1657: 50). Hughes, describing slave funerals in the 1730s and 1740s, reported that "most young people sing and dance, and make a loud noise with rattles, as they attend the corpse to its interment" (1750:15). In the late eighteenth century Pinckard (1806;1:270–274) and Orderson (1842:37) also stressed or alluded to the importance of various forms of musical expression in the mortuary complex. One of the clauses in the "slave consolidation act" of 1826 prohibited "any heathenish or idoltarous music, singing, or ceremonies" at slave funerals (*Parliamentary Papers* 1826–27a:210) although it is not known what specific effects this clause had on individual plantations.

In a unique reference, Pinckard wrote that on reaching the burial ground "the corpse was taken from the hearse, and borne by eight Negroes, not upon their shoulders, but upon four clean white napkins placed under the coffin. The body was committed to the grave, immediately on reaching it" (1806;1:271–272).

INTERMENT

Under normal circumstances, plantation managements apparently did not interfere with interment and postinterment behavior. It was not until the 1820s, as noted above, that legislative action simultaneously tried to encourage the Christianization of slaves and to eliminate "heathenish" practices.

The historical sources and the archaeological evidence agree that slaves were buried in freshly excavated graves—the universal practice among West African peoples—and not, for example, in surface or above-surface sites. We do not know how it was decided who would be buried under a house and how specific locations in plantation communal burial grounds were selected. Only Hughes reported a particular custom surrounding the excavation of a grave: "If . . . in digging a grave, they find a stone which they cannot easily get out, they immediately conclude that the deceased is unwilling to be buried there; therefore they dig elsewhere, until they find a place more propitious to the supposed inclination of the dead" (1750:15).[24] We do not know if this custom also applied to slaves buried under house floors. Similarly, the historical sources provide no information on the rules, if any, governing who was charged with digging the grave. In graves excavated under houses, perhaps the gravediggers stood in a special relationship, kinship or otherwise, to the deceased, and there may have been a similar norm with respect to gravesites in plantation communal burial grounds. Among West African peoples, the gravediggers were often kinsmen, of one kind or another, of the deceased.

Pinckard observed that "the body was committed to the grave, immediately on reaching it, without either prayer or ceremony; and the coffin, directly, covered with earth" (1806;1:272). However, some "ceremony" may have taken place during interment, especially of the more Africanized plantation slaves during earlier periods. In Jamaica, in the early eighteenth century at least, gravesite rituals were performed at interment and if the decedent "be one whose circumstances could allow it, or if he be generally beloved, the Negroes sacrifice a hog in honour of him; which they contribute to the expenses of among themselves . . . the nearest relation kills it, the entrails are buried, the four quarters are divided, and a kind of soup made, which is brought in a calabash or gourd, and, after waving it three times, it is set down; then the body is put in the ground" (Leslie 1740:307–310, quoted in Patterson 1967: 196–197).[25]

ORIENTATION AND POSITION OF THE CORPSE

The historical sources for Barbados yield a little information on the selection and preparation of gravesites, but they do not mention the specific manner in which the corpse was interred in the ground. The archaeological record from Newton cemetery provides the only information on such practices. Our data show that consideration was given to the positioning and directional orientation of the body. Of the ninety-two burials, body orientation could be ascertained in fifty-eight cases. Fifty-five (95 percent of the sample) were buried along an east-west axis (in seventeen cases the head was to the east, and in thirty-eight cases it was to the west). Only three were laid out in a north-south position with the head to the north, but we have not been able to ascertain if this orientation had any cultural significance.[26]

The reasons for the east-west pattern are not clear. East-headed burials may suggest some emphasis on orientation toward Africa, which lies east of Barbados. Because east-headed burials (without coffins) were generally earlier than those headed west they were more likely to have been of African-born individuals (or first-generation creoles), and, as discussed earlier, a widespread belief was that through death one returned to Africa. However, there were some relatively early coffinless burials headed west, and west-headed burials were the most common type. Unless we can assume that these burials reflected emphasis on the eyes' facing east, the significance of orientation in relation to the direction of Africa must remain entirely conjectural.

If value was attached to the direction in which the eyes faced, the slaves may have adopted the European practice, but, perhaps, with a different underlying rationale since most slaves were not Christians. The nineteenth-century English anthropologist Edward Tylor reported that the standard "Christian usage of digging graves east and west, which prevailed through mediaeval times, is not yet forgotten. The rule of laying the head to the west, and its meaning that the dead shall rise looking toward the east . . . still remain established in modern European religion" (1958:509–512; cf. Ariès 1974:8). H. J. Rose also noted "the usual practice throughout Christendom" of placing the body with the head to the west so that the deceased would "rise facing the Lord," to the east, "on the Second Coming" (Rose 1922:127; cf. Genovese 1974: 198). This orientation pattern, which was followed in Anglican practice, may be reflected in the west-headed burials at Newton that tend to be later than the east-headed ones. At any rate, West African data indicate a variety of orientation practices (and explanations), including east-west positioning, and the possibility of West African influence cannot be discounted.[27]

African sources also suggest that sometimes the direction of the feet was emphasized in body orientation practices. For example, among some peoples of Sierra Leone, "the body is buried . . . with the feet facing eastward, so that the thunderstorms which blow from the east may 'blow the spirit back to its former home'" (McCulloch 1950:84). Among the Edo of the Benin kingdom in Nigeria "the corpse is laid in the grave with the feet pointing to the west, that is towards... the old port of Benin, where the dead are believed to embark in canoes and cross the sea to the spirit world which lies beyond the dome of the sky" (Bradbury 1965:104).

In general, we assume that Newton slaves, especially in the earlier periods, subscribed to beliefs that were fundamentally African. Because of the variety of African practices in orientation, however, it is probably better to view orientation patterns (and, for that matter, many other features of the mortuary complex) as generalized features related to ideas concerning the passage of the soul, rather than to interpret them rigidly as representing any single set of beliefs or reflecting a particular African cultural tradition.

With two exceptions, Newton burials were found in extended, supine positions. Although extended-supine interments were apparently highly characteristic of Christian and Northern European burial practices (see, for example, Hazlitt 1965:285; Boase 1972:112; Hartley and Elliot 1926, plate 17; Rose 1922:127), they were also found in West Africa where flexed and lateral burials were also common.[28] In such West African burials, hands were commonly placed near the head or under the cheeks, most often in the "sleeping" position. The African data on hand positioning are generally very sparse, but we can assume that when burials were extended and supine the hands were placed along the sides or over the pelvic or chest area, as in European practice. In no case were the hands placed under the head or cheeks at Newton cemetery; this is undoubtedly related to the fact that we found no flexed burials (aside from one that was partially flexed), a feature that might have been expected given the African influences on the mortuary complex in general. At Newton cemetery we observed a variety of hand positions: in some burials hands were at the sides or folded over the chest or pelvic area; in others each hand was in a different position. We could not find, however, any statistically significant patterning among the various hand positions.

Explaining the single prone burial in Newton cemetery also raises a problem. Burial 9 was not only interred in a prone position, but also was the solitary interment in Mound 1; these unique features suggest that the woman possessed some unusual but unknown characteristics. We were unable to find any indication of prone burial positions in Europe or in the West Indian historical literature. Our survey of the West African ethnographic literature yielded only one specific reference to prone burials, and this reference suggests a broad explanation, involving a negatively viewed death, for the prone burial in Newton cemetery.

Among some Coastal Bantu peoples of the Cameroons, as among

other West African peoples, "abnormal" burial rites were performed for albinos, twins, firstborn children dying as infants, and
"for persons with supernatural powers." In particular, there was a
belief, apparently shared by neighboring peoples, in "a special
form of witchcraft" called *Nyongo*. The "people believed to have
Nyongo ... [were] buried face downward so that if they attempt
to come out of their graves they will move in the wrong direction"
(Ardener 1956:90, 105–106). We are not maintaining that Burial 9
can be specifically explained in terms of *Nyongo*, but a special
feature such as this is suggestive, especially when combined with
broader evidence from West Africa that people with unusual
characteristics or negatively viewed traits were buried differently
from others. Burial 9 may have been viewed as a special type of
witch or Obeah woman and her interment probably reflected an
African cultural influence. The late seventeenth- or early eighteenth-century date of the burial coincides with a period when most
Barbadian slaves were either African-born or first-generation
creoles.

GRAVE GOODS

The historical sources on Barbados do not mention if slaves were
buried with nonorganic materials, such as tobacco pipes, pottery,
jewelry, or other objects, or organic goods, such as food or drink.
In 1687–88, however, Hans Sloane observed that when Jamaican
slaves died "their country people make great lamentations, mourn-
ings, and howlings about them expiring, and at their funeral throw
in rum and victuals into their graves, to serve them in the other
world. Sometimes they bury it in gourds, at other times spill it on
the graves" (1707;1:xlviii). John Taylor, whose account of Jamaican slave life was also based on a residence during 1687 and 1688,
reported: "When those slaves die they make a great adoe at their
burials for having caryed them to the grave in a very mournfule
manner ... both men & women which accompany the corpse sing
and howle in a sorrowfull manner in their own language till being
com to the grave, into which the[y] gently put the corpse, and
with it casadar bread, rosted fowles, sugar, rum, tobacco, & pipes
with fier to light his pipe withall,[29] and this they doe ... in order
to sustain him in his journey beyond those pleasant hills in their
own country [Africa] whither they say he is now goeing to live
at rest" (1688;2:544). By 1687–88, many Jamaican slaves had come
from Barbados or had been transported from the West African
Gold Coast (Patterson 1967:134–135), and the placement of grave
goods may have been an aspect of the interment "ceremonies"

alluded to by seventeenth-century commentators on Barbadian slave life.

In the early 1720s, while at a slave trading post on the Gold Coast, John Atkins learned from an African trader who spoke some English that "the putting up of a few necessaries with the corps [*sic*], such as they loved, is our way of respecting the deceased"; the "necessaries" included "pipes, tobacco, brandy, or whatever else the deceased loved or wanted" (1735:80, 85–86). We gathered information on burial practices from some sixty to seventy West African cultures, but the literature mentioned only one broad group, the Ashanti and related Gold Coast peoples, that used tobacco pipes as grave goods. Ellis reported that goods interred with the wealthy included "gold ornamented pipes" (1887:240) while Ffoulkes noted that in the burial of a chief, "inside the coffin, and near the head, are placed a pipe (if the chief was a smoker), or snuff, etc., and all his best jewels" (1909:158, 155–156).

West African peoples commonly placed goods inside the grave with the corpse. These goods could variously include food and drink, pottery containers, fine cloths and clothing, mats, kola nuts, tobacco, money, beads, cowry shells, jewelry (such as copper rings and bracelets), gold dust, soap, and other personal articles or possessions such as knives. They were viewed as presents or gifts to the ancestors the deceased was about to meet, as necessities to assist on his journey and residence in the spirit world, to keep him from being ashamed at having insufficient possessions in his new home, or to help him maintain the same position in the afterlife that he enjoyed before death.[30] The quality and quantity of these goods, of course, often varied according to the wealth and status of the deceased. Placing offerings or goods inside the graves can be distinguished from placing food and goods on top of the filled-in grave during interment rites. Both practices, however, could exist in the same society and occur during the same burial.

Although the literary sources on Barbados fail to report if organic and nonorganic materials were interred with burials, the archaeological evidence clearly indicates the practice. The amount of artifactual material associated with individual burials, however, was quite limited. We found the largest percentage of grave goods with the earlier burials—that is, those burials that occurred when there were a greater number of African-born slaves or first-generation creoles. The function of burial artifacts may have related to African or African-type beliefs, but we cannot archaeologically demonstrate if grave goods reflected the slaves' religious beliefs in an afterlife.

Furthermore, there was no overall correlation between the presence or absence of grave goods and particular age or sex groups. In general, we do not know to what extent, if any, interment and postinterment procedures and ritual for adults varied with the sex and status of the slave in his or her community. As we discussed in chapter 2, Obeah practitioners had great influence and probably prestige in their communities in Barbados (as in Jamaica; see Brathwaite 1971:162–163, 219; Patterson 1967:182–190). The uniquely large quantity of materials associated with Burial 72 (see chapter 5) suggests that he was some type of an Obeah man or at least someone who enjoyed a special status within the Newton slave community. However, Burial 9, which was interred by itself in Mound 1 and was roughly contemporaneous with Burial 72, may have been a witch or negatively viewed Obeah woman, and completely lacked artifactual material.

No other sociologically defined status or wealth distinctions among the slaves can be suggested by the archaeological evidence. Indeed, if we rely only on this evidence, any distinctions among slaves, as indicated by the historical record and described in chapter 4, would be overlooked. On the other hand, the archaeological evidence showing the existence of grave goods (and patterning in body orientation) provides a good illustration of the limitations of the historical sources.

The archaeology also allowed us to examine the possibility that slaves placed coins over the eyes of the dead at the time of burial. A Barbadian writer reported in 1942 that particular types of copper coins "were often used by the people to close the eyes of their dead and they still occasionally come to light when old burial grounds are disturbed for building or other purposes" (Aspinall 1942:113). The coins were minted in 1788 and 1792, apparently for use as tokens on some Barbadian plantations; referred to as the "Pineapple" and "Neptune" pennies, respectively, the coins are collectively known as the "Barbados Pennies" (Pridmore 1965:77, 82–84; 1962). Primary historical sources do not mention this use of coins in slave burials, and excavations at Newton and elsewhere in Barbados did not yield any type of coinage. Thus, the origin of the custom during the slave period is not supported by written or archaeological evidence.[31]

GRAVESITE RITUALS

Documentary data about the treatment of the grave after the body had been interred are limited. In the 1796 urban funeral of a slave washerwoman, Pinckard observed that after placement in the grave, the coffin was immediately "covered with earth. In doing this, much decent attention was observed. The mould was not shovelled in roughly with the spade . . . but was first put into a basket, and then carefully emptied into the grave; an observance which might be adopted in England"—thus suggesting the non-European nature of this practice (1806;1:272; cf. Genovese 1974: 200). While the grave was being filled "an old negro woman chanted an African air, and the multitude joined her in the chorus. It was not in the strain of a hymn . . . but was loud and lively, in unison with the other gaieties of the occasion." Pinckard went on:

> From the moment the coffin was committed to the earth, nothing of order was maintained by the [funeral] party. The attendants dispersed in various directions, retiring, or remaining, during the filling up of the grave, as inclination seemed to lead. When the whole of the earth was replaced several of the women, who had staid to chant, in merry song, over poor Jenny's clay, took up a handful of the mould, and threw it down again upon the grave of their departed friend, as the finishing of the ceremony, crying aloud "*God bless you, Jenny! good-by! remember me to all friends t'other side of the sea, Jenny! Tell 'em me come soon! Good-by, Jenny, good-by! See for send me good —— to-night, Jenny! Good-by, good night, Jenny, good-by!*" All this was uttered in mirth and laughter, and accompanied with attitudes and gesticulations expressive of any thing but sorrow or sadness (1806;1:273).[32]

Pinckard's description points to the importance attached to grave dirt, an importance confirmed by other observers in different contexts. Pinckard, however, was the only one to provide any information on what transpired during and after the grave was filled; thus the extent to which his description can be extended to the funerals of plantation slaves in the same period (as well as earlier and later ones) is a matter of speculation. However, the significance of grave dirt and postinterment rites honoring the dead make it likely that similar activities took place at plantation burial grounds.[33]

Indeed, Barbadian slave customs, at least in earlier periods, were probably similar to Jamaican practices. In 1687–88, John Taylor observed that after offerings had been placed in the grave, Jamaican slaves "fill up the grave, and eat and drink thereon, singing in their own language [and] verey dolefully desirring the dead corpse (by kissing the grave) to acquaint their father, mother, husband, & other relations of their present condition & slavery as he passes thru their countrey towards the plesant mountains, which message they bellow out to the dead corpse in a dolefull sound, and goe kiss the grave & depart (1688;2:544). Another Jamaican source, dating from the early eighteenth century, described how while the body was covered "with earth, the attendants scream out in a terrible manner, which is not the effect of grief, but of joy." Sometimes a hog had been sacrificed and a "soup" prepared; "after the grave is filled up, they place the soup ... at the head, and a bottle of rum at the feet. In the meantime cool drink ... is distributed amongst those who are present; one half of the hog is burned while they are drinking, and the other is left to any person who pleases to take it ... and so the ceremony ends" (Leslie 1740:307–310, quoted in Patterson 1967:196–197; as previously suggested, these practices were West African in character).

GRAVE MARKERS AND MOUNDS

Our archaeological investigations at Newton and elsewhere on the island suggest that grave markers or gravestones were not erected or placed over gravesites in plantation burial grounds. Moreover, only one written source mentions grave markers of any kind for plantation slaves. Although the absence of such references is not conclusive, the fact that grave markers are not mentioned supports the interpretation suggested by the archaeological record.

The manager of Newton requested of the plantation's owner to send from England "if there be not much expense in it ... a small plain stone for the head of ... [the] grave" of George Saer (Newton Papers 523/381-1), although the records do not reveal whether the stone was actually sent. Saer was a Christian and a much-valued slave, and chances are that the "handsome funeral" given him by the plantation manager in 1798 included a churchyard burial. Because gravestones involved expenditures, it is very unlikely that plantation managements regularly provided them. They probably were given only to highly valued Christian slaves destined for churchyard burial.[34]

Although graves do not appear to have been marked in any particular way, the archaeological investigations indicate that in some cases earth was added to the grave after interment. The written record for Barbados provides no information, but an authoritative Jamaican source during the last half of the eighteenth century reported that after "the space of a month" another ceremony took place that involved, among other elements, laying "a considerable heap of dirt over the grave, which is called covering it" (Long 1774;2:421–422, quoted in Patterson 1967:197. See also sources cited in Brathwaite 1971:217–218, and details on the "tombing ceremony" in early twentieth-century Jamaica; Beckwith 1969:84).

This activity apparently had socioreligious significance, but it could also have been performed to compensate for the settling-in of the grave, a common phenomenon. In either event, the amounts of earth involved in the construction of the large, permanent mounds at Newton (see chapter 5) imply more labor than simply filling a settled-in grave would have required. Whatever the significance of these mounds, the archaeological evidence indicates that the practice of mound building in Barbados was relatively uncommon.[35]

POSTINTERMENT

The documentary evidence strongly suggests that behavior following interment was as or even more important as interment itself. In Barbados, as in Jamaica, postinterment rites were not only widespread but also a vital aspect of the whole mortuary complex.

Neither the historical sources nor the archaeological record suggest that slaves practiced exhumation and secondary burials, a custom found in Europe from the Middle Ages to the sixteenth and seventeenth centuries (Ariès 1974:18–22), but which seems to have been uncommon in West Africa. But a fundamental element in the Barbadian mortuary complex, which Europeans invariably found to be the most exotic and alien, was the "barbarous ceremony of strewing the grave of a friend with provisions to help the dear defunct on his journey to his native lands" (Colthurst 1835–38:48). "I ... never suffer a Christian [slave] to be buried any other way than as he ought to be," wrote the Anglican catechist to the Codrington slaves in 1789, "on which occasions I strictly prohibit any of their rude customs to be afterwards practised over the corpse" (quoted in Bennett 1958:97). Although there are implications that these "idolatrous ceremonies and customs" were occurring in the seventeenth century (Gunkel and Handler 1969:7; see also Atkins 1676b), the earliest specific references to them occur in the 1720s. In a 1729 letter, an Anglican minister complained that insufficient care was "taken to restrain the Negroes ... from what they call their plays (frequently performed on the Lords days) in which with their various instruments of horrid music howling and dancing about the graves of the dead, they [give] victuals and strong liquor to the souls of the deceased to keep them (as they pretend) from appearing to hurt them" (Holt 1729a; see also Bennett 1958:80–81). The letter writer did not imply that these "plays" were of recent vintage nor confined to certain plantations (although he was especially concerned with the Codrington plantations); moreover, neither implication is given by Griffith Hughes when he generalized on similar ceremonies from the mid-1730s through the 1740s: "Some days after [interment], especially on their feasts, they strew at night some of the dressed victuals upon the graves of their deceased parents, relations, or friends" (1750:15).

Although some offerings of food and drink may have been made at the time of interment (as occurred in a number of West African cultures), the major rites occurred sometime after the day of the burial, according to Hughes and other sources. In fact, Philip Madin, who observed the funeral of a Barbadian plantation slave in 1779, specifically noted that on "the day after his interment a number of ... [the slaves] went to stroke up his grave, as they call'd it." We are not sure what this expression meant (although it might have alluded to, in part, the construction of some type of mound). About nine or ten days later "they went again to carry some victuals and drink to the grave, pretending that the deceased expects it from them, and that if they don't do so they will dream of him and he will come and trouble them" (1779:22).

Viewing dreams as omens was an important aspect of Barbadian slave culture (as it was in African cultures and in parts of the British isles—see, for example, Campbell 1900:268–276; Dyer 1878:206–233). However, Madin's observation alludes to a West African belief that delaying postinterment ceremonies might bring about deleterious social or personal consequences for those who were obliged to perform the ceremonies (see, for example, Busia 1954:201; Little 1954:115; Rattray 1927:166; Forde and Jones 1950:27). Madin also learned from the owner of the slave who died about another incident in which a slave woman "who had buried her husband, and after some time having neglected this ceremony she took it into her mind that her husband was displeased with her, for neglecting him, and used to dream that he came and told her she did not love him" (1779:22–23). Madin implied that offerings were also made on occasions subsequent to the immediate postinterment period. The novel *Creoleana*, perhaps in exaggerated form, also mentions such practices: "It was no unusual thing to see, as each Sunday returned, hundreds—nay, thousands of these poor deluded creatures 'throwing victuals' and with drumming, dancing and riot practising frenzied incantations over the graves of their deceased relatives and friends" (Orderson 1842:37–38). Similarly, periodic offerings were also suggested in 1788 by a planter who mentioned that the "faith" of the slaves was "demonstrated by their funeral rites and their anniversary celebrations of them to departed friends" (Steele 1789:28). During the eighteenth century, at least, these "anniversary celebrations," or "heathen sacrifices at the graves of the dead" (Holt 1729b), appear to have been more or less regularly performed on Sundays, when slaves were freed from work demands on plantations. Offerings of food and drink on top of the graves were intrinsic features of these rites. Robert Nicholls, a Barbadian-born Anglican minister (who left Barbados as a young man and returned in 1768 for a two-year residence), also specifically reported that "the principal feasts... [the slaves] ever give... are after the funerals of their friends, when they scatter some provisions on the grave and eat the rest themselves with a view, as I understand, of holding communion with the dead" (1790:332).

The historical sources provide no information on what norms governed the termination of the mourning period, or at what point and under what circumstances postinterment rites ceased, if they did, for a particular decedent. Nor do they indicate if the mourning period required other practices, such as special ritual taboos or body decoration. In West Africa, a wide variety and diversity of special customs were associated with the mourning period. The people most intimately involved in these practices were kinsmen and affines, such as wives. The historical sources for Barbados suggest that persons who stood in a special relationship to the deceased were primarily responsible for performing the postinterment rites; however, the participants were also drawn from the wider slave community and bore no special relationship to the deceased other than the fact that they were his or her friends and peers.

By the late 1820s, under legal and acculturative pressures, open performance of gravesite rites appear to have waned (see Colthurst 1835–38:48; Society for the Conversion 1829). In 1832 the Archdeacon of Barbados may have suggested their virtual disappearance, at least in their more dramatic form: "I have reason to think that the indecent revellings and the disorderly and demoralizing dances on the Lord's day, formerly so common in this colony, are at present of comparatively rare occurrence" (Eliot 1833:84–87).

Whatever the specific ethnographic details at any given period, and whenever gravesite rites ceased to be a characteristic feature of plantation slave culture, these rites were clearly widespread and of fundamental significance to plantation slaves for much of the period of slavery; furthermore, this ritual complex, involving at its core the propitiation and veneration of the spirits of the dead, must be viewed in light of the influence of the West African heritage on the culture of Barbadian slaves—a heritage that universally stressed, albeit with varying emphasis and elaboration, the vital role of the ancestors in socioreligious thought and practice.[36]

GRAVE DIRT AND OATHS

The influence of the African heritage and the sacred value attached to gravesites is also suggested by the importance of grave dirt and its role in the ordeal used in establishing innocence. Griffith Hughes first documented and most elaborately described the vital role of grave dirt in ordeals:

> [In] their method of clearing themselves from imputed crimes ... the Negroes take a piece of earth from the grave of their nearest relations, or parents, if it can be had; if not, from any other grave. This being mingled with water, they drink it, imprecating the divine vengeance to inflict an immediate punishment upon them; but in particular, that the water and mingled grave-dust which they have drank (if they are guilty of the crime) may cause them to swell, and burst their bellies. Most of them are so firmly persuaded that it will have this effect upon the guilty, that few, if any (provided they are conscious of the imputed crime), will put the proof of their innocency upon the experiment (1750:15–16).[37]

The seriousness with which slaves regarded the ordeal when grave dirt was employed was capitalized on by whites when they required slaves to testify in legal proceedings. The ordeal became, in effect, a means of swearing an oath in the European sense of the term.

Although slaves were legally prevented from testifying against whites until 1831, they were sometimes called on to give evidence in cases involving themselves or freedmen. If required to testify at a "slave court," where capital and minor offenses were tried in front of white judicial officials (there was no jury at a slave court), baptized slaves testified under oath in the same manner as whites. However, as a British parliamentary commission was told in 1823, nonbaptized slaves were "sometimes sworn on grave dirt according to a superstition" (Dwarris 1827:86). This practice had been going on for many years. In 1783, for example, a Barbadian newspaper reported a case (cited in K. Watson 1975:173) in which two plantation slaves were accused of having stolen a heifer from a neighboring plantation. The crime was a felony punishable by death. The testimony of Cromwell, a slave on one of the plantations, established the guilt of one of the accused and the innocence of the other. The wife of the guilty man, however, challenged Cromwell's testimony and urged the justices of the peace trying the case to "swear Cromwell on a Negro grave." Cromwell was made to stand on a grave and the woman "mixed some of the dirt in a glass of spirit and prostrating herself upon the grave . . . crying and kissing it, invoked the dead within, saying 'Oh Molly, if Cromwell swears true, well, bless and prosper him so long as he lives; but if he swears falsely . . . I beg you all to follow him close, and never let him rest, night or day, till he goes to hell, where he will belong to.' "

Cromwell reluctantly drank the mixture. When reexamined he changed his testimony "and implicated the individual whose innocence he had previously established. His testimony was then corroborated by the real culprit."

Some whites questioned whether an oath taken by a non-Christian was as efficacious as one sworn on the Bible. One writer strongly believed in the power of such an oath and explained: "their grave dirt is the same as the dust of the tabernacle, for their burial place is called the Negroes church. They mix both [water and grave dirt] together, and set the deponent on the grave, putting the mixture in his hand, which he drinks, and then he is charged by an oath of cursing, to which he replies, amen. And they think . . . that the perjured person will swell and rot, and become a curse among them" (*Barbados Mercury*, February 7, 1784). And arguing in 1787–88 that slaves should be permitted to give evidence in all courts, a planter was confident that "the solemnity of that oath ["by grave dirt"] appears to be connected with their ideas of the survivance of departed souls, and of future rewards and punishments under the decrees of the Divine Power" (Steele 1787–88, in Dickson 1814:83).

AFRICAN INFLUENCES AND CHANGES IN MORTUARY PATTERNS

We have suggested the influence of the West African cultural heritage on the mortuary patterns of plantation slaves throughout this chapter. Aside from specific practices and beliefs that the historical sources mention and the archaeological evidence suggests, whites who reported on the mortuary complex in general terms stated or implied that what they observed or heard about was essentially non-European. In 1779, for example, a visiting Englishman observed that the slaves participating in a plantation funeral had "some singularities peculiar to themselves" (Madin 1779:22). Over a century earlier the island's governor reported that slaves buried their dead "and not without ceremonies of their own" (Atkins 1676b). In general, the evidence indicates that in Barbados, as in other areas of the British Caribbean, the most fundamental elements in the mortuary complex throughout most of the slave period were African in form and origin; moreover, although these elements were most pronounced in the beliefs and behavior of African-born or nonbaptized slaves or both, they were also found among other plantation slaves.

The strength of African traditions in slave life was directly or indirectly emphasized by writers who reported, however briefly and ethnocentrically, on slave culture. In the early eighteenth century, for example, John Oldmixon wrote that "few" slaves "shew any disposition to hearken to the doctrine of Christians. They are so fond of their own idolatry" (Oldmixon 1741;2:130; cf. Frere 1768:125). Hughes succinctly stated the influence of African traditions during the 1730s and 1740s: "Our slaves, in their mirth and diversions, differ according to the several customs of so many nations intermixed... The Negroes in general are very tenaciously addicted to the rites, ceremonies, and superstitions of their own countries, particularly in their plays, dances, music, marriages, and *burials. And even such as are born and bred up here, cannot be intirely weaned from these customs*" (1750:15–16; italics supplied).

African traditions must have been as strongly pronounced in earlier periods. As the years progressed, however, more slaves were creoles and they were increasingly "weaned from these customs." But even by 1788, when most slaves were Barbadian-born, the governor, in reporting how "Negroes are superstitiously attached to the burial places of their ancestors and friends," noted: "for tho' they seem to have no system of religion, nothing like the worship of any diety, in some instances their superstition is inconceivable" (Parry 1789a:17). "So superstitious are some of them," Madin reported (1779:22), referring to beliefs surrounding death. In 1812 a group of planters observed how Christian "moral and religious instruction" would act as "a means of counteracting the baneful effects of superstition" (Society for the Improvement 1811–16:123). "There is no characteristic more strongly marked in the Negro," Rolph emphatically observed in 1833, "than their superstitious veneration for the dead" (1836:38). The "superstitious" beliefs and "heathenish ways" (Porteus 1807:174[38]), as ethnocentrically perceived by whites, implied a magicoreligious complex that was fundamentally non-European—that is, Afro-creole or African.

In discussing the African or African-like components of the mortuary complex of plantation slaves, we relied to a considerable degree on the published literature relating to the cultures of West Africa—the region that was the ancestral home of most Afro-American populations in the West Indies—although we do not claim that our coverage was exhaustive. The information in this literature is largely based on ethnographic studies conducted during the twentieth century, "thus the data from contemporary Africa are projected back in time and are assumed to be relevant to Africa (and Barbados) of another epoch" (Handler and Frisbie 1972:35). This assumption presupposes a cultural conservatism in West Africa—a conservatism especially evident in, for example, music and motor behaviors associated with musical expression (Merriam 1967:107–108; Mintz 1970:5). Although cultural patterns in traditional, nonliterate, or nonindustrialized societies undergo a less rapid rate of change than under modern conditions and in industrialized societies,[39] "even in phases of extensive technical and social change such as the peoples of Africa...have experienced over the past century, traditional beliefs and standards continue to exert a powerful influence" (Forde 1954: vii–viii; cf. Busia 1954: 191). West African cultures, like many others—including those of Western Europe—were conservative with respect to the ideological and behavioral system surrounding death, but aspects of mortuary complexes changed,[40] not only as a result of European contacts and influences, but also as a result of the influences that African cultures had on one another over the past few centuries.[41]

We believe it remains legitimate to question the extent and ways in which the specific cultural patterns in twentieth- or late nineteenth-century Africa can be used to indicate what existed on the continent during the seventeenth and eighteenth centuries when the slave trade to the British West Indies was the most intensive. It is not possible to deal with this question here. Although we do not maintain that ethnographic data from modern or relatively modern Africa are conclusive evidence, we believed these data are useful (at least on a general and nonspecific ethnic group level) in suggesting the cultural patterns of African origin that were found among Barbadian slaves. More conclusive proof, of course, could only be arrived at by a comprehensive and systematic reconstruction of the mortuary patterns that existed in West Africa (especially among the peoples chiefly involved in the slave trade) during the seventeenth and eighteenth centuries.

Some of the more distinctive general and specific features of African influence on the Barbadian slave mortuary complex included the emphasis that slaves placed on the funeral and the central role of the funeral in socioreligious life; the importance attached to ancestors, and the manifestation of this importance in interment and postinterment rites; sacrifices or offerings of food and drink at gravesites during these rites; goods interred with the corpse; the sacred nature of gravesites and the expression of this in ordeals

210

and oaths; the apparent norm that interment and, especially, post-interment rites be performed, at the minimum, by close kin or affines; the value attached to locating burial sites close to the houses of the living and interment under the houses; the prominent role of various forms of musical expression; the custom of "carrying the corpse"; and such beliefs as the emphasis on witchcraft or sorcery as causes of death, the survival of the soul, and its migration to a spirit world where the dead reside and the ancestors are rejoined.

Many African peoples believed that the afterworld was similar to the temporal one and that the social status held while alive was perpetuated after death. The evidence suggests that Barbadian (and West Indian) slaves added a new dimension to this belief that was, in effect, a function of their status in the New World. Not only did they subscribe to the notion of a return to the "other side of the sea" (Africa), but they also felt that death (including suicide) was a release from slavery which elevated them to a state of freedom in the afterlife. Other values, beliefs, and practices related to their status as plantation slaves were influenced by the European and Euro-creole environment—for example, the value that some slaves attached to burial in Christian churchyards, and the conception of baptism as a device to achieve such burials. Plantation managements could make a "handsome burial" an element in the plantation reward system by merely capitalizing on a fundamental strain in the African or African-type component of the slaves' cultural system. Plantation communal burial grounds were a concomitant of the plantation system itself (some African societies had communal burial grounds but only for particular kin groups). The timing of burials in the evenings and nights, as well as the performance of postinterment rites on Sundays, were responses to the demands of plantation labor schedules.

Other features of European origin entered the mortuary complex, especially in the later years of the slave period and particularly, but not uniquely, with baptized slaves. For example, palls, coffins with metal furniture (including handles), horse-drawn hearses, gravestones (at least for those interred in church burial grounds), and certain characteristics of the funeral procession, including, in some cases, its ambience, walking in pairs, types of attire for mourners, and, of course, the Christian rituals for baptized slaves. Aside from Christian slaves, European influences were, perhaps, to some extent manifest in other areas of the mortuary complex, such as the way in which the corpse was oriented and positioned in the grave (we expected more flexed burials from an African-type population than we found in Newton cemetery).

Some items of European origin were incorporated but in a non-European pattern; for example, various artifacts, such as clay tobacco pipes, were of European manufacture, but using them as grave goods was characerically African.

We generally lack detailed comparative information on the mortuary customs of white creoles and those of European birth in Barbados. From the information that is available, however, including numerous wills not cited here, it appears safe to assume that the mortuary complex of the island's white population did not significantly deviate from European practices in basic features. A number of these features also appeared in the slave mortuary complex. We are aware, of course, that on a general level a number of mortuary features were shared by both European and African populations in the Old and New Worlds, and that various elements of the Barbadian slave complex were no more unique to West Africa than they were to the British Isles.

In West Africa and the British Isles, funerals and the disposition of the dead were important socioreligious and cultural features. Characteristic features and phases of the funeral and burial varied with, among other factors, the status and wealth of the deceased (and even the manner of death, such as suicide). In both areas the corpse was formally prepared for interment by being washed, dressed in clothes or shrouding, or was covered in some manner. The body was watched over in a wake or wakelike atmosphere. Other rules stipulated where and how the dead should be buried, processions of one kind or another accompanied the corpse to the burial place, and excavated graves were widely used. In both areas, the corpse was oriented in an east-west direction (although in Africa, there was apparently greater variation in orientation patterns) and was rarely buried in a prone position. White or dark colors signified death or mourning, prescribed mourning practices were followed, persons in close relationships to the deceased were expected to behave in particular ways, and food and drink were consumed by mourners. West Africans and Europeans also shared a variety of broadly defined beliefs such as witchcraft, sorcery, and notions of a soul, afterlife, and spirit world.[42]

In sum, in a wider context, as Melville Herskovits suggested many years ago, "given traits of New World Negro ... behavior, are ascribable equally to European and African origin. This may well be viewed as but a reflection of the fact that deep beneath the differences between these varied civilizations of the Old World lie common aspects which, in generalized form, might be expected to emerge in situations of close contact between peoples, such as

Europeans and Africans, whose specialized cultural endowments are comprehended within the larger unity" (1958:18). In illustrating the "Old World cultural province" Herskovits noted, among other features, shared elements of folklore, and "certain aspects" of magic, ordeals, the role and forms of divination, and conceptions of the universe. Various dimensions of the mortuary complex can also be included.

These shared broad cultural features and patterns facilitated the acculturative process between African and European populations. However, in stressing the African-like nature of the Barbadian slave mortuary complex, we are not only emphasizing that specific features were distinctively African (for example, burials under houses, the role of the ancestors, and postinterment rites at gravesites), but also that the qualitative nature of the mortuary complex and the distinctive patterning of its constituent elements gave it an African appearance. This appearance is attested to by viewing particular elements and the way in which they were combined and in the reactions of whites to slave funerary and religious practices. Whites' reactions, which often stressed or alluded to the exotic or alien qualities of significant mortuary features, underscored the African nature of these features.

The African influence on the mortuary complex was especially pronounced in the earlier periods of slavery. By the late eighteenth century, when most of Barbados's slaves had been born on the island, European elements were more visible,[43] and the complex itself was creole. Although some of its elements resembled or replicated Old World antecedents, the complex had its own contours and patterning and included elements that were distinctively a function of the New World environment and the plantation slave system. As much as European traditions may have influenced the mortuary complex (especially among baptized slaves and in the later periods of slavery), during the entire slave period and for most of the island's slaves, the mortuary complex "strongly reflected the African traditions from which it ultimately derived" (Handler and Frisbie 1972:40).

It is difficult and, perhaps, unnecessary, to "locate the particular areas in West Africa from which the different [mortuary elements and] rites . . . came," Patterson concluded from his study of Jamaican slave life. We generally concur with respect to Barbados and, like Patterson, also stress that "it is more fruitful to regard the rites described in Jamaica as syncretisms of what existed all over West Africa. In the light of the known uniformity of these rites in this area of Africa such syncretisms would certainly not be unlikely" (1967:198). Patterson may exaggerate the "uniformity" of West African mortuary patterns, and more interethnic or tribal group diversity existed than his statement implies; nonetheless, in mortuary patterns, as well as more generally in religious belief and behavior, a number of broad cultural features, including "basic assumptions about social relations" and "basic assumptions and expectations about the way the world functions phenomenologically" (Mintz and Price 1976:5), were widespread and found in most, if not all, of the societies of the region.

These cultural features included, for example, the concept of the great gods, including a creator god; nature deities; the general responsiveness of deities to human actions; propitiation and veneration of the ancestors, the ancestral cult, and the active role of the dead in the lives of the living; oaths and ordeals involving ancestors or other deities; food and small animal (particularly chicken) ritual sacrifice; the concept of the afterlife or spirit world and souls (including multiple souls); basic shared premises about causality and the efficacy of magical and divinatory techniques; religious ritual associated with medical practices; the profound belief in witchcraft and sorcery; and the central role and significance of the funeral and rites attending the disposition of the dead (Herskovits 1962:101–103, 110–111; Bohannan and Curtin 1971:173–185; Parrinder 1961; Mintz and Price 1976:23. One authority has also noted the "remarkable similarities among symbols used in ritual throughout sub-Saharan Africa"; Turner 1973:1105).

We believe that the specific differences in mortuary practices and other cultural features among West African ethnic groups are, as Hammond has written, "less significant for an understanding of Afro-American cultural history than are the underlying similarities which unite them" (1970:196). Our archaeological data on interment practices also supports this view. We did not find evidence for the range of behavior that could have been expected if the slaves were maintaining broadly different mortuary patterns, rather than synthesizing fundamentally common West African features.[44]

"In terms of our current knowledge," Mintz and Price have recently written, "it seems reasonable to expect that almost any sub-system of an Afro-American culture ... would be highly syncretic in terms of its diverse African origins, as well as in terms of inputs from European ... sources; and we must expect it to possess a built-in internal dynamism and a marked adaptiveness to changing social conditions as well" (1976:32). As the "common [cultural] aspects in generalized form" (Herskovits 1958:18) shared by Africans and Europeans facilitated the process of acculturation between these groups, at least in mortuary patterns, so the "under-lying similarities" in West African socioreligious and mortuary belief and behavior provided the foundation on which African slaves from varying traditions constructed a mortuary complex in the New World setting.

"However one may choose to define a generalized West African 'heritage' shared by the slaves transported to any New World colony," and whether or not this heritage "will have to be defined ... by focusing more on values, and ... 'cognitive orientations'... and less on ... the more formal elements stressed by Herskovits" (Mintz and Price 1976:5–7), the West African homelands clearly influenced the mortuary patterns of Barbadian slaves to a con-siderable degree. Despite the lack of many details on these patterns, the mortuary complex also formed an important and patterned component of slave culture. Only the most superficial historical research could maintain otherwise, and argue in more general terms, as a modern anthropological study of Barbados has done, that "under the conditions of the slave plantation [the slaves] ... were able neither to re-establish African culture nor to develop new independent patterns. With emancipation, they could have had no choice but to accept the [English] culture that already existed in the island" (Greenfield 1966:171). Slaves, of course, could not reestablish a specific African culture, but "Africans did not arrive on the shores of the New World with blank minds onto which were impressed ... English culture patterns in the 1830s. Although the social system of the slave society was harsh and highly restrictive, slaves developed a complex of behavioral patterns that by any anthropological characterization was cultural" (Handler 1969b: 337).

Clearly in Barbados, as in Jamaica and the Leeward Islands, "the majority of the slaves ... retained a very strong African element in their culture" (Goveia 1965:248). In general features, however, by the late eighteenth century, this culture was not "wholly African," but was creolized.[45] Barbadian slave culture had developed from the interaction between Africans and their descendants (wherein the plantation community was of crucial importance), and from the absorption of European or Euro-creole culture ele-ments in the process of adapting to the conditions of the plantation system and wider features in the island's sociocultural and physical environments.

7/ The Ethnohistorical Approach to Slavery

ARCHAEOLOGICAL data and information derived from written sources (supplemented on occasion by ethnographic observations) have enabled us to describe various dimensions of the plantation system and slave life and to view cultural changes that took place during the slave period. A great deal of our information could only be acquired from the written record, but archaeology was the sole source of data for certain areas of investigation. This was particularly evident in our discussion of slave mortuary patterns. The documentary sources were crucial for ascertaining the nature of pre- and post-burial behavior, though only the archaeology provided data about interment of the body in the grave and the use of grave goods. Other areas of interest, such as the use of coffins and the placement of clay pipes with the deceased, were approached by combining written and archaeological sources. In general, archaeology can make definite contributions to the study of plantation slavery and slave culture because it yields information and generates questions not available in the documentary sources. It nonetheless has limitations because many aspects of plantation slavery and slave life did not leave archaeological traces.

We are conscious of the relative uniqueness of our data base and our methodological approach, given the geographical area and the cultural affiliations of the population of our study. We are also open to the possibility that we may not have chosen, in terms of Barbados's heavy agricultural depradation of archaeological resources, an optimum locale in which to examine the archaeological nature of slavery. However, Higman conducted slave period archaeology in uncultivated areas of Jamaica (1974, 1975, 1976a) and encountered many of the same interpretative problems (although his archaeological work to date has been considerably less extensive than our work in Barbados and thus an assumption of general similarity of results may be somewhat premature). The impact

216

of agriculture on Barbados's archaeological past may have been less substantial than our work has led us to believe.

Subsequent studies will probably alter some of our tentative and occasionally speculative conclusions. These conclusions advocate the use of the ethnohistorical approach for studying slave cultures and also have broader implications for archaeological objectives in the study of ahistoric and prehistoric populations. In this chapter, we utilize the synthesis of archaeological and historical data presented in earlier chapters to briefly examine the theoretical and methodological bases of archaeological, anthropological, historical, and ethnohistorical approaches to the study of slave cultures. In distinguishing between ethnohistorical and archaeological approaches to the study of slavery, this chapter also emphasizes the methodological contrast between our study and studies traditionally conducted by many historical archaeologists.

THE ETHNOHISTORICAL METHODOLOGY

Within the framework of the research described in this book, ethnohistory is viewed as an approach to "gathering, preparing, and analyzing oral and written traditions. The aims for which these methods are employed are those of cultural anthropology in general, and have to do with theories of culture. Therefore, ethnohistory itself cannot be considered an independent discipline" (Carmack 1972:234). Ethnohistory, then, is an approach to describing and understanding culture and cultural processes and, like archaeology, is defined primarily by a methodological criterion. Methodologically, ethnohistory is not solely the companion of archaeology, ethnography, or history, but may also supplement such fields as historical linguistics or paleobiology (Carmack 1972:232). Though none of these fields employs an ethnohistorical approach in every research situation, the most significant aspect of ethnohistory is its flexibility in bringing seemingly diverse sources of data to bear on particular problems.

In her study of a Tlingit community, Frederica de Laguna concluded "that archaeological, ethnological, and historical data, if combined and analyzed together, can give a deeper insight than any one type of material or any one methodology alone" (1960: 200). "It is indeed this methodological consideration, the appraisal of the factors involved in coordinating a multifaceted approach that enhances the significance of the study" (Baerreis 1961:58). Baerreis reemphasized this position in defining the archaeological approach to ethnohistory as "the means for coordinating diverse kinds of data in the solution of anthropological problems . . . For archaeology, an ethnohistoric approach serves as a means whereby a fundamental link in the broad narrative of man's culture history is achieved" (p. 70).

Barbados plantation rewards or incentives are excellent examples of the improved level of interpretation derived from integrating archaeological and historical data. Prior to our archaeological research, written sources yielded fragmentary information that indicated the various types of rewards or incentives and some of the social contexts in which they were allocated. These data, however, were dispersed throughout notes dealing with other dimensions of plantation slavery.

In trying to interpret the archaeological remains from Newton cemetery, we had to account for apparently disparate allocations of artifacts in association with interments, particularly the presence or absence of whole clay pipes and coffins. During the archaeological analysis, notes from written sources were reexamined to isolate references to types of excavated artifacts. In the early stages of analysis we found that pipes and tobacco were sometimes distributed to slaves as rewards and that material assistance at the time of burial was sometimes given to certain slaves. We began to suspect that the occurrence of particular artifacts, such as coffins, with interments may have been a manifestation of plantation rewards or incentives. As a result, the notes were more intensively reexamined, the presence of a reward-incentive system was established to a degree not previously understood, and the function of various archaeological materials as remnants of this system was inferred. In this case, the step-by-step articulation of the historical and archaeological data utilized the historical data for a purpose for which they were not initially intended; furthermore, this articulation produced an interpretation that would have been difficult or delayed on the basis of historical data alone and probably impossible if only archaeological data had been available.

In this instance, applying the ethnohistorical approach suggested a new perspective. Though the historical data were necessary to define the existence of the slave system before questions about rewards and incentives could even be asked, the encounter with specific archaeological data, for which the presence or absence of certain artifactual materials suggested cultural explanations, led to a useful organization and analysis of the historical data.

Thus, our archaeological research attempted to adhere to the ethnohistorical approach by employing historical and to some extent ethnographic data to complement analyses of archaeological data. This is clearly seen when contrasting the integrated discussion in chapter 6 with the principally archaeological account in chapter 5. Until recently, investigations that recovered historic period data by archaeological methods have often ignored the broader cultural implications of the data. As Robert Ascher (1974:7) has noted, the development of prehistoric archaeology has produced many techniques for improving our understanding of the more recent historical past, but these techniques have often not been applied. Likewise, many of the theoretical considerations given to prehistoric sites have been omitted or ignored when considering historical materials in traditional historical archaeology or historic sites archaeology.

HISTORICAL ARCHAEOLOGY

Despite the types of some of our artifactual material and other superficial similarities, our research was explicitly not historical archaeology as this field has usually been defined. Larrabee's definition of historical archaeology is typical: "Historical archaeology is ... concerned with archaeological sites which can somehow be linked with written historical data. This means sites affected by or belonging to the Europeans who came to the New World after Columbus. The excavation of Viking sites is not normally included in the field" (1969:70; see also Fontana 1965; Dollar 1968). Larrabee also contended that "Historic Sites Archaeology is *not* limited to the 19th century. It can start as far back as 1500 A.D. in the Caribbean" (1969:70). Larrabee was presumably thinking of early European-Amerindian contact sites or European settlements in the Caribbean, but our project treated a different subject than normally of concern to historical archaeology. We focused on a captive population that developed an African-based creole culture in an essentially European-dominated societal and institutional context.

Larrabee also stressed that "Historic Site Archaeology is very interdisciplinary" (1969:71), although multidisciplinary might have been a better term in his context. In either case, the interdisciplinary nature of historic site archaeology, according to Larrabee, is its "unique" use of documents related to archaeology, its ability to find artifacts in documented, undisturbed contexts, the use of facts developed from historic sites to extend archaeology into chronologically earlier periods, and its use of historically documented archaeological data to refine and control techniques in prehistoric studies.

Larrabee's definition and description of historical archaeology overlaps with Baerreis's definition of ethnohistory (1961) in several areas. However, Baerreis emphasizes anthropological concepts and applications with regard to historically related archaeological data. Moreover, being interdisciplinary or multidisciplinary does not evolve simply from using historical documents, but rather from integrating written or ethnographic data with those from archaeology to interpret and enhance the cultural understanding of excavated materials.

The apparent lack of concern with the cultural aspects of historical data is also clearly manifest in Larrabee's brief discussion of the use of historical archaeological controls to refine controls in other fields. His discussion refers only to such technical analytical methods as radiocarbon and remnant magnetism dating and ignores cultural questions (1969:72). Larrabee is not the only historical archaeologist to have implicitly, if not explicitly, rejected the anthropological implications of the data.

Not all historical archaeologists, however, are oblivious to cultural emphases. Schuyler, for example, strongly argues for the inclusion of historical archaeology within the broader discipline of anthropology: "there is no evidence of anything particularly new about the basic approaches of our discipline (Historical Archaeology) from either an anthropological or historical point of view . . . The future development of our field . . . does not lie in . . . attempts to gain specific data . . . but in making Historic Sites Archaeology, including artifacts and documents, an integral part of anthropology" (1970: 83, 86). Schuyler also stresses that the study of Vikings should be included in definitions of historical archaeology (1970:84); if the documentary and artifactual aspects of historical archaeology are included within the broader methodological range of ethnohistory, resulting research foci are not on particular geographical areas or temporal periods, but on particular problems in which an integrative approach significantly improves research, analysis, and interpretation.

"The study of historic sites using an anthropological approach," Stone has recently written, "is a relatively new procedure" that can be accounted for by several reasons:

> the most important of which is the relatively short period of time during which historic sites have been investigated by qualified persons who employ systematic archaeological techniques of excavation and analysis. Secondly, historic site archaeologists have traditionally been more interested in evaluating a site's structural evidence for reconstruction and restoration purposes, an activity which provides rapid and visible results for the benefit of project sponsors, rather than in studying artifacts and their significance for comprehensive site interpretation. This emphasis has limited both the interpretation of cultural phenomena which characterize these sites and the comparative value of artifact descriptions presented in

many historic site reports... The results of research thus far
have clearly shown that one must have a working knowledge
of both anthropological and historical methods and objectives
(1974:1–2).

Various writings in recent years have considered the relationship
between historical archaeology and prehistoric archaeology, on the
one hand, and historical archaeology and anthropology, on the other
(see, for example, Walker 1967a, 1974); however, there has apparently been no detailed discussion of the relationship between
ethnohistory and historical archaeology. An exception is a very
brief discussion by Brain, Toth, and Rodriguez-Buckingham in
which they characterized historical archaeology "as customarily...
confined to our own Euro-American history" whereas "Ethnohistoric archaeology... refers to the contemporary native contexts and
benefits from the addition of ethnographic data, methods and
interpretations, a perspective we are not traditionally wont to apply
to ourselves" (1974:232). Such statements ignore a conception of
ethnohistory as a methodology applicable to particular situations
and ignore that it is not a discipline confined by limits of time,
geographical space, or the cultural group being studied. Its utilization of historical and ethnographic data in conjunction with archaeological data defines the ethnohistorical method, regardless of whether
the object of the study or the source of documentation is European,
Amerindian, descriptive, or archaeological. The fact that archaeologists have not been "wont to apply" ethnohistoric methods and
data to the study of North American colonial history has been one
of the major obstacles to accepting an anthropological approach to
the study of historical period archaeological data.

The artifactual base from Newton plantation (coffin handles,
clay pipes, china, glass beads, and other historical European materials) is generally similar to that recovered by historical archaeologists from post-European contact sites in North America. We also
share interests with historical archaeologists in chronology and descriptive accuracy. However, as a result of the structuring of our
research, we have asked questions of our data that are usually not
posed in historical archaeology but which have been frequently
examined through the methodology of ethnohistory. Measured
against Baerreis's definition of ethnohistory, our major areas of interest in Barbados (domestic activities, mortuary practices, the survival or modification of African cultural traditions, and cultural
change) are perfectly suited to investigation by an ethnohistorical
methodology.

In general, the inability of either history or archaeology to individually deal effectively with the problem of slave culture lies in the limits of the data. The written record is fragmentary, selective, and biased and the slaves themselves did not contribute to this record. Although archaeological data can illuminate some areas of behavior not covered in or obscured by the written records, they also have limitations. Some are practical ones, such as the preservation of cultural materials over time, while others are related to theoretical and conceptual limits of the archaeological record as a basis for interpreting past human behavior.

THE ARCHAEOLOGICAL RECORD

Since 1962, L. R. Binford and various scholars influenced directly and indirectly by him (see, for example, King 1973) have advocated that all vestiges of past cultures are reflected by artifactual remains. Support for this absolutist position has declined among those who initially adhered to it; today this position is held by relatively few professional archaeologists, although Binford (1975) has recently forcefully restated his earlier views. Trigger (1971) and Watson, LeBlanc, and Redman (1971), among others, speak for a majority who accept a more moderate approach that recognizes possible limitations in the archaeological record. This approach does not automatically define areas of archaeological limitation, but maintains that under particular conditions and specific circumstances certain types of data may not be preserved consistently and thus certain types of behavior cannot be detected archaeologically. This allows us to identify specific areas of possible archaeological limitation, to evaluate data gathered and methodologies used, and to make adjustments for future attempts to obtain similar sorts of information. In some cases, we may also recognize that certain behavior patterns are outside the archaeological domain.

Some of the practical limitations of our archaeological record reflect the fact that Barbados is a small island that has experienced heavy population densities, intensive agricultural exploitation and reuse of land, and the recycling of nonperishable building materials over long periods. Hurricanes and the tropical environment have also taken a toll. As noted in chapter 3, we have only to contrast the drawing of the yard area at Ashford plantation (figure 6) or the map of Staple Grove (figure 5) with the archaeological findings to realize what has been destroyed or altered since emancipation. Daily activities during the slave period also affected the archaeological record, through either redistribution of nonperishable items or changing patterns of settlement and land utilization.

The archaeological record on Barbados reflects the struggle between the island's limited surface area and its dense population. The slaves had no choice in settlement pattern. The criteria for locating slave villages were partially agricultural (not having people occupying good agricultural land) and largely a matter of social control. The result of locating the villages near the plantation yard and the house of the owner or manager was intensive reuse of a limited area for slave habitation. After emancipation, when the ex-slaves were moved to the peripheries of the plantations, the limits of local resources dictated that materials should not rest unused or that land should be unproductive. Available building materials were reused and former slave villages became the sites of new buildings or storage for machinery or equipment or were placed under cultivation. Thus, the limitations of the archaeological record in reflecting slave life on Barbados are partially practical problems of preservation that may or may not be encountered in other situations.

Regardless of preservation, however, no artifactual remains were independently characteristic of slave culture and status. Positive delineation and isolation of data indicative of slave status and slave culture lay at the heart of our analytical problems with the archaeological data from Barbados in general and the data from Newton plantation in particular. Though the written record established that the plantations on which we worked existed prior to 1834 and were, indeed, slave plantations, the archaeological data alone, without the support of documentary evidence, did not reflect an institution or behavioral system identifiable as slavery. This problem presents a major obstacle to any purely archaeological study of slavery and has also confronted others who have worked with the remains of slave cultures.

In Jamaica, for example, Higman noted that despite documentary evidence that slaves lived at New Montpelier estate the artifactual materials recovered from house excavations did not reveal the social status of the occupants. The artifacts alone could not identify a slave system (1976a, 1974, 1975). In their excavation of a slave cabin in Georgia, Ascher and Fairbanks recognized that archaeology might recover data that were not found in literary sources or oral traditions (1971). They chose their excavation site, however, because historical sources documented the location of slave cabins, not because they independently arrived at the conclusion that the structural remains they excavated were those of a slave house. Their objective was to gain an archaeological insight into known slave remains, not to test whether such remains were actually indicative of slave habitation. Otto (1975) has also indicated that his choice of slave areas to be excavated was based on documentary evidence.

Discussing a different form of slavery from the Old World, Siegel (1947:5) also recognized the inseparable link between documentary resources and the archaeological study of slavery.

Although archaeological data clearly supplement historical data on the institution of slavery once the presence of slavery is known, the initial identification of a slave system in a society and at a particular site, or areas to be excavated, depends on historical proof.

The historical data from Barbados indicated that most slaves were buried in plantation areas set aside for such purposes. There was no specific documentary mention of a slave burial ground at Newton, and in this sense the archaeological research helped to validate the generalization derived from the historical record. Whites were also sometimes buried on plantations, but their graves were usually clearly marked, and they were not buried in the same areas as slaves. Information from Barbadian informants also supported a belief that Newton cemetery was slave in origin. Though the characteristics of the burials were not wholly European, the artifactual material of glass beads, clay pipes, and coffin hardware indicated we were dealing with an historical population. Although metric cranial analyses of the skeletal population were not conducted, they undoubtedly would have demonstrated the Negroid physical identity of the population, but they would not have indicated that the individuals were slaves. All evidence supported a strong inference but nothing archaeological was independently diagnostic of a slave cemetery.

As we noted in chapter 5, it was generally difficult to identify archaeological materials reflecting the African background of the slaves. Historical evidence, of course, showed that many Africans and their descendants lived in Barbados during the slave period. Because most of these persons were slaves, we could assume with relative assurance that artifactual materials reflecting African motifs and patterns were slave-related; thus one means of identifying slave culture would be through identification of artifacts reflecting African technical or decorative traditions. However, we were unable to define an artifactual complex diagnostic of the slave population. This lack of African data in material remains is particularly disturbing considering the size of the Barbadian slave population and its African cultural heritage, a heritage clearly manifest in other areas of behavior such as, for example, mortuary patterns (see chapter 6) and music (Handler and Frisbie 1972).

One of the problems, then, in dealing with the artifacts recovered from the archaeological research was determining what was and what was not a part of the slave milieu. Slave manufactures reflecting African cultural traditions would most likely have been of either ceramic or organic materials, because these were the most readily available resources on the island. We found no organic material and could not identify any ceramics with decorative or manufacturing aspects distinctive of African derivation. Some non-wheel pottery was found, but its cultural affiliation is uncertain. (Some of the metal jewelry objects and various artifacts associated with Burial 72, discussed in chapter 5, possibly were manufactured in Africa or were influenced by African craft traditions.)

Similar problems in identifying slave artifacts are seen in Mathewson's study of Afro-Jamaican pottery (1972b). The ceramics were culturally distinguishable from English manufactured ceramics and some were clearly derived from African ceramic traditions. It is not, however, discernible from the pottery itself that it was made by slaves, although this was not a concern in Mathewson's study. Higman's work in Jamaica has also failed to identify archaeological material uniquely indicative of slavery, and Otto (1975) has made a similar observation about his research off the Georgia coast. In observing the cultural materials recovered from excavations at the Kingsley plantation in Florida, Fairbanks reported:

> It was surprising that no surely African elements in the material culture could be identified. It has long been known that blacks ... did manage ... to leave survivals of their language and other behavioral traits ... which survive in Afro-American culture until the present. I felt that the special circumstances of Kingsley being a slave-importing station, and ... [the owner's] permissive attitude toward his charges, would assure that some elements of African material culture would have been recreated in the plantation situation. Pottery, ornaments, game pieces, or ritual objects might well be expected in such a milieu. We found nothing, however, that could surely be identified as such (1974:90).

Why no African-type materials were found in such differing slave situations as Barbados and the American South is not fully clear. Similar observations in these areas, however, suggest that verifying archaeological slave complexes cannot be dependent on survivals or materials derived from African backgrounds.

In interpreting artifacts of slavery or any other artifactual remains, the archaeological context is fundamental. Schiffer (1972) detailed several ways in which an artifact may move through a society. The two parts of his model of most importance to our study are procurement and lateral cycling. Applied to slavery situations, procurement is the manner in which slaves or other members of a slave society obtained material items from commercial or natural sources. Lateral cycling is the passing of items from one segment of the society to another, possibly with a change in function, prior to any permanent discard from active use.

Barbadian slaves procured a large percentage of their nonfood materials from sources equally available to whites and free non-whites. To varying degrees, all segments of society utilized such locally available raw materials as wood, clay, and gourds. Slaves obtained such imported items as cloth, clay pipes, and some tools and cooking utensils by such means as theft, plantation allocation and rewards or incentives or by purchase and exchange on the internal marketing system. In other cases, as artifactual materials were discarded by planters and other free persons, they were laterally cycled into the slave or lower free classes and reused before their final archaeological deposition. At Newton, the glass objects associated with Burials 55 and 60, the door hinges with Burial 33, the partial ceramic vessel from Mound 2, and interred broken pipes are possible examples of such lateral cycling. Fairbanks also reported that china dishes found in the Kingsley slave quarters were almost certainly discards from the planter's table (1974:79). The money Barbadian slaves acquired from the sale of cash crops or stolen goods, the birth premiums paid mothers whose children survived their first month, the money given to various plantation officers, and the wages earned by slave tradesmen who were hired out also facilitated the entry of goods into the slave milieu by permitting slaves to purchase products from white and freedman shopkeepers and others. In brief, any patterns of purchase, trade, exchange, or gift-giving would have tended to blur absolute artifactual distinctions between the nonslave and slave segments of the island's population.

One of our major interpretative problems was assigning shared artifactual material to a particular segment of a stratified, complex society—in this case distinct social groups that, for archaeological purposes, occupied more or less the same area and separately, but concurrently, used many of the same resources. Fairbanks faced this problem on the Kingsley plantation and the problem is also seen in Otto's work in Georgia on dietary patterns (1975). Otto found the remains of domestic and wild foods used by planters, overseers, and slaves. His excavations were conducted in refuse middens associated with habitation areas of the three groups; the areas were located through documentary evidence and by analogy to other coastal plantations. Otto concluded that status differences could not be discerned among all three groups on the basis of either food or the remains of food procurement equipment. In all three cases, procurement equipment was present in approximately equal quantities. Minor differences were seen in the concentration of certain fish and turtle species at the planter's house, but these items were equally present in the slave and overseer areas. The contrast derived from Otto's archaeological data is between slaves and overseers as a group, and planters as a group, rather than overseers and planters as opposed to slaves or, alternatively, a tripartite distribution.

In Barbados (and apparently in other slave site studies) the artifact assemblages (such as imported and local ceramics, glass beads, clay pipes, hardware) consisted of materials available to and utilized by the slaves as well as other population segments: planters, middle and lower class whites, and freedmen of various socioeconomic strata. Various societal segments probably used the same types of artifacts, or indeed on many occasions the *same* artifact was discarded by one segment of society, acquired by another, and by a variety of other means transmitted vertically as well as horizontally through the society.

ARCHAEOLOGY AND SLAVERY

None of the archaeological data from Newton and other plantations investigated in Barbados are solely indicative of slavery and slave status. The limited comparative data from other research on slaves suggest this generalization may be acceptable from an archaeological perspective. One problem in identifying the physical remains of slaves and artifacts indicative of slave culture is that slave status did not give people distinctive phenotypes or genotypes; nor did it give them material goods that were not found among other segments of the society. A somewhat different perspective on this problem might be derived from envisioning a grave in which two complete human skeletons, one an adult male and the other an adult female, were found. Once we have described their age, sex, manner of interment, and whether or not grave goods were found, we are left with the possibility of social interpretation: were they husband and wife, brother and sister, queen and courtesan, or lovers? We can never know, for these are arranged, genetic, and contractual human relationships that leave no artifactual remains. Despite extensive data on the Newton interments, the archaeological data as such do not establish if the individuals found in the concentrated burial areas, such as Mound 2 and 30N9W, were kinsmen, or what the relationships were, if any, between the adult men and women, or whether the adult in the multiple Burial 69–70 (regardless of whether it was male or female) was a parent of the interred child. Furthermore the

227

archaeological data do not even establish that these persons were slaves.

An extreme but nonetheless useful illustration of potential difficulty in archaeological interpretation of status or social position was the interment of King Faisal of Saudi Arabia. At the time of his assassination in the spring of 1975, Faisal was one of the world's wealthiest men and the undisputed leader of his society and government. Although preinterment behavior differed somewhat from what would have occurred had a person of lesser status and prestige died, burial customs were those of the Islamic sect to which Faisal belonged. His body was wrapped in a simple shroud and was interred in a graveyard where commoners as well as royalty are buried. Like other graves in the cemetery, Faisal's had a small mound and was encircled by unmarked stones (*New York Times*, March 27, 1975; *Time*, April 7, 1975). Subsequent excavation in the cemetery would yield the physical remains of other members of Saudi royalty, including Faisal's father, but they would be indistinguishable from the many other interments in the same area.

Lewis Binford has contended that "the formal structure of artifact assemblages together with the between element contextual relationships should and do present a systematic and understandable picture of the *total extinct* cultural system" (1962a:219) and that "there has been as yet no attempt to assess the limitations of the archeological record for yielding different kinds of information" (1968:22). We submit, however, that our study of plantation slavery and slave culture is such an assessment of limitation for one broad area of archaeological research. "Even if all the material items in a culture are related to its non-material aspects, the archaeological remains may be so limited, altered, or destroyed that a complete description of the past cannot be reconstructed from them ... because the complete past is simply not reflected in the material that remains" (Watson, LeBlanc, and Redman 1971:21).

In Barbados and in archaeological research on slave cultures elsewhere, the means for extracting a more useful body of data has been to utilize historical records dealing with slavery in the specific instances under investigation. Once historical documents have established the existence of slavery, excavated materials have contributed to the study of slave cultures and provide a new perspective on the written sources. The same perspective would have been impossible on the basis of the excavated materials alone. Slavery is an institution of variable structure that cannot be inferred, deduced, or otherwise derived from purely archaeological remains. A search of the literature of prehistory has revealed a glaring lack of mention of slavery, not because prehistorians have been methodologically naive, as Binford (1968:23) has maintained, but simply because archaeological data do not identify slave status and slavery. The fact that there were blacks in Barbados who were free, Amerindians who were either free or slave, and poor whites who were free or indentured servants (but who lived at the same low economic level as some freedmen and even black slaves) is also a cause for interpretative concern when only artifactual or skeletal remains are used.

Although the archaeological record has definite limitations, archaeology can in fact contribute to the sociocultural history of "inarticulate" peoples (Ascher 1974:10–11) who left no written records and about whom documentary sources are often silent, contradictory, or biased. We believe that plantation slavery and slave culture can be most profitably explored through the ethnohistorical approach advocated in this book and that our work has shown more detailed results than might have been obtained by employing only one source of data or a single methodology. At the same time, the excavation results from Barbados and other New World slave sites clearly indicate that archaeologists who do not employ the ethnohistorical approach cannot effectively deal with the problem of slavery and slave culture. As Trigger has noted in a more general vein, "Archaeologists must learn to live with the realization that their desire to study whole cultural systems cannot be realized. This, however, is not meant to be an unconstructive comment. On the contrary, the real weakness of much modern archaeology can be attributed to the tendency of many archaeologists to treat their discipline as being merely the 'past tense of ethnology' or a kind of 'paleoanthropology,' rather than defining its goals in terms of the potentialities of its data" (1971:332).

Our study has shown the substance of Trigger's remarks to be true for plantation slavery and slave life. In general, we have defined certain limits to one area of archaeological endeavor; we also believe that we have defined new directions in the study of plantation slavery and slave culture that can be undertaken by applying an archaeological methodology within the ethnohistorical framework.

Appendix A

Excavation Summary: Newton Cemetery

The tabular summary of the excavated cultural and human skeletal materials from Newton cemetery in this appendix is divided into three groups: (1) lines 1–9 provide data on the location and context of interment and basic data on the skeletal materials; lines 10–12 provide additional information on burials interred with coffins; (2) lines 13–21 summarize associated artifactual materials for which some form of chronological data exist; (3) lines 22–29 summarize artifactual materials for which chronological data are currently lacking.

SYMBOLS USED IN TABLE, OTHER THAN THOSE DESCRIBED IN EXPLANATORY NOTES

— Recovered data were insufficient to make a determination for particular burials in this category of information.

0 Absence of the characteristic or artifact, in lines 8–29.

Y Presence of characteristic or artifact, in lines 8, 9, 11.

? Provisional identification.

EXPLANATORY NOTES

Line 1: Location. The square or mound (M: mound) where each interment was found; see figure 9.

Line 2: Articulated or Disturbed. The condition of the burial at the time of excavation; A: fully articulated skeleton, D: disturbed skeleton (generally disturbed to the extent that subsequent interpretation was impaired), A–D: skeleton that was largely articulated for interpretive purposes, but which had been partially disturbed.

Line 3: Orientation. The direction of the head of the individual; N: north, W: west, E: east. These directions are generalized, but few individuals varied more than 5° from the true measurement.

Line 4: Body position. S: supine; P: prone; F: flexed; S* (Burial 46): the individual may have been interred on its left side.

Line 5: Coffin use. C: coffin; NC: no coffin; P: possible coffin.

Line 6: Age. I: infant; C: child; AD: adolescent; YA: young adult; A: adult; OA: old adult. Age was primarily determined from dental criteria described in chapter 5. An "old adult" is strictly a relative estimation and includes individuals from approximately age 30 upward.

Line 7: Sex. Sex was ascertained by applying criteria described in chapter 5; M: male; F: female. The poor preservation of many burials often made sexing impossible even where postinterment disturbance was not a factor.

Line 8: Dental pipewear.

Line 9: Filed incisors.

Line 10: Coffin handles. The number of coffin handles associated with particular burials.

Line 11: Metal plates over chests. Though assumed to be part of the coffin, the exact function of these plates is unknown.

Line 12: Nails and tacks. The number of nails and tacks with individual burials; N: nails, T: tacks, Fe: iron, and Cu: copper—followed by the number of each. In some cases the presence of nails and tacks was used to infer coffin use although coffin handles were absent. Evidence for nails or tacks was found with Burial 36, but poor preservation made more specific identification impossible.

Line 13: Whole pipes. The number of whole pipes (bowl or bowl fragment attached to a full or partial stem) found with each burial. The two pipes listed with Burial 83 could have been associated with that burial or Burial 81. With the exception of the pipe with Burial 72, all pipes are of white clay.

Line 14: Pipestem or bowl fragments. The number of pipe fragments found in generalized contexts and usually not in direct association with a burial.

Line 15: Buttons. The number of buttons found with individual burials; S: shell, B: bone. A metal button was found in square 15N3W but its burial association could not be determined.

Line 16: Lead glazed slipware (combed yellow). Number of sherds with individual burials; date range, 1670–1795.

Line 17: Buckley Ware. Number of sherds with individual burials; date range, 1720–1803.

Line 18: Plain white delftware. Number of sherds with individual burials; date range, 1640–1800.

Line 19: Creamware. Number of sherds with individual burials; date range, 1762–1820.

Line 20: Pearlware (blue and green edged). Number of sherds with individual burials; date range, 1780–1830.

Line 21: Burslem stoneware. Number of sherds with individual burials; date range, 1705–40.

Line 22: Locally made glazed redware. Number of sherds with individual burials. The number given for Burial 22 refers to a large fragment of the original vessel, reconstructed from several sherds (see figure 24).

Line 23: Plain redware. Number of sherds with individual burials.

Line 24: Nonwheel-made ceramics. Number of sherds with individual burials.

Line 25: Glass beads. Number with individual burials.

Line 26: Iron knives. Number with individual burials.

Line 27: Finger rings. Number with individual burials.

Line 28: Glass fragments. Number with individual burials.

Line 29: Other artifacts. The number and type with individual burials.:* other artifacts associated with Burial 72 (see chapter 5).

Burials

Line	1	2	3	4	5	6	7	8
1	18N24W	M 2	M 2	M 2	M 2	M 2	M 2	M 2
2	D	D	A	D	A	A-D	D	A
3	W	—	W	—	W	W	—	W
4	S	—	S	—	S	S	—	S
5	C	P	P	P	C	C	C	C
6	YA	OA	YA	—	OA	YA	—	YA
7	—	M	M	F	M	F	M	F
8	0	—	Y	—	Y	0	—	0
9	0	—	0	—	0	0	—	0
10	0	0	0	0	8	4	3	4
11	0	—	0	0	0	0	0	Y
12	N-Fe 40 T-Cu 1	N-Fe 8 T-Cu 1	N-Fe 8	N-Fe 3	N-Fe 25	N-Fe 40	N-Fe 22 T-Fe 6	N-Fe 12 T-Fe 3
13	0	0	0	1	0	0	0	1

Burials

Line	1	2	3	4	5	6	7	8
14	2	1	2	0	1	2	2	0
15	0	0	0	0	0	0	0	0
16	0	0	0	0	0	0	0	0
17	0	0	0	0	0	0	0	0
18	0	0	0	0	0	1	0	0
19	1	0	0	2	0	6	12	4
20	0	0	0	0	0	3	5	2
21	0	0	0	0	0	0	0	0
22	2	0	0	0	0	0	3	0
23	10	0	2	0	0	8	11	4
24	0	0	0	0	0	0	0	0
25	0	0	0	0	0	0	0	0
26	0	0	0	0	0	0	0	0
27	0	0	0	0	0	0	0	0
28	0	0	0	0	0	1	0	0
29	0	0	0	0	0	0	0	0

Burials

Line	9	10	11	12	13	14	15	16
1	M 1	M 2	M 2	M 2	M 2	M 2	M 2	M 2
2	A	A	D	D	D	D	A-D	D
3	W	W	—	—	N	—	W	—

	Burials							
Line	9	10	11	12	13	14	15	16
4	P	S	—	—	—	—	S	—
5	NC	C	—	—	C	P	C	C
6	YA	YA	C	—	YA	C	OA	C
7	F	F	—	—	M	—	—	F?
8	Y	Y	—	—	0	—	—	—
9	0	0	—	—	0	—	—	—
10	0	9	—	—	2	—	2	6
11	0	0	—	—	0	—	0	0
12	0	N-Fe 27 T-Fe 22	—	—	N-Fe 8	—	N-Fe 13 T-Cu 1	N-Fe 22
13	0	1	0	0	0	0	0	0
14	2	2	0	0	2	0	0	3
15	0	0	0	0	0	0	0	0
16	0	0	0	0	0	0	4	0
17	0	2	0	0	0	0	0	0
18	0	0	0	0	1	0	1	1
19	0	0	0	0	2	0	1	3
20	0	0	0	0	0	0	0	1
21	0	0	0	0	0	0	0	0
22	0	0	0	0	0	0	0	0
23	1	13	0	0	4	0	10	10
24	0	0	0	0	0	0	0	0

Burials

Line	9	10	11	12	13	14	15	16
25	0	0	0	0	0	0	0	0
26	0	0	0	0	0	0	0	0
27	0	0	0	0	0	0	0	0
28	0	0	0	0	0	0	0	1
29	0	0	0	0	0	0	0	0

Burials

Line	17	18	19	20	21	22	23	24
1	M 2	M 2	M 2	M 2.	M 2	M 2	M 2	M 2
2	D	D	D	A	D	A-D	D	A-D
3	—	—	—	W	—	W	—	W
4	—	—	—	S	—	S	—	S
5	C	C	C	C	C	C	P	P
6	IC	OA	I	OA	I	YA	OA	YA
7	—	—	—	M	—	F	—	M
8	—	—	—	—	—	0	0	0
9	—	—	—	—	—	0	0	0
10	—	—	3	4	with	1	0	1
11	—	—	0	Y	burial	0	0	0
12	—	—	N-Fe 8	N-Fe 9	20	N-Fe 8	N-Fe 4	0
13	0	0	0	1	0	0	0	0
14	0	0	0	1	0	1	1	2

Burials

Line	17	18	19	20	21	22	23	24
15	0	0	0	0	0	0	0	0
16	0	0	1	0	0	0	0	0
17	0	0	0	0	0	0	0	0
18	0	0	0	0	0	0	0	0
19	0	0	0	0	0	1	0	1
20	0	0	0	0	0	0	0	0
21	0	0	0	0	0	0	0	0
22	0	0	0	0	0	1	0	0
23	0	0	4	3	0	2	0	1
24	0	0	0	0	0	0	0	0
25	0	0	0	0	0	8	0	0
26	0	0	0	0	0	0	0	0
27	0	0	0	0	0	0	0	1
28	0	0	0	0	0	0	0	0
29	0	0	0	0	0	0	0	0

Burials

Line	25	26	27	28	29	30	31	32
1	M 2	M 2	M 2	M 2	M 2	M 2	M 2	M 2
2	D	D	D	A	D	D	A	D
3	—	W	W	W	—	—	W	—
4	—	S	—	S	S	S	S	—

Burials

Line	25	26	27	28	29	30	31	32
5	P	P	P	C	P	NC	C	P
6	YA	YA	OA	YA	YA	OA	YA	—
7	—	—	M	—	—	M	F	—
8	0	0	Y	0	—	Y	—	—
9	0	0	0	0	—	0	—	—
10	—	0	1	4	3	see	7	—
11	—	0	0	0	—	burial	Y	—
12	N-Fe 2 T-Cu 1	N-Fe 6	N-Fe 2 T-Fe 1	N-Fe 25 T-Fe 16	N-Fe 47 T-Fe 12 T-Cu 1	29	N-Fe 36 T-Fe 2	— —
13	0	0	0	2	0	0	0	0
14	0	0	1	1	3	0	2	0
15	0	0	0	0	0	0	S-5	0
16	0	0	0	0	0	0	6	0
17	0	0	0	0	0	0	0	0
18	0	0	0	0	0	0	2	0
19	0	0	0	0	6	0	14	0
20	0	0	0	0	0	0	1	0
21	0	0	0	0	0	0	0	0
22	0	0	0	0	0	0	0	0
23	0	0	0	4	5	0	17	0
24	0	0	0	0	0	0	0	0
25	0	0	0	0	0	0	0	0

	Burials							
Line	25	26	27	28	29	30	31	32
26	0	0	0	1	0	0	1	0
27	0	0	0	0	0	0	0	0
28	0	0	0	0	0	0	1	0
29	0	0	0	0	0	0	6 copper fasteners	0

	Burials							
Line	33	34	35	36	37	38	39	40
1	27.5N25W	M 3	M 3	31N37W	M 2	M 2	M 2	M 2
2	A	A-D	A-D	A	D	D	D	D
3	W	E	N	W	—	—	—	—
4	S	S	S	S	—	—	—	—
5	P	P	NC	P	P	C	P	NC
6	YA	YA	OA	YA	OA	OA	YA	YA
7	M	F	M	M	—	—	—	—
8	0	0	Y	Y	0	0	—	Y
9	0	0	Y	0	0	0	—	—
10	0	0	0	0	0	3	0	0
11	0	0	0	0	0	0	0	0
12	N-Fe 16	N-Fe 11	N-Fe 2	Y	N-Fe 9 T-Fe 3	N-Fe 6 T-Fe 1	0	0
13	1	1	0	0	0	1	0	0
14	0	0	0	0	0	0	0	0

Burials

Line	33	34	35	36	37	38	39	40
15	0	0	0	0	0	0	0	0
16	0	0	0	0	0	0	0	0
17	0	0	0	0	0	0	0	0
18	0	0	0	0	0	0	0	0
19	0	0	1	0	0	0	0	0
20	0	0	0	0	0	0	0	0
21	0	0	0	0	0	0	0	0
22	0	0	0	0	0	0	0	0
23	0	1	1	0	1	2	0	0
24	0	0	0	0	0	0	0	0
25	0	0	0	31	0	0	0	0
26	0	0	0	1	0	0	0	0
27	0	0	0	0	0	0	0	0
28	0	0	1	0	0	1	0	0
29	2 metal door hinges	0	1 metal belt buckle	0	0	0	0	0

Burials

Line	41	42	43	44	45	46	47	48
1	M 2	M 2	18N15W	33N57W	15N3W	27N12W	36N42W	36N42
2	D	D	A-D	A-D	D	A-D	D	A-D
3	—	—	E	E	E	E	W	N

	Burials							
Line	41	42	43	44	45	46	47	48
4	—	—	S	S	—	S*	S	S
5	NC	NC	NC	NC	NC	NC	NC	NC
6	—	YA	YA	OA	C	YA	OA	OA
7	—	—	F	M	—	M?	—	F?
8	—	0	0	0	—	Y?	0	Y?
9	—	0	0	0	—	0	0	Y
10	—	—	0	0	0	0	0	0
11	—	—	0	0	0	0	0	0
12	—	—	0	0	0	N-Fe 1	0	0
13	0	0	1	0	0	0	0	0
14	0	0	0	1	0	0	0	0
15	0	0	0	1	0	0	0	0
16	0	0	0	0	0	0	0	0
17	0	0	0	0	0	0	0	0
18	0	0	0	0	0	0	0	0
19	0	0	0	0	0	0	0	0
20	0	0	0	0	0	0	0	0
21	0	0	0	0	0	0	0	0
22	0	0	0	0	0	0	0	0
23	0	0	7	3	2	1	0	1
24	0	0	0	0	0	0	0	0
25	0	0	0	0	0	0	0	0

Burials

Line	41	42	43	44	45	46	47	48
26	0	0	0	0	0	0	0	0
27	0	0	0	0	0	0	0	0
28	0	0	0	0	1	0	0	1
29	0	0	0	0	0	0	0	0

Burials

Line	49	50	51	52	53	54	55	56
1	30N9W	30N9W	30N9W	30N9W	30N9W	30N9W	30N9W	30N9W
2	D	D	D	D	D	A-D	A	A
3	—	—	—	—	W	W	E	W
4	—	—	—	—	S	S	S	S
5	—	—	—	—	C	C	NC	C
6	C	YA	YA	—	YA	YA	OA	YA
7	—	—	—	—	M	F	M	M
8	—	—	—	—	0	0	0	0
9	—	—	—	—	0	0	0	0
10	—	—	—	—	6	5	0	8
11	—	—	—	—	0	0	0	Y
12	—	—	—	—	N-Fe 43 T-Fe 19	N-Fe 22 T-Fe 9	N-Fe 4 T-Fe 1	N-Fe 21 T-Fe 2
13	0	0	0	0	0	0	2	0
14	0	0	0	0	1	1	0	0
15	0	0	0	0	0	0	0	0

242

Burials

Line	49	50	51	52	53	54	55	56
16	0	0	0	0	0	0	0	0
17	0	0	0	0	0	0	0	0
18	0	0	0	0	0	0	0	0
19	0	0	0	0	0	0	0	0
20	0	0	0	0	0	0	0	0
21	(2 association with specific burial indefinite)				0	0	0	0
22	0	0	0	0	0	0	0	0
23	0	0	0	0	1	2	1	1
24	0	0	0	0	0	1	0	0
25	0	0	0	0	0	0	8	0
26	0	0	0	0	0	0	1	0
27	0	0	0	0	0	0	0	0
28	(5 association with specific burial indefinite)				0	2	7	1
29	0	0	0	0	0	1 metal fastener	1 metal fastener, 1 glass object	2 copper earrings

Burials

Line	57	58	59	60	61	62	63	64
1	30N9W	30N9W	30N9W	30N9W	30N9W	30N9W	30N9W	30N9W
2	D	A	D	A	A	D	A	A
3	—	W	—	W	E	—	E	W

APPENDIX A

Burials

Line	57	58	59	60	61	62	63	64
4	—	S	—	S	S	—	S	S
5	—	C	—	NC	NC	—	NC	C
6	—	OA	AD	OA	AD	A	—	OA
7	—	M	—	F	F?	—	—	M
8	—	Y	0	—	—	—	Y	Y
9	—	0	0	—	—	—	0	0
10	0	7	0	0	0	0	0	11
11	0	Y	0	0	0	0	0	Y
12	0	N-Fe 9	T-Fe 1	N-Fe 4	N-Fe 2	N-Fe 2	0	N-Fe 17 T-Fe 4
13	0	0	0	0	0	1	0	0
14	0	1	0	1	0	1	0	1
15	0	0	0	0	0	0	0	B-4 S-2
16	0	0	0	0	0	0	0	0
17	0	0	0	0	0	0	0	0
18	0	0	0	0	0	0	0	0
19	0	0	0	0	0	0	0	0
20	0	0	0	0	0	0	0	0
21	0	0	0	0	0	0	0	0
22	0	0	0	0	0	0	0	0
23	0	0	0	0	0	0	0	0
24	0	0	0	0	0	0	0	0

Burials

Line	57	58	59	60	61	62	63	64
25	0	2	81	287	313	0	62	0
26	0	0	0	0	0	0	0	0
27	0	0	0	0	0	0	2	0
28	0	2	0	1	0	0	0	0
29	0	2 iron fasteners	0	1 glass object, 1 copper-covered wood fragment	0	0	0	0

Burials

Line	65	66	67	68	69	70	71	72
1	30N9W	21N9W	21N9W	21N9W	21N9W	21N9W	21N9W	36N66W
2	D	A	D	D	A	A	A	A
3	—	W	E	E	W	W	W	E
4	—	S	S	F	S	S	S	S
5	—	NC	NC	NC	P	P	C	NC
6	YA	A	A	—	OA	C	A	OA
7	—	M	—	—	M	—	F	M
8	0	0	—	—	Y	0	Y	Y
9	0	0	—	—	0	0	0	0
10	0	0	0	0	0	with	3	0
11	0	0	0	0	0	burial	0	0
12	0	N-Fe 3	0	0	N-Fe 11	69	N-Fe 4 T-Fe 3	N-Fe 4

Burials

Line	65	66	67	68	69	70	71	72
13	0	0	0	0	0	0	0	1
14	0	1	1	0	0	0	0	0
15	0	0	0	0	0	0	0	0
16	0	0	0	0	0	0	0	0
17	0	0	0	0	0	0	0	0
18	0	0	0	0	0	0	0	0
19	0	0	0	0	0	0	0	0
20	0	0	0	0	0	0	0	0
21	0	0	0	0	0	0	0	0
22	0	0	0	0	0	0	0	0
23	0	1	0	0	0	0	1	0
24	0	0	0	0	0	0	0	0
25	0	0	0	0	0	0	0	14
26	0	0	0	0	0	0	0	1
27	0	0	0	0	0	0	0	3
28	0	0	0	0	0	0	0	0
29	0	0	0	0	1 metal fastener	0	0	*

Burials

Line	73	74	75	76	77	78	79	80
1	24N15W	36N66W	36N30W	24N15W	24N15W	27N54W	21N3W	M 2
2	A	D	A	A	A	A	A	D

Excavation Summary: Newton Cemetery

				Burials				
Line	73	74	75	76	77	78	79	80
3	E	—	E	W	E	E	E	W
4	S	S	S	S	S	S	S	S
5	NC	NC	NC	NC	NC	NC	NC	C
6	AD	OA	A	AD	A	YA	OA	AD
7	M?	M	F	M?	—	M	—	—
8	0	Y	Y	Y	Y	Y	—	0
9	0	0	0	0	0	0	—	0
10	0	0	0	0	0	0	0	0
11	0	0	0	0	0	0	0	0
12	0	0	0	0	0	0	N-Fe 4	N-Fe 3
13	0	1	0	0	1	0	0	0
14	1	0	0	0	0	0	0	0
15	0	0	0	0	0	0	0	0
16	0	0	0	0	0	0	0	3
17	0	0	0	0	0	0	0	0
18	0	0	0	0	0	0	0	0
19	0	0	0	0	0	0	0	13
20	0	0	0	0	0	0	0	0
21	0	0	0	0	0	0	0	0
22	0	0	0	0	0	0	1	9
23	0	0	0	1	0	0	9	26
24	0	0	0	0	0	0	0	0

Burials

Line	73	74	75	76	77	78	79	80
25	0	1	0	0	88	0	0	0
26	0	0	0	0	0	0	0	0
27	0	0	0	0	0	0	0	0
28	0	0	0	0	0	0	0	1
29	0	0	0	0	0	0	0	0

Burials

Line	81	82	83	84	85	86	87	88
1	M 2	M 2	M 2	M 2	M 2	24N33W	M 2	M 2
2	D	D	A	A	A	D	A-D	A
3	—	W	W	W	W	E	W	W
4	—	S	S	S	S	S	S	S
5	—	NC	C	C	C	P	P	P
6	YA	C	A	C	OA	A	A	OA
7	M	—	F	—	M?	—	—	—
8	0	—	Y	—	Y	0	Y?	Y
9	0	—	0	—	0	0	0	—
10	0	0	0	0	0	0	0	0
11	0	0	0	0	0	0	0	0
12	N-Fe 2	N-Fe 7 or	N-Fe 6	N-Fe 4	N-Fe 4	N-Fe 3	N-Fe 3	N-Fe 4
13	1	0	1	0	1	0	0	0
14	1	0	2	0	0	0	0	0

Burials

Line	81	82	83	84	85	86	87	88
15	0	0	0	0	0	0	0	0
16	0	0	0	0	0	0	0	0
17	0	0	0	0	0	0	0	0
18	0	0	0	0	0	0	0	0
19	0	0	0	0	0	0	0	0
20	0	0	0	0	0	0	0	0
21	0	0	0	0	0	0	0	0
22	0	1	1	0	0	0	0	0
23	0	0	0	1	0	0	0	0
24	0	0	0	0	0	0	0	0
25	0	0	0	0	0	0	4	0
26	0	0	0	0	0	1	0	0
27	0	0	0	0	0	0	0	0
28	1	0	0	0	0	0	0	0
29	0	0	0	0	1 copper pin	0	0	0

Burials

Line	89	90	91	92
1	M 2	24N33W	17.5N4W	18N24W
2	A	D	D	D
3	W	E?	W	—
4	S	—	S	—

Burials

Line	89	90	91	92
5	P	C	P	—
6	AD	A	—	C
7	—	F	—	—
8	—	—	0	—
9	—	—	0	—
10	0	0	0	0
11	0	0	0	0
12	N-Fe 4	N-Fe 11	N-Fe 11	0
13	1	1	0	0
14	0	1	0	0
15	0	0	0	0
16	0	0	0	0
17	0	0	0	0
18	0	0	0	0
19	0	0	0	0
20	0	0	0	0
21	0	0	0	0
22	0	0	0	0
23	0	0	0	0
24	0	0	0	0
25	0	0	0	0
26	0	0	0	0
27	0	0	0	0
28	0	0	0	0
29	0	0	0	0

Appendix B

Clay Pipes from Newton Plantation Excavations

Crawford H. Blakeman, Jr., and Robert V. Riordan

White clay tobacco pipes are common finds at New World historical sites. Great quantities were manufactured in Europe, and large numbers were exported to the New World colonies. Clay pipes were inexpensive and were used by both sexes and all classes of society (Pritchard 1923:169, Oswald 1951:153). Over the years, pipe styles and manufacturing techniques gradually changed. The broad outlines of these changes are known today, and historical records give the names of many pipemakers and the periods during which they worked. Research over several decades has developed the potential of pipes as a source of chronological information for historic archaeology.

Historical sources record the use of pipes by Barbadian slaves, and numerous cases of characteristic dental wear in adult skeletons caused by the use of clay pipes attest to frequent pipe use by Newton slaves (see chapter 5). Of the ninety-two burials, seventeen (23 percent of the cemetery's adult population) had associated pipes. In addition, pipestem fragments and bowl fragments were found in the fill surrounding thirty-six of the ninety-two individuals. One whole pipe and twenty-eight pipe fragments were also recovered from the surface and general fill of the cemetery lot.

As objects of fired clay, pipes, like pottery, were subject to a high degree of accidental breakage. For whites, it was probably easier to replace pipes (because they were cheap) than to guard excessively against their breakage. The life of a pipe may also have been governed to some extent by hygenic considerations: Spence noted that "at one time it was the practice for pipes to be handed round from man to man, which unhygenic custom was somewhat mitigated by the more fastidious breaking off a small length of the stem before taking their turn" (1955:62). We are uncertain how much this last factor may have influenced the lifespan of the pipes used by slaves, but stems were undoubtedly shortened both accidentally through breakage and purposefully to gain fresh mouthpieces.

251

Most frequently pipes were broken in normal use before being discarded. As Iain Walker has noted, "the discovery of whole pipes in archaeological contexts is virtually unknown" (1967b:188). In general the pipes found by archaeologists at historic sites were originally discarded only when they became unfit for additional use. The manner of their disposal and subsurface crushing probably further altered most pipes from their condition at the time of their disposal. At Jamestown, for example, by 1954 "only three or four complete stems" had been located among about 50,000 stem fragments and 5,000 "bowls or major portions of bowls" (Harrington 1954). Although the sample is considerably smaller, the pattern at Fort Shantok in Connecticut is somewhat similar; 201 specimens were recovered, including 30 bowl fragments and 170 stem fragments, but only 1 whole pipe was found in the backdirt (Salwen 1966). The record is probably similar at other sites, but in most instances precise frequencies have not been published.

The feature that is perhaps unique about the sample of twenty-one whole pipes (defined as a significant portion of the bowl and a section of attached stem) from Newton cemetery is that the pipes are essentially the same as they were when last used by their owners. Artifacts deposited as grave goods are probably far more likely to survive in complete form than are similar objects that were casually discarded. An undisturbed cemetery has not been the usual type of site investigated by historic archaeologists; parts of a single pipe may be widely and irretrievably separated in the fill of an old house site or a fort bastion. Pipes interred with burials at Newton cemetery were subjected to the usual dangers to preservation inherent in burial, and bowls were broken and long stems fractured. In undisturbed graves, however, the pieces remained in place and pipes could be reconstructed.

The average stem length (measured from the point where the back of the bowl begins to ascend from the stem to the end of the stem) for the twenty-one whole pipes is 9.5 centimeters. The range extends upward to 24.5 centimeters for a pipe with Burial 89 (figure 32E).

The pipe sample at Newton cemetery spans several generations of the pipemaker's art. For a collection of pipes from a single location, the Newton sample is remarkable for the time it covers and the diversity of its origin.

DATING THE PIPES

Pipes provide the best archaeological data for the dating of Newton cemetery. Three characteristics of the pipes are independently datable: pipe bowl forms, stem bore diameters, and makers' marks. When analyzed in conjunction with one another, these three traits can provide an estimate for the date of manufacture of the pipes and, by extension, they can be used to date the cemetery itself.

Using these pipe attributes to date the cemetery depends on two assumptions: first, that the pipes were buried with their original owners or users, or, at least, contemporaneously with the life of their original owners or users—that is, the pipes found in burial association were not heirlooms interred with someone who lived long after the date of the pipes' manufacture; and second, that the breakage rate of the pipes was relatively high, and that an individual had not used the particular pipe buried with him for a long period of time. If either of these assumptions is not valid for the Barbadian slave population, then the pipe dates will not accurately reflect the dates of the burials in Newton cemetery.

In *The Pipe Book*, Dunhill (1924:204–224) reported that during the seventeenth and eighteenth centuries in England the replacement rate of pipes was high. This pattern of usage would be consistent with both our assumptions. In England, however, pipes were cheap and easy to obtain. Therefore, people felt no pressure to use pipes after they were broken or damaged. In contrast, Barbadian slaves probably could not rapidly replace their pipes and may have been more careful to prevent breakage. Slaves also probably used pipes after they were partially broken, as the wear at the tip of broken stems in some Newton examples seems to show. To the extent that this long-term usage of pipes may have existed at Newton, the dates which we have derived from the pipe analysis may be too early for the actual interments of the individuals in the cemetery. The pipe dates should be taken as a baseline for dating the burials in the cemetery. The magnitude of the lag that may have existed between the manufacture of the pipes and their actual deposition in the cemetery would determine the time difference between the pipe dates and the cemetery dates; at present this lag is problematic.

BOWL FORM DATES

Dunhill (1924) noted that the earliest English clay pipes were very small because of the cost of tobacco in Elizabethan England. These early pipes had heels (figure 29), barrel-shaped bowls, and an obvious obtuse angle between the stem and the bowl.

By the end of the seventeenth century the bowls had spurs rather than heels, a smaller angle between stem and bowl, and simpler curves. This shift in bowl form was one of the most obvious trends

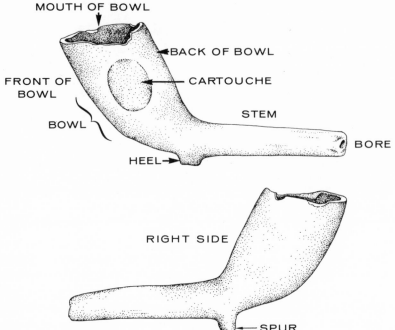

LEFT SIDE

MOUTH OF BOWL

BACK OF BOWL

FRONT OF BOWL

CARTOUCHE

STEM

BOWL

BORE

HEEL→

RIGHT SIDE

SPUR

Figure 29. Composite drawing of white clay tobacco pipe, illustrating principal parts.

in pipe development to those who studied clay pipes. Oswald systematized the classification of pipe bowl forms and fit such changes into a chronological framework. His two articles (1951, 1961) are the best sources for dating pipes by their bowl forms.

We encountered two problems in using Oswald's typology to date the Newton pipes. The most troublesome problem was the lack of consistency of the outline drawings in the two articles. For example, a bowl form that, according to the text, was the same in both articles would in some cases be obviously different when the outline drawings in the two articles were compared. The second problem involved establishing priorities in making the classifications. In several cases the pipes from Newton could fit into more than one of Oswald's groups, depending on which bowl traits were considered as the primary criteria for classification. Oswald does not make it clear if the traits should be considered hierarchically in making bowl form classifications, or if the best compromise form should be selected by equally weighing all bowl traits. He apparently did not intend his typology to be either rigid or absolute.

Therefore, we made bowl form classifications on the basis of the best general fit of Oswald's types.

To circumvent problems in bowl classification which might have arisen because of the individual biases of one analyst, we independently classified the bowls. We then compared results and made a joint effort to resolve discrepancies.

The median date for the bowl form for each of the twenty-one whole pipes is given in table 20. Although all but one pipe were found in close association with burials, the given dates do not imply that a burial was made at a specific time. The bowl dates and bowl form classes are not secure enough to date individual events. In-

TABLE 20. Burials with whole pipes from Newton cemetery excavations.

	Burials					Whole pipes			
Burial	Location[b]	Head orientation	Coffin	Dental pipeware	Pipe number	Bore diameter (64ths)	Median bowl date	Bowl date range	Figure
4	Mound 2	—	P	—	—	4	1815	1780–1850	31*A*
8	Mound 2	W	+	n	—	5	1815	1780–1850	30C
10	Mound 2	W	+	+	—	5	1815	1780–1850	30B
20	Mound 2	W	+	—	—	5	1815	1780–1850	31C
28	Mound 2	W	+	n	1	5	1705	1680–1730	30*A*
28	Mound 2	W	+	n	2	5	1705	1680–1730	30D
33	field	W	P	n	—	6	1695	1680–1720	32*A*
34	Mound 3	E	P	n	—	7	1690	1670–1710	31D
38	Mound 2	—	+	n	—	5	1705	1680–1730	31B
43	field	E	n	n	—	6	1705	1680–1730	32C
55	field	E	n	n	1	5	1705	1680–1730	34D
55	field	E	n	n	2	5	1705	1680–1730	34C
62	field	—	—	—	—	7	1700	1680–1720	33B
74	field	—	n	+	—	7	1695	1680–1710	33C
77	field	E	n	+	—	8	1680	1670–1690	33*A*
81 [or 83]	Mound 2	—	—	n	1	6	1705	1680–1730	34B
[81 or] 83	Mound 2	W	+	+	2	6	1680	1670–1690	34*A*
85	Mound 2	W	+	+	—	5	1745	1710–1780	32B
89	Mound 2	W	P	—	—	5	1730	1690–1770	32E
90	field	E?	+	—	—	7	1700	1680–1720	33D
—[a]	field	—	—	—	—	7	1645	1620–1670	32D

[a] Pipe had no burial association; it was excavated between Mounds 1 and 2.
[b] Field refers to nonmound areas. See figure 9 for burial locations.

stead, the burials will be examined in groups, and the pipe bowl forms will be used to establish the period during which it was most likely that the burials as a group were made.

The total range of the median dates of the bowls from Newton is 170 years, from 1645 to 1815, which includes most of the slave period in Barbados. The bowl forms of the whole pipes are illustrated in figures 30–34.

The mean of the median dates for the bowls from several groups of burials in table 21 indicate that the most likely period for the major use of the cemetery was from the end of the seventeenth century through the first half of the eighteenth. If the bowl dates are accurate it would appear that Mound 2 was in use later than the rest of the cemetery. Consistent with this later use of Mound 2 is the fact that none of the bowls found outside of Mound 2 have a post-1705 median date, and only one bowl in Mound 2 is dated pre-1705.

Therefore, the bowl form dates suggest that although the cemetery may have been used for nearly 175 years, the primary use of the cemetery was probably in the first half of the eighteenth century or later, depending upon the lag between pipe manufacture and deposition. Also the means of the median bowl dates indicate

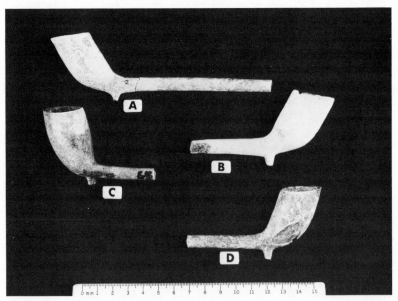

Figure 30. Whole pipes with burials, Newton cemetery. *A:* Burial 28, pipe 1; *B:* Burial 10; *C:* Burial 8; *D:* Burial 28, pipe 2. (See table 20 for dates.)

TABLE 21. Dates of pipe bowls from grave lots at Newton cemetery.

Grave lot	Burials	Pipes	Mean of median bowl dates
Mound 2	9	11	1749
Field (nonmound)	7	8	1698
Head to east	7	7	1697
Head to west	8	10	1741
Coffin	8	10	1742
Coffinless	5	6	1697
Head to east, coffinless	5	6	1697
Head to west, coffin	7	9	1747
Total number of burials with datable bowls	17	21	1722

that cemetery usage can be divided into two phases: near the turn of the eighteenth century burials were made in the general field area; and during the second quarter of the eighteenth century burials were made in Mound 2 (see figures 8 and 9).

PIPESTEM DATES

Unlike bowls, which are rarely preserved intact (and which must be whole if they are to be dated), pipestems are often preserved

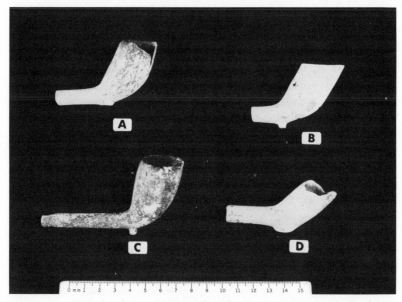

Figure 31. Whole pipes with burials, Newton cemetery. *A:* Burial 4; *B:* Burial 38; *C:* Burial 20; *D:* Burial 34. (See table 20 for dates.)

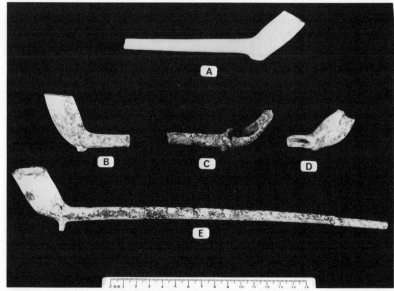

Figure 32. Whole pipes with burials, Newton cemetery. *A:* Burial 33; *B:* Burial 85; *C:* Burial 43; *D:* no burial association; excavated between Mounds 1 and 2; *E:* Burial 89. (See table 20 for dates.)

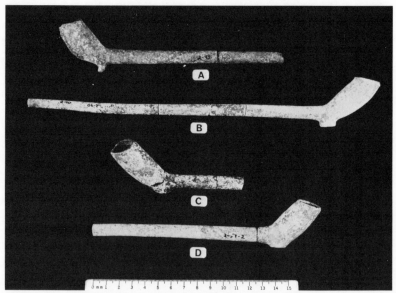

Figure 33. Whole pipes with burials, Newton cemetery. *A:* Burial 77; *B:* Burial 62; *C:* Burial 74; *D:* Burial 90. (See table 20 for dates.)

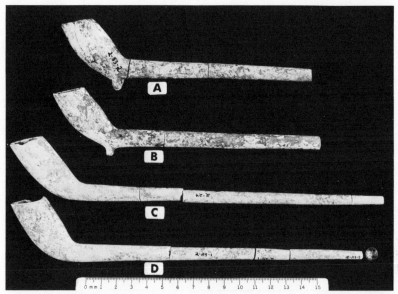

Figure 34. Whole pipes with burials, Newton cemetery. *A:* near Burials 81 and 83, pipe 2; *B:* near Burials 81 and 83, pipe 1; *C:* Burial 55, pipe 2; *D:* Burial 55, pipe 1, with glass object as found in association. (See table 20 for dates.)

and can be dated even if they are in fragmentary form. Harrington (1954) was the first to date stem fragments by measuring the stem bore diameter. His initial article stimulated an outburst of revisions and rebuttals dealing with the accuracy and validity of utilizing bore diameters as dating devices (see, for example, Binford 1962b, 1972; Chalkley 1955; Hanson 1971, 1972; Harrington 1955; Heighton and Deagan 1972; Walker 1965).

While examining pipestems from dated archaeological contexts, Harrington observed a tendency toward a decrease in bore diameter through time. When these data were tabulated, he found that bore diameters consistently decreased from a maximum of nine sixty-fourths of an inch to a minimum of four sixty-fourths of an inch between 1620 and 1800 (figure 35). He believed this trend resulted from the increase in stem lengths in the seventeenth and eighteenth centuries: "What really counts however, is whether there is a time-hole size correlation. Archaeological evidence shows quite conclusively that such is the case . . . It was due to a change in pipe styles. As the stem grew longer and slimmer, the hole became smaller in diameter; probably due entirely to mechanical limitations" (1955). Whether the stem length and bore diameter are causally

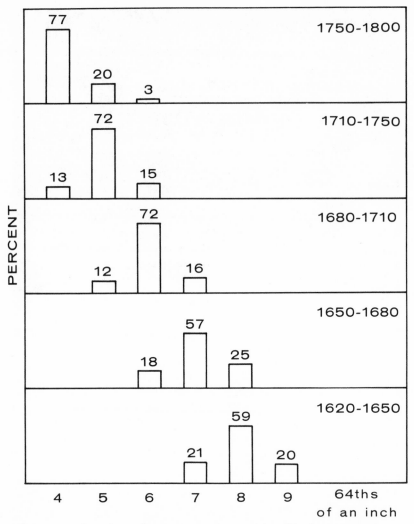

Figure 35. Stem bore diameters and dates. (After Harrington 1954.)

related in this way is not of importance for our purposes because our primary interest is that the trend occurred and that the bore diameters can be used for dating.

However, like bowl form classification, Harrington's bore diameter method can be used only to assign specific pipes to relatively broad time periods. Moreover, we must consider the possibility that a bore diameter may vary over the length of the stem to such a degree that a single stem may fall into two or more date groups. And Harrington's chart leaves some question of how to interpret the results obtained from measuring the bore diameters from a site. Harrington has clearly identified a trend, but he has not provided a method for chronologically placing any specific site that does not closely match one of his five histograms (figure 35).

There are two ready solutions to the problem that a stem bore may vary over the length of the stem. One solution is to measure the bore diameter of each stem section of the whole pipes to determine the probability of the problem occurring. Another solution is to use a relatively large increment for measuring the bore diameters. Large increments will mask minor bore variations along the length of the stem while discriminating the differences of chronological significance. Harrington used $\frac{1}{64}$-inch increments, partially because it was easy to obtain drill bits in $\frac{1}{64}$-inch divisions. Harrington (1955) also used $\frac{1}{128}$-inch increments and obtained essentially the same results. Therefore, it appears that the $\frac{1}{64}$-inch increment is large enough to cover the minor diameter variations of a single bore and small enough to be chronologically meaningful. Harrington's data are presented only in $\frac{1}{64}$-inch increments. In the collection of whole pipes from Newton cemetery, bore diameter variations on long stems were not of such a magnitude that any stem would be thrown into two 64th-inch categories by measuring the bores of several different pieces of the same stem.

Binford (1962b) provided a solution to the problems of broad time periods and interpreting the results of bore measurements. Using Harrington's original data, Binford computed a regression formula with the date as the dependent variable and the bore diameter as the independent variable. Binford's formula is $Y = 1931.85 - 38.26X$ (where Y equals the mean date of the collection of pipes, and X equals the mean bore diameter of the stem fragments measured in $\frac{1}{64}$-inch units). Binford (1962b) also suggested that the standard deviation of the bore diameters could be used to compute the probable span of the period during which the pipes were deposited.

In attempting to refute or revise the Binford formula, Hanson (1971) and Heighton and Deagan (1972) developed other formulae for computing site dates from bore diameters. Binford (1972:245), however, has effectively shown that Hanson's formulae are not as accurate as the original regression formula. Hanson (1972:255–256) has raised serious questions about the accuracy of the data on which the Heighton and Deagan formula was based. Therefore, Binford's seems to be the best formula presently available for calculating dates for groups of pipestems. Between 1680 and 1760, his formula yields dates that are more consistent with dates obtained by other means than do any of the other proposed pipe bore formulae. We used the Binford formula to calculate dates from the bores of pipestems.

In applying his formula, Binford (1962b) noted two potential sources of error. First, if the stem sample is not random (that is, if it is artificially skewed), the date obtained will be skewed. Binford associated this skewing with differential efficiency in the trade network by which pipes were supplied. For example, if pipes were more abundant in a later period than in an earlier one solely because of an increase in the efficiency in the method of obtaining the pipes, then the date would be skewed toward the later period because of the abundance of pipes from that period. There is no reason to suspect that this type of error would have greatly affected the analysis of pipes from Newton. Although the specific patterns of pipe exports from Britain are not known, British trade continued throughout the period of slavery, and there do not appear to have been significant variations in the general types of material goods exported to Barbados. As an independent check on the possibility that there was a shift in the logistics of pipe supplies, we examined the number of burials with pipes in different periods, as these periods were defined by the bowl form dates. Burial orientation appears to be chronologically significant as indicated by the bowl form analysis. Seven (33 percent) of the twenty-one burials with head orientations to the east had pipes, but only eight (22 percent) of the thirty-seven west-headed burials had pipes. The density of whole pipes per burial was 0.33 for head-to-east burials and 0.27 for head-to-west burials. The bowl dates suggest that the west-headed burials have Binford dates that are too early. Possibly the sample of pipes was skewed in favor of the earlier period of use of the cemetery, making the Binford dates slightly too early.

Binford (1962b) also stated that a dating error could be caused by the presence of non-English pipes. Harrington's and Binford's dating methods were based on collections of English-made pipes, and pipes of Dutch or Colonial American manufacture would not necessarily fit the bore diameter pattern of the English ones. (None of the excavated pipes appear to be Dutch or American; moreover, most of the marked pipes can be identified as English.) The imposition of the navigation acts would have reduced the probability of large numbers of Dutch pipes coming to Barbados after the 1650s. However, a brisk trade existed between Barbados and the mainland colonies in the seventeenth and eighteenth centuries, and the possibility that American-made pipes might have been included in that trade must be kept in mind. The actual scale and intensity of the importation of American pipes, if any, and its overall effect on the dates from Newton, is presently unknown.

All the bore diameters of the stems and stem fragments from Newton were measured by Blakeman in an attempt to obtain a consistent measurement. Measurements were made in $\frac{1}{64}$-inch increments by using the butt end of drill bits, as Walker (1965) suggested. The stems of twenty-one whole pipes and seventy-three stem fragments were measured.

The only stems that were definitely associated with specific burials were those of the twenty whole pipes found with the burials. All other pipestems were included either in burial fill or were on the surface of the site. The stem fragments found in the burial fill probably predate the burials and were only incidentally included in the fill.

The Binford formula was used to calculate the dates for several groups of pipes and stem fragments (tables 22 and 23). The dates obtained from the whole pipes in burial association agree with the bowl dates (table 24), in terms of the relative sequence of the

TABLE 22. Dates derived from whole pipes using the Binford formula.

Grave lot	Pipes	Mean	Standard devia-tion	Date	Date range ($\pm 2\sigma$)
Mound 2 pipes in definite burial association	11	5.1	0.51	1737	1698–1776
Mound 2, all pipes	12	5.3	0.72	1731	1676–1786
Field (nonmound)	8	6.4	0.99	1688	1612–1764
Coffin	10	5.4	0.74	1725	1668–1782
Coffinless	6	6.3	1.10	1690	1606–1774
Head to east	7	6.4	1.05	1686	1606–1766
Head to west	10	5.3	0.46	1729	1694–1764
Head to east, coffinless	6	6.3	1.10	1690	1606–1774
Head to west, coffin	9	5.2	0.42	1732	1700–1764
Total number of whole pipes	21	5.8	1.02	1711	1633–1789

burial groups and of the actual absolute dates indicated. The bowl dates and the bore dates were independently derived and need not be consistent; the fact that they are consistent strengthens the argument for the accuracy of the dates.

A problem arises, however, in examining the dates calculated from the stem fragments found in the fill. With the exception of the

TABLE 23. Dates derived from whole pipes plus stem fragments using the Binford formula.

Grave lot	Pipes and frag- ments	Mean	Standard devia- tion	Date	Date range ($\pm 2\sigma$)
Mound 2 burials	56	5.9	1.3	1707	1608–1806
Field (nonmound)	34	6.6	0.87	1678	1611–1745
Head to east	13	6.5	0.93	1685	1614–1756
Head to west	42	6.4	1.38	1689	1583–1795
Coffin	42	6.2	1.06	1694	1613–1775
Coffinless	15	6.6	1.20	1679	1587–1771
Head to west, coffin	33	6.2	0.49	1695	1656–1732
Head to east, coffinless	8	6.4	0.99	1688	1612–1764
Total number of datable stems	93	6.2	1.43	1696	1587–1805

Mound 2 dates, all fragments yield seventeenth-century dates. The relative burial sequence within the cemetery is still supported by the stem fragment dates, but the absolute differences are greatly reduced and the stem fragment dates do not agree well with the bowl dates. This reduction of date differences is probably to be expected. It is likely that stem fragments from grave fill are the remains from previous, disturbed burials. Stem fragments from the fill would be expected to date earlier than the undisturbed burials. Inclusion of the disassociated stem fragments in the dating calculation, then, introduces an error factor that can best be avoided

TABLE 24. Mean bowl dates and mean bore dates from pipes at Newton cemetery.

Grave lot	Mean bowl date	Mean bore date	Year differential
Mound 2 burials	1749	1737	12
Field (nonmound)	1698	1688	10
Head to east	1697	1686	11
Head to west	1741	1729	12
Coffin	1742	1725	17
Coffinless	1697	1690	7
Head to east, coffinless	1697	1690	7
Head to west, coffin	1747	1732	15
Total sample of datable pipes	1722	1711	11

by considering only those whole pipes in firm burial associations.

There are two major probable explanations for the large number of early stem fragments: either stem fragments were introduced with fill from other areas on the estate or a number of early burials with pipes were later disturbed but were not identified in our excavations. A number of disturbed burials indicated interments prior to those completely or partially intact burials that we recovered with associated whole pipes.

In general, by using only the whole pipes, the dates calculated for the burial groups, by both Binford's formula and the mean of the median bowl dates, are consistent and differ by only seventeen years at the maximum (table 24). In all cases the bowl dates are more recent than the bore dates, but both methods of dating indicate a base date of late seventeenth- to mid-eighteenth-century cemetery use, and both suggest gradual changes in patterns of field and mound interments.

MAKERS' MARKS

Of the twenty-one whole pipes associated with skeletal remains, nine had bowls with discernible makers' marks, and one bowl had extensive relief decoration. Eight of these pipes were found in Mound 2: seven were assignable to specific disturbed or undisturbed burials; one was from the fill in the western section of the mound and apparently had been separated from its burial association by subsequent use of the mound. Only two marked pipes came from nonmound burials (Burials 43 and 55). (Besides makers' marks and relief decoration, blank cartouches were found on two pipes, one from a burial in Mound 2 and one from Burial 55.)

Our analysis of pipestem and bowl form chronology suggests that Mound 2 was most intensively used as a burial place during the second quarter of the eighteenth century. The standard deviations of the stem dates also suggest that some interments took place before and after this period of intensive use. Makers' marks potentially offer an independently datable characteristic of clay pipes, providing that the marks can be correctly identified. Because most of the marked pipes are from Mound 2, the dates of manufacture suggested by the marks provide a check on the interpretation of the mound that is independent of the chronology derived from stems and bowls.

Problems exist in exploiting the dating potential of makers' marks. The products of some makers became very popular and the marks were used for a long period. The best known case of this is the TD mark, which was used from the mid-eighteenth to the twentieth centuries (Walker 1966). Variations of the mark exist, but the chronology of these changes is unknown. Another source of difficulty lies in the identification of certain marks with specific pipemakers. We may know that two or more men with similar initials were making pipes at different times, but we do not know which man made a certain pipe with a mark bearing those initials. Even when explicit chronological information can be elicited from a maker's mark, the difficulty of inferring the time lag between the date of a pipe's manufacture and the date of its interment introduces an additional source of caution in using these dates.

Pipes marked TD were associated with Burials 4 and 10. The marks were impressed on the backs of the bowls, inside impressed circles, only portions of which remain visible in both cases (figure 36B, C).

Atkinson (1962:182–183) cites examples of English pipes with TD initials from the early seventeenth century, with the mark located on the heels of bulbous-shaped pipes. Walker's study of TD pipes indicates that the modern TD mark began to be used in the 1750s, probably by a London pipemaker named Thomas Dormer (1966:100). Pipes bearing this mark became extremely popular, leading to the plagiarization of the mark by other makers. Styles of TD marks range from unadorned impressed initials to initials accompanied by ornamental heraldic devices. The multiplicity of styles is well documented by Walker who reports examples of simple impressed initials appearing in dated contexts from the nineteenth century (1966:91).

Without a sequential stylistic chronology for TD marks, it is impossible to conclude more than that it is highly likely that Burials 4 and 10 were interred after 1750. Moreover, the bowl form of the pipe with Burial 10 (figure 30B) suggests that the burial may date from the late eighteenth or early nineteenth century.

One pipe with an impressed RT mark on the back of the bowl (figure 36G; see also pipe 1, figure 34B) was found in the fill of the western section of Mound 2, lying directly alongside another, undecorated pipe (pipe 2, figure 34A). A nearby disturbed burial (Burial 81) may have been the original association of these pipes. Because the association was uncertain, we are using the RT pipe as an indicator of the possible period of use of the immediate area of the mound.

The bowl of the pipe with Burial 43 was broken (figure 32C). A piece that probably came from the back of the bowl contains the letter R in the same style as that on the RT pipe from Mound

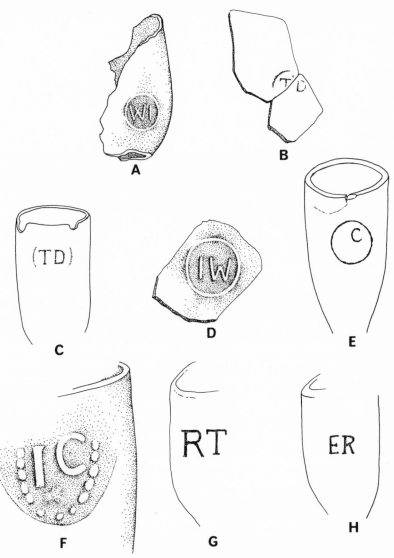

Figure 36. Makers' marks on excavated pipes, Newton cemetery. Not drawn to scale.

2. The bowl portion containing the rest of the mark was missing; it seems likely, however, that this is also an RT pipe.

RT pipes were the products of the Tippet family of Bristol (Walker 1971:73). There were three Robert Tippets: the first gained his freedom from apprenticeship in 1660 and probably died in the 1680s; the second Robert Tippet (son of the first) gained his freedom in 1678 and lived until at least the second decade of the 1700s; the third (son of the second) became a freeman in 1713, but the date of his death is unknown. The widow of the first Robert Tippet was also active in the business during the 1680s and 1690s.

Walker wrote that "certainly all New World Tippet pipes seem to have a medallion" (1971:74), but this assertion is contradicted by the example from Mound 2 (figures 36G; 34B), and perhaps also by the pipe with Burial 43. Walker also noted that "Omwake [1958:12] tentatively suggested that the second Robert may have started with the impressed RT on the back of the bowl, later adding the medallion on the side, and that the third Robert may have used the medallion without the RT" (Walker 1971:73). If Omwake's suggestion about the third Robert Tippet is correct, then the RT pipe from Mound 2 was probably made by either the first or second Robert, and probably dates to a span of years covering the late seventeenth to early eighteenth centuries. If a short time lag between the pipe's manufacture and interment is assumed, and if the association of the pipe with Burial 81 is correct, then Burial 81 was probably interred not much later than about 1720. Burial 88 was immediately underneath 81 and was probably responsible for the disturbance of Burial 81; Burial 88 was probably interred sometime after 1720.

Tippet pipes may have been produced later in the eighteenth century, after the family's interest ended, by a firm or firms using the Tippet molds. Tippet pipes have been found in North American contexts dated from ca. 1740 to 1780 (Hanson and Hsu 1975:141). If this is so, Burial 81 may have been interred later in the eighteenth century than the suggested date of around 1720. At the same time, the median bowl date for both RT pipes is 1705 and the bore-hole diameters of both measure six sixty-fourths of an inch, which further suggests an early eighteenth-century date.

In addition to the TD pipe mentioned above, two other pipes were found with the disturbed remains of Burial 4. One is a fragmentary bowl with the initials WI in raised letters inside a raised circle on the right side of the bowl (figure 36A). This pipe could have been the product of either William Jackson of London, an apprentice in 1720 who would have been making his own pipes by 1730, or William Ilsley of Reading, Berkshire, who was working in 1756 (Leonard H. Gant, personal communication). The third pipe with Burial 4 is decorated by leafy branches and grape clusters molded in relief over the entire bowl surface (figures 37; 31A); there is no discernable maker's mark on the bowl. The leaf design

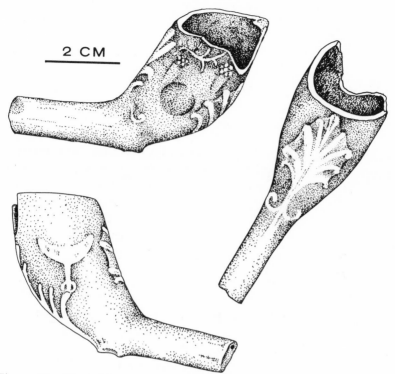

2 CM

Figure 37. Pipe with relief design, Burial 4, Newton cemetery.

was quite conventional during the eighteenth century, and the pipe dates to around the middle of the century (Leonard H. Gant, personal communication). All three pipes from Burial 4 can be interpreted as having been made after 1750 if we favor the William Ilsley origin for the WI mark.

A bowl fragment from Burial 23 is marked with a raised IW inside a raised circle (figure 36D). Pritchard (1923:175) identifies a mark with these initials as having belonged to John Wall of Bristol who was working from the 1640s to the 1660s; Wall generally produced bulbous-shaped bowls with his mark on the heel. This description, however, does not fit the Burial 23 pipe. Atkinson (1965:256) lists IW as one of the molded letter marks used in London around 1700, but he apparently is referring to pipes with marks placed on the sides of the heel. The Burial 23 pipe was marked on the right side of the bowl. Gant has suggested that the mark may be that of John White, a Bristol pipemaker who received his freedom in 1754 and whose products could date from as late as the 1770s or later (personal communication).

Burial 28 had two marked pipes. The mark on one pipe is molded in relief on the right side of the bowl with IC set inside a circle composed of raised dots (figures 36F; 30A). The mark is possibly that of Isaac Carey of Bristol, who became a freeman in 1756 (Leonard H. Gant, personal communication). On the second pipe with Burial 28 (figure 30D), the back of the bowl, close to the mouth, has a C set off-center inside a circle (figure 36E). To the left of the C, and slightly below it, there is a very faint impression of what appears to be an I (not illustrated in figure 36E), but the impression is too faint to decipher the letter with certainty. The mark, however, may also be that of Isaac Carey.

Burial 55 was the only nonmound burial with a marked pipe. The letters ER are deeply impressed on the back of the bowl (figures 36H; 34C). The bowl form corresponds most closely to Oswald's 9B form, without a spur (1961:61), suggesting an early eighteenth-century date, and the ER mark was probably that of Edward Randall, a London pipemaker whose products date between 1700 and 1740 (Leonard H. Gant, personal communication).

Milling or rouletting around the mouth of the pipe bowl is another indicator of the period of manufacture of an English pipe. Milling was a common practice during the seventeenth century, and it did not continue much after 1700 (Walker 1967b:191). Milling is found on only one of the marked pipes, the RT pipe from the western section of Mound 2 (see figure 34B). Also in the western section of Mound 2 were two other milled pipes, one with Burial 90 and the other found next to the RT pipe. Three other examples of milled pipes came from nonmound Burials 33, 34, and 74.

The identified makers' marks tend to expand the period of intensive use of Mound 2 into the first and third quarters of the eighteenth century. The tentativeness of some of our identifications makes an explicit adjustment of the bore dates impossible, but the direction of this evidence favors the interpretation that the period of most intensive use includes the third quarter of the eighteenth century.

SURFACE FINDS FROM UPPER WELL FIELD

Though we are primarily concerned with the excavations in Newton cemetery, we also discuss the marked bowls and stems found on the surface in an area of artifact concentration in the plantation's Upper Well field (figure 4). Two bowls were found. One is marked RT but differs from the excavated RT pipe. Besides the letters RT impressed on the back of the bowl, it also has two faint and partially obscured marks below; these marks may be portions of letters. Furthermore all impressed marks are enclosed in an impressed circle (figure 38*A*). The lower letters are possibly JO, perhaps an unrecorded mark of Jane or J(o)ane Tippet, widow of the first Robert Tippet (Walker 1971:73). Like the excavated RT pipe, this pipe bowl has milling around the mouth.

Another bowl was fragmentary and only consists of a portion of the right side of the bowl. On the bowl fragment, the mark ARVEY is in raised letters arranged circularly around a raised five-point star (figure 38*B*). The mark may be that of the Harvey family, three generations of which worked in Bristol during the eighteenth century. A John Harvey received his freedom in Bristol in 1725; another Harvey, probably his son, was working in Dover in 1756 (Leonard H. Gant, personal communication).

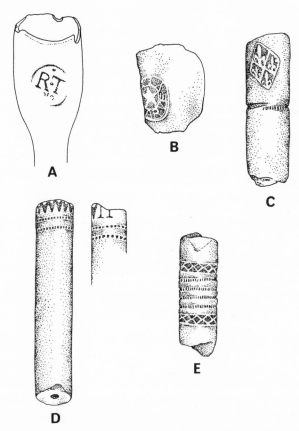

Figure 38. Pipestem and bowl fragments, surface collected from Upper Well field, Newton plantation.

Three decorated stems were also found in Upper Well field. One stem has four depressed bands; the inner two have milling along both sides of each band, while the outer two bands are filled with raised Xs (figure 38E). Toward one end of the second stem there are two milled lines with a series of impressed triangles and two adjacent Ts; each triangle contains a single raised circle (figure 38D). Walker illustrates a similar stem (1971:92). The third stem has a poorly executed impressed line (the ends do not meet) filled halfway around with milling; toward one end of the stem fragment a stamped diamond contains four nested diamonds, each diamond filled by a raised fleur-de-lis (figure 38C). A similar design from the Hallowes site in Virginia is described and illustrated by Buchanan and Heite (1971:44). All three stems have design elements that were typical of Dutch pipes from 1680 to 1720 (Leonard H. Gant, personal communication), although Walker cautions that nearly identical decoration was produced on stems made in Bristol (Walker 1967b:193). Walker also notes that rouletting on Dutch pipes is commonly accompanied by a series of impressed pendant triangles, as shown in the example illustrated in figure 38D.

The five marked bowl and stem fragments suggest use of the area in Upper Well field sometime during the early eighteenth century or, in any event, during the slave period. Moreover, this area in Upper Well field is almost certain to have been inside Newton's slave village, according to the manager's description of the plantation in 1796 (see chapter 4).

SUMMARY AND INTERPRETATION

For the analysis of clay pipes from Newton cemetery we used three sources of data with chronological implications: bore sizes, bowl forms, and makers' marks. We were particularly concerned with deriving information on the period during which the cemetery was in use, and on any temporal shifts in the patterns of mortuary behavior. As previously noted, recognition of the limitations of each type of data must be taken into account when reaching chronological conclusions.

The dates derived from bore sizes and bowl forms indicate that the cemetery was most intensively used from the last part of the seventeenth century through the first half of the eighteenth. By using the two standard deviation ranges of the bore sizes from whole pipes, it appears likely that the cemetery was not used much after the third quarter of the eighteenth century, and that its use began soon after the establishment of the plantation in the 1650s and 1660s. The expansion of the later part of the range agrees with the evidence of the makers' marks.

Temporal changes in slave mortuary patterns are also indicated by the pipe dates. The head-to-east, coffinless burial pattern was replaced by the head-to-west, coffin pattern. The shift in body orientation and coffin use appear to have occurred nearly simultaneously at Newton. Of the ninety-two burials excavated, only Burials 60 and 66 were west-headed with no coffin, and none were east-headed with a coffin. The mean bowl and bore size dates suggest that this shift may have occurred during the first two decades of the eighteenth century.

The practice of burial in an accretional mound was apparently the latest pattern in mortuary practices. In Mound 2, all the burials whose orientations could be identified were west-headed. The latest dates calculated from the pipes are from Mound 2 burials; these dates suggest that the mound was probably used during the first three quarters of the eighteenth century. Furthermore, all but two of the marked pipes are from this mound, and these marks, as well as milling around the mouths of some bowls, tend to support this chronology. The RT mark and milling are probably early eighteenth century, while the TD marks seem the most certain indicators of post-1750 interments. Burials 4, 8, 10, and 20 in Mound 2 are probably among the latest in the cemetery, their dates based on the bowl forms and marks of the associated pipes. The possibility also exists that these four burials were interred as recently as the early nineteenth century; this assumption does not, however, conclusively dispute the third-quarter eighteenth-century date provided by the two standard deviation range of bore size dates.

Despite some of the chronological ambiguities in this discussion, it is significant that nothing in the pipe data suggests a dating of Newton cemetery that is later than 1834; the data therefore directly support the inference that the cemetery was, in fact, a slave burial ground.

Appendix C

Classification and Description of Beads from Newton Cemetery

Our classification of the different types of European manufactured glass beads found in Newton cemetery is based on the taxonomic system developed by Lyle Stone (1974), which defines four levels of differentiation: class (C), series (S), type (T), and variety (V). According to Stone, "classes are based on differences in method of manufacture. Series are based on differences in structure. Types are distinguished on the basis of combinations of shape and surface characteristics. Variety distinctions are based on differences in glass color, the number, color, and form of glass appliques, and on the degree of translucency" (1974:89).

After we had classified the Newton beads or had placed some in groups of "unidentified" types or varieties, we sent a sample collection to William L. Minnerly at the Michigan State University Museum. Minnerly's careful examination of our classification resulted in the correction of a number of erroneous identifications and the placement of unidentified beads into new taxa in Stone's system. Minnerly observed that several of our misidentifications were caused by our failure to remove or consider heavy surface patinations. He noted that this common mistake is easily remedied by using intense light and high levels of magnification. Where Minnerly designated new taxa, they are noted below along with his description of principal characteristics.

BEAD TYPE DESCRIPTIONS (ADAPTED FROM STONE 1974; ALL MEASUREMENTS IN MILLIMETERS)

Class I Hollow-Cane Method
Series A Simple Construction
Type 1 Convex Shape

Variety b: turquoise (Munsell: greenish-Blue, 2.5B, 5/6), translucent
Figure 26B, S

72 specimens
Dimensions: Stone's published ranges: length, 10.3–15.9; width, 8.0–9.0; bore, 1.2–1.9. Dimensions of type specimen: length, 1.0; width, 6.0; bore, 3.5
Surface: highly polished, glossy
Distribution: Burial 59 (34); Burial 61 (1); Burial 63 (37)

Variety e: blue (Munsell: Blue, Purple-Blue, 10.0B, 3/4)
Figure 26T
166 specimens
Dimensions: (type specimen only) length, 2.0; width, 3.5; bore, 1.5. Stone's published ranges: length, 1.3–1.9; width, 2.2–3.0
Surface: highly polished, glossy
Distribution: Burial 61 (127); Burial 77 (39)

Variety f: light blue (Munsell: Blue, 5.0B, 6/6)
Figure 26R
42 specimens
Dimensions: (type specimen only) length, 2.5; width, 3.5; bore, 2.0. Stone's published ranges: length, 2.7; width, 2.9
Distribution: Burial 22 (7); Burial 60 (4); Burial 61 (1); Burial 36 (30)

Variety g: clear
Figure 26C
1 specimen
Dimensions: length, 2.5; width, 3.0; bore, 2.5. Stone's published ranges: length, 2.3; width, 3.1
Surface: polished, glossy
Distribution: Burial 61 (1)

Variety k: clear, cloudy
Figure 26U
7 specimens
Dimensions: (type specimen only) length, 7.5; width, 1.0; bore, 4.0. Stone's published ranges: length, 2.2; width, 2.7
Surface: polished, glossy
Distribution: Burial 61 (1); Burial 77 (6)

Variety q: light green (Munsell: bluish Blue-Green, 7.5BG, 6/4)
Figure 26V
46 specimens
Dimensions: (type specimen only) length, 2.5; width, 3.5; bore, 2.0. Stone's published ranges: length, 1.0–3.2; width, 2.3–4.7
Surface: dull
Distribution: Burial 61 (46)

Variety w: light blue (Munsell: greenish Blue, 2.5B, 7/6)
Figure 26*W*
2 specimens
Dimensions: (approximate measurements from fragmentary type specimen) length, 1.0; width, 2.5; bore, 2.0. Stone's published ranges: length, 1.6; width, 2.1
Surface: dull
Distribution: Burial 61 (2)

Variety y: white
Figure 26*X*
14 specimens
Dimensions: (type specimen only) length, 2.5; width, 3.5; bore, 1.5. Stone's published ranges: length, 1.0–2.4; width, 2.1–3.8
Distribution: Burial 77 (14)

Type 3 Round

Variety g: yellow/amber (new taxon from Minnerly)
Figure 26*ee*, *aa*
5 specimens
Dimensions: length, 3.5–10.5; width, 5.0–8.0; bore, 2.0–2.5
Surface: dull
Distribution: Burial 60 (4); Burial 72 (1)

Type 4 Barrel

Variety b: dark brown, opaque
Figure 26*D*, *E*
193 specimens
Dimensions: fall within Stone's published ranges; length, 6.6–11.5; width, 8.0–12.2; bore, 2.0–3.1
Surface: semiglossy with considerable wear
Distribution: Burial 59 (11); Burial 60 (152); Burial 61 (21); Burial 63 (9)

Type 9 Tubular, fibrous structure

Variety d: white, opaque
Figure 26*I*
7 specimens
Dimensions: fall within Stone's published ranges; length, 11.4–12.3; width, 3.4–3.5; bore, 1.3
Surface: dull

Distribution: Burial 55 (1); Burial 58 (1); Burial 61 (2); Burial 77 (3)

Variety e: white, opaque (new taxon from Minnerly)
Figure 26*bb*
9 specimens
Dimensions: (type specimen only) length, 10.5; width, 6.0; bore, 2.0
Surface: dull
Distribution: Burial 59 (3); Burial 61 (1); Burial 63 (5)

Type 10 Globular

Variety a: dark brown, opaque
Figure 26*G*
35 specimens
Dimensions: fall within Stone's published ranges; length, 7.7–11.9; width, 11.4–13.9; bore, 2.6–3.0
Surface: glossy to dull, with patina; appears black
Distribution: Burial 55 (1); Burial 60 (34)

Type 11 Globular to barrel (Stone wrote: "This is a problematical type designation because specimen shape varies from nearly doughnut to barrel to globular. All specimens are very small in relation to other necklace beads, although they are longer than the majority of seed beads"; 1974:96.)

Variety c: red, translucent (addition to Stone; from Minnerly)
Figure 26*H*
1 specimen
Dimensions: length, 3.5; width, 9.0; bore, 3.0
Surface: polished glossy
Distribution: Burial 59 (1)

Type 12 Round to oblong; multifaceted, cut or ground surfaces
Variety d: clear, translucent (addition to Stone; from Minnerly)
Figure 26*A*
2 specimens
Dimensions: (Stone's published ranges) length, 7.3–9.2; width, 8.8–9.4; bore, 1.7–2.3. Dimensions of type specimen: length, 13.0; width, 4.5; bore, 5.0
Surface: dull with slight patina; numerous air-bubble pits
Decoration: facets irregularly spaced and shaped; vary from 5 to 6 sides; occur only on median surface
Distribution: Burial 63 (2)

Series B Compound Construction
Type 2 Doughnut, 3 layers of glass

Variety a: red (Munsell: Red, 5.OR, 5/6), opaque
Figure 26*Y*
65 specimens
Dimensions: fall within Stone's published ranges; length, 1.0–3.5; width, 2.0–3.9; bore, 0.6–1.1
Structure: inner layer, light green translucent glass; center layer, red opaque glass; outer layer, clear glass veneer
Surface: semiglossy
Distribution: Burial 58 (1); Burial 59 (32); Burial 60 (1); Burial 61 (5); Burial 77 (26)

Variety c: blue (addition to Stone; from Minnerly)
Figure 26*F*
1 specimen
Dimensions: length, 16.5; width, 4.0; bore, 2.5
Structure: hollow cane and compound construction; also fibrous structure and untumbled ends
Surface: "I am assuming the minute amount of red substance adhering to the exterior surface is what remains of a glass veneer" (Minnerly, personal communication).
Distribution: Burial 63 (1)

Variety d: red and green (new taxon; from Minnerly)
Figure 26*cc*
135 specimens
Dimensions: (type specimen only) length, 27.0; width, 8.0; bore, 3.0
Structure: Minnerly writes: "hollow cane and compound construction, having two layers of glass which are twisted and exhibit fibrous structure. There is no clear glass veneer over the two glass layers. There is no corresponding type in Stone (1974); this might best be considered a ... 'Cornaline d'Aleppo' variant" (personal communication).
Distribution: Burial 60 (86); Burial 61 (49)

Series C Complex Structure
Type 1 Convex

Variety e (addition to Stone; from Minnerly)
Figure 26*Z*
2 specimens

Dimensions: length, 17.0; width, 7.0; bore, 3.0
Structure: "hollow cane and complex construction; twelve white glass rod insets appear within the single glass layer" (Minnerly, personal communication).
Distribution: Burial 63 (2)

Type 3 Globular

Variety g: brown, opaque; 3 circumferential white glass insets
Figure 26J
5 specimens
Dimensions: fall within Stone's published ranges; length, 6.2–10.8; width, 9.5–11.1; bore, 2.2–2.9
Shape: doughnut to semibarrel
Surface: dull
Decoration: 3 irregularly spaced, white insets extend around circumference of bead; insets jog irregularly and join at different intervals
Distribution: Burial 60 (1); Burial 63 (4)

Class II Mandrel Wound Method
Series A Simple Construction
Type 1 Faceted ("All CII,SA,T1 Varieties exhibit 8, 5-sided pressed facets. A series of 4 facets encircle each bead end and join at the center to form an apex, or line of maximum circumference. The 2 rows of facets are normally offset. Bead shapes vary, depending on degree of facet modification from oval, through round, to elongate. All specimens exhibit circumferential surface striations, indicative of the mandrel-wound technique of manufacture. All specimens are semi-translucent to translucent. The major distinguishing feature between varieties is color"; Stone 1974:104.)

Variety a: blue (Munsell: purplish Purple-Blue, 7.5PB, 3/10)
Figure 26K
17 specimens
Dimensions: (type specimen only) length, 7.0; width, 9.0; bore, 4.0. Stone's published ranges: length, 7.5–11.1; width, 11.0–12.0; bore, 3.0
Distribution: Burial 61 (15); Burial 72 (2)

Variety f: amber (Munsell: Yellow-Red Yellow, 10.0YR, 6/8)
Figure 26L

4 specimens
Dimensions: (type specimen only) length, 9.0; width, 10.0; bore, 4.0. Stone's published ranges: length, 8.3–10.0; width, 9.0–11.6; bore, 3.4
Distribution: Burial 61 (4)

Variety h: clear
Figure 21
9 specimens
Dimensions: length, 7.5–9.0; width, 9.5–10.5; bore, 4.0–4.5. Stone's published ranges: length, 9.0–11.3; width, 9.9–11.7; bore, 3.0
Distribution: Burial 72 (9)

Variety j: milk white
Figure 26M
13 specimens
Dimensions: (type specimen only) length, 9.0; width, 11.0; bore, 3.5. Stone's published ranges: length, 9.9–10.4; width, 10.0–10.2; bore, 2.6
Distribution: Burial 87 (4); Burial 61 (7); Burial 63 (1); Burial 72 (1)

Variety k: red/amber (new taxon; from Minnerly)
Figure 26dd
3 specimens
Dimensions: length, 4.0–5.0; width, 4.0–5.5; bore, 2.5–3.5
Surface: dull
Distribution: Burial 61 (3)

Type 2 Nodular, "mulberry" ("All CII,SA,T1 beads exhibit molded glass knobs over their entire surface. The knobs generally occur in either 2 or 3 circumferential rows. The basic bead shape is barrel, although this has been modified by molding to produce knobs. Knobs on different specimens vary considerably in number, size, and shape. Many specimens exhibit circumferential surface striations. Several specimens exhibit longitudinal grooves which may be mold seams. The major distinguishing feature . . . is color"; Stone 1974: 101.)

Variety a: grey blue (Munsell: Purplish Purple-Blue, 7.5PB, 3/2)
Figure 26N
1 specimen
Dimensions: length, 8.0; width, 10.0; bore, 3.0. Stone's published ranges: length, 5.7–7.5; width, 8.7–10.0; bore, 3.1–3.4
Distribution: Burial 61 (1)

Type 6 Convex; highly visible circumferential striations

Variety a: clear, translucent
Figure 26O
1 specimen
Dimensions: (Stone's published ranges) length, 16.0–20.0; width, 13.4–15.0; bore, 3.4–3.6. Dimensions of type specimen: length, 1.1; width, 9.5; bore, 4.5
Surface: dull, highly patinated; very noticeable circumferential grooves wind around the bead between the ends
Distribution: Burial 22 (1)

Type 8 Round; highly visible circumferential striations

Variety a: clear to cloudy, semitranslucent
Figure 26P
3 specimens
Dimensions: fall within Stone's published ranges; length, 7.5–20.2; width, 8.9–18.5; bore, 2.2–3.4
Surface: dull to semiglossy; several have silver patina; circumferential striations common and deep in many cases
Distribution: Burial 61 (3)

Type 10 Doughnut-shaped; highly visible circumferential striations

Variety e: clear to cloudy; semitranslucent
Figure 26Q
1 specimen
Dimensions: length, 4.5; width, 11.0; bore, 4.5. Stone's published ranges: length, 4.3–7.9; width, 10.6–12.4; bore, 2.4–3.5
Distribution: Burial 60 (1)

Appendix D

A Comparison of the Historical and Archaeological Populations at Newton Plantation

The relationship between the historical and archaeological populations at Newton suggests that interment practices were selective at the plantation and that a consequential number of slaves were not buried in the cemetery.

The plantation area containing the cemetery (figure 4) was gridded into 246 three-meter-square units during the 1973 field season. Randomly located excavations in sixteen of these units (figures 8 and 9) yielded thirty-eight burials, an average of 2.31 per unit. Taking these 2.31 individuals as the average number for each of the sixteen randomly excavated units, and assuming the reliability of an admittedly small sample, an extrapolation for all 246 excavation units yields a total cemetery population of 568 or 570. This figure does not include the possibility of burials in partial squares intersecting cart roads or the possibility that some slaves were buried in immediately contiguous fields, outside of what we recognize as the cemetery area. To balance the possibility of these extra burials, many of the squares included in the same grid had bedrock either showing or immediately below the grass cover, and these squares could not have contained burials. Overall, it appears that an estimate of 570 interments is a reasonable maximum for the main cemetery area. It should be explicitly indicated, however, that if the total number of actual interments were to fall below 570, the case for selectivity in burial practices is increased; if the burials are in excess of 570, the case is decreased.

In comparing the projections of the archaeological population with slave deaths at Newton, a major problem involves establishing the actual number of deaths over the duration of the plantation's history during the slave period because, as we suggested in chapter 5, the cemetery appears to have been used for most if not all of this period.

Although the number of deaths prior to 1796 is unknown, such data are available for all but two years of the 1796–1833 period

Table 25. Slave deaths by sex: Newton plantation.

Year	Males	Females	Total[a]	Year	Males	Females	Total
1796–1797	3	2	5	1817	2	4	6
1797–1798	1	2	3	1818	3	6	9
1798–1799	1	1	4	1819	8	3	11
1799–1800	7	4	11	1820	2	2	4
1800–1801	6	2	8	1821	6	8	14
1803–1804	1	1	5	1822	8	4	12
1806	—	—	5	1823	4	1	5
1807	—	—	10	1824	5	5	10
1808	1	5	6	1825	12	17	29
1809	1	4	5	1826	10	12	22
1810	6	12	18	1827	5	2	7
1811	3	9	12	1828	8	13	21
1812	2	4	6	1829	9	11	20
1813	1	1	2	1830	5	4	9
1814	1	3	4	1831	4	6	10
1815	0	4	4	1832	5	2	7
1816	8	2	10	1833	5	3	8
Total	42	56	118	Total	101	103	204

Sources: 1796–1804, Newton Papers (523/315, 116, 128, 131-1, 282, 567, 586, 593). 1806–1833, Newton Plantation (1805–1841). From 1796 to 1804, the annual period reported was from August 1 to July 31; in other years a calendar year was usually used.

[a] Sex is not reported for 2 slaves in 1798–1799, for 3 in 1803–1804, for 5 in 1806, and for 10 in 1807.

(table 25); the number of deaths in the two unknown years (1801–02 and 1805) can be estimated by interpolating the average of the number of deaths in the known preceding and following years. Combining the 322 reported deaths (table 25) with the additional ten estimated deaths yields 332 deaths during 1796–1833, an annual average of 9.2 (median 7.5) deaths during the thirty-six year period that witnessed the end of slavery.

By the way in which figures were reported in the historical sources, the annual number of deaths cannot be precisely correlated with the plantation's annual live population. Using the figures given in tables 6 and 25, however, we estimate a high average annual death rate of 3.4 percent of the total population (median 3.0 percent; range 0.8 to 9.5) during the 1796–1833 period. There is no reason to suspect that the annual death rate would have been less in earlier periods and, indeed, it may have been greater.

Establishing a reasonable estimate of the number of deaths for the period prior to 1796 is difficult because no death figures are available in the manuscript sources. From 1776 to 1795, population figures are available for only four years: 1776, 1782, 1783, and 1784 (table 6). Using the average of these four years, 247.7, to approximate the annual average population from 1776 to 1795 and applying the estimated annual death rate of 3.4 percent to this average yields an estimate of 8.4 deaths per annum, or a total of 176 deaths during the twenty-year period (using the median estimated annual death rate of 3.0 percent yields 7.4 deaths per annum, or 148 deaths). If the average number of annual deaths, as calculated from the figures for 1796–1833, is applied the result is 184 deaths from 1776 to 1795 (using the median figure for 1796–1833, the total number of deaths from 1776 to 1795 would have been 150).

The total number of 332 deaths from 1796 to 1833 added to the estimates of the number of deaths from 1776 to 1795 produces an overall estimate of the total number of deaths for the 1776–1833 period of between 516 at the highest and 480 at the lowest.

The final problem involves estimating the total number of deaths from the beginnings of the plantation to 1775. For purposes of this discussion, 1670 is taken as a certain baseline date for the full operation of Newton as a plantation (although, as discussed in chapter 4, the plantation was formed in earlier years). However, during the 106-year period from 1670 to 1775, population figures exist only for 1740 and 1750, and in both years the population is recorded as 171 (table 6). Although the admittedly slim evidence indicates that Newton's population expanded in the 1750s or 1760s (probably through new purchases), and the 171 average is questionable throughout the 1670–1775 period, we accept 171 as a working estimate. This estimate would not be inconsistent with the slave populations on many other medium to large plantations (see table 3), and we assume that if it is an overestimate it would be balanced by the apparently higher death rates (which we assume, but cannot statistically demonstrate) during the early years of slavery. The estimated annual average death rate of 3.4 percent (as calculated for the 1796–1833 period) applied to the population figure of 171 yields 5.8 deaths per annum, or a total of 615 deaths for the 1670–1775 period; if the estimated annual median death rate of 3.0 percent is applied to the figure of 171, the annual number of deaths would have been 5.1, or 541 total deaths for the 106-year period.

In all, we estimate that from 1,021 to 1,131 slaves died at Newton plantation between 1670 and 1833. These figures are close to double the number of the 570 interments we projected for the total cemetery population on the basis of the skeleton population that was excavated. Allowing for errors in our estimates, we nonetheless believe the data indicate that a significant (but nonquantifiable) number are missing from the cemetery. We thus conclude that interment in the cemetery was selective and that certain members of the slave population, particularly most infants and small children, were interred differently or buried elsewhere.

This conclusion is independently supported by correlating historical data on age at the time of death with the relative age groups of the skeletal population. Qualitative evidence from Barbados in general indicates that the mortality rates of infants and small children were high, and that newborn infants were particularly vulnerable to death during their first month. In the late 1780s, for example, Governor Parry reported "there is no doubt that more ... [slave children] die in a state of infancy, that is under seven years, than of other children, in proportion to the number born of each" (Parry 1789b), and in 1812 a committee of planters complained that "of the [slave] children who are born, there is infinitely too great a proportion that die in the month" (Society for the Improvement 1811–16: 138; see also chapter 4, note 16). For Newton, age data at the time of death are available for 83 percent of those who died in the thirty-three year period from 1796 to 1800–01, 1803–04, and from 1806 to 1832 (table 26). It can be assumed that age attributions given in the manuscript sources were not as precise for older people as they were for younger categories, especially because Newton's managers were explicitly concerned with the natural increase of the slave population during this period.

As shown in table 26, at least 41.7 percent of the deaths were in the age ten and under group (at least 37.1 percent were five and under), which, for purposes of identifying the skeletal population, included small children and infants. Of the ninety-two excavated skeletons, eighty-two were assigned a relative age, and twelve (14.6 percent) of these were identified as small children or infants; only one skeleton (or possibly two) was clearly identifiable as an infant (see Appendix A). Because these statistics suggest that infant and small child interments in the cemetery were not proportionate to the number of such deaths reported in the manuscript sources, many infants and small children must have been buried elsewhere.

The selective pattern of interment at Newton is also suggested by a comparison of the sex of the archaeological population with the sex of decedents as reported in the manuscripts. As shown in table 25, sex data are available for 302 of the 322 slaves who died during the thirty-four years from 1796–97 to 1800–01, 1803–04, and 1806–33. Of this total, there were 159 female deaths, or 52.6 percent—a

TABLE 26. Slave population by age at time of death: Newton plantation, 1796 to 1800–01, 1803–04, 1806 to 1832.

Age	Deaths	
	Number	Percentage
5 and under[a]	97	37.1
6–10	12	4.6
11–15	3	1.1
16–20	3	1.1
Unknown but 20 or under	22	8.4
Unknown but 21 or over	7	2.7
21–30	14	5.3
31–40	24	9.1
41–50	17	6.6
51–60	22	8.4
61 and over	40	15.3
Total	261	

Sources: Same as table 25. Although records show 314 deaths at Newton for these years (see table 25), ages at death are available for only 261 persons or 83 percent of the total deaths reported.

[a] Many in this category were infants, roughly under 2.

percentage that favorably compares with the percentage of females in the living population during this period (table 6). However, the number of females in the skeletal population was disproportionately low. Of the ninety-two excavated individuals, sex was assignable to thirty-nine with a reasonable degree of confidence. Only fifteen (38 percent) were identified as females; another seven were provisionally sexed as four males and three females (Appendix A). The provisional identifications added to the ones in which we have greater confidence yields nineteen females, also 41 percent of the skeletal population, for which some kind of sex identification was made. This percentage, however, was lower than we would have expected from the historical data on the sex of decedents, and, as discussed in chapter 5, lower than what would be found in a normal population.

When the population estimates and actual figures from manuscript sources are compared with the projections and findings of the archaeological research, it is apparent that not all dead slaves were buried in the cemetery area. Moreover, the population profile reconstructed from the excavated interments reveals a very low percentage of small children and infants and a lower percentage than might have been expected of females. These facts suggest that interment practices were age-related and probably also sex-related.

Our data preclude an explanation for the presence in the cemetery of small children and infants, especially those few in multiple burials with adults. However, despite the lack of historical descriptions or data on the mortuary treatment of slave infants and small children, African ethnographic materials suggest what might have happened at Newton (and, presumably, other Barbadian plantations). West African cultures generally either buried small children and infants apart from adults or cast their bodies into the bush. As we stressed in chapter 6, the slave mortuary complex manifested many African influences. It is reasonable to assume that, especially in the earlier years of the slave period, African traditions also influenced the disposition and burial of small children and infants. The possibility of differential treatment for children and infants, especially as projected from archaeologically recovered skeletal remains, is supported on a more general level by a wide range of cross-cultural data. Kenneth Weiss, for example, has written: "In taking an aged skeletal series as representative of a population, one must assume ... that the remains are representative of the population age distribution. Burial customs quite often systematically violate these assumptions as regards juveniles ... Many ethnographical reports describe differential burial practices which systematically underrepresent infants and juveniles; they are often buried separately, their burial sites are usually not excavated, and perhaps not even found" (1971:12).

Most infants and small children at Newton may have been buried in a special area of the cemetery, in an area bordering the cemetery, or in an area of the plantation removed from the cemetery or the slave village. We assume that the social conventions of the white planters would have prohibited the bodies of infants and small children from being simply discarded and exposed on the surface of their plantations; moreover, it is likely that similar conventions were later followed by creolized slaves. Following the practices of West African cultures, it is unlikely that infants and small children were buried near or under the floors of the houses in the slave village. The fact that such burial sites existed in Barbados, as attested to by reliable historical sources quoted in chapter 6, also probably accounts for some of the adult interments we assume are missing from the cemetery. However, we found no evidence for such burials in the area of Newton's slave village or slave village sites on other plantations that were test-excavated.

Some Newton slaves were buried in churchyards, but, as discussed in chapter 6, baptized slaves were a small minority of the Barbadian slave population during the entire slave period. The burials of Christian slaves largely took place toward the end of this period and many of these slaves were interred on plantations rather than in churchyards.

Finally, the adults that are apparently missing from Newton cemetery may be buried in another cemetery on the plantation. Although this is a logical possibility, we provisionally discard it because it is not suggested by the archaeological investigations or the historical source materials. Moreover, our interviews and conversations with Barbadians who had a longstanding and intimate acquaintance with Newton never yielded any suggestion of another cemetery or even an allusion to the discovery of human bones while agricultural activities were pursued in various plantation fields.

In general, the excavated population displays so little consistency with respect to physical, cultural, or artifactual characteristics that we find it difficult to select a common denominator or denominators which would explain why some slaves were interred in the cemetery and others excluded. African burial practices suggest a possible explanation for infants and small children but, assuming that some adults were interred close to houses in the village or under house floors, neither the archaeological nor the historical data assist in interpreting why they were interred in these sites while others were buried in the cemetery area. No burials were found outside of the cemetery, which further inhibits an explanation.

We believe that an understanding of how decisions were made in locating burial sites depends not only on slave cultural values and norms, but also on a knowledge of how access to the cemetery was controlled and how and if the planters themselves affected interment decisions. Information on these topics is not within our data. Thus, a comparison between Newton's historical and archaeological populations raises a variety of questions pertaining to mortuary behavior and cultural norms and indicates that selective criteria were applied in interment. However, we are presently unable to more fully describe or analyze the selection procedures, particularly those involving interment in the cemetery itself.

Notes

1. Introduction

1. In this book we distinguish among several common terms: *slave society*, "the whole community based on slavery, including masters and freedmen as well as slaves" (Goveia 1965:vii); *slavery*, the institution that structured the slave society and the relationships between its population segments; and *slave*, the sociolegal status or position and the holder of that position. *Culture* is used in the anthropological sense. Although many anthropological definitions of culture exist, for present purposes we conceive of *slave culture* as comprising the behavioral and ideological patterns (and their material products) that were shared by the slave group and socially learned and transmitted. (Using culture in this sense, of course, does not imply that slave culture was static or that various aspects of it were unique to the slave population.)

2. The historical research is part of a wider project that is designed to produce an intensive and holistic ethnographic account of a West Indian slave population; the project treats the entire period of slavery to achieve maximum insight into developmental processes. The project is particularly concerned with the values, traditions, material life, and behavior of the slaves: how they reacted to their status, developed a cultural tradition (and the influences on and changes in this tradition), and interacted with each other as well as with populations of European ancestry. In more general terms, the project is concerned with the processes by which Africans and their descendants lost, modified, or retained their cultural heritages in New World environments characterized by plantation economies, colonialism, and institutionalized chattel slavery.

3. Sidney Mintz has recently summarized these broader issues: "The history of the masses has always posed problems for the historian; the masses, characteristically, do not write about themselves—if, indeed, they are able to write at all—and those who observe them as contemporaries necessarily do so from a perspective that is bound to conceal many of the realities of social life. In the case of enslaved masses, living in the midst of the free and more powerful, the problem is quite possibly compounded... The end of... research [on slavery] is, among

289

other things, the documentation of a past not only obscure, but obscured" (1975:484, 494).

4. In this book, *creole* refers to anyone, regardless of racial or ethnic ancestry, who was born in the West Indies in general or Barbados in particular. Creole culture is comprised of those beliefs and behavioral patterns which developed in the New World. Despite the often marked resemblance of these patterns to their Old World antecedents, creole culture has its own distinctive elements and patterning (see, for example, Brathwaite 1974).

2. BARBADOS: GEOGRAPHY, ECONOMY, DEMOGRAPHY, AND HISTORY

1. In Barbados a plantation is generally considered as any land unit over 10 acres, and a "peasant" holding as a unit of 10 acres or less; relatively few peasant holdings, however, are more than 1 acre, and very few plantations are less than 50 acres.

2. For example, according to the 1960 West Indies population census, whites comprised 2.3 percent of the population in Saint Vincent, 1.9 percent in Trinidad and Tobago, and 1.3 percent in Antigua; in the remaining territories the proportion was under 1 percent (Ifill 1964). Although more recent figures on these territories from the 1970 census were not available at the time of writing, it can be assumed that today these percentages are somewhat smaller.

3. We conducted test excavations in a cave at one plantation in 1972 because local informants reported that the cave had once been used by black slaves. Although no evidence of slave occupation was found, extensive remains of Amerindian occupation were encountered. A report on these excavations is currently being prepared for publication.

4. A very small number of Amerindian slaves, including a few from the North American mainland, persisted throughout the seventeenth century. Despite their limited population, Indians made some important and enduring contributions to the island's culture, especially in areas related to the domestic arts and the exploitation of plant life (Handler 1970).

5. European indentured servants were found on Barbadian plantations throughout the seventeenth century, albeit in decreasing numbers as the years progressed. From 1679 to 1684, there were about 2,300 indentured servants, about 11 to 12 percent of the total white population (British Museum 1684; Dunn 1972:88). There appear to have been a few indentured servants by the middle of the eighteenth century, but none by the 1770s and early 1780s, if not earlier (Dickson 1789:44). Many descendants of indentured servants, however, continued to live in Barbados throughout the period of slavery as poor farmers called "militia tenants." Plantations were obliged to send to the parochial units of the island's militia one militiaman for every 30 to 50 acres of plantation land; in return for their services, the plantation allotted 2 or 3

acres to each tenant for cultivating provisions and minor cash crops and raising small livestock.

Other descendants of indentured servants became small farmers. They were known as "ten-acre planters" or "ten-acre men," "so called from the early practice of granting ten acres of land to those white indentured servants who had fulfilled the period of their servitude...by various subdivisions and junctions, those lots now [in the 1770s and 1780s] contain from one or two acres up to twenty or thirty" (Dickson 1814:528).

6. In 1709, seventy-seven men claimed to own two-thirds of all the land and slaves on the island (*Letter from Considerable Proprietors of Barbados* 1709).

7. For example, in the early eighteenth century, John Oldmixon, an English historian who was very familiar with Barbados described the "goods which are all brought from England or Ireland." These included Osnaburg, "vast quantities [of which are]...consumed by the servants and slaves whose cloathing is made of this sort of linnen"; "linnen of all sorts for the planters and their families"; "broad cloth and kersies for planters' and overseers' use"; "silks and stuffs for the ladies and household servants"; "red caps for slaves, male and female"; "stockings and shoes for masters and servants"; gloves, hats, "millenary-ware," wigs, laces, woolens, and silks; beef, pork, peas, beans, oats, and "bisket"; wine "of all sorts," beer, ale, pickles, candles, butter, and cheese; "iron ware for mills and sugar works," including whip saws, hand saws, files, axes, hatchets, chisels, adzes, hoes, pick axes, mat hooks, planes, gouges, augers, hand bills for cutting sugar cane, drawing knives, and nails; powder and shot; "leaden ware"; "all sorts of Birmingham ware" and "brasiary ware," both of which "rust, canker, and are eaten up in a few years"; "copper ware for the sugars is a very good commodity"; "all sorts of India goods and toyes, coals, pantiles, hearthstones, hoops; and, in a word, everything that's proper for an English market, or fair, will sell there." To this list, the writer added the caution that before shipment goods should be "well packed, especially millenary ware, glasses, and all goods that are easily broken, or [the buyer] will unload rubbish instead of merchandize" (1708; 2:154–62).

Over sixty years later, a Barbadian provided a relatively detailed partial inventory of the "goods sent from Great Britain to Barbados [which] are chiefly" woolens, linen, manchester velvets, silk, iron, brass, copper, leather, laces, hats, wigs, shoes, stockings, china, glass, earthen wares, pictures, clocks, watches, jewels, plate, gold and silver lace, medicines, oats, peas, beans, cheese, bacon, starch, oatmeal, gunpowder, bricks, tiles, lead, paint, oil, coals, cordage, sugar pots and drips, hoops, pewter, soap, candles, snuff, cut tobacco, clay smoking pipes, cards, refined sugar, wine, beer, ale, cider, perry, spice, fruit, tea, pickles, guns, swords, pistols, walking canes, horses, mules, grinding stones, paving stones, books, toys, stationery, cutlery, "Birmingham and haberdashery" wares, coaches, chariots, chaises, "all sorts of household goods, etc. besides the supplies from Ireland, and the very considerable importations of timber, fish etc. from the Northern colonies" (Frere 1768:120–21).

8. Detailed lists of exports from about forty-two North American ports (about thirty-seven in the thirteen colonies) from 1768 to 1772 provide a good idea of the range and types of materials sent from the thirteen colonies (Public Record Office 1768–1773). These export lists, however, only refer to "the British and Foreign West Indies" as a group, and do not specify particular islands. The lists mention a wide assortment of foodstuffs, timber and timber products, and other raw and manufactured organic materials. Iron (bars, wrought, pig, and cast) is also mentioned and, starting in 1770 and 1771, the lists show that small quantities of unspecified "earthenware" were exported from Philadelphia. In 1772 small quantities of earthenware were also exported from Boston, Rhode Island, New London, and New York, and larger quantities from Philadelphia and Charlestown. We do not know if any of this "earthenware" arrived at Barbados.

9. Except for coins. The silver and gold coins used in the British West Indies during the seventeenth and eighteenth centuries were largely of Spanish and Portuguese Brazilian origin; copper currency, of French origin, "came into circulation in the British islands towards the end of the seventeenth century and formed the principal *negroe money* until ...the Imperial reforms during the nineteenth century" (Pridmore 1965:8–12). However, we found no coins during our archaeological research.

10. The number of reexported slaves is difficult to ascertain, but reexports took place throughout most of the slave trade period. Slaves were shipped from Barbados to the British North American colonies, the Spanish colonies in the Caribbean and elsewhere, and British and French Caribbean colonies. More slaves were probably reexported in later periods than in earlier ones (see, for example, Dickson 1814:440; J. Brathwaite 1789). From June 1682 to June 1683, 307 slaves were reexported (British Museum 1684); 226 were reexported in 1748–1750 (Pitman 1917:72–73); and from 1783 to 1788, "about 2,600," an annual average of 433, were reexported (Barbados Assembly 1790). Over sixteen years, from 1788 to 1800 and 1802 to 1804, 26,027 slaves were accounted as imports, but 21,525 were reexported—an average of 1,345 per year (Public Record Office 1805). In a letter, dated May 1805, appended to these figures, Governor Seaforth of Barbados explained: "It would be erroneous in any calculation to count upon the importation of slaves, as many cargoes are sold for exportation, and on consequence of such sale are subject to the duty, and therefore appear under the head of imports, altho' not landed in the island" (*ibid.*).

11. With the new data provided by Roger Anstey (1975), Curtin (1975) has recently revised some of his figures for the British slave trade, but he does not break down these new figures by territories to which slaves were exported.

12. In addition to slaves who arrived directly from African areas, a

relatively small number occasionally came to Barbados from the West Indian colonies. These slaves included persons who accompanied their masters who settled or visited Barbados, were captured in English military campaigns against Dutch or French possessions, or who ran away from neighboring islands during the seventeenth and eighteenth centuries (see, for example, *Letter from Barbados* 1673:6; Codrington 1699; Oldmixon 1741;2:63; Frere 1768:77–78; Pinckard 1806; 1:382–383). Apparently the few slaves who came after the abolition of the slave trade were brought from other British West Indian territories (see table 1).

13. During the late seventeenth and early eighteenth centuries an indeterminate number of Barbadian slaves originated in southeast Africa, primarily Madagascar, from where the English Caribbean and North American colonies "imported large numbers" of slaves "especially between 1675 and 1690" (Curtin 1969:125). Slaves from Madagascar were brought during "two relatively short periods of time," from the 1670s until 1698 and from 1716 to 1721 when acts of Parliament discontinued the trade (Platt 1969:548). The Madagascar trade was very small in relation to that of western Africa (table 2), but at certain periods Malagasy slaves appear to have been significant in Barbados.

In 1676, for example, a communication from the Directors of the Dutch East India Company advocated increasing the slave trade with Madagascar by noting that the English "appear ... to be in the habit of supplying the island of Barbados from that island" (quoted in S. Patterson 1975:168); and in 1684, a governmental account of Barbados implied the significance of the Madagascar trade when it reported that "Negroes [are] brought thither from the coast of Guiny, Cormantine, & Madagascar" (British Museum 1684). The Royal African Company claimed that 700 Malagasy slaves were imported in March 1679 (Platt 1969:549), of a total 1,425 slave imports (Public Record Office 1679); although the number of Malagasy imports in 1679 was "probably inflated" (Platt 1969:549), these slaves could have accounted for as much as 49 percent of the Royal African Company's imports during that year. The Company also maintained that during a two-month period in 1681 it sold between 900 and 1,000 Malagasy slaves at Barbados. Although this number was also "probably inflated" (Platt 1969:549), during 1681 a total of 1,501 slaves were brought to the island (Harlow 1926:317); Malagasy slaves could have thus accounted for as much as 59.9 percent to 66.6 percent of the total. The percentage of Malagasy slave imports was probably lower; however, in 1681 Barbados's governor stressed "that in the preceding seven years many slaves" had come from Madagascar (Plate 1969–549). At the minimum, 1,741 Malagasy slaves were imported between May 1682 and May 1687. During 1717, 1718, and 1719 a number of ships arrived from Madagascar, but available figures are limited to only five vessels which brought 1,658 slaves (Platt 1969:556, 557–558); in these three years, a total of 16,365 slaves came to the island (Barbados Department of Archives 1726), and thus at least 10 percent, and probably more, of Barbadian slave imports during this short period originated in Madagascar.

These imprecise figures suggest that Barbados received a proportionately greater number of Malagasy slaves than were involved in the British trade in general; moreover it appears that these slaves were especially important during the first phase of the Madagascar trade, from the 1670s to 1698. It is not known, however, what proportions or numbers stayed on the island (and were not reexported), and the extent to which Malagasy slaves influenced the development of Barbadian slave culture is uncertain. In any event, after 1721 apparently no slaves from Madagascar arrived in Barbados; by the mid-1730s through the 1740s, Griffith Hughes, a well-informed observer of Barbados's slave population, spoke of the Madagascar trade in the past tense when he reported that "formerly some slaves [were] brought hither from the island of Madagascar" (1750:14).

14. "There is a great deal of difference between the Negroes," wrote John Oldmixon in the early eighteenth century: "those that are born in Barbados are much more useful men, than those that are brought from Guinea. Mr. Ligon [in 1647–50] could not make this observation, the colony was too young; but the creolian Negroes are every way preferable to the new comers (whom they call saltwater Negroes) ... The children that come over young from Africa are also better servants, when they are grown up, than those that come thence men or women" (1741;2:133).

About fifty years later, a group of Barbadian planters reported: "Very little service can be performed by new negroes from the first three or four years, and with every indulgence the hazard of seasoning them is so great that there have been instances where not above two or three in ten have survived a course of more than six or seven years servitude" (Codrington Attorneys 1762). Referring to the late eighteenth and early nineteenth centuries, the Bishop of London, deriving his information from persons familiar with Barbados, flatly stated: "Creole slaves ... are far superior in fidelity, obedience, docility, and industry to the African Negroes" (Porteus 1807:191–192).

15. Figures on the white population in 1715 are based on a census of that year (Shilstone 1945:14; Molen 1971); the slave population for 1716 is given in Hugh Hall (1714–17) and apparently derives from official returns, which also are the basis for the figures on slaves in 1757 (Pinfold 1762). Statistics on the white population in 1757 were published in *Parliamentary Papers* (1789). The island's deputy-secretary believed the 1757 figures were very "imperfect" and "fall at least ⅓ d short of the real numb[e]r of inhabitants" (quoted in McCusker 1970:749). Figures for 1802–03 were reported to Governor Seaforth by the island's treasurer (see Pinckerton Papers 1804).

16. Figures on the slave population for 1817–32 derive from registry returns published in *Parliamentary Papers* (1824, 1826, 1830, 1833a,

1833b). Figures for freedmen and whites are from 1825–29 (*Parliamentary Papers* 1830).

17. Compensation was claimed for 83,146 slaves, but was awarded for 82,807; the latter figure is usually taken to represent the number of slaves at emancipation (see *Parliamentary Papers* 1835 and 1837–38; and Schomburgk 1848:146). Figures on whites and freedmen are given in Handler (1974:18–19).

Freedmen began to emerge as a group during the last half of the eighteenth century. They were persons of African or mixed racial ancestry who were either freeborn or manumitted from slavery. In the late eighteenth century, freedmen comprised about 1.1 percent of the population, by 1800 about 2.7 percent, and around 1834 approximately 6.3 percent (Handler 1974:18–19). Although legally free, and thus accorded a variety of privileges and rights that were not extended to slaves, freedmen were denied other privileges and rights because of their racial ancestry. Freedmen were scattered throughout the island's parishes, but most lived in the Bridgetown area where they became heavily involved in small shopkeeping activities and the skilled trades. For a variety of reasons freedmen seldom participated in agricultural activities.

18. We follow common social anthropological practice in distinguishing between the household as a residential group, in which its members lived together, and the family as a group based on kinship criteria. The two groups were sometimes coterminous in slave culture, but, as in all human societies, the family was generally more extensive than the household. By definition, members of the same household lived on the same plantation, whereas members of the same family could live in different household units on the same plantation or be dispersed over more than one plantation. In a so-called simple nuclear family unit, for example, the father could have been living on one plantation, and the mother and children by him could have been living on another; the mother and children could have formed a household unit, while the father, on his plantation, could have been living in another household, coresident with a woman who was not the mother of his children.

We cannot determine the frequency distribution of the various household types found among Barbadian plantation slaves but from the available information, common types included an adult man and woman with the younger children of one or both adults, an adult couple without resident children, a mother and her children by the same man or different men. There were also single-person households and households comprised of unrelated adults of the same sex. (It can be noted that, in what is perhaps the most detailed study yet published of household structure in a British West Indian slave population, Higman has isolated thirteen household types among 814 slaves on three Jamaican properties in 1825. The most common type was composed of a man, a woman, and her children; 1973a:534–535; 1974:42–43.)

Data on household size are also very limited. An 1823 estimate mentions that "an average number of about four persons" inhabited the slave houses on Barbadian plantations (Barbados Council 1824:114), which agrees with figures from six different plantations over the 1796–1824 period. Although it is difficult to say how representative these plantations were, they are the only ones for which we could obtain figures on the number of houses as well as the number of slaves. The plantations contained 30, 32, 41, "upwards of 70," 76, and "nearly 80" houses, a total of about 328; 1,246 slaves inhabited these houses, an average of 3.8 persons per house (Bennett 1958:100–101; J. W. Jordan 1824; Rolph 1836:53; Barbados Assembly 1818:41, 42).

19. The sources convey the impression that most practitioners (not believers) of Obeah were men, but the evidence for Obeah women is unequivocal. Aside from the Barbados Council's observation that most plantations had "some old man or woman" who practiced Obeah, an 1806 law making Obeah a felony, punishable by death, stressed "the wicked acts of certain Negro and other slaves going under the appelation of Obeah men and women" (Public Record Office 1806); a similar act of 1818 also mentioned "persons going under the appelation of Obeah men and women" (Public Record Office 1818).

"Of their arts we know nothing," reported the Barbados Council (1789). Although several references to Obeah in the historical literature mention or allude to the use of poisons and other materials, only Walduck and Hughes described the practice in any detail. Both their descriptions noted the use of various material objects. Walduck reported that Obeah persons used "bones," "shells," "images of clay, wax, dust, and those stuck with pins, old iron, tobacco pipes ... strings ... Basket[s]ful of such trumphery I have took away from them upon searching their houses and burnt them" (1710–12). Griffith Hughes, describing the period from the mid-1730s to the late 1740s, noted the use of "pieces of glass, rusty nails, and splinters of sharp stones ... earthen basons ... different kinds of leaves, and ... soap" (1750:15).

In one form or another Obeah "is still practiced in Barbados and still remains a felony on the statute books" (K. Watson 1975:169). In 1976, an elderly Barbadian reported to Handler that in his youth, around World War I, Obeah men and women were very common. They were paid to ascertain the cause of death (especially in cases of suspected poisoning), to cure some ill, and sometimes even to cause harm to someone else. Karl Watson, a Barbadian, has recently reported that grave dirt (which, during the days of slavery, was used in ordeals and oaths—see chapter 6) "still forms an integral part in the lexicon of Obeah ... This was considered to have special magical powers and, controlled by the initiated, could be harmful" (1975:169; cf. Genovese 1974:200).

20. Figures in this paragraph were derived from information in Barbados Department of Archives (1803–04; 1780–1834); Bishop (1759); J. Brathwaite (1789); Dickson (1814:157); Lowther Plantation (1756, 1825–35); Newton Papers (523/131–1, 278, 969–2, 984); Oliver (1910–20,

1:67); Parry (1789c); Pasfeild (1727); Society for the Propagation of the Gospel (1740); Steele (1789:35); and White (1972).

21. We are concerned here with the number of individual working units, not with the number of proprietors.

22. At the end of slavery Barbados, along with other British West Indian territories (with the exception of Antigua), went through four years of "Apprenticeship." The Apprenticeship period was initially conceived and justified as a transitional phase during which the ex-slaves would gradually become accustomed to working and living as freemen. The act of emancipation declared that all emancipated slaves above age six were to become apprentices to their former masters until 1838 or 1840, depending on whether they had been domestic or field slaves. They were obliged to give a certain number of working hours to their masters who, in turn, were obliged to pay them for their labor. Although apprenticeship brought in its wake a number of institutional modifications, it bore such close resemblance to slavery and caused so many problems that it was terminated for everyone on August 1, 1838.

3. The Archaeological Project: Methodology and Survey Summary

1. These data and their analyses are on file with the Department of Anthropology, Southern Illinois University at Carbondale.

2. Slaves frequently cultivated the small plots of land surrounding their houses, but on some plantations additional acreage was occasionally set aside for slave use. This land, the Negro garden, was planted in food crops. For example, at Ashford plantation, the nine acres "cultivated by the Negroes for their own use" in 1812 were distinct from the plantation's Negro yard (Society for the Improvement 1811–16:38–39). Although "on many plantations the Negroes have no ground at all" (p. 112), when such additional acreage was allocated it was called either the "Negro garden" or "Negro ground." This land could be located at the periphery of a plantation or adjacent to the slave village, but present information makes it difficult to establish which was the most common practice.

3. We are especially indebted to Mrs. Mildred Hart Higgins, of Fairfield, Connecticut, who owns the original drawing and who made a photocopy of it for inclusion in this book. A detailed drawing of an early plantation yard is very rare. The Ashford drawing was included among some family papers which had belonged to Mrs. Higgins's father, Henry Francis Hart, who had been born in Barbados and who came to the United States in 1896. Henry Francis Hart was a descendant of a former owner of Ashford by the same name. According to Mrs. Higgins (personal communications, February 5 and 26, 1972), the drawing is in a "ladies journal" that also includes other drawings and poems; the album's dedication to Mrs. Henry Hart is dated May 9, 1845. The draw-

ing of Ashford is not dated, but its caption reads "Ashford. The Estate of Henry Hart Esq. Barbados."

As a result of detailed research conducted in the Barbados Department of Archives's collection of deeds and wills as well as in other sources, Darla White established that Ashford was first purchased by Henry Francis Hart in April 1837. At the time of purchase, the plantation included 129 ex-slaves and comprised 299 acres (White 1972; see also Barbados Department of Archives, Deed Books, vol. 293, p. 236). The drawing of Ashford was thus made sometime between 1837, the year the plantation was purchased by Hart, and probably 1845, the date of the dedication in the "ladies journal." The features and distribution of buildings depicted in the drawing probably would have been quite similar had the drawing been made prior to emancipation in 1834.

4. For example, in 1796, Sampson Wood, the manager of Newton, sarcastically reported that "generally" in Barbados "the managers dwelling house is ... situated where they enjoy the sight of all the doors of the [yard] buildings at one view; if nothing is wrong in the day time, all must be secure—they suppose—and from ... their front door, they give their directions [to the slaves] with a stentorial voice without the trouble of motion, and they never get up to go out or even about the grounds but on horse-back" (Newton Papers 523/288). Wood complained that these practices led to inefficient security and increased theft.

5. Stone-walled houses (some of which are inhabited) with wood shingle roofs can be seen in Barbados today, especially in parts of the parishes of Saint Peter and Saint Lucy. In a sense, Barbadians are correct when they refer to these as "slave houses," but it is erroneous to assume that such houses were characteristic and typical of the island's slave population. Although there is some evidence that stone houses appeared in the seventeenth century—for example, the schedule of a plantation owner's will in January 1678 mentions "7 negro houses of stone" (Barbados Museum and Historical Society 1953:27)—they were not numerically significant compared to the wattle-and-daub houses until the early nineteenth century.

6. Historical sources showed that wattle-and-daub houses were the most common type on the New Montpelier estate in the 1820s. Although their archaeological field season was very brief, Higman and his associates were working in undisturbed contexts, but their "search for yards composed of wattled houses was inconclusive" (Higman 1974:44–45); a subsequent short period of fieldwork also did not yield evidence of wattle-and-daub houses (Higman 1975).

7. The English slave trader, Captain Thomas Phillips, gives a good indication of what these stones may have been. Describing Whydah in Dahomey, where he acquired slaves in 1694 for shipment to Barbados, he reported: "The negroes ... bread is made of Indian or Guiney corn ground, which they do between two stones call'd the cancy stones and rubber, and is made as follows. First they place the cancy stone, which is smooth and broad, shelving in a frame; then put on it thirty or forty grains of

Indian corn after it has lain some time soaking in water; then with the rubber (which is a small stone big enough for one to grasp in his hand) they bruise the corn, and continue rubbing it till it is reduc'd to a meal (much as our painters grind their paint), often sprinkling water thereon to moisten it. Of the said meal temper'd with water they make round lumps like dumplins, which they boil in an earthen crock, or bake o'er the fire on an iron or stone; and this they call cancy which ... is the diet of the generality" (1746:237–238). Before arriving at Whydah, Phillips stopped at the Gold Coast, not far from Axim, where he acquired "some cancy-stones, for our slaves to grind their corn upon" during the middle passage (p. 218).

8. Dickson, who was in Barbados during the 1770s and early 1780s, provided a unique piece of information in his discussion of black carpenters: "On the doors of some of the Negro huts, I have observed wooden locks, at once simple and well contrived, and which it was impossible to open, without the wooden key, which had two or three square, polished prominencies, adapted to the internal parts of the lock, which I have also seen, but it cannot be explained without a model" (1789:74).

4. NEWTON PLANTATION: HISTORY AND THE SLAVE POPULATION

1. While we were test-excavating in one area of the island, a plantation owner told us that human bones from a possible slave cemetery had been unearthed in earlier years at Newton. On a brief visit to the plantation, Newton's manager showed us the area where he thought the cemetery was located. The location was confirmed by an elderly worker whose grandparents had also worked on the plantation. As a child, the worker remembered being told of a place where the "old people" had been buried, and he showed us a number of precise spots where we eventually found interments (see chapter 5).

2. The major part of the collection was acquired in 1960 and 1961, and a detailed list of its contents was prepared by Christine E. Micklem (1969).

In June 1974, the University of London purchased approximately eighty-three documents that date from 1683 to 1702 for its Newton collection (Newton Papers 523/1054–1117). These documents, mostly letters and some legal papers that contain little information on slaves, were consulted by Handler soon after their purchase and have been recently cataloged by Rowan Watson (1975).

3. All the report says about this map is "You [the owners] will be so good as to turn to your plan of Newton plantation and follow me according to the alphabetical division of the fields as there arranged"; the manager described each field's acreage, agricultural state, and potential (Newton Papers 523/289).

4. Because Barbados lacked major rivers and surface springs were irregularly distributed Barbadians largely relied on rainwater that was

collected in ponds and cisterns; wells were also excavated to tap underground springs or streams. Cisterns, usually built next to the plantation house to collect the rain funneled through roof gutters, and wells were the major sources of water for whites. Slaves were compelled to use the ponds (sometimes sharing these with the plantation's livestock). Ponds were formed in natural depressions or were constructed, usually by taking advantage of an incline or slope in the terrain. Reliance on ponds could be precarious, especially in low rainfall areas of the island; evaporation was a problem and in times of drought or during the dry season, the slaves would inevitably suffer. In 1799 one of Newton's fields was named Well House and another Negroe pond (Newton Papers 523/129). Today the former comprises Lower Well and Upper Well fields (see figure 4), but the "Negroe pond" name no longer exists.

5. The hurricane of October 1780 was one of the most devastating in the island's history (the only earlier one of apparently comparable force occurred in 1675). "Nothing has ever happened," an eyewitness reported, "that has caused such universal desolation. No one house ... is exempt from damage. Very few buildings are left standing on the estates. The depopulation of the Negroes ... is very great" (*Gentleman's Magazine* 1780).

We have no other specific information on how the 1780 hurricane affected Newton, but the plantation was certainly well within the area of major damage. The owner of Grove plantation, about five miles northeast of Newton, provided a particularly vivid account that suggests how Newton may have been affected: "The dwelling house, boiling house, curing house, corn house, manager's house, Negroes' houses and stable were all levelled with the ground, nor did any [other] building escape [damage] ... 3 Negroes were killed outright ... and 3 others died soon afterwards ... The lower grounds [of land] appeared like a sea, and the upper were washed and robbed of a great part of the soil. The few trees that remained were totally deprived of their leaves; vegetation seemed to be annihilated, and the whole country [of Barbados] was a blank and dreary waste" (Senhouse 1935:204, 205).

In 1831, another massive hurricane engulfed the island. Seven of Newton's slaves were killed (Newton Plantation 1805–1841). The southern portions of Barbados were particularly hard hit, and Christ Church, Newton's parish, ranked third in the value of losses and sixth in the number of slaves killed (Schomburgk 1848:440, 696–697).

6. Michael J. Chandler, Barbados Government Archivist, derived this information from a survey of seventeenth-century deeds and land conveyances located in the Barbados Department of Archives (personal communications, January 29 and October 22, 1974).

7. As best as we can tell, the northeastern Newton plantation is not shown with a mill on Forde's map (suggesting its smaller size), but two cattle mills are identified with the southwestern one. By 1687, however, the latter had two windmills that were still functioning in 1693, albeit

in need of repairs; in addition, in May 1693, a new cattle mill was constructed for emergencies in the event the winds failed (Newton Papers 523/1106; Bate 1693).

8. The earliest account of the state of Newton plantation appears to be in a 1693 letter from Richard Bate, the plantation's attorney, to Barbara and John who were then resident in London. However, it provides only fragmentary information on miscellaneous topics. In general, unless otherwise noted, information on the history of Newton plantation's ownership is based on the will of Samuel Newton, June 16, 1684 and will of Barbara Newton, June 19, 1694 (recopied Wills Books, RB 6/12, fol. 514 seq. and RB 6/2, fol. 175 seq., Barbados Department of Archives), and a variety of documents among the University of London's Newton Papers.

9. This map was later reprinted but Tony Campbell (1965:15, 17), presumably following Shilstone (1938:63), incorrectly identifies a 1717 printing as its first publication.

10. Bentley Gibbs derived this information on the establishment of the Newton tenantry from data in the Newton journals located in the Barbados Museum (personal communication).

11. "So called," William Dickson wrote, "from their having been formerly given to pigeons, and other feathered stock; but which are now discovered to be very good food for men; and, by many white people, are preferred to any kind of European peas" (1789:13).

12. Death was the major factor accounting for losses in Newton's slave population from the late 1700s to emancipation. During this period, however, about seven or eight slaves were also lost to the plantation through manumission, sale, or successful escape.

13. Unless otherwise noted, the following discussion of work roles and labor organization at Newton is based on materials for the years 1776, 1782, 1783, 1796, 1803, 1817, and 1820 (Newton Papers 523/270, 271, 272, 288, 285, 275, and Newton Plantation 1805–1841).

14. In fifty-one cases, which include thirty different plantations over the period 1781–1834, there was a total of 9,766 slaves; 3,954 of these persons, or 40 percent, were first and second gang members. In no case were gang members less than 30 percent of a plantation's total slave population; in 26 cases (50.9 percent) they comprised between 30 and 39 percent; in 19 cases (37.2 percent), 40 to 49 percent; in 5 cases (9.8 percent), 50 to 59 percent; and in only one case were they 60 percent. Thus, in slightly more than half the total cases, the effective labor force, the first and second gangs, constituted between 30 and 39 percent of all the slaves on a plantation. See Bennett (1958:12); Harewood Archives (1834); Rolph (1836:53); Society for the Improvement (1811–16); Barbados Department of Archives (Deed Books, vol. 287, pp. 322–328); Guinea Plantation (1820); and Newton Papers (523/119, 276, 285).

These figures generally confirm an estimate given by the agent for Barbados in the late 1780s; he reported to a British parliamentary committee that "in any given plantation the working Negroes amount to about one third of the whole number" (J. Brathwaite 1789; cf. Parry 1789b).

15. No ranger is listed for Newton in 1784, but in that year, the average value of all slaves at Seawell was £33: the highest valued slave (£80) was a carpenter; next were the two coopers (£70) and third (£60) was a nineteen-member group that included the ranger, driver, head boiler, cook, four masons, and eleven male members of the first gang (Newton Papers 523/278).

16. The "premium" given to women whose infants survived their first month was a major type of monetary reward or incentive that slaves received (although it was not the only type; see, for example, Bennett 1958: 18, 95). Infanticide may not have been uncommon (see Thome and Kimball 1838:58, 77), but natural causes were the major reasons for infant mortality, and "of the children who are born, there is infinitely too great a proportion that die in the month" (Society for the Improvement 1811–16:138). Whatever the specific causes of infant mortality, there is some evidence that by the 1770s or early 1780s planters awarded a small sum of money to a mother "upon the birth of her first child if it survives one month" (Gibbes 1797:86–87), but, as Dickson observed, "this is not the ordinary practice" (1789:12). The practice increased, however, and on a number of plantations was extended to cover all month-old infants. In 1798, for example, Newton's manager emphasized: "I encourage their breeding as much as I can . . . when [mothers] . . . bring me their child after the month I present them with a dollar" (Newton Papers 523/381-1). Newton's financial accounts over subsequent years show "birth premiums" of a dollar (equivalent to six shillings, three pence local currency) paid to "women for bringing out . . . newborn babies" (Newton Plantation 1805–1841). The premium Newton paid for each newborn child and the reason for the payment appear to have been standard throughout the island, at least on middle- to large-scale plantations (see, for example, *The Christian Remembrancer* 1823:408; Barbados Council 1824:109, 114–115; and Lowther Plantation 1825–35).

17. An incident that occurred at Newton in the early 1790s illustrates this view of field labor. The manager before Sampson Wood had disciplinary problems with some members of a slave family who had been traditionally nonfield laborers. After a "quarrel with the family," the manager "put them into the field by way of degradation and punishment, and left them there . . . with the mockery of putting them into the field's list" (Newton Papers 523/288). "Such is the difference between the treatment of house and field-negroes," wrote William Dickson, "that *to turn a house negro into the field*, is universally considered as a *punishment;* and, on some plantations, it is a very severe punishment. If a house-negro ever choose, or seem to choose, to go into the field, it is to flee from unsupportable domestic tyranny" (1789:7).

18. At Newton, for example, the plantation's work log from May 1796 to April 1797 shows that one of the plantation's three cooper-

carpenters did no agricultural work while the other two worked in the fields for only twenty-three days; the plantation's two masons performed agricultural work for only nineteen days (Newton Papers 523/110).

19. The work role and ranking of slaves was reflected in, among other things, the amounts of food they received from plantation managements. For example, the Reverend Davies, who had lived in Barbados from about 1756 to 1770, observed that "a grown Negro" received "from seven to nine pints of corn" per week, but "some of the principal slaves had as far as twelve pints" (1791:185). A more detailed illustration of the relationship between role or rank and food supplies was gathered from information that a plantation manager provided a House of Assembly committee in 1816 or 1817. On his plantation the driver, ranger, and head carter each received weekly fifty-six pounds of yams or potatoes, twenty pints of corn, five pints of molasses, one pound of salt fish, and one-half pint of salt; the senior tradesmen and second class drivers received forty pounds of yams or potatoes, thirteen pints of corn, two pints of molasses, and the same amount of salt fish and salt. In contrast, field laborers received twenty-eight pounds of yams or potatoes, ten pints of corn, one and one-half pints of molasses, one-half pound of salt fish, and one-quarter pound of salt. Weekly allowances were even lower for other categories of slaves: house servants and "slaves in light employment," for example, were only given twenty-two pounds of yams or potatoes and seven pints of corn, and older children received sixteen pounds of yams or potatoes and four pints of corn. House servants and "slaves in light employment" were given the same amounts of salt fish and salt as the field laborers, but slightly less molasses, and older children were not supplied with salt fish or molasses (Barbados Assembly 1818:47).

20. For example, in 1833 Lowther plantation paid eighteen shillings and nine pence "to Prince, the field overseer, as a reward for his good conduct" (Lowther Plantation 1825–35). In 1796, Newton's head driver received about £8½ and the others somewhat less; the coopers were given £9½ and the distiller close to £2 (Newton Papers 523/113). In 1805, Dickey Bird, Newton's head driver, received a year's "allowance" of £10 and in one month during 1806 he received £2 as "part" of his "allowance" (Newton Plantation 1805–1841). On the Codrington plantations in the late 1700s, the head drivers received annual "cash rewards" of a little over six shillings, but their "nineteenth century successors received handsome annual gifts of £20 and two pairs of shoes" (Bennett 1958:18).

21. About six weeks after this letter was written, the only slave revolt (which had been planned for months) in Barbados's history erupted in the parishes of Saint Philip and Christ Church. Seawell, whose manager had received a similarly inscribed plate, was considerably damaged as a result of rebel action and suffered a financial loss of over £2,600, including the value of seven slaves who were killed or executed

303

for their participation in the revolt (Newton Papers 523/766,781). A few months after the revolt, the attorney for Newton and Seawell wrote that during the uprising Seawell's slaves "were the most refractory set, I may venture to say, in the parish of Christ Church," but "the Negroes at Newton...conducted themselves with great propriety" (523/773). It is difficult to say, however, what would have happened at Newton, for the revolt was put down before it had spread to the plantation.

It is a reflection of white self-delusion about the motivations and aspirations of slaves that only one or two days before the revolt erupted the attorney wrote in a letter to Thomas Lane complaining about emancipationist activities in England: "The slaves of this island were never so happy...as of this moment...They are now more enlightened and enjoy more comforts and luxuries unknown to many of their masters 25 years ago" (Newton Papers 523/765-1).

22. This and the following sections on clothing, shelter, and medical care are based on a variety of sources, some of which are cited in the text. Other sources employed for these sections include (but are not restricted to) the following: Alleyne (1801a, 1802a); Barbados Assembly (1818:42, 43, 46, 47, 49, 50); Barbados Assembly (1790:4); Barbados Council (1789); Bayley (1832:90); *The Christian Remembrancer* (1823); Clarke (1832); Coleridge (1832:126); Davies (1791:181, 185); Douglass (1755;1:118, 123–24); Gibbes (1786:20–22); Gunkel and Handler (1969, 1970); Littleton (1689:19–20, 28); Oldmixon (1741;2:131, 134, 161); Parry (1789b); Rees (1790:247–48); Society for the Improvement (1811–16); and Towne (1726).

23. Imported rice, which became the staple food of Barbados's working class after emancipation, was only occasionally distributed to plantation slaves through the eighteenth century or so and then usually reserved for infants or invalids. However, rice consumption began to increase by the 1820s (see, for example, Lowther Plantation 1825–35; Newton Papers 523/831).

24. As on other Barbadian plantations, Newton's slaves occasionally received herring (sometimes imported from Britain), but herring was less frequently distributed than cod or mackerel. During 1796–97, Newton's slaves received herring, in unspecified amounts, on three days.

25. During the preemancipation decades of the nineteenth century, Barbadian slaves also grew small amounts of such cash crops as ginger, cotton, aloes, and arrowroot for the local and export market. Although direct evidence is lacking, Newton's slaves possibly were also engaged in such production because the plantation manager cultivated small amounts of arrowroot for his own use (Handler 1971b:71–73).

26. For example, a severe drought over "the last two or three years," wrote the manager of Seawell in 1821, has "nearly ruined many of our planters, for independently of small crops, their plantations have not yielded food for their Negroes"; "from this misfortune," he added, both

Seawell and Newton "have been exempt" (Newton Papers 523/850), although both the plantations were affected at other times.

27. An anonymous observer, commenting on the food preferences of Jamaican plantation slaves in the early 1770s, stressed that "a cat is generally esteemed a peculiar dainty" (Higman 1976b:15).

28. Newton's work log from May 1796 to April 1797 shows that at least one member of the first gang was in the "sick house" every day, but, on the average during each month, close to seven gang members were confined on a daily basis; taking the first and second gangs together, an average of 8.5 persons were in the "sick house" daily during each month of the twelve-month period. These figures do not include other plantation slaves, such as tradesmen or domestics, who also reported sick (Newton Papers 523/110).

5. Newton Plantation: Archaeological Investigations

1. Surface collections were also made in a number of other fields at Newton. Some of these fields, such as Lower Duck Pond and Upper Well, are shown in figure 4; the other fields, not shown, are more distant from the plantation yard. We made collections in different parts of the plantation to contrast distributions of surface archaeological materials between suspected former habitation areas and nonhabitation areas. A major concentration of china, redware pottery, and pipestem fragments was found in Upper Well field near an area that was reported to be the former site of one or more windmills and other plantation structures that are no longer standing.

2. In Jamaica, Higman and his associates worked in areas that were not in agricultural use, but they encountered difficulties in locating remains of domestic structures in unplowed areas. They found surface evidence of stone house structures but no remains of wattle-and-daub or other subsurface, nonmasonry structures (1974:45; 1975; 1976a). It is also significant in terms of the decisions we made in the process of our work, that the disturbed soil in which testing was carried out did not exceed one foot in depth, and even such depths would be easily included within the zone of deep plowing in Barbados.

3. The undisturbed skeletons conform to what Sprague (1968:481) refers to as articulated, and the disturbed, but still partially in place, skeletons as "secondary" (Cleland 1971:7). Because "secondary" often implies planned redeposition of the total remains, the term "semiarticulosis" proposed by Bass (1962:43) is more appropriate. The disarticulated and sometimes unassociated bone concentrations are "residual" (Cleland 1971:7) in the sense that the remains represent the residue of subsequent behavior at the site and not the primary interment of a bone mass.

4. A short, round fragment of wood (approximately 5.5 centimeters long and 2 centimeters at its widest) was associated with Burial 60; this piece of wood was located approximately 16 centimeters from the right hand and roughly parallel to it (figure 13). The wood appears to repre-

sent the bottom end of a cane or a staff or perhaps the handle to some other, undefined, artifact. One end of the wood is severely jagged and was obviously broken off from a larger piece. From the broken end, the wood fragment slightly tapers to the tip into which a piece of iron, perhaps a large nail, had been inserted (under X ray, the outline of the inserted piece of iron is visible, but its exposed tip is severely corroded and its shape could not be ascertained). A thin (approximately 1 millimeter) sheet of copper completely encases the wood, lending further support to the suggestion that the wood fragment was once the bottom end of a cane or staff.

5. The specimen with the Burial 55 pipe weighs 0.3368 grams (on a Mettler balance) and measures 3.6 millimeters high and 8.0 millimeters in diameter at the base. It was found lying, apex down, exactly at the mouthpiece end of the pipestem, as shown in figure 34D. The pipe and glass object apparently were undisturbed since their original interment with Burial 55. The specimen with Burial 60, weighing 0.3813 grams and measuring 3.6 millimeters high and 8.3 millimeters at the base, was lying next to the end of a 4.5-centimeter length of pipestem. This section of pipestem clearly was not an original mouthpiece, and was not found attached to a bowl or additional stem fragment. The section may have been disturbed since the original interment; if so, its association with the glass object may have been fortuitous.

A refractive index determination by the X ray and Optics Laboratory at Southern Illinois University showed that both objects were definitely glass with a specific gravity of 3.5 to 3.7, and a hardness of 7. The analyst concluded that the glass was unusually heavy or hard and suggested that glass of this type would not normally be manufactured in modern times.

6. We use the term "multiple interment" to refer to two or more people buried in the same place at the same time; "simultaneous burial" refers to bodies buried in clearly distinct spaces but at the same time. Burials 69 and 70 (figure 17) constitute a multiple interment while Burials 56, 58, and 64 (figures 14 and 15) were a simultaneous burial.

7. Although broken when excavated, the pipe is complete except for a small portion missing from the back of the bowl. The bowl mouth is not perfectly circular, but it is approximately 3.2 centimeters across the diameter of the mouth to the outer edges, and approximately 3.4 centimeters from the top of the mouth to the point of the base where the bowl joins the stem. Internally, the bowl is funnel-shaped and tapers from an approximately 2.1-centimeter diameter at the mouth to approximately 0.8 centimeters at the base where it joins the bore hole of the stem. The bore hole is also tapered, from 0.9 centimeters at the opening to an approximately 0.5 centimeter diameter where it enters the base of the bowl. Measured externally, the stem is approximately 3.8 centimeters long and 1.9 centimeters wide.

The pipe may have been used with its short clay stem or a detachable stem of some perishable material could have been inserted into the bore hole to enlarge the total stem size. The small bridge between the back of the bowl and the top of the stem has an approximately 0.3-centimeter hole; it may be that this hole was used for tying or lashing the detachable stem to the pipe (Ozanne 1962:54) or, perhaps, for stringing the pipe and carrying it on a belt—or hanging it in some other way from the body—when not in use.

The pipe is made of buff-colored clay and contains quartz and clay temper inclusions, unlike the white clay used in tobacco pipes of European manufacture. There is no evidence of a seam on either the stem or the bowl, suggesting that the pipe was not made in a mold despite its relatively elaborate appearance and the regularity of most of its decorative features.

Around its outer circumference, the bowl is decorated with nine equally spaced flutes. The outer circumference of the stem has three groups of incised lines; each group, in turn, is comprised of three lines. A relief dot is set inside a circular punctation or impression between each group of lines; three of these dots are on each side and on the bottom of the stem. Four shallow and roughly circular punctations are on the blunt heel of the stem; the fact that these are not equidistant from each other may be additional evidence that the pipe was handmade, rather than having been cast in a carefully patterned mold.

8. Slaves often slept on a rough board or plank that rested directly on the earthen floors of their houses, and wooden doors were found in at least some slave houses; moreover, in the mid-1820s, for example, Newton's financial accounts show small sums expended for pairs of "hinges for Negro houses" (Newton Plantation 1805–1841). The historical sources, however, do not mention the use of doors in mortuary practices. It is, perhaps, of some relevance to note that a late nineteenth-century account of mortuary practices among Yoruba-speaking peoples reported that "on the afternoon of the third day of the wake the body is placed on some boards, or on a door taken off its hinges, covered with a rich native cloth, and borne at a trot through the streets by the men." The account implied that the corpse was not interred on this platform, although it noted that "a coffin is sometimes used, but not often" (Ellis 1894:158).

9. According to elderly Barbadian informants, white clay pipes were commonly smoked, especially by the working class, well into the twentieth century. The pipes were frequently smoked very close to the bowls after the stems had broken. A 1789 Jamaican source quoted by Brathwaite, mentions that some planters on that island supplied their slaves with, among other goods, "short tobacco pipes" (1971:232). Jamaican plantation slaves, "of both sexes," reported another late eighteenth-century observer, "regale themselves with smoking tobacco, the effect of which enables them to subsist a considerable time without food" (Higman 1976b:16).

10. Walduck indicated another secondary use of pipes. He reported that Obeah sorcerers made "images of clay, wax, dust" and then stuck

these with "pins, old iron, tobacco pipes in several parts, according as they design to grieve the patient" (1710–12).

11. The importation of earthenware sugar pots to Barbados may have started by the 1650s (Barbados Museum and Historical Society 1940b: 70, 72), but we have been unable to find statistics reflecting the number of such imports during the slave period. However, English export statistics for the eighteenth and nineteenth centuries show that from 1740 to 1780, 9,578,832 "glass and earthenware pieces" were exported from England to Barbados; although the records do not separate these types, it is likely that a significant number were sugar pots and jars (into which the molasses dripped). Similarly, from 1814 to 1834, England exported 4,354,186 "earthenware" items to Barbados. Of this total, 4,195,799, or 96.3 percent, were described as "common earthenware"; the records offer no breakdowns on the types of this "common earthenware," but we assume that a significant percentage was composed of sugar pots and jars. (Debbie Teglia gathered these statistics from the Customs Records, Series 3, vols. 35–80, and Series 9, vols. 1–28, in the Public Record Office, London.) We do not know how much of the imported earthenware was reexported to other Caribbean territories, but Barbadian plantations clearly used a great number of sugar pots and jars and frequently calculated sugar production by the number of pots they filled. For example, on Newton in 1799, the crop yielded 4,911 "pots of sugar" (Newton Papers 523/129), and in 1797 the manager of Lower Estate plantation reported "I have already made 3,000 pots" (Yearwood 1949:116). On Lowther plantation in 1756 the inventory listed 1,300 "sugar pots" (Lowther Plantation 1756), and there were about 5,000 on the Codrington plantations in 1739 (Society for the Propagation of the Gospel 1739). Although a number of plantations produced pots, island production could not meet the demand, and sugar pots and jars are indicated as standard items on import lists (Pinfold 1762; Frere 1768:121); jars were sometimes glazed (Alleyne 1801c).

12. An Anglican minister in Barbados during the 1670s also alluded to the use of pottery within the slaves' belief system: they place "confidence in certain figures, and ugly representations... (which very decently... they usually enshrine in some stately earthen potsherds), the fugitives and runaways believing these deities able to protect them in their flight, and from discovery" (Godwyn 1680:33).

13. On Antigua, in particular, some of the household wares made during the slave period were still being manufactured in the early 1960s (Handler 1964; Flannigan 1844;2:4; see also Handler 1963a:148). There is also some indication that pottery was made on Nevis in the eighteenth century (Rymer 1775:4–5).

14. For example, the inventory of one of the Codrington plantations in 1739 included "a pot-house"; "1 kiln in use"; "488 sound potts"; "923 hooped potts"; "380 cracked potts"; "300 sound jarrs"—all these vessels were in the "pot-house." In addition, the "curing house" (where the pots were placed while the molasses drained from the sugar) contained

"2110 jarrs, 244 old jarrs, 76 jarrs with molasses, 300 old potts" (Society for the Propagation of the Gospel 1739; see also Handler 1963a:136–139).

15. Mathewson also speculated that the earliest Africans in Jamaica acquired some information from Arawaks on local clays and pottery technology (1972b:56). The seventeenth-century Amerindians imported to Barbados from Guiana and other Caribbean islands made some contributions to the island's culture, particularly in areas related to the exploitation of plant life and the domestic arts, but there is no evidence that they contributed to the development of a ceramic tradition among Africans or Europeans (Handler 1970).

16. Noël Hume pointed out that silver (and gold) rings are "very rarely" found in archaeological contexts in North American colonial sites, "though those of brass are not uncommon. But...little attention has been afforded them and no acceptable chronology has been established" (1970:265).

17. Neptunes were large brass pans or basins that were common for many years in the European trade with West Africa. Abundant quantities were imported. In addition to their utilitarian functions, neptunes were also used in sacrificial rituals and burials (see, for example, Herbert 1973:187). Although a variant spelling (or typographical error), Phillips's "anilias" were obviously manillas, copper or brass bracelets that were apparently first introduced to Africa by the Portuguese in the early sixteenth century, if not before. Manillas were used to purchase slaves and ivory. Later the British and other Europeans manufactured these items for the African trade. Phillips indicates that Africans also made manillas, and the objects became a medium of exchange among a number of West African groups (see, for example, Roth 1903:5–6; Talbot 1932:282–284).

18. We did not have the services of a trained physical anthropologist in the field, and budgetary limitations prevented us from shipping the entire skeletal inventory to the United States for further study. We were unable to obtain storage space in Barbados for the bones, and we reluctantly back filled most of the postcranial material. Some cranial and all dental materials, however, were sent to the United States for additional analysis.

19. Reports on skeletal remains of other slave populations are rare. Dailey discussed approximately fifteen partial skeletons found eroding from the shoreline at Cinnamon Bay in Saint John, the Virgin Islands: "the skeletons are very incomplete, sometimes comprising only the cranium or a few fragmented bones from the post cranial skeleton... and all appear to have been predominantly Negroid" (1974:1). The fragmentary nature of these remains makes it difficult to compare them with the Newton sample. As at Newton, the Cinnamon Bay material shows very few pathologies and no marked anomalies. Only one case of probable pipewear was observed, although dental material was incomplete for many of the individuals. In his general observations,

Dailey noted that the Cinnamon Bay cemetery "takes on additional significance ... because we know virtually nothing about the stature, diseases and non-metrical variations of black population[s] during the slave period" (1974:11).

6. The Mortuary Patterns of Plantation Slaves

1. Secondary materials on the mortuary patterns of slaves in other areas of the Caribbean are meager. For example, in a lengthy article dealing with eighteenth-century plantation burial grounds in Haiti, Gabriel Debien, the doyen of historians of slavery in the French Antilles, was only able to write about whites and freedmen. His primary sources rarely mentioned baptized slaves and, in particular, there was "not a word on the burials of non-Christian slaves. But, Christians or not, they had their own funerals to which they were deeply attached and which they organized among themselves, with processions, rituals, and special chants. Will one ever be able to specify in detail of what these funerals consisted?" (1974a: 539–540, our translation). Debien's recently published volume on slavery and slaves in the French West Indies does not even mention mortuary patterns (1974b).

The scholarly literature for the United States also sparsely treats mortuary patterns, although several recent major studies of slavery have discussed in varying degrees slave sociocultural life. In one exception, Eugene Genovese's *Roll, Jordan, Roll*, the ethnographic details mainly relate to the later phases of the slave period (1974:194–202; cf., for example, Blassingame 1972; Fogel and Engerman 1974; Mullin 1972; Rawick 1972; and Wood 1974).

2. The Incorporated Society for the Conversion and Religious Instruction and Education of the Negro Slaves in the British West Indian Islands was founded by the Church of England in 1794, but did not become active in Barbados until the early 1820s, when one missionary was assigned to work among plantation slaves.

3. In Jamaica, in the late 1700s—if not earlier—"interment took place in Negro burial grounds, if these were provided by the authorities, or 'promiscuously in the fields, and [near] their near and dear relations at the back of their huts, and sometimes under their beds'" (Brathwaite 1971:216). In 1816, a Jamaican planter reported that the "Negroes are always buried in their own gardens" (Lewis 1834:97). The location of graves varied among West African peoples; some areas had communal burial grounds belonging to particular family groups. However, interment under the house or room of the deceased was widespread. See, for example, Bascom (1969:66–67); Herskovits (1938;1:359); McCulloch (1950:46); Ardener (1956:87); Field (1961:199); Parrinder (1961:109); Manoukian (1950:53); Rattray (1927:161); Talbot (1932: 255); Thomas (1910:44); Manoukian (1952:43); and Forde and Jones (1950:27). The practice in Barbados and Jamaica was undoubtedly of African derivation.

4. If these reports accurately reflect the intensity of "attachment to

the burying places of their ancestors" they raise the question of what might have happened in the immediate postemancipation period when the slave villages began to be abandoned and plantation tenantries were established. Citing an 1838 letter from the governor of Barbados, Riviere has written that ex-slaves "revered their burial grounds to the extent that a major ambition was to die on the estates where their relations had been interred, so that they too would be buried there" (1972:4). The movement to the tenantries, however, does not seem to have been marked by friction or a reluctance to abandon the slave villages, which may suggest that the practice of burial under houses had waned significantly by emancipation.

5. This raises the possibility that Newton burials also may have been made in Lower and Upper Well fields, the area between the excavated cemetery and the slave village nearer the Negro yard fields (see figure 4). Although limited testing was done on the periphery of the village site, no burials were found; moreover, no burials were located during test excavations at slave village sites at other plantations.

6. Planters and slaveowners in general prohibited or discouraged baptism. Differences in baptismal rates between earlier and later periods can be illustrated by the statistics from Saint Michael, the parish which usually had the largest number of slave baptisms. Over the eighteen-year period, from 1670 to 1687, thirty-four "mulattoes and Negroes"—mostly nonplantation slaves—were baptized (Dunn 1972:255), an annual average of 1.8. From 1791 to 1817, 4,901 slaves were baptized, approximately 185 each year (Garnett 1817). Especially from the late eighteenth century to the emancipation period, baptism as a vehicle for a church burial was apparently a positive value shared by certain elements of the slave population (Parry 1789a:18; Dickson 1814; Hutchins 1817; and Rolph 1836:38).

7. Passed during a period of general reform in the slave code, the "Sunday and marriage act" also encouraged slaveowners or their agents to "endeavor to instruct their slaves in the principles of the Christian religion" and "cause to be baptized by any clergyman of the established Church of England, all their slaves" (*Parliamentary Papers* 1826–27b). By 1832, however, the Anglican archdeacon of Barbados stressed that "there are still proprietors who have not encouraged or authorized the baptism of a single Negro"; he found the 1826 law "quite feeble and inoperative" (Eliot 1833:161–162).

8. The written sources do not indicate if baptized slaves (and freedmen) were buried in places apart from whites in Anglican church or chapel grounds. They may have been separated, however, especially in the earlier periods. Moreover, we are uncertain if there was another burial ground in Bridgetown for unbaptized slaves. In Pinckard's 1796 description of the funeral of an apparently unbaptized slave, a "burial ground" in Bridgetown is referred to several times (1806; 1:270–74). A separate cemetery for unbaptized slaves may have existed, but in earlier periods both baptized and unbaptized slaves may have been in-

terred in the same cemetery in Bridgetown, a cemetery which was apart from that in which whites were interred. We also do not know if unbaptized slaves were buried apart from baptized ones in plantation cemeteries, although we suspect that no locational distinctions were made.

9. Non-Anglican whites generally were buried on their own land or in sectarian burial grounds. During the seventeenth century, Anglicans were buried in parish churchyards, but "many others," noted the governor in 1680, "bury their dead in the gardens and other spots near their houses...the distance from the [parish] church being often so great that those who live far off know not how to get the corpse down" (Atkins 1680b). As the island's road network improved, it became more customary to transport the corpse to the church for the funeral service and interment. Some planter families, however, continued to maintain private vaults on their plantations, and in such cases the corpse was removed back to the plantation for interment after the church service. In other cases planters may not have had family vaults, but in their wills planters still directed that their remains be interred on their plantations (Barbados Museum and Historical Society 1945:173). By the early nineteenth century plantation burials seemed to have waned considerably (Lucas 1953:25). Burial vaults or individual graves of former plantation owners are occasionally found on Barbadian plantations today, but the areas in which whites were buried were separate from the slave burial grounds.

Sometimes slaves attended the parish church for the funeral services of an owner or the actual interment at the plantations and sometimes participated in the funeral processions of their owners (Orderson 1842: 209–210; Hutchins 1817; Handler 1975:26; cf. Dunn 1972:329). Whether or not they participated in the funerals of whites (or of fellow baptized slaves), slaves in general had ample opportunities to witness white funerals and Christian burial practices.

10. The historical sources on Barbadian slave mortuary practices implicitly or explicitly refer to the burials of adults, and the general pattern in the burial of infants and small children is unclear. Moreover, the burials of infants and very small children were inexplicably lacking from Newton cemetery although historical population data on Newton's slaves indicate that many more infants died than the cemetery data suggest; historical sources on Barbados in general also confirm the pattern of infant mortality (see Appendix D).

11. Although commonly labeled Obeah, descriptions in the historical sources often prevent making a distinction between these phenomena. However, there is a technical distinction that has sociological implications. In sorcery, "evil magic" is performed against others, but "the acts themselves are usually of such a nature that they can be performed by anyone. They are termed magical...because there are no grounds in terms of Western science for believing them able to accomplish the ends claimed for them." On the other hand, "witchcraft is a

312

mystical and innate power, which can be used by its possessor to harm other people. Often it is thought that the witch need merely wish to harm his victim and his witchcraft then does this, or it may be enough for him to merely feel annoyance or jealousy against someone for the power to set itself in operation without his being aware of the fact that it has done so" (Middleton and Winter 1963:3).

12. "Lodging this opinion in their hearts," Ligon wrote, "they make it an ordinary practice, upon any great fright, or threatening of their masters, to hang themselves" (1657:51). Several other observers of Barbadian slave life also believed that this conception was directly related to slave suicide (Drax 1755:56–57; Pinckard 1806; 1:274–275). Similar observations were made about Jamaican slaves (Taylor 1688; 2:545; Sloane 1707;1:xlviii, liii; Stewart 1823:281; Lewis 1834:100; and Patterson 1967:196, 265).

In both Barbados and Jamaica, suicide appears to have been common, especially among African-born slaves during the seventeenth and early eighteenth centuries. The sources do not convey the impression that slaves viewed suicide as a disgraceful or negative act.

Attitudes toward suicide varied among West African peoples, who sometimes made distinctions in terms of the motivations that impelled one to suicide. For example, among the Yoruba "when a man finds life burdensome, disgraceful, and perilous ... and consequently commits suicide, he is given great credit and honour. But when out of shame for a mean act he commits suicide, his corpse is considered abominable and cast into the bush unburied" (Ajisafe 1924:32). Similarly, in Ashanti, Rattray reported that although suicide was regarded as a "capital sin ... under certain circumstances ... [it] was considered as honourable and acclaimed as praiseworthy" (1929:299).

Where distinctions were made between types of suicide, burial rites varied within the same West African society. In other societies all suicides appear to have been buried differently from others. There is no information on whether the Barbadian mortuary patterns surrounding slave suicides were any different from those of nonsuicides.

13. Loading newly purchased slaves aboard his ship at Whydah in Dahomey in 1694, Captain Thomas Phillips reported: "The negroes are so wilful and loth to leave their own country, that they have often leap'd out of the canoes, boat, and ship, into the sea, and kept under water till they were drowned to avoid being taken up and saved by our boats, which pursued them; they having a more dreadful apprehension of Barbadoes than we can have of hell ... We had about 12 negroes did wilfully drown themselves, and others starv'd themselves to death; for 'tis their belief that when they die they return home to their own country and friends again" (1746:235).

Writing about Jamaican slaves in 1688, Sloane also reported how "the Negroes from some countries [in Africa] think they return to their own country when they die in Jamaica ... imagining they shall change their condition, by that means from servile to free" (Sloane 1707; 1: xlviii;

see also Taylor 1688; 2:543–545); similar beliefs involving a return to Africa, freedom, and a rejoining with kinsmen and friends were reported by later observers (Lewis 1834:100, 344–45; Stewart 1823:280–81; and Leslie 1740:307–10).

14. "When we abstract certain general principles out of the many religions of Africa, we find that these religions do not differ either from Islam or Christianity to an extent that would preclude a measure of accomodation under contact"; one of these "general principles" is a belief in a "Great God" (Herskovits 1962:178).

15. A magistrate, writing in 1836, implied that the notion of a decedent's taking a "journey to his native lands" still existed in Barbados during the 1820s, if not later (Colthurst 1835–38:48). If the dating of his comment is correct (the context makes it difficult to interpret chronologically with precision), it suggests that creoles also adhered to this belief: by 1817, 93 percent of the slave population was Barbadian-born, and the percentage increased over subsequent years.

16. Not all slaves, however, were buried in a ritualistic context according to the behavioral norms of slave culture. In 1718, for example, a visiting English Quaker witnessed the "dismal sight [of] ... a mastif dog eating the carcase of a negro man. The dog had eaten off one of his arms and torn his face and bowels and was eating the fat of his thighs as we came by" (Cadbury 1943:123). An American sailor who spent a short time in Barbados in the early 1760s, reported that he had "seen at high water mark, the heads of slaves, fixed upon sharp pointed stakes, while their unburied carcases were exposed to be torn by dogs and vultures on the sandy beach" (Benson 1828:42). In 1806, an English army officer recorded in his journal: "A poor miserable starved black woman laid herself down at our door, having been driven away from that of our opposite neighbor ... In the evening she died and was taken off and thrown into a hole like a dog" (Handler 1975:26).

It is impossible to estimate how many slaves were not buried according to customary procedures. In some cases, such as when a slave was executed for a crime, a ritualistic burial may have been prevented by the white authorities; in others the slaves may have been divorced, for whatever reasons, from a plantation community or lacked community social ties.

17. All cultures in West Africa seem to have had formally defined procedures in preparing the corpse, but practices varied between ethnic groups as well as within the groups themselves (for example, as a function of the rank or status of the deceased). The procedures included washing the corpse, rubbing it with oil, straightening its limbs, shaving the heads of males, dressing the body in fine cloths or clothing and personal jewelry, and sometimes placing food and material goods by the corpse to prepare for the journey of its soul.

Barbadian informants today report that traditionally each rural area had an old woman who was paid to prepare the corpse for burial. The woman washed and dressed the corpse, regardless of sex, and the cloth with which it was washed was then placed in the coffin and buried; nothing else would be placed in the coffin or grave. On the night before the burial a wake would usually be held at the home of the deceased, but we have no evidence if wakes were a part of the slave mortuary complex.

18. Throughout Western Europe during the Middle Ages, white was the color of mourning for both sexes. Black started being used in the fifteenth century and by the eighteenth it was the universal color, although white was also used in various clothing accessories such as scarves, gloves, and hat bands (Habenstein and Lamers 1962:169–170; Morley 1971:63–64; Besant 1925:270–272; Ashton 1883:35–46).

In Africa greater variation apparently occurred. In some areas, dark colors, such as blue and red, were used to signify mourning, while other areas used white. Sometimes color was a function of sex or status; for example, among coastal peoples in the Cameroons, blue was the color for men (Ardener 1956:88). Although red clay was generally the sign of mourning among the Ashanti, priests wore white and also sprinkled themselves with white clay (Rattray 1927:175, 195, 214; see also Ellis 1887:241, 1890:160; Talbot 1932:240; Habenstein and Lamers 1963:235; Thomas 1916:126, 129; Herskovits 1938;1:390).

19. The horse-drawn hearse was of obvious European derivation. Originally only used for persons of distinction in Britain, by 1690 the horse-drawn hearse was common in funeral processions (Habenstein and Lamers 1962:356; Besant 1925:270–272).

20. One early eighteenth-century observer noted the use of coffins in Jamaica, but he also implied that they were not necessarily employed when he mentioned burial in a "coffin, or whatever the body happens to be wrapt in" (Leslie 1740:307–310, quoted in Patterson 1967:196); the coffin was apparently more characteristic by the late eighteenth and early nineteenth centuries (Brathwaite 1971:216; Senior 1835:46).

Coffins were not commonly used in Britain until the seventeenth century. By 1650, however, interments without coffins were frequent among the "humbler classes," and for the remainder of the seventeenth century, uncoffined burials were not at all uncommon. Although coffins were more widespread in the eighteenth century, they were still not considered mandatory. Many people, especially among the poor, were still buried without coffins; as late as 1820, a coffin was not an absolute necessity for a burial. In England and Europe in general, though coffins (whether of wood, stone, or lead) have some antiquity, especially in the burials of persons of wealth and high status, "the popular practice of coffined burials developed only in the last several hundred years" (Habenstein and Lamers 1962:169, 119, 125, 171; Hazlitt 1965:250; Boase 1972:110; Burton 1962:230; Campbell 1900:241; Besant 1925:270–272). We do not know how common coffins were for whites in Barbados, although coffins were used from an early period (Walduck 1710–12).

Coffins are now fairly widespread in West Africa, but most observers attribute their use and distribution to European contact and influence,

315

or believe that the use of coffins is of modern, or relatively modern, derivation. Some West African peoples traditionally employed containers, such as baskets (Field 1961:200). In general, however, coffins or containers (not mats of one kind or another) seem to have had a very restricted distribution. We found only one case of coffins used in pre-European conquest times in Dahomey, but coffins were confined to kings or, possibly, other persons of royalty (Herskovits 1938;1:354; cf. Rattray 1927:159).

21. Aside from references to attendants being buried with royalty or persons of high status it has been generally difficult to ascertain how widespread multiple interments were in West Africa. The few cases in which double interments are cited refer to women dying in childbirth (Rattray 1927:58; Parrinder 1961:96; Ellis 1887:234; Henry 1910: 250). We do not know if any specific practices were followed in Barbados with respect to slave mothers who died in childbirth.

22. In contrast, Walduck described the funerals of Barbadian whites in 1710: "Their burial...keeps pace with ye rest of their follys... there is plenty of eating and drinking and smoking tobacco (for their best feasts are always made at their funerals). And there is more good victual, wine, and ale devoured that day than all the whole parish eats and drinks in a whole month afterwards...there is always carried to the church, 10 or 12 gallons of burnt wine or a pail full or 2 of rum-punch to refresh the people (for a funeral sermon makes them squeamish) where as soon as the corpse are interred they sit around the liquor in the church porch, drink to the obsequies of the defunct, smoke, drink until they are as drunk as tinckers...After they are buried, there is no care taken of the graves or ye churchyards. Hogs has routed up childrens and dogs carried away their bones. The town people make fire of the rotten coffins, the church porches is a stable for horses, and they lie as promiscuously under ground as they lived above" (1710–12).

The persistence of this kind of funeral atmosphere is attested to by observations made by two Methodist missionaries over a century later: "the funeral solemnities of deceased friends so calculated to lead to serious thoughts and induce rational consideration produce no such salutory effects among these thoughtless and unfeeling lovers of pleasure. The house of mourning is prostituted to the purposes of feasting, excess, and foolish mirth. Of this astonishing and deplorable fact we have been eye witnesses or we should have thought it utterly incredible" (Shrewsbury and Nelson 1821b).

23. Music was important in the culture of Jamaican slaves and was also present in their mortuary complex (Brathwaite 1971:216–218, 220–232; Patterson 1967:196–197). Various forms of musical expression and instrumentation were also characteristic of mortuary complexes in West African cultures.

24. We failed to identify a similar custom among West African peoples but the practice appears to be African.

25. This custom was probably of African derivation. West African in-

terment ceremonies commonly involved such elements as the sacrifice of small animals and scattering or placing food and other goods on the grave, as well as the consumption of food and drink by the funeral participants at the gravesite. Such practices could occur before the grave was filled in or immediately afterward. See, for example, Field (1961:200); Ellis (1887:240); Thomas (1910:41); Bascom (1969:68); Little (1954:115); Rattray (1927:163).

26. In seventeenth-century England, according to one source, the graves of those who died honorable deaths were oriented east-west, while those considered to have died dishonorably were interred in a north-south position (Hazlitt 1965:285–286).

In a number of African cultures funerary rites and grave locations differed for people who had died in special or unusual ways (for example, by suicide, in pregnancy, from lightning, or execution for a crime) or who possessed abnormal physical characteristics (such as albinos and hunchbacks). We have been unable to ascertain to what extent, if any, such special burials affected body orientation. The few sources that report a northern head orientation suggest that orientation was sex-linked and not related to other circumstances surrounding death (for example, Mangin 1921:84; Monteil 1924:183; Littlewood 1954:124; Meek 1931:114; and East 1939:332; see also note 27, this chapter). Two of the three north-headed burials in Newton cemetery were males (Burials 13 and 35); the sex of the third (Burial 48) was provisionally classified as female.

27. Specific information on body orientations in the West African literature is difficult to find. Even when such information is given, it is ambiguous if the orientation of the head is being referred to, or the way in which the face was positioned. For example, a burial whose head was oriented toward the north could have its face pointed toward the west or the east, and this distinction is frequently not made clear in the literature. However, there were variations among West African peoples and some placed greater emphasis on orientation than others. In Dahomey, for example, the head was oriented south, toward the sea (Herskovits 1938; 1:359). "The orientation of the grave and the body does not seem to follow a uniform rule" for the Ashanti although "all Ashanti agree that the corpse should not lie facing the village." In some cases people were buried facing east, in others, west (Rattray 1927:162–163). In some cases at least, among the Ashanti the pattern seems to have been sex-linked. Males faced east and females faced west. This sexual distinction was also found in other West African cultures; see, for example, Thomas (1916:129); Parrinder (1961:107); Cardinall (1920:104, 108); Meek (1931:74); Rattray (1932:352, 391). Among some peoples of the Cameroons, the head pointed north (Littlewood 1954: 124), while others emphasized an east direction (Dugast 1954:149). One source reports that the heads of Bambara males are oriented south and those of females are placed facing north (Monteil 1924:183), but another source reports that heads faced east (Dieterlen 1951:250). Daryll

Forde has suggested that an eastern facial orientation is a Moslem practice that became widespread among non-Islamic peoples in West Africa (Forde 1955:44; cf. Rose 1922:127).

28. Both extended and flexed positions were widespread in West Africa. The latter may have been more common, but both positions could occur within the same geographic and cultural areas. Flexed burials were generally associated with placement of the corpse on its side, that is, in a lateral position. Although lateral positioning was common, supine burials also appear to have been frequent. Occasionally persons were also buried in seated positions. See, for example, Cardinall (1920:108, 109); Rattray (1932:391, 1927:150, 162); Ardener (1956:90); Littlewood (1954:124); Dugast (1954:9); Herskovits (1938;1:359); Ellis (1890:158–59); Talbot (1932:236); Little (1951:192); Meek (1931: 74); Gunn (1953:97, 1956:20).

29. Citing Ligon (1657:47–53), Richard Dunn implies (1972:251) that similar offerings were placed in graves in Barbados; although this is probably true, Ligon does not mention these offerings. We examined the contents of the bowls of whole pipes found in Newton cemetery but observed no carbonized material—this suggests the pipes were not lit when placed in the graves.

30. See, for example, Herskovits (1938;1:368, 374–375, 378–379); Thomas (1916:122); McCulloch (1950:45); Nkeita (1969:14); Forde (1951:29); Manoukian (1950:53); Habenstein and Lamers (1963:225, 232); Parrinder (1961:109); Dugast (1954:149); Field (1961:200); Herbert (1973); Little (1951:139, 193); Rattray (1927:149, 150, 156); Danquah (1928:234); Talbot (1932:235); Bascom (1969:67); and Busia (1954:201).

31. An elderly Barbadian informant recalled that around the time of World War I, coins were placed over the eyes of the deceased before rigor mortis had set in, but these coins were later removed and were not buried. While excavating a late nineteenth- to early twentieth-century black burial ground in South Carolina, Combes uncovered a burial in which a penny had been placed over each eye. Some general similarities with various burials at Newton included the lack of grave markers and the intrusion of graves "through burials previously interred" (1974:54, 55–56).

32. There are some interesting and perhaps nonfortuitous parallels between this scene and the funeral dirges of the Akan peoples in West Africa (Nkeita 1969).

33. Orderson described the funeral of a white plantation owner in *Creoleana*. The interment of the corpse in the family vault "called forth from the negroes of the plantation one of those vociferous lamentations by which that class of persons was formerly so accustomed to display their feelings...this loud wailing...This thrilling, piercing cry..." (1842:210).

34. Inscribed gravestones were common in the British Isles and Colonial America from the seventeenth century. Although in the seven-

teenth and early eighteenth centuries "a grave marker in the West Indies was a status symbol . . . and the people memorialized were mostly from the planter or merchant classes" (Dunn 1972:330), early gravestones of whites can be found in Barbadian cemeteries today. Gravestones of the European type were not found traditionally in West Africa. Some West African peoples marked graves, but such markers ranged from stones and pots to hoe handles and miniature dwelling huts erected over graves. See Dugast (1954:149); Meek (1931:74); Gunn (1956:33, 134, 1953:27, 47, 97); Talbot (1932:236); Cardinall (1920:109); Thomas (1916:130); and Rattray (1932:390).

35. We found it difficult to ascertain if mounding of graves was a widespread West African characteristic. Most sources we consulted either do not mention mounding or specify that the grave was leveled, thus implying that mound construction was not common. A few sources indicate that mounds were constructed among some Nigerian peoples (Bohannan and Bohannan 1953:79; Gunn 1956:134) although the practice may have occurred elsewhere (Field 1961:41, 121).

36. Aspects of the postinterment rites seem to have survived in Barbados in the form of a gathering on the ninth day after burial. A Barbadian informant told us that up until around the time of World War I and probably later, mourners congregated at the house of the deceased nine days after burial and sang hymns during the whole of the day. The "ninth day" was observed for adults of either sex, but never for children. The "ninth day" ceremony observed in modern Jamaica "bears striking resemblance to the post-burial ceremonies of West African peoples" (Patterson 1967:198; cf. Simpson 1957).

Postinterment ceremonies, including the so-called second burial, with such elements as offerings and consumption of food and drink at gravesites, were widespread in West African cultural systems. The particulars of these ceremonies varied within societies and from society to society, as did the periods at which the ceremonies were expected to be performed. For example, among coastal peoples of the Cameroons, ceremonies took place on the third and ninth days after burial. If the decedent were considered important, supplementary rites occurred six months to a year later (Ardener 1956:86, 88, 90, 91). Ibo-speakers of southeastern Nigeria conducted final mortuary rites several months or even years after death (Forde and Jones 1950:27). Some Ashanti practiced postinterment ceremonies on the sixth, fifteenth, and fortieth days after death and finally on the first anniversary (Rattray 1927:165; cf. Nkeita 1969:15). See also, for example, Forde (1951:29); Bascom (1969:68); McCulloch (1950:41, 46, 74); Little (1954:115); Ottenberg (1968:197–198); Field (1961:201); Bradbury (1965:104); Thomas (1910: 43); Manoukian (1952:43–44); Parrinder (1961:109–110); and Herskovits (1938;1:350–402).

Jamaican slaves also practiced post interment rites (Brathwaite 1971: 217–18; Patterson 1967:197–98). The parallels between Jamaican and Barbadian slave rites on one hand and West African cultures on the other are too great to be fortuitous. The idea, if not the particulars of these ceremonies, is clearly attributable to West African cultural systems.

37. Ordeals (particularly those involving swallowing a substance) and oaths were important elements of West African legal systems and were regarded with considerable gravity. There were many types of ordeals and oaths. Although we have been able to find little specific evidence for the use of grave dirt in West African cultures, the Barbadian practice was apparently of African derivation. For example, the importance of the ancestors in oath-taking is noted among the Gã of the Gold Coast: "it is more serious to swear by the dead than by the gods. The penalties for violating oaths sworn by a dead father, a long-dead chief, or by all the dead slain in some specific battle are extremely heavy... When a chief wishes to swear fealty to the ideals of his forerunners he goes and eats some of the earth over their burial-place" (Field 1961:197). Among the Yoruba, creditors of the deceased could not make their claims after burial unless they could prove that they were absent at the time of death, were under restraint, or had not heard of the death. In such cases, "if swearing is necessary, some earth from the grave of the deceased is put in drinking water for the claimant who swears... and then drinks the water with the earth in it" (Ajisafe 1924:82; see also Bascom 1969:67). In one of several trials by ordeal in Dahomey, the "accused takes some earth in his hand, calls on the spirits of the dead of his sib, and eats it. If he is guilty, he is believed doomed to die in seven, or in sixteen days" (Herskovits 1938;2:20).

The use of grave dirt in ordeals was reported from early eighteenth-century Jamaica (Leslie 1740:308, quoted in J. Williams 1932:180); this use persisted into the postemancipation period, and grave dirt was also "drunk with blood and water by the Kromanti Negroes in order to make an oath inviolable" (Beckwith 1969:109). In a planned slave revolt in Antigua during the mid-1730s, slaves were "bound by oaths" whose "general tenour... was to kill the whites"; the oaths involved "drinking a health in liquor with grave-dirt and sometimes cock's blood infused." Slaves who took this oath were creoles and Africans, the latter primarily persons "born on the Gold Coast" (Mathew 1737:11–12). In her study of Akan slave rebellions in the British Caribbean, Monica Schuler considers the Antiguan oath a "traditional Akan oath," and mentions the use of similar grave-dirt oaths in revolts or plots in Jamaica in 1760 and Saint Croix in 1759; she implies, however, that the oath was also employed in other rebellions and plots in the British colonies (1970).

38. Referring to the late eighteenth and early nineteenth centuries, the Bishop of London (who had apparently never visited Barbados but who derived his information from persons knowledgeable about the island) discussed the factors that inhibited full Christianization of the slaves on the Codrington plantations. Slaves always have "a strong natural propensity" to "revert to their heathenish ways... and when this propensity is continually inflamed by the solicitations of their uncon-

verted brethren, or the arrival of new companions from the coast of Guinea, it frequently becomes very difficult to be resisted, and counteracts, in a great degree, all the influence and exhortations of their religious teachers" (Porteus 1807:174–175).

39. The French social historian Philippe Ariès has recently remarked that "historians today are discovering the quasi-static nature of traditional cultures." He also suggested that Western attitudes to death and mortuary practices remained essentially the same from the Middle Ages to the late eighteenth century (1974:2).

40. See, for example, Bascom (1969:65–66, 67); Nkeita (1969:5–18); Habenstein and Lamers (1963:225, 231); Ardener (1956:86–90); Manoukian (1950:92); Herskovits (1938;1:352–402); and Rattray (1927:177–181).

41. See, for example, Bohannan and Curtin (1971:223–343); Forde (1960); and Murdock (1959). The Ottenbergs have observed that West Africa "has undergone so much change and development that it is difficult to estimate the relative influence of different cultural traditions in molding the life of the people. Many important group migrations obviously took place in West Africa, though it is frequently impossible to trace these in detail" (1960:116).

42. Sometimes it is difficult to find precise information on specific elements of various European or British mortuary practices; moreover, within the British Isles, as in Africa, there were regional variations in particular beliefs and practices. Some of the sources we have employed to ascertain European beliefs and practices during the seventeenth, eighteenth, and early nineteenth centuries include Ariès (1974); Ashton (1883); Andrews (1897); Burton (1962); Besant (1925); Boase (1972); Campbell (1900); Dyer (1878); Habenstein and Lamers (1962); Hartley and Elliot (1926); Hazlitt (1965); Owen (1959); Pine (1967); Morley (1971); Hole (1947); Grant (1961); Sidney (1891); Porter (1969); and Wimberly (1927).

43. We are specifically concerned here with the possible influence of European and Euro-creole beliefs and practices on slave culture, but we do not mean to imply that slave patterns had no effect on Euro-creole culture (see, for example, Brathwaite 1974:17–21).

44. We do not mean to imply, of course, that the mortuary complex was monolithic. The archaeological and historical evidence indicate that variations in behavioral detail occurred among slaves on the same plantation within broad time periods and variations probably existed between populations on different plantations. As with all human groups, individual patterns of behavior varied within broadly defined cultural dictates, but we suspect that there was less variation in mortuary features than would be found in a free, more economically stratified population.

45. For an interesting and thoughtful analysis of the process of creolization and its implications for understanding West Indian cultures, both past and present, see Brathwaite (1974; cf. Mintz and Price 1976).

References

Most of the manuscript and printed primary sources are described in *A Guide to Source Materials for the Study of Barbados History, 1627–1834* (Handler 1971a), which also discusses the archival repositories and provides library locations for the printed works.

In this list of references, brackets have been supplied when a title is not given in a report and we have constructed a title; when supplementary information has been inserted into a title; and when a place, date, or author of a publication and an author or date of a manuscript are not given in the item, but where these data have been established on the basis of internal or other evidence. In addition, the following abbreviations are employed:

MANUSCRIPT COLLECTIONS AND ARCHIVAL REPOSITORIES

BM	British Museum, London
CO	Colonial Office Group, Public Record Office, London
MMSA	Methodist Missionary Society Archives, London
PRO	Public Record Office, London
USPGA	United Society for the Propagation of the Gospel Archives, London
WIC	West India Committee Library, London

PUBLICATONS

CHSAP	The Conference on Historic Site Archaeology Papers (Columbia, South Carolina)
CSPCS	Calendar of State Papers, Colonial Series, America and West Indies (London)
JBMHS	Journal of the Barbados Museum and Historical Society (Bridgetown)
PP	Parliamentary Papers (London)

Abbitt, Merry W.
  1973 The eighteenth-century shoe buckle. In *Five artifact studies. Colonial Williamsburg occasional papers in archaeology,*

vol. 1, ed. Ivor Noël Hume. Williamsburg: Colonial Williamsburg Foundation.

Abstract of Evidence before a Select Committee
1791 *An abstract of the evidence delivered before a select committee of the House of Commons in the years 1790 and 1791; on the part of the petitioners for the abolition of the slave trade.* London.

Academia de Ciencias de Cuba
1970 [Report on excavations at Ingenio Taoro, 1969–70.] Havana: Department of Anthropology. Mimeographed.

Accola, Richard M.
1972 Artifact association study on Barbados. Logan Museum, Beloit College. Typescript.

Account of a Voyage to Jamaica
1776 *An account of a voyage to Jamaica, with a description of some of the Caribbee islands, and various matters relative to the island of Jamaica and its inhabitants, etc. etc.* Dublin.

Account of the Number of Negroes
1709 *An account of the number of Negroes delivered in to the islands of Barbados, Jamaica, and Antego, from the year 1698 to 1708.* [London.]

Ajisafe, A. K.
1924 *The laws and customs of the Yoruba people.* London: G. Routledge.

Alleyne, Abel
1741 Letter to the Society for the Propagation of the Gospel, July 14. *Letter books,* vol. B8, no. 48, USPGA.

Alleyne, John F., Letters
1801a Alleyne to Smith, December 6. WIC.
1801b Alleyne to Wiltshire, November 23. WIC.
1801c Alleyne to Storey, September 24. WIC.
1802a Alleyne to Smittens, January 7. WIC.
1802b Alleyne to Allen, January 15. WIC.
1802c Alleyne to T. Daniel and Sons, July 28. WIC.
1803 Alleyne to T. Daniel and Sons, April 4. WIC.

Andrews, William
1897 *England in the days of old.* London.

Anstey, Roger
1975 The volume and profitability of the British slave trade, 1761–1807. In *Race and slavery in the Western hemisphere: quantitative studies,* ed. Stanley L. Engerman and Eugene D. Genovese, pp. 3–31. Princeton: Princeton University Press.

Ardener, Edwin
1956 *Coastal Bantu of the Cameroons*. In Ethnographic survey of Africa: Western Africa, Part 11, ed. Daryll Forde. London: International African Institute.
Ariès, Philippe
1974 *Western attitudes toward death*. Baltimore: Johns Hopkins University Press.
Armson, F. G. A.
1975 An account of Seawell plantation and the people who owned it. Barbados Museum Library. Typescript.
Ascher, Robert
1974 Tin*can archaeology. *Historical Archaeology* 8:7–16.
Ascher, Robert, and Charles H. Fairbanks
1971 Excavation of a slave cabin: Georgia, U.S.A. *Historical Archaeology* 5:3–17.
[Ashley, John]
1732 *The British empire in America, consider'd. In a second letter from a gentleman of Barbadoes, to his friend in London*. London.
Ashton, John
1883 *Social life in the reign of Queene Anne*. London.
Aspinall, Algernon
1942 Rachel Pringle of Barbados. *JBMHS* 9:112–119.
Atkins, John
1735 *A voyage to Guinea, Brazil, and the West Indies*. London.
Atkins, Jonathan
1675 Letter to Sir Joseph Williamson, October 3. CSPCS 1675–1676:294–295.
1676a An account of His Majesty's island of Barbadoes and the government thereof. February. CO 1/36, no. 20.
1676b Answers to the 32 queries by the Lords of Trade and Plantations. July 4. CO 1/37, no. 67.
1677 Letter to Lords of Trade and Plantations, May 13–23. *CSPCS* 1677–1680:85.
1680a Letter to Lords of Trade and Plantations, October 26. *CSPCS* 1677–1680:618–621.
1680b Further answers to the 32 queries of the Lords of Trade and Plantations on the state of Barbados, March 26. CO 1/44, no. 45.
Atkinson, D. R.
1962 Maker's marks on clay tobacco pipes found in London. *Archaeological News Letter* 7:55–62. London.

1965   Maker's marks on clay tobacco pipes found in London, Part two. *Archaeological News Letter* 7:249–256. London.

Authentic History of the West Indies

1810   *Authentic history of the English West Indies; with the manners and customs of the free inhabitants ... with the treatment and condition of the Negroes ... etc.* London.

Ayer Mss.

[1651]   An essay evenly discussing the present condition and interest of Barbadoes. Ms. 276, Newberry Library, Chicago.

Baerreis, David A.

1961   The ethnohistoric approach and archaeology. *Ethnohistory* 8:49–77.

Barbados Assembly

1790   *Report of a committee of the General Assembly upon the several heads of enquiry, etc. relative to the slave trade.* London.

[1818]   *The report from a select committee of the House of Assembly, appointed to inquire into the origin, causes, and progress, of the late insurrection.* Barbados.

Barbados Census

1950   *West Indian census 1946: part C, census of the colony of Barbados, 9th April, 1946.* Kingston, Jamaica: The Government Printer.

1960   *West Indies population census 1960: series C, Barbados.* Port-of-Spain, Trinidad: Central Statistical Office.

1972   *Commonwealth Caribbean population census 1970: preliminary bulletins, Barbados.* Barbados: Barbados Statistical Service.

Barbados Council

1654–58   Minutes of the Barbados council. 2 vols. PRO. Typescript.

1789   Replies to queries 6, 15, 22, 23, 24, and 25. In *Report of the Lords of the committee of Council ... concerning the present state of the trade to Africa ... and the effects and consequences of this trade ... in Africa and the West Indies,* Part 3. PP, vol. 26.

1824   *A report of a committee of the council of Barbadoes appointed to inquire into the actual condition of the slaves in this island.* London.

Barbados Council and Assembly

1834   A memorial of the council and assembly of Barbados, in explanation of a supplemental bill to the act for the abolition of slavery. November 4. *PP* 1835, vol. 50, rept. 278, pp. 80–84.

Barbados Department of Archives

1700–1833 Parochial registers, burials. RL 1/1, 2, 3, 4, 6, 7, 21, 25, 29, 32, 35, 38, 39, 48, 49, 56.

1726 List of vessels that have imported Negroes to Barbados, March 29, 1708–March 1726, certified October 5, 1726. Duplicates of shipping returns, CO 33/15.

1803–04 Records of Drax Hall plantation: inventory. Z9/11/5.

1780–1834 Estate inventories, originals.

Barbados Museum and Historical Society

1934 Extracts from the Barbadian newspaper, 1826–27. *JBMHS* 2:93–101.

1935 The Librarian's notes. *JBMHS* 3:127–128.

1936 Extracts from the Barbadian newspaper, 1832–33. *JBMHS* 4:22–33.

1940a Old plantation customs. *JBMHS* 7:109–115.

1940b Hooper of Barbados. *JBMHS* 7:69–82.

1942 Thornhill of Barbados. *JBMHS* 9:90–101.

1945 Tales of old Barbados. *JBMHS* 12:171–178.

1953 Quaker records: Settle-Taylor. *JBMHS* 21:26–28.

Barbados Sugar Producers' Association

1970 *Barbados sugar industry review*, no. 4. Barbados.

Barton, G. T.

1953 *The prehistory of Barbados*. Barbados: The Advocate Company.

Barton, Kenneth J.

1954 The Buckley potteries: excavations at Prescot's pottery. *Flintshire Historical Journal* 16:63–87.

Bascom, William

1969 *The Yoruba of Southwestern Nigeria*. New York: Holt, Rinehart and Winston.

Bass, William M.

1962 The excavation of human skeletal remains. In *Field handbook on the human skeleton*, by R. F. G. Spier, pp. 39–51. Columbia: Missouri Archaeological Society.

Bate, Richard

1693 Letter to Barbara and John Newton, May 31. In Richard Pares, Barbados history from the records of the Prize Courts. *JBMHS* 6 (1938):10–20.

Bayley, F. W. N.

1832 *Four years residence in the West Indies during the years 1826, 7, 8, and 9*. London.

Beckford, William
  1790 *A descriptive account of the island of Jamaica.* 2 vols. London.
Beckwith, Martha W.
  1969 *Black roadways: a study of Jamaican folk life.* New York: Negro Universities Press.
Bennett, J. Harry
  1958 *Bondsmen and bishops: slavery and apprenticeship on the Codrington plantations of Barbados, 1710–1838.* University of California Publications in History, vol. 62. Berkeley and Los Angeles: University of California Press.
Bennett, John
  1738 *Two letters and several calculations on the sugar colonies and trade.* London.
Benson, John
  [1828] *A short account of the voyages, travels and adventures of John Benson.* No place of publication.
Besant, Walter
  1925 *London in the eighteenth century.* London: A. and C. Black.
Binford, Lewis R.
  1962a Archaeology as anthropology. *American Antiquity* 28: 217–225.
  1962b A new method of calculating dates from kaolin pipe stem samples. *Southeastern Archaeological Conference Newsletter* 9:19–21.
  1968 Archaeological perspectives. In *New perspectives in archaeology*, ed. Sally R. Binford and Lewis R. Binford, pp. 5–32. Chicago: Aldine.
  1972 The "Binford" pipe stem formula: a return from the grave. *CHSAP* 6 (1971):230–253.
  1975 Sampling, judgment, and the archaeological record. In *Sampling in archaeology*, ed. James W. Mueller, pp. 251–257. Tucson: University of Arizona Press.
Bishop
  1759 Deed of sale to Gibbons, March 22. MCRO, Acc. 621, Box 5, Greater London Record Office, London.
Blake, Nicholas
  1669 Letter to the king, February 28. *CSPCS* 1699:590–593.
Blassingame, John W.
  1972 *The slave community: plantation life in the antebellum South.* New York: Oxford University Press.

Boase, T. S. R.
1972 *Death in the middle ages.* New York: McGraw-Hill.
Bohannan, Laura, and Paul Bohannan
1953 *The Tiv of Central Nigeria.* In Ethnographic survey of
Africa: Western Africa, Part 8, ed. Daryll Forde. London:
International African Institute.
Bohannan, Paul, and Philip Curtin
1971 *Africa and Africans.* Garden City, N.Y.: Natural History
Press.
Boothby, Jeremiah
1814 Letter to Smith, February 26. Box 1814–1815, no. 124,
MMSA.
Bradbury, Ray E.
1965 Father and senior son in Edo mortuary ritual. In *African
systems of thought,* ed. M. Fortes and G. Dieterlen, pp.
96–121. London: International African Institute, Oxford
University Press.
Bradnack, Isaac
1804 Letter to Wesleyan Missionary Society, July 21. Box 1803–
1813, no. 190, MMSA.
Brain, Jeffrey, Alan Toth, and Antonio Rodriguez-Buckingham
1974 Ethnohistoric archaeology and the DeSoto entrada into the
Lower Mississippi Valley. *CHSAP* 7 (1972):232–289.
Brathwaite, Edward
1969 Caribbean critics. *New World Quarterly* 5:5–12. Kingston,
Jamaica.
1971 *The development of Creole society in Jamaica 1770–1820.*
Oxford: Clarendon.
1974 *Contradictory omens: cultural diversity and integration in
the Caribbean.* Mona, Jamaica: Savacou Publications.
Brathwaite, John
1789 Replies to queries 5, 6, 12, 15, 22, 23, 24, 25, 34, 37, in *Report of the Lords of the committee of Council ... concerning the present state of the trade to Africa ... and the effects and consequences of this trade ... in Africa and the
West Indies,* Part 3. PP, vol. 26.
Bridenbaugh, Carl, and Roberta Bridenbaugh
1972 *No peace beyond the line: the English in the Caribbean
1624–1690.* New York: Oxford University Press.
British Museum
1684 An account of Barbados and the government thereof.
Sloane Mss. 2441.

1714–16   Voyage to Guinea, Antegoe, bay of Campeachy, Cuba, Barbados, etc., 1714 to 1716. Additional Mss. 39946.

[Browne, Benjamin]
1926   *The yarn of a Yankee privateer.* Edited by Nathaniel Hawthorne, introduction by Clifford Smyth. New York: Funk and Wagnalls.

Browne, Patrick
1789   *The civil and natural history of Jamaica.* London.

Buchanan, William T., and Edward F. Heite
1971   The Hallowes site: a seventeenth-century yeoman's cottage in Virginia. *Historical Archaeology* 5:38–48.

Bullen, Adelaide K., and Ripley P. Bullen
1945   Black Lucy's garden. *Bulletin of the Massachusetts Archaeological Society* 6:17–28.

Bullen, Ripley P.
1966   Barbados and the archaeology of the Caribbean. *JBMHS* 32:16–19.

Bullen, Ripley P., and Adelaide K. Bullen
1968   Barbados archaeology: 1966. *Proceedings of the Second International Congress for the Study of Pre-Colombian Cultures in the Lesser Antilles,* pp. 134–144. Barbados: Barbados Museum and Historical Society.

Burns, Alan
1954   *History of the British West Indies.* London: George Allen and Unwin.

Burton, E.
1962   *The Jacobeans at home.* London: Secker & Warburg.

Busia, K. A.
1954   The Ashanti of the Gold Coast. In *African worlds: studies in the cosmological ideas and social values of African peoples,* ed. Daryll Forde, pp. 190–209. London: International African Institute, Oxford University Press.

Cadbury, Henry J., ed.
1943   A Quaker account of Barbados in 1718. *JBMHS* 10:118–124.

Calendar of State Papers
1734   Account of new Negroes and wine imported into Barbados, August 8, 1723–September 13, 1734. *CSPCS* 1734–1735: 288.

Campbell, John G.
1900   *Superstitions of the highlands and islands of Scotland.* Glasgow: James MacLehose & Sons.

Campbell, Tony
  1965   *The printed maps of Barbados.* The Map Collectors' Series
         (Third Year), no. 21. London: Map Collectors' Circle.
Cardinall, A. W.
  1920   *The natives of the northern territories of the Gold Coast.*
         London: G. Routledge.
Carmack, Robert M.
  1972   Ethnohistory: a review of its development, definitions,
         methods, and aims. In *Annual review of anthropology,*
         vol. 1, ed. Bernard Siegel, pp. 227–246. Palo Alto, Calif.:
         Annual Reviews.
Chalkley, J. F.
  1955   Tobacco pipe stem hole dating—factors of proof and certi-
         tude. *Bulletin of the Archaeological Society of Delaware*
         7:3–10.
Chandler, John
  1968   Plantation field names in Barbados. *JBMHS* 32:133–143.
Chandler, Michael J.
  1965   *A guide to records in Barbados.* Oxford: Basil Blackwell.
The Christian Remembrancer
  1823   Treatment of slaves in Barbadoes. 5:406–408.
Clarke, Forster
  1823   Plan of treatment of the Negroes on the estates in Barbados,
         1823. *JBMHS* 2(1934):29–31.
  1828   Letter to the secretary of the Society for the Propagation
         of the Gospel, May 7, 1828. *Annual Report* [for 1827], pp.
         218–219. London: Society for the Propagation of the Gos-
         pel in Foreign Parts.
Cleland, Charles E.
  1971   *The Lasanen site, an historic burial locality in Mackinac
         county, Michigan.* Publications of the Michigan State Uni-
         versity Museum, Anthropological Series, vol. 1, no. 1. East
         Lansing.
Cline, Walter
  1937   *Mining and metallurgy in Negro Africa.* General series in
         anthropology, no. 5, ed. Leslie Spier. Menasha, Wisc.:
         George Banta.
Codrington, Colonel
  1699   Letter to Council of Trade and Plantations, July 10. *CSPCS*
         1699:337–338.
Codrington Attorneys
  1762   Letter to D. Burton, May 28. Letter Books, vol. B6, no. 69,
         USPGA.

Coleridge, Henry Nelson
1832 *Six months in the West Indies in 1825*. London.
Colleton, Peter
1673 Letter to the Council for Trade and Plantations, May 28. *CSPCS* 1669–1674:495–496.
Colley, Thomas
1779 Account of visit to the West Indies, etc. with Philip Madin, 1779. Miscellaneous mss., Box P, Society of Friends Library, London.
Colthurst, John B.
1835–38 Journal as a special magistrate in the islands of Barbados and Saint Vincent, July 1835–August 1838. Ms. U.1.2, Boston Public Library.
Combermere, Lord
1818 Letter to Lord Bathurst, January 3. CO 28/87.
Combes, John D.
1974 Ethnography, archaeology and burial practices among coastal South Carolina blacks. *CHSAP* 7 (1972):52–61.
Commissioners for Trade and Plantations
1750 *Papers laid before the honourable House of Commons . . . for the better securing, improving, and extending the trade to Africa*. London.
1734 *Representation from the commissioners for Trade and Plantations, to the . . . Lords . . . in Parliament . . . relating to the state of the British islands in America*. London.
Connell, Neville
1957 Furniture and furnishings in Barbados during the 17th century. *JBMHS* 24:102–121.
1959 18th century furniture and its background in Barbados. *JBMHS* 26:162–190.
Cooper, Ashley, and Gerard Hawtaine
1652 Award of the arbitrators between Sir Anthony Ashley Cooper and Gerard Hawtaine and inventory of stock, etc. on plantations in Barbados, June 18. Shaftesbury Papers, 30/24/49, no. 1, PRO.
Cracknell, Everil M. W., ed.
1934 *The Barbadian diary of Gen. Robert Haynes, 1787–1836*. Medstead, N.H.: Azania Press.
Crowe, Mitford
1708a Letter to the Council of Trade and Plantations, June 27. *CSPCS* (1706–June 1708):772–773.
1708b Letter to the Council of Trade and Plantations, August 17. *CSPCS* (June 1708–1709):65–66.

Cruickshank, J. Graham
1935   Field names in Barbados. *JBMHS* 2:166.
Cundall, Frank, ed.
1934   *Lady Nugent's journal*. London: Institute of Jamaica.
Curtin, Philip
1969   *The Atlantic slave trade: a census*. Madison: University of Wisconsin Press.
1975   Measuring the Atlantic slave trade. In *Race and slavery in the Western hemisphere: quantitative studies*, ed. Stanley L. Engerman and Eugene D. Genovese, pp. 107–128. Princeton: Princeton University Press.
Dailey, R. C.
1974   Osteological analysis of human skeletal remains from the Virgin Islands. Tallahassee: Florida State University. Mimeographed.
Danquah, Joseph B.
1928   *Gold Coast: Akan laws and customs and the Akim Abuakwa constitution*. London: G. Routledge.
Dark, Philip J. C.
1973   *An introduction to Benin art and technology*. Oxford: Clarendon.
Davies, Kenneth G.
1957   *The Royal African Company*. London: Longmans, Green.
Davies, Reverend
1791   Testimony, in *Minutes of the evidence taken before a committee of the House of Commons ... appointed to take the examination of witnesses respecting the African slave trade*. PP, vol. 34, no. 746, pp. 185–189.
Debien, Gabriel
1974a   Petits cimetières de quartier et de plantation à Saint-Domingue au XVIIIe siècle. *Revue Française d'Histoire d'Outre-Mer* 61:522–541.
1974b   *Les esclaves aux Antilles Françaises (XVIIe–XVIIIe siècles)*. Basse-Terre, Guadeloupe, and Fort-de-France, Martinique: Societé d'Histoire de la Guadeloupe and Societé d'Histoire de la Martinique.
Declaration of Inhabitants of Barbados
1826   *A declaration of inhabitants of Barbados, respecting the demolition of the Methodist chapel*. Barbados.
Declaration Set forth by the Lord
1651   *A declaration set forth by the lord lieutenant general and the gentlemen of the councell and assembly occasioned from the view of a printed paper, entitled, an act prohibit-*

ing trade with the Barbados, Virginea, Bermudes and Antegoe. Hagh.

Dickson, William

1789   *Letters on slavery.* London.

1814   *Mitigation of slavery in two parts.* London.

Dieterlen, Germaine

1951   *Essai sur la religion Bambara.* Paris: Presses Universitaires de France.

Dollar, Clyde D.

1968   Some thoughts on theory and method in historical archaeology. *CHSAP* 2 (1967):3–30.

Dorson, Richard

1961   Ethnohistory and ethnic folklore. *Ethnohistory* 8:12–30.

Douglass, William

1755   *A summary, historical and political, of the … present state of the British settlements in North America.* 2 vols. London.

Drax, Henry

1755   Instructions for the management of Drax-Hall and the Irish-Hope plantations [written between 1670 and 1682]. In *A treatise upon husbandry or planting,* by William Belgrove, pp. 51–86. Boston.

Dugast, I.

1954   Banen, Bafia, and Balom. In *Peoples of the Central Cameroons.* Ethnographic survey of Africa: Western Africa, Part 9, ed. Daryll Forde, pp. 132–169. London: International African Institute.

Dunhill, Alfred

1924   *The pipe book.* London: A. & C. Black.

Dunn, Richard S.

1969   The Barbados census of 1680: profile of the richest colony in English America. *William and Mary Quarterly* 26:3–30.

1972   *Sugar and slaves: the rise of the planter class in the English West Indies, 1624–1713.* Williamsburg, Va.: The Institute of Early American History and Culture, University of North Carolina Press.

Dutton, Richard

1681   Answers to the heads of inquiry respecting Barbados, June 11. *CSPCS* 1681–1685:70–72.

Dwarris, Fortunatus

1827   *Substance of three reports of the commission of inquiry into the administration of civil and criminal justice in the West Indies.* London.

Dyer, T. F. T.
  1878   *English folk-lore*. London.
East, Rupert, ed.
  1939   *Akiga's story: the Tiv tribe as seen by one of its members*. London: International Institute of African Languages and Cultures, Oxford University Press.
Ebanks, R. C.
  1974   Letter to editor, January 29. *Jamaica Journal* 8:2.
Eliot, Edward
  1833   *Christianity and slavery*. London.
Ellis, Alfred B.
  1887   *The Tshi-speaking peoples of the Gold Coast of West Africa*. London.
  1890   *The Ewe-speaking peoples of the Slave Coast of West Africa*. London.
  1894   *The Yoruba-speaking peoples of the Slave Coast of West Africa*. London.
Fairbanks, Charles H.
  1974   The Kingsley slave cabins in Duval county, Florida, 1968. *CHSAP* 7 (1972):62–93.
Fewkes, J. Walter
  1922   A prehistoric island culture area of America. *Thirty-fourth annual report of the Bureau of American Ethnology*. Washington, D.C.
Ffoulkes, Arthur
  1909   Funeral customs of the Gold Coast colony. *Journal of the African Society* 8:154–164.
Field, M. J.
  1961   *Religion and medicine of the Gã people*. 2nd ed. London: Oxford University Press. (First ed. 1937.)
Flannigan, Mrs.
  1844   *Antigua and the Antiguan: a full account of the colony and its inhabitants*. 2 vols. London.
Fogel, Robert W., and Stanley L. Engerman
  1974   *Time on the cross: the economics of American Negro slavery*. 2 vols. Boston: Little, Brown.
Fontana, Bernard L.
  1965   On the meaning of historic sites archaeology. *American Antiquity* 31:61–65.
Forde, Daryll
  1951   *The Yoruba-speaking peoples of South-western Nigeria*. Ethnographic survey of Africa: Western Africa, Part 4, ed. Daryll Forde. London: International African Institute.

1954   Introduction. In *African worlds: studies in the cosmological ideas and social values of African peoples,* ed. Daryll Forde, pp. vii–xvii. London: International African Institute, Oxford University Press.

1955   The Nupe. In *Peoples of the Niger-Benue confluence.* Ethnographic survey of Africa: Western Africa, Part 10, ed. Daryll Forde, pp. 17–52. London: International African Institute.

1960   The cultural map of West Africa: successive adaptations to tropical forests and grasslands. In *Cultures and societies of Africa,* ed. Simon Ottenberg and Phoebe Ottenberg, pp. 116–138. New York: Random House.

Forde, Daryll, and G. I. Jones

1950   *The Ibo and Ibibio-speaking peoples of South-eastern Nigeria.* Ethnographic survey of Africa: Western Africa, Part 3, ed. Daryll Forde. London: International African Institute.

Forde, Richard

[1675]   *A new map of the island of Barbadoes.* [London.]

[Frere, Henry]

1768   *A short history of Barbados from its first discovery and settlement to the present time.* London.

Garnett, William

1817   Report to Lord Combermere, July 2. CO 28/86.

Genovese, Eugene D.

1974   *Roll, Jordan, roll: the world the slaves made.* New York: Pantheon Books.

Gentleman's Magazine

1780   Account of the hurricane in Barbadoes. 50:621–622.

[Gibbes, Philip]

1786   *Instructions for the treatment of Negroes, etc. etc. etc.* London.

1797   *Instructions for the treatment of Negroes, etc. etc. etc.* London (Reprint with additions of 1786 ed.).

Godwyn, Morgan

1680   *The Negro's and Indians advocate.* London.

Goveia, Elsa

1965   *Slave society in the British Leeward islands at the end of the eighteenth century.* New Haven: Yale University Press.

Government of Barbados

1961   *Report for the years 1958 and 1959.* Barbados: Government Printing Office.

Grant, I. F.
1961   *Highland folk ways*. London: Routledge & Paul.
Greenfield, Sidney M.
1966   *English rustics in black skin*. New Haven: College and University Press.
Guinea Plantation
1820   Inventory, 1820. Privately held manuscript in Barbados.
Gunkel, Alexander, and Jerome S. Handler, eds.
1969   A Swiss medical doctor's description of Barbados in 1661: the account of Felix Christian Spoeri. *JBMHS* 33:3–13.
1970   A German indentured servant in Barbados in 1652: the account of Heinrich von Uchteritz. *JBMHS* 33:91–100.
Gunn, Harold D.
1953   *Peoples of the plateau area of Northern Nigeria*. Ethnographic survey of Africa: Western Africa, Part 7, ed. Daryll Forde. London: International African Institute.
1956   *Pagan peoples of the central area of Northern Nigeria*. Ethnographic survey of Africa: Western Africa, Part 12, ed. Daryll Forde. London: International African Institute.
Gutman, Herbert G.
1975   *Slavery and the numbers game: a critique of* Time on the cross. Urbana: University of Illinois Press.
Habenstein, Robert, and William M. Lamers
1962   *The history of American funeral directing*. Milwaukee: Bulfin.
1963   *Funeral customs the world over*. Milwaukee: Bulfin.
Hall, Hugh, Jr.
1714–17   Diary in almanac form, of weather observations, 1714–1717. Manuscript division, New York Public Library.
Hall, Richard
1764   *Acts, passed in the island of Barbados*. London.
1924   *A general account of the first settlement and of the trade and constitution of the island of Barbados, written in the year 1755*. Edited with a foreword by E. M. Shilstone. Barbados.
Hammond, Peter
1970   West Africa and the Afro-Americans. In *The African experience, vol. 1: Essays*, ed. John N. Paden and Edward W. Soja, pp. 195–209. Evanston, Ill.: Northwestern University Press.
Handler, Jerome S.
1963a   A historical sketch of pottery manufacture in Barbados. *JBMHS* 30:129–153.

1963b Pottery making in rural Barbados. *Southwestern Journal of Anthropology* 19:314–334.

1964 Notes on pottery-making in Antigua. *Man: A Record of Anthropological Science* 64:150–151.

1965 Some aspects of work organization on sugar plantations in Barbados. *Ethnology* 4:16–38.

1966 Small-scale sugar cane farming in Barbados. *Ethnology* 5:264–283.

1967 Father Antoine Biet's visit to Barbados in 1654. *JBMHS* 32:56–76.

1969a The Amerindian slave population of Barbados in the seventeenth and early eighteenth centuries. *Caribbean Studies* 8:38–64.

1969b Review of *English rustics in black skin*, by Sidney M. Greenfield. *American Anthropologist* 71:335–337.

1970 Aspects of Amerindian ethnography in 17th century Barbados. *Caribbean Studies* 9:50–72.

1971a *A guide to source materials for the study of Barbados history, 1627–1834*. Carbondale: Southern Illinois University Press.

1971b The history of arrowroot and the origin of peasantries in the British West Indies. *Journal of Caribbean History* 2:46–93.

1974 *The unappropriated people: freedmen in the slave society of Barbados*. Baltimore: Johns Hopkins University Press.

1975 Memoirs of an old army officer: Richard A. Wyvill's visits to Barbados in 1796 and 1806–7. *JBMHS* 35:21–30.

Handler, Jerome S., and Charlotte J. Frisbie

1972 Aspects of slave life in Barbados: music and its cultural context. *Caribbean Studies* 11:5–46.

Hanson, Lee H.

1971 Kaolin pipe stems: boring in on a fallacy. *CHSAP* 4 (1969):2–15.

1972 A few cents more. *CHSAP* 6 (1971):254–263.

Harewood Archives

1834 Barbados compensation [for slaves on Belle, Mount, Thicket, and Fortescue plantations]. Earl of Harewood Archives, Leeds Archives Department.

Harlow, Vincent T.

1926 *A history of Barbados 1625–1685*. Oxford: Clarendon.

Harrington, J. C.

1954 Dating stem fragments of seventeenth and eighteenth

century clay tobacco pipes. *Quarterly Bulletin of the Archaeological Society of Virginia* 9, no. 1.

1955 A comment on "A critique and rebuttal of the paper dating stem fragments of 17–18 century clay tobacco pipes" by John F. Chalkley. *Quarterly Bulletin of the Archaeological Society of Virginia* 9, no. 4.

Hartley, D., and M. M. Elliot

1926 *Life and work of the people in England: the sixteenth century.* New York.

Hawtayne, G. H.

1893 A cavalier planter in Barbados. *Timehri* 7:16–43. Georgetown, British Guiana.

Hazlitt, William C.

1965 *Faiths and folklore of the British Isles.* New York: B. Blom (Reprint of 1905 ed.).

Heighton, Robert F., and Kathleen A. Deagan

1972 A new formula for dating kaolin pipestems. *CHSAP* 6 (1971):220–229.

Hendy, James

1784 *A treatise on the glandular disease of Barbados.* London.

Hendy, T. W. B.

1833 *An attempt to prove the fallacy of inflicting corporal punishment ... as preparatory to its extinction in West-India slave discipline.* Bridgetown, Barbados.

Henry, Joseph

1910 *L'âme d'un peuple Africain: les Bambara, leur vie psychique, éthnique, sociale, religieuse.* Münster: Aschendorff.

Herbert, Eugenia W.

1973 Aspects of the use of copper in pre-colonial West Africa. *Journal of African History* 14:179–194.

Herskovits, Melville J.

1938 *Dahomey: an ancient West African kingdom.* 2 vols. New York: J. J. Augustin.

1958 *The myth of the Negro past.* Boston: Beacon Press.

1962 *The human factor in changing Africa.* New York: Knopf.

Higman, Barry W.

1973a Household structure and fertility on Jamaican slave plantations: a nineteenth century example. *Population Studies* 27:527–550.

1973b Slave family structure in the British West Indies, 1800–1834. History Department, University of the West Indies, Mona, Jamaica. Mimeographed.

1974   A report on excavations at Montpelier and Roehampton. *Jamaica Journal* 8:40–45.

1975   Report on excavations at New Montpelier, St. James, Jamaica, 22–24 March and 3–18 August, 1975. History Department, University of the West Indies, Mona, Jamaica. Mimeographed.

1976a Report on excavations at New Montpelier, St. James, Jamaica, 28 December 1975 to 10 January 1976. History Department, University of the West Indies, Mona, Jamaica. Mimeographed.

1976b *Characteristic traits of the Creolian & African Negroes in Jamaica, &c. &c.* [first published in the *Columbian Magazine*, Kingston, Jamaica, 1797]. Mona, Jamaica: The Caldwell Press.

Hillary, William
1766   *Observations on the changes of the air and the concomitant epidemical diseases in the island of Barbadoes.* London.

Hodges, Henry
1964   *Artifacts.* London: John Baker.

Holder, Henry E.
1788   *A short essay on the subject of Negro slavery, with particular reference to the island of Barbados.* London.

Hole, Christina
1947   *English home-life 1500 to 1800.* London: Batsford.

Holt, Arthur
1729a Letter to Bishop Gordon, March 7. Fulham Papers, vol. xv, fols. 266–267, Lambeth Palace Library, London.

1729b Letter to H. Newman, February 18. Letter books, vol. B6, no. 62, USPGA.

Hughes, Griffith
1750   *The natural history of Barbados.* London.

Hughes, William
1672   *The American physitian.* London.

Hull, John
1671   Letter from Barbados to Edward Mann in London, Nov. 1, 1671. In *The journals of George Fox*, ed. John L. Nickalls, pp. 596–599. London: Cambridge University Press.

Huskisson, W.
1827   Letter to J. Skeete, October 18. *PP*, 1828, vol. 27, unnumbered rept., pp. 37–41.

Hutchins, J.

1817   Letter to Lord Combermere, June 30. CO 28/86.

Ifill, Max B., ed.
    1964   *Caribbean economic almanac 1964–1966*. Port-of-Spain, Trinidad: Economic and Business Research Information and Advisory Service.

Innes, Frank C.
    1967   Plantation and peasant farms, Barbados 1627–1960. Ph.D. dissertation, McGill University.

Inniss, B. deL.
    1961   *The yield of sugar cane in Barbados in 1961*. Department of Science and Agriculture Bulletin 31 (new series). Barbados.

Instructions for the Management of a Plantation in Barbadoes
    1786   *Instructions for the management of a plantation in Barbadoes; and for the treatment of Negroes; etc. etc. etc.* London.

Jeffrey, Reginald W., ed.
    1907   *Dyott's diary, 1781–1845*. 2 vols. London.

Jelks, Edward B., et al.
    1967   The Gilbert site: a Norteño focus site in northeastern Texas. *Bulletin of the Texas Archaeological Society* 37.

Jordan, G. W.
    1816   *Copies of a letter containing queries respecting the state of the silver and copper coins of Barbados*. London.

[Jordan, J. W.]
    1824   *An account of the management of certain estates in the island of Barbados*. London.

King, Thomas F.
    1973   Reply to Kautz. *American Antiquity* 38:351.

Labat, Jean Baptiste
    1722   *Nouveau voyage aux isles de l'Amérique*. 6 vols. Paris.

Laguna, Frederica de
    1960   The story of a Tlingit community: a problem in the relationship between archaeological, ethnological and historical methods. Bureau of American Ethnology *Bulletin* 172.

Lange, Frederick W., and Charles R. Rydberg
    1972   Abandonment and post-abandonment behavior at a rural central American house-site. *American Antiquity* 37:419–432.

Larrabee, Edward M.
    1969   Historic site archaeology in relation to other archaeology. *Historical Archaeology* 3:67–74.

Lenihan, Daniel
  1974 Archaeological resource management plan, Virgin Islands
        National Park. Mimeographed.
Leslie, Charles
  1740 *A new history of Jamaica.* London.
Letter from Barbados
  1673 *A letter sent from Barbados to a friend in London. Being
        a true relation of the surrender of the island of Tobago.*
        London.
Letter from Considerable Proprietors of Barbados
  1709 *A letter from the most considerable proprietors of the is-
        land of Barbados, to the several persons in Great Britain . . .
        requesting their application to the . . . House of Commons,
        for establishing the African trade by a joint stock.* [Lon-
        don.]
Lewis, Matthew Gregory
  1834 *Journal of a West India proprietor, kept during a residence
        in the island of Jamaica.* London.
Ligon, Richard
  1657 *A true and exact history of the iland of Barbados.* London.
Little, Kenneth L.
  1951 *The Mende of Sierra Leone.* London: Routledge and Ke-
        gan Paul.
  1954 The Mende in Sierra Leone. In *African worlds: studies in
        the cosmological ideas and social values of African peoples,*
        ed. Daryll Forde, pp. 111–137. London: International Afri-
        can Institute, Oxford University Press.
[Littleton, Edward]
  1689 *The groans of the plantations . . . relating more particularly
        to the island of Barbados.* London.
Littlewood, Margaret
  1954 Bamum and Bamileke. In *Peoples of the central Cameroons.*
        Ethnographic survey of Africa: Western Africa, Part 9,
        ed. Daryll Forde, pp. 53–131. London: International Afri-
        can Institute.
Long, Edward
  1774 *The history of Jamaica.* 3 vols. London.
Lowenthal, David
  1957 The population of Barbados. *Social and Economic Studies*
        6:445–501.
  1972 *West Indian societies.* New York: Oxford University Press.
Lowther Plantation
  1756 The Barbadoes plantation—accompts. Commencing Jan-

uary 1st 1756 and ending December 31, 1756. Additional mss. 43507, fols. 1–5, BM.

1825–35 An abstract of the accounts of Lowther's plantation in Barbados, 1825, 1827, 1828, 1829, 1833, 1835. Additional mss. 43507, fols. 7–30, BM.

Lucas, Nathaniel
 1946 The Lucas manuscript volumes in the Barbados public library. *JBMHS* 13:161–182.
 1949 The Lucas manuscript volumes in the Barbados public library. *JBMHS* 16:38–53.
 1952 The Lucas manuscript volumes in the Barbados public library. *JBMHS* 20:32–44.
 1953 The Lucas manuscript volumes in the Barbados public library. *JBMHS* 21:13–25.
 1956 The Lucas manuscript volumes in the Barbados public library. *JBMHS* 23:68–81, 111–126.

McCulloch, M.
 1950 *Peoples of Sierra Leone protectorate*. Ethnographic survey of Africa: Western Africa, Part 2, ed. Daryll Forde. London: International African Institute.

McCusker, John J.
 1970 The rum trade and the balance of payments of the thirteen continental colonies, 1650–1775. Ph.D. dissertation, University of Pittsburgh.

McFarlane, Suzanne B.
 1975 The ethnoarcheology of a slave community: the Couper plantation site. M.A. thesis, University of Florida.

MacGregor, Evan J. M.
 1836 Letter to Lord Glenelg, December 6. *PP* 1837–38, vol. 48, rept. 215.

Madin, Philip
 1779 Account of his journey to the West Indies with Thomas Colley, 1779. Miscellaneous mss., Box W, Society of Friends Library, London.

Mangin, Eugene
 1921 *Les Mossi*. Paris.

Manoukian, Madeline
 1950 *Akan and Ga-Adangme peoples of the Gold Coast*. Ethnographic survey of Africa: Western Africa, Part 1, ed. Daryll Forde. London: International African Institute.
 1952 *The Ewe-speaking people of Togoland and the Gold Coast*. Ethnographic survey of Africa: Western Africa, Part 6, ed. Daryll Forde. London: International African Institute.

Massiah, Joycelin
  1976   The population of Barbados [1970]. Institute of Social and Economic Research, Cave Hill, Barbados. Typescript.
Mathew, William
  1737   Letter to council of trade and plantations, enclosing a report on the slave conspiracy in Antigua, January 17. *CSPCS* 1737:10–13.
Mathewson, R. Duncan
  1972a History from the earth: archaeological excavations at Old King's House. *Jamaica Journal* 6:3–11.
  1972b Jamaican ceramics: an introduction to 18th century folk pottery in West African tradition. *Jamaica Journal* 6:54–56.
  1973   Archaeological analysis of material culture as a reflection of sub-cultural differentiation in 18th century Jamaica. *Jamaica Journal* 7:25–29.
Maycock, James Dottin
  1830   *Flora Barbadensis.* London.
Maynard, George F.
  1821   Barbadoes, parish of St. Thomas ... a return of the population. *PP* 1823, vol. 18, rept. 80, p. 43.
Mayo, William
  1722   *A new and exact map of the island of Barbadoes in America.* London.
Meek, Charles K.
  1931   *Tribal studies in Northern Nigeria.* London: Kegan Paul, Trench, Trubner.
Meggers, Betty, and Clifford Evans
  1956   The reconstruction of settlement pattern in the South American tropical forest. In *Prehistoric settlement patterns in the New World,* ed. G. R. Willey, pp. 156–164. Viking Fund Publications in Anthropology 23. New York: Wenner-Gren Foundation for Anthropological Research.
Merriam, Alan P.
  1967   The use of music as a technique of reconstructing culture history in Africa. In *Reconstructing African culture history,* ed. Creighton Gabel and Norman R. Bennett, pp. 83–114. Boston: Boston University Press.
Micklem, Christine E.
  1969   University of London Library MS. 523. The Newton papers: a handlist. University of London Library. Mimeographed.

Middleton, John, and E. H. Winter, eds.
 1963 *Witchcraft and sorcery in East Africa*. London: Rout-
       ledge and Kegan Paul
Mintz, Sidney W.
 1970 Foreword. In *Afro-American anthropology: contemporary
       perspectives*, ed. Norman E. Whitten, Jr., and John F.
       Szwed, pp. 1–16. New York: The Free Press.
 1975 History and anthropology: a brief reprise. In *Race and
       slavery in the Western hemisphere: quantitative studies*,
       ed. Stanley L. Engerman and Eugene D. Genovese, pp.
       477–494. Princeton: Princeton University Press.
Mintz, Sidney W., and Douglas Hall
 1960 The origins of the Jamaican internal marketing system.
       Yale University Publications in Anthropology 57:3–26.
Mintz, Sidney W., and Richard Price
 1976 *An anthropological approach to the Afro-American past:
       a Caribbean perspective. ISHI Occasional Papers in Social
       Change* 2. Philadelphia: Institute for the Study of Human
       Issues.
Modyford, Thomas
 1662 Extracts of letters . . . , 1662. *CSPCS* 1661–1668:123–124.
Molen, P. A.
 1971 Population and social patterns in Barbados in the early
       eighteenth century. *William and Mary Quarterly* 28:287–
       300.
Moll, Herman
 1708 A new map of the island of Barbadoes. In *The British
       empire in North America*, by John Oldmixon, vol. 2, p. 1.
       London.
Monteil, Charles V.
 1924 *Les Bambara du Ségou et du Kaarta*. Paris: LaRose.
Morley, John
 1971 *Death, heaven and the Victorians*. London: Studio Vista.
Morton-Williams, Peter
 1964 The Oyo Yoruba and the Atlantic trade 1670–1830. *Journal
       of the Historical Society of Nigeria* 3:25–45.
Mullin, Gerald W.
 1972 *Flight and rebellion: slave resistance in eighteenth-century
       Virginia*. New York: Oxford University Press.
Murdock, George P.
 1959 *Africa: its peoples and their culture history*. New York:
       McGraw-Hill.

Neblett, William
  1817   Letter to Lord Combermere, June 24. CO 28/86.
Newton Papers (Ms. 523, University of London Library)
  110   Work log, Newton Plantation, May 5, 1796–April 26, 1797.
  111   Work log, Seawell Plantation, April 25, 1796–April 25, 1797.
  113   Newton journal, 1797.
  116   Land and stock accounts, Newton plantation, 1798.
  119   "Disposition of the several fields of Seawell plantation," 1798.
  128-1 "An account of the several fields according to the plot, of Newton plantation," 1799.
  129   Boiling house account, Newton plantation, 1799.
  131-1 "An account of the several fields according to the plot, of Seawell plantation," 1800.
  270   "List of Negroes on Newton," May 2, 1776.
  271   "List of Negroes on Newton," 1782.
  272   "List of Negroes on Newton," July 28, 1783.
  275   "List of Negroes on Newton," 1820.
  276   "List of Negroes on Seawell," April 15, 1791.
  277   "Valuation of Newton," June 7, 1784.
  278   "Valuation of Seawell," June 7, 1784.
  285   "List of Negroes on Seawell," [1803].
  287   Valuation of Newton plantation, May 11, 1803.
  288   Sampson Wood, "Report on the Negroes," Newton plantation, July 1796.
  289   Sampson Wood, "Report on the lands," Newton plantation, July 2, 1796.
  290   Sampson Wood, "Report on the buildings at Newton," June 24, 1796.
  315   Wood to Lane, July 20, 1797.
  316   Wood to Lane, July 20, 1797.
  321   Wood to Lane, September 8, 1797.
  340-1 Wood to Lane, May 7, 1798.
  345   Wood to Lane, June 22, 1798.
  352-1 Wood to Lane, July 18, 1798.
  353   Wood to Lane, July 21, 1798.
  381-1 Wood to Lane, October 19, 1798.
  401   Wood to Lane, April 22, 1800.
  423   Wood to Lane, October 21, 1800.
  434   Wood to Lane, February 10–13, 1801.
  441   Miler to Lane, May 25, 1801.
  459   Wood to Lane, December 19, 1801.

496-1 Wood to Lane, August 24, 1802.

567 A. Wood to Lane, March 19, 1804.

585 Haynes to Lane, September 13, 1804.

586 Farrell to Lane, September 13, 1804.

593 Farrell to Lane, November 29, 1804.

601 Haynes to Lane, April 7, 1806.

630 Haynes to Lane, March 9, 1807.

633 Haynes to Lane, June 7, 1807.

653 Haynes to Lane, April 10, 1808.

690 Jane [or Jenny] Lane to Lane, March 4, 1813.

694 Haynes to Lane, May 13, 1813.

703 Blackman to Lane, August 18, 1813.

709 Haynes to Lane, October 21, 1813.

741 Haynes to Lane, January 26, 1815.

745 Haynes to Lane, March 24, 1815.

759 "Presented to Mr. Robert Reece ... by Thomas Lane," October 1815.

761 Reece to Lane, March 3, 1816.

765-1 Haynes to Lane, April 13, 1816.

766 Haynes to Lane, April 25, 1816.

773 Haynes to Lane, July 2, 1816.

781 Haynes to Lane, September 23, 1816.

811 Haynes to Lane, October 18, 1818.

831 Haynes to Lane, June 23, 1820.

850 Reece to Lane, June 9, 1821.

899 Reece to Lane, July 31, 1823.

969-2 Release of Seawell plantation, part of the conveyance of the plantation from John and Elizabeth Newton to Anthony Lynch, July 16, 1756.

970 "A List of the slaves belonging to the estate of Samuel Newton esquire, taken the 8th day of June 1740."

976 Indenture between John and Thomas Lane and "Jenny, a free black woman," May 8, 1818.

984 Printed notice of sale of Searles-Tyrwhitts plantations at Court of Chancery in London, November 28, 1801.

1068 Cryer to Newton, June 16, 1686.

1106 Partial inventory of the estate of Barbara Newton, February 17, 1688.

1110 "The case of Barbara Newton, widow, the relict of Colonel Samuel Newton, dec'd.," [1695].

Newton Plantation

1805–1841 Journal. vol. 1. Barbados Museum Library.

Nicholls, Robert B.
1790 Testimony, in *Minutes of the evidence taken before a committee of the House of Commons ... for the abolition of the slave trade*. PP, vol. 30, pp. 325–360.

Nkeita, J. H.
1969 *Funeral dirges of the Akan peoples*, 2d ed. New York: Negro Universities Press.

Noël Hume, Ivor
1970 *A guide to artifacts of colonial America*. New York: Knopf.

Oldmixon, John
1708 *The British empire in America*, 1st ed. 2 vols. London.
1741 *The British empire in America*, 2nd ed. 2 vols. London.

Oliver, Vere L., ed.
1910–20 *Caribbeana: being miscellaneous papers relating to the history, genealogy, topography and antiquities of the British West Indies*. 6 vols. London.

Omwake, H. G.
1958 Kaolin pipes from the Schurz site. *Bulletin of the Archaeological Society of Connecticut* 29:3–13.

Orderson, J. W.
1842 *Creoleana: or, social and domestic scenes and incidents in Barbados in days of yore*. London.

Oswald, Adrian
1951 English clay tobacco pipes. *The Archaeological News Letter* 3:154–159.
1961 The evolution and chronology of English clay tobacco pipes. *The Archaeological News Letter* 7:55–62.

Ottenberg, Simon
1968 *Double descent in an African society: the Afikpo village-group*. Seattle: University of Washington Press.

Ottenberg, Simon, and Phoebe Ottenberg, eds.
1960 *Cultures and societies of Africa*. New York: Random House.

Otto, John S.
1975 Status differences and the archaeological record—a comparison of planter, overseer, and slave sites from Cannon's point plantation (1794–1861), St. Simons Island, Georgia. Ph.D. dissertation, University of Florida.

Owen, Trefor
1959 *Welsh folk customs*. Cardiff: National Museum of Wales.

Ozanne, Paul
1962 Notes on the early historic archaeology of Accra. *Transactions of the Historical Society of Ghana* 6:51–70.
Parliamentary Papers
1789 *Report of the Lords of the committee of Council ... concerning the present state of the trade to Africa ... and the effects and consequences of this trade ... in Africa and the West Indies*, vol. 26. London.
1814–15 *Papers relating to the West Indies*, vol. 7, rept. 478, pp. 1–24. London.
1823 *Slave population*, vol. 18, rept. 80. London.
1824 *Slave population*, vol. 24, rept. 424. London.
1826 *Slave population*, vol. 28, rept. 353. London.
1826–27a An act to repeal several acts and clauses of acts respecting slaves, and for consolidating and bringing into one act, the several laws relating thereto, October 1826. In *Papers ... in explanation of the measures adopted ... for the melioration of the condition of the slave population in ... the West Indies*, vol. 25, unnumbered rept., pp. 205–230. London.
1826–27b An act for the encouragement of baptisms and marriages amongst the slaves, and for the due observance of ... Sunday, Christmas day, and Good Friday, October 1826. In *Papers ... in explanation of the measures adopted ... for the melioration of the condition of the slave population in ... the West Indies*, vol. 25, unnumbered rept., pp. 277–278. London.
1830 *Slave population in the colonies*, vol. 21, rept. 674. London.
1831–32a *Report from the select committee on the extinction of slavery throughout the British dominions*, vol. 20, rept. 59, pt. 2. London.
1831–32b *Slave population. Extracts from returns*, vol. 47, rept. 660, pp. 21–31. London.
1833a *Slave registration*, vol. 26, rept. 539. London.
1833b *Slave population (slave registries)*, vol. 26, rept. 700. London.
1835 *Slavery abolition proceedings*, vol. 51, rept. 420. London.
1837–38 *Accounts of slave compensation claims*, vol. 48, rept. 215, pp. 171–202. London.
Parrinder, Geoffrey
1961 *West African religion*. London: Epworth Press.
Parry, David
1789a Extract of a letter from Governor Parry to the right

honourable Lord Sydney, August 18, 1788. *PP* 1789, vol. 26, pp. 13–24.

1789b   Replies to Queries 6, 12, 15, 19, 49, in *Report of the Lords of the committee of Council . . . concerning the present state of the trade to Africa . . . and the effects and consequences of this trade . . . in Africa and the West Indies,* Part 3. *PP,* vol. 26.

1789c   An account of 22 plantations in Barbados, 1788 . . . situated in almost every different part of the island. *PP* 1789, vol. 26, p. 39.

Pasfeild, Samuel

1727   An inventory and valuation of the Negroes, etc. on the estate of Samuel Pasfeild . . . 20th day of April 1727. Ms. U.l.21, no. 30, Boston Public Library.

Patterson, Orlando

1967   *The sociology of slavery: An analysis of the origins, development and structure of Negro slave society in Jamaica.* London: MacGibbon and Kee.

Patterson, Sheila

1975   Some speculations on the status and role of the free people of colour in the Western cape. In *Studies in African social anthropology,* ed. Meyer Fortes and Sheila Patterson, pp. 159–205. London: Academic Press.

Peckover, Edmund

1742–43   Journal of travels in North America and Barbados, 1742–1743. *London Yearly Meetings,* vol. 9, pp. 322–339, Society of Friends Library, London.

Phillips, Thomas

1746   A journal of a voyage made in the *Hannibal* of London, ann. 1693, 1694, from England, to . . . Barbadoes. In *A collection of voyages and travels,* ed. A. Churchill, vol. 6, pp. 187–255. London.

Philopatris

[1748]   *Answers to the objections against the proposals of the Royal African Company for settling the trade to Africa. In a second letter to a member of Parliament. March 31, 1748.* [London.]

Pinckard, George

1806   *Notes on the West Indies.* 3 vols. London.

Pinckerton Papers

1804   Slaves taxed [in Barbados, 1802–1803]. Pinckerton Papers, Ms. 1711, fol. 75, National Library of Scotland, Edinburgh.

Pine, L. G.
1967 *Tradition and custom in modern Britain.* London: Whiting & Wheaton.

Pinfold, Charles
1762 Answers . . . to the queries proposed by the Lords of Trade and Plantations. June 1. Kings Mss. 205, fols. 456–473, BM.

Pitman, Frank W.
1917 *The development of the British West Indies 1700–1763.* New Haven: Yale University Press.

Platt, Virginia
1969 The East India Company and the Madagascar slave trade. *William and Mary Quarterly* 26:548–577.

Porter, Enid
1969 *Cambridgeshire customs and folklore.* London: Routledge & K. Paul.

Porteus, Beilby
1807 *An essay towards a plan for the more effectual civilization and conversion of the Negroe slaves, on the trust estate in Barbados.* London.

Postlethwayt, Malachy
1745 *The African trade, the great pillar and support of the British plantation trade in North America.* London.

Postma, Johannes
1970 The Dutch participation in the African slave trade: slaving on the Guinea coast, 1675–1795. Ph.D. dissertation, Michigan State University.
1975 The origin of African slaves: the Dutch activities on the Guinea coast, 1675–1795. In *Race and slavery in the Western hemisphere: quantitative studies,* ed. Stanley L. Engerman and Eugene D. Genovese, pp. 33–49. Princeton: Princeton University Press.

Price, Richard
1976 *The Guiana Maroons: a historical and bibliographical introduction.* Baltimore: Johns Hopkins University Press.

Pridmore, F.
1962 Notes on colonial coins. The Barbados issues of 1788 and 1792. Are they coins or private tokens? *JBMHS* 30:14–19.
1965 *The coins of the British commonwealth of nations to the end of the reign of George VI 1952. Part 3. Bermuda, British Guiana, British Honduras and the British West Indies.* London: Spink.

Pritchard, John E.
1923 Tobacco pipes of Bristol of the XVIIth century and their

makers. Bristol and Gloucestershire Archaeological Society *Transactions* 45:165–191.

Public Record Office (London)

[1667] Some observations on the island Barbadoes. CO 1/21, no. 170.

1673 List of the most eminent planters in Barbados. CO 1/30, no. 42. ii.

[1679] Certificate of the number of Negroes imported into Barbados by the Royal African Company, December 1, 1678 to December 1, 1679. CO 1/44, no. 245.

1679/80 Census of Barbados, 1679. Supplied by Governor J. Atkins to the Lords of Trade and Plantations in March–April 1680. CO 1/44, no. 45.

1692 To his excellency Collonel James Kendall . . . [report on slave plot], November. CO 28/1, fols. 202–205.

1710 A list of Negroes, mills, cattle-mills, and pott kilns, July 1710. CO 28/13, no. 189.

1712 A list of the inhabitants men women and children . . . belonging to the several parishes of this island. August 16. CO 28/14, no. 21.

1768–1773 An account of the exports from the several ports in North America to the British and foreign West Indies. January 5, 1768–January 5, 1773. Customs 16/1.

1788 An account of the number of slaves imported into this island. March 8, 1781–March 13, 1788. CO 28/61, no. 202.

1805 An account of slaves imported and exported in the island of Barbados. CO 28/72, no. 61.

1806 An act for the punishment of such slaves as shall be found practising Obeah. November 4. CO 30/18, no. 262.

1817 An abstract account of the slave population. October 31. CO 28/86.

1818 An act for the better prevention of the practice of Obeah. June 28. CO 30/20, no. 367.

1823 Statement of baptisms and burials in the island of Barbados from the 1st January 1822 to 31st December 1822, inclusive [forwarded by Governor Henry Warde, February 27, 1823]. CO 28/92, no. 11.

Rattray, R. S.

1927 *Religion and art in Ashanti.* Oxford: Clarendon.

1929 *Ashanti law and constitution.* Oxford: Clarendon.

1932 *The tribes of the Ashanti hinterland.* 2 vols. Oxford: Clarendon.

Rawick, George P.
1972 *The American slave: a composite autobiography. Vol. 1. From sundown to sunup: the making of the black community.* Westport, Conn.: Greenwood.

Rawlin, William
1699 *The laws of Barbados.* London.

Rees, Thomas G.
1790 Testimony, in *Minutes of the evidence taken before a committee of the House of Commons ... for the abolition of the slave trade.* PP, vol. 30, pp. 247–264.

Renny, Robert
1807 *An history of Jamaica.* London.

Riviere, W. Emanuel
1972 Labour shortage in the British West Indies after emancipation. *Journal of Caribbean History* 4:1–30.

Roach, C. N. C.
1936–39 Old Barbados. *JBMHS* 3:137–148, 211–222; 4:12–21, 53–67, 109–122, 167–179; 5:3–11, 85–100, 130–143; 6:26–40, 74–86, 139–151, 191–197.

Rolph, Thomas
1836 *A brief account, together with observations, made during a visit in the West Indies ... in parts of the years 1832–3.* Dundas, Upper Canada.

Rose, H. J.
1922 Celestial and terrestial orientation of the dead. *Journal of the Royal Anthropological Institute* 52:127–140.

Roth, H. Ling
1903 *Great Benin.* Halifax, England: F. King & Sons.

Royal African Company
[ca. 1700] The Royal African Company do humbly propose for the regaining and preservation of the trade to Africa as followeth ... Sloane Mss. 2902, fols. 88–89, BM.

Rymer, James
1775 *A description of the island of Nevis.* London.

Salwen, Bert
1966 European trade goods and the chronology of the Fort Shantok site. *Bulletin of the Archaeological Society of Connecticut* 34:5–39.

Samuel, Wilfred S.
1936 *A review of the Jewish colonists in Barbados in the year 1680. Transactions of the Jewish Historical Society of England* 12.

Sauer, Carl O.
1966   *The early Spanish Main.* Berkeley and Los Angeles: University of California Press.

Schiffer, Michael B.
1972   Archaeological context and systematic context. *American Antiquity* 37:156–165.

Schomburgk, Robert
1848   *The history of Barbados.* London.

Schuler, Monica
1970   Akan slave rebellions in the British Caribbean. *Savacou* 1:8–32. Kingston, Jamaica.

Schuyler, Robert L.
1970   Historical and historic sites archaeology as anthropology. *Historical Archaeology* 4:83–89.

1974   Sandy Ground: an archaeological sampling in a black community in metropolitan New York. *CHSAP* 7(1972):13–51.

Scott, John
[1668]   The description of Barbados. Sloane Mss. 3662, fols. 54–92, BM.

Senhouse, William
1788   Letter . . . to Mr. Granville Sharp, dated Barbadoes, February 27, 1788. In *Report of the Lords of the committee of Council . . . concerning the present state of the trade to Africa . . . and the effects and consequences of this trade . . . in Africa and the West Indies,* Part 3. PP 1789, vol. 26.

1935   The autobiographical manuscript of William Senhouse [ca. 1791]. *JBMHS* 2:115–134, 191–209.

[Senior, Bernard M.]
1835   *Jamaica, as it was, as it is, and as it may be.* London.

Shepherd, Jill
1974   Redlegs—myth and reality. *West Indies Chronicle* 89:144–145.

Sheridan, Richard B.
1972   Africa and the Caribbean in the Atlantic slave trade. *American Historical Review* 77:15–35.

1974   *Sugar and slavery: an economic history of the British West Indies 1623–1775.* Baltimore: Johns Hopkins University Press.

Shilstone, E. M.
1933   Historic sites re-visited—1, Andrews plantation, St. Joseph, its cemetery and history. *JBMHS* 1:90–98.

1938   A descriptive list of maps of Barbados. *JBMHS* 5:57–84.

1945   The population of Barbados. *JBMHS* 13:3–20.

1956   *Monumental inscriptions in the burial ground of the Jewish synagogue at Bridgetown, Barbados.* London: The Jewish Historical Society of England.

1966   The Jewish synagogue Bridgetown, Barbados. *JBMHS* 32: 3–15.

Shrewsbury, W. J., and J. Nelson

1821a   Letter to Wesleyan Missionary Society, November 8. Box 1821–1822, no. 102, MMSA.

1821b   Letter to Wesleyan Missionary Society, January 10. Box 1821–1822, no. 250, MMSA.

Sidney, William C.

1891   *England and the English in the eighteenth century.* 2 vols. Edinburgh.

Siegel, Bernard J.

1947   *Slavery during the third dynasty of Ur.* American Anthropological Association Memoir 66.

Simmons, Henry P.

1833   *A letter to the Right Hon. Earl Grey, on the West India question.* Liverpool.

Simpson, George E.

1957   The nine night ceremony in Jamaica. *Journal of American Folklore* 70:329–335.

Skey, Joseph

1816   Some remarks upon the structure of Barbadoes, as connected with specimens of its rocks. *Transactions of the Geological Society* 3:236–242. London.

Sloane, Hans

1707   *A voyage to the islands Madera, Barbados, Nievis, S. Christophers and Jamaica,* vol. 1. London.

Smalridge, John

1711   Letter to Smalridge, March 11. Letter books, vol. A6, no. 67, USPGA.

Smith, Captain John

1630   *The true travels, adventures, and observations of Captain John Smith.* London.

Smith, M. G.

1956   Community organization in rural Jamaica. *Social and Economic Studies* 5:295–312.

Snow, C. T.

1969   Excavations at Casey's house. Archaeological Research Report, National Park Service. Mimeographed.

Society for the Conversion and Religious Instruction and Education of the Negro Slaves in the British West India Islands
  1829   Returns to questions addressed to the clergy of the diocese of Barbados and the Leeward Islands, up to December 31, 1828: island of Barbados. *Report for the Year 1828*. London.
Society for the Improvement of West India Plantership
  1811–16   Minute book [June 1, 1811–April 6, 1816]. Raymond Richards Collection of Miscellaneous Historical Material, University of Keele Library, Staffordshire, England.
Society for the Propagation of the Gospel in Foreign Parts
  1739   Inventory of the Codrington plantations, February 25. Letter books, vol. B8, no. 16a, USPGA.
  1740   A List of Negroes belonging to the honourable society. September 5. Letter books, vol. B8, nos. 35–36, USPGA.
South, Stanley
  1964   Analysis of the buttons from Brunswick Town and Fort Fisher. *Florida Anthropologist* 17:113–133.
  1972   Evolution and horizon as revealed in ceramic analysis in historical archaeology. *CHSAP* 6 (1971):71–116.
Spence, George C.
  1955   Notes on clay tobacco pipes and clay tobacco pipe makers in Cheshire. *Lancashire and Cheshire Antiquarian Society Transactions* 56:45–66.
Sprague, Roderick
  1968   A suggested terminology and classification for burial descriptions. *American Antiquity* 33:479–485.
Starkey, Otis P.
  1939   *The economic geography of Barbados*. New York: Columbia University Press.
  1961   *Commercial geography of Barbados*. Office of Naval Research, Technical Report 9. Bloomington: Department of Geography, Indiana University.
Steele, Joshua
  1787–88   Letters of Philo-Xylon. In *Mitigation of slavery in two parts*, by William Dickson. London, 1814, pp. 65–142.
  1789   Queries from . . . Governor Parry, answered by a planter of 1068 acres . . . in the island of Barbados. *PP*, vol. 26, pp. 24–36.
Stewart, J.
  1823   *A view of the past and present state of the island of Jamaica*. London.
Stone, Lyle M.
  1971   Rosary and glass beads. In *The Lasanen site: an historic*

burial locality in Mackinac County, Michigan, ed. Charles E. Cleland, pp. 74–85. Publications of the Museum, Anthropological Series, vol. 1. East Lansing: Michigan State University.

1974 *Fort Michilimackinac 1715–1781: an archaeological perspective on the revolutionary frontier.* Publications of the Museum, Anthropological Series. East Lansing: Michigan State University.

Sturge, Joseph, and Thomas Harvey

1838 *The West Indies in 1837,* 2nd ed., rev. London.

Sturge, C. Dickinson

1908 Friends in Barbadoes. *Journal of the Friends Historical Society* 5:43–46.

Substance of the Evidence on the Petition

1775 *The substance of the evidence on the petition presented by the West-India planters and merchants, ... as it was introduced ..., and summ'd up by Mr. Glover.* New York.

Talbot, P. Amaury

1932 *Tribes of the Niger delta.* London: Frank Cass.

Taylor, John

[1688] Historie of his life and travels in America. Containeing a full geographical description of the island of Jamaica. 3 vols. West India Reference Library, Institute of Jamaica, Kingston. Manuscript.

Thomas, Northcote W.

1910 *Anthropological report on the Edo-speaking peoples of Nigeria. Part 1: Law and custom.* London: Harrison & Sons.

1916 *Anthropological report on Sierra Leone.* London: Harrison & Sons.

Thome, J. A., and J. H. Kimball

1838 *Emancipation in the West Indies.* New York.

Towne, Richard

1726 *A treatise of the diseases most frequent in the West Indies.* London.

Trigger, Bruce

1971 Archaeology and ecology. *World Archaeology* 2–3:321–336.

True State of the Case

[1644] *A true state of the case between the heires and assignes of Sir William Courteen ... and the late earl of Carlisle, and planters in the island of Barbadoes, ... and others, exhibited in Parliament.* [London.]

Turner, Victor W.
1973   Symbols in African ritual. *Science* 179:1100–1105.
Tylor, Edward B.
1958   *Religion in primitive culture.* New York: Harper & Row (reprint of chapters 11–19 of *Primitive culture*, 2nd ed., London, 1873).
Uchendu, Victor
1965   *The Igbo of Southeast Nigeria.* New York: Holt, Rinehart and Winston.
United Brethren
1790–1836   *Periodical accounts relating to the missions of the church of the United Brethren.* 13 vols. London.
United Nations
1974   *Statistical yearbook 1973.* Paris: UNESCO Press.
Vernon, K. C., and D. M. Carroll
1966   *Soil and land-use surveys, no. 18: Barbados.* Trinidad: The Regional Research Centre of the British Caribbean at the Imperial College of Tropical Agriculture, University of the West Indies.
Vines, Richard
1947   Letter to John Winthrop, July 19, 1647. In *Winthrop papers*, vol. 5, 1645–1649, pp. 171–172. Boston: The Massachusetts Historical Society.
Walduck, J.
1710–12   Letters to J. Petiver, November 1710–September 1712. Sloane Mss. 2302, BM.
Walker, Iain C.
1965   Some thoughts on the Harrington and Binford systems for statistically dating clay pipes. *Quarterly Bulletin of the Archaeological Society of Virginia* 20:60–64.
1966   TD pipes—a preliminary study. *Quarterly Bulletin of the Archaeological Society of Virginia* 20:86–102.
1967a   Historic archaeology—methods and principles. *Historical Archaeology* 1:23–24.
1967b   Clay pipes from the fortress of Louisburg. *Archaeology* 20:187–193.
1971   An archaeological study of clay pipes from the king's bastion, fortress of Louisburg. *Canadian Historic Sites, Occasional Papers in Archaeology and History*, no. 2, pp. 56–122.
1972   Comments on Stanley South's "Evolution and horizon as revealed in ceramic analysis in historical archaeology." *CHSAP* 6 (1971):127–157.

1974 Binford, science, and history: the probabilistic variability of explicated epistemology and nomothetic paradigms in historical archaeology. *CHSAP* 7 (1972):159–201.

Waller, John A.
1820 *A voyage in the West Indies.* London.

Warner, Thomas
1636 Letter to secretary of state, September 10. CO 1/9, fols. 49–50.

Watson, Karl
1975 The civilized island: Barbados, a social history 1750–1816. Ph.D. dissertation, University of Florida.

Watson, Patty Jo, Steven A. LeBlanc, and Charles L. Redman
1971 *Explanation in archaeology.* New York: Columbia University Press.

Watson, Rowan
1975 University of London Library ms. 523. The Newton papers: a handlist of the second deposit with an index to the whole collection. University of London Library. Mimeographed.

Watts, David
1966 *Man's influence on the vegetation of Barbados 1627 to 1800.* Occasional Papers in Geography 4. Hull, England: University of Hull.
1968 Origins of Barbadian cane hole agriculture. *JBMHS* 32:143–151.

Weiss, Kenneth M.
1973 *Demographic models for anthropology.* Society for American Archaeology Memoir 27. Washington, D.C.

Werner, O., and Frank Willett
1975 The composition of brasses from Ife and Benin. *Archaeometry* 17:141–156.

Weslager, C. A.
1954 The excavation of a (colonial) log cabin. Near Wilmington, Delaware. *Bulletin of the Archaeological Society of Delaware 6.*

West India Committee Circular
1911 Values in Barbados in 1828 [Clapham plantation]. *The West India Committee Circular* 29:396–397.

West Indies Chronicle
1973 Barbados supplement. *West Indies Chronicle*, vol. 88 (November).

Whistler, Henry
1655 A journall of a voardge from Stokes Bay ... for the West Inga. Sloane mss. 3926, BM.

White, Darla
  1972   Histories of Ashford, Bourbon, Guinea, and Staple Grove
         plantations. Logan Museum, Beloit College. Typescript.
Willett, Frank
  1967   *Ife in the history of West African sculpture.* New York:
         McGraw-Hill.
Williams, Eric
  1961   *Capitalism and slavery.* New York: Russell and Russell.
Williams, Joseph J.
  1932   *Voodoos and Obeahs: phases of West India witchcraft.*
         New York: Dial Press.
Willoughby, William
  1664   Letter to the king, June 17. *CSPCS* 1661–1668:215–216.
  1666   Letter to the king, May 12. *CSPCS* 1661–1668:382–383.
  1668   Letter to the lords of council, July 9. *CSPCS* 1661–1668:
         586–588.
Willyams, Cooper
  1796   *An Account of the campaign in the West Indies in the
         year 1794.* London.
Wimberley, L. C.
  1927   *Death and burial lore in the English and Scottish popular
         ballads.* University of Nebraska Studies in Language, Litera-
         ture, and Criticism 8. Lincoln, Nebraska.
Winthrop, Henry
  1929   Letter to John Winthrop, October 15, 1627. In *Winthrop
         Papers,* vol. 1, 1498–1628, pp. 361–362. Boston: Massachu-
         setts Historical Society.
Wood, Peter H.
  1974   *Black majority: Negroes in colonial South Carolina.* New
         York: Knopf.
Yearwood, Seale
  1949   Letters to A. Frere, March 1796 and April 26, 1797. *JBMHS*
         16:113–117.

Index